Modern Central Asia has become a synonym for energy geopolitics, and India is involved in it. Dr Pradhan's new book takes readers through the history of India's energy hunt in Central Asia that went on for decades; it involves intricate details of exploration bids in Kazakhstan – initially driven by strategic consideration and how Nazarbayev astutely used India as a pawn in the delicate balancing act between the various suitors competing for the energy reserves in Kazakhstan.

—***Ambassador Phunchok Stobdan, former Indian Ambassador to the Republic of Kyrgyzstan***

The author has traced the critical role energy plays in developmental processes, innovation and its impact on human lives. India being a net importer of energy, relies partly on Central Asian energy resources for its needs and has crafted a policy and a strategy to procure this vital resource, but there are other players who are scrambling for Central Asian energy. The author has discussed in a scholarly way the presence and interplay of major powers in their effort to procure energy. In trying to understand the geopolitics of energy and India's approach the author has presented a detailed and objective analysis.

—***Professor Nirmala Jodhi, Former Professor, Centre for Russian and Central Asian Studies, School of International Studies, JNU, New Delhi***

India and Central Asian states share a strong historical bond and an exceedingly superb friendship since antiquity. But their trade and economic relations are still at infancy despite being connected through the Silk Road. Although India's relationship and diplomatic ties with the countries of Central Asia after the disintegration of the Soviet Union have been relatively strong yet India was dubbed disinterested due to its shyness in taking part in the energy game taking place in the region. This book in this premise is timely as it vividly discusses the energy security dimension between India and Central Asia, both from bilateral and multilateral perspectives. I am sure scholars and experts would benefit immensely from the pragmatic investigations of this book in the energy domain.

—Professor Akbota Zholadasbekova, Vice-Rector,
L. N. Gumilyov Eurasian National University,
Nur-Sultan, Kazakhstan

GEOPOLITICS OF ENERGY IN CENTRAL ASIA

This book focuses on the geopolitics of Central Asia which has emerged as the new fertile ground for oil and energy resources. It analyses the scramble for energy and control over the region by many nations and their diplomatic manoeuvrings to ensure energy sufficiency and economic growth.

The book provides a quantitative analysis of the Central Asian energy potential and offers an understanding of the unique position that each country occupies in the geopolitics of oil and energy in the region. It looks at aggressive foreign policies by countries such as the United States, China, the European Union, Japan, Israel, Iran and Pakistan, focusing primarily on India's position and strategies in the region within the new great game. The book further examines the dynamics between Central Asia and India and India's policies for geopolitical engagement and diversification of energy sources.

This volume will be of interest to researchers and students of political studies, international relations, economics, sociology and Asian studies. It will also be useful for policymakers and professionals working in the field of energy security and geo-economics.

Ramakrushna Pradhan is Assistant Professor of Political Science and International Relations, in the Department of Social Science, Fakir Mohan University, Balasore, Odisha, India. A Ph.D from the Centre for Russian and Central Asian Studies, School of International Studies, Jawaharlal Nehru University, Dr. Pradhan also served as Visiting Professor also served in the Department of Regional Studies, Faculty of International Relations, L. N. Gumilyov Eurasian National University, Nur-Sultan, Kazakhstan. He has also worked in the position of Associate Editor in *Eurasian Report*, an area study research journal, and as a Research Associate with the Eurasian Foundation, New Delhi. Some of his recent publications include *Geopolitics of Central Asia: China–US Engagement* (2010), *Geopolitics and Energy Diplomacy* (2016) and *Geopolitics of Energy and Pipeline Diplomacy in Central Asia: Policy Options for India* (2018).

GEOPOLITICS OF ENERGY IN CENTRAL ASIA

India's Position and Policy

Ramakrushna Pradhan

Routledge
Taylor & Francis Group
LONDON AND NEW YORK

First published 2021
by Routledge
2 Park Square, Milton Park, Abingdon, Oxon OX14 4RN

and by Routledge
52 Vanderbilt Avenue, New York, NY 10017

Routledge is an imprint of the Taylor & Francis Group, an informa business

British Library Cataloguing-in-Publication Data
A catalogue record for this book is available from the British Library

Library of Congress Cataloging-in-Publication Data
Names: Pradhan, Ramakrushna, author.
Title: Geopolitics of energy in Central Asia: India's position and policy/Ramakrushna Pradhan.
Description: Abingdon, Oxon; New York, NY: Routledge, 2021. | Includes bibliographical references and index.
Identifiers: LCCN 2020039842 (print) | LCCN 2020039843 (ebook) | ISBN 9780367110345 (hardback) | ISBN 9780367695897 (paperback) | ISBN 9781003142423 (ebook)
Subjects: LCSH: Energy industries–Asia, Central. | Energy policy–Asia, Central. | Energy policy–India. | Geopolitics–Asia, Central. | Asia, Central–Relations–India. | India–Relations–Asia, Central. | Asia, Central–Strategic aspects.
Classification: LCC HD9502.A78452 P74 2021 (print) | LCC HD9502.A78452 (ebook) | DDC 333.790958–dc23
LC record available at https://lccn.loc.gov/2020039842
LC ebook record available at https://lccn.loc.gov/2020039843

ISBN: 978-0-367-11034-5 (hbk)
ISBN: 978-0-367-69589-7 (pbk)
ISBN: 978-1-003-14242-3 (ebk)

Typeset in Bembo
by Deanta Global Publishing Services, Chennai, India

Dedicated to my beloved wife and son
Punya Prabha and Harshit

CONTENTS

FIGURES

TABLES

PREFACE

The age we live in is the age of energy. Its centrality lies in its complexities as it has been the single most moving force behind economic development worldwide, technological innovation and transformation. To be honest, energy is what keeps the world going. It has been the sole driver of the growth, development, prosperity and well-being of mankind and a source of military power and determinant of people's welfare through all ages. History shows evidence that the success of any civilization or state is the result of its access to ample energy. Energy is, therefore, called a "universal currency" as anything can be done through energy and, in turn, it can be responsible for the survival of human life and civilized existence. No other element has shaped the history of the world in the past one hundred years so much as the competition and conflict to control and administer oil and energy.

The revelation of the secret of 20th-century prosperity is attributed to cheap oil and energy. As we enter the 21st century, these energy resources continue to be the determining factor of the success of both the developing and developed world. However, the challenge before countries in the 21st century, unlike the 20th century, is that the sources of energy deposits are well known but the resources are finite. Besides, the direct link between energy security and economic growth has further accentuated the resource scramble in the significant energy bastions of the world. It should be noted here that in the last 40 years the world's demand for energy has grown by 95 per cent while future energy demand is projected to grow by 90 per cent because of increasing demand from developing countries like India and China. The fight has even become aggressive as the number of consumers has increased while oil and petroleum have started to dry up, as claimed by the Club of Rome thesis and Peak Oil theory. All the above factors have further encouraged the powerful countries of the world to engage in aggressive competition for the resource scramble, whereas the newly developing countries have also left no stone unturned to meet their domestic demands by diversifying their supply sources of equity oil. While there are two categories of consumers – the Western capitalist club – the developed countries – and the Eastern emerging economies – the developing countries – the supplying countries are also categorized into two clubs as those who are suppressed and those who can be suppressed. Those who are strong exert their policies, thereby giving rise to oil diplomacy which becomes effective as it concerns the indispensable unit, crude oil. Those who can be suppressed are targeted by influential players, mainly those who import oil, to access cheaper ways to import oil or to gain strategic control over the reserves. Thereby, this gives rise to power-play surrounding the supply of crude oil in the world. This precisely has set the milieu to link India – one of the fastest-growing economies of the world – with Central Asia – the latest geographical landscape of world energy.

It is no wonder that India – with an economy expected to grow at 10 per cent for the next 25 years has developed a ravenous appetite for energy. India accounting for 2.4 per cent of the world's total land surface and around 16 per cent of the total world population is also the third-largest growing economy in the world. With the rapid rise of population and industrialization, the main challenge before India, therefore, is to maintain sustainable growth at a rate of 8–10 per cent GDP over the next quarter-century to meet its developmental goals for poverty eradication, food security, rural development, education and health. India had an average growth rate of GDP at 7 per cent in the last decade and has attained a growth rate of 7.1 per cent up to March 2017 despite demonetization. Further, to catch up with the rest of Asia and to eradicate poverty, it is essential on the part of India to continue to grow at about 8–10 per cent or more over the next 25 years or so. To maintain this pace of growth, India will have to increase its energy consumption by at least 4 per cent annually. The energy requirement for such sustained annual growth poses a major challenge. According to the Integrated Energy Policy of Government of India, it needs to increase its primary energy supply by a factor of three or four and its electricity generation capacity/supply by a factor of five to six compared to its 2004 level.

Increasingly, frustrated by the dismal performance of India's domestic energy sector, India's diplomatic setup has opened up its arms to become actively involved in helping India achieve energy sufficiency in the last few years. Diversifying and expanding its international sources of energy has been a major Indian policy thrust for the past decade. Since then there is a growing recognition that energy security needs to be a critical component of India's foreign policy as India's continued economic success hinges around this. It is also believed that India's energy security can be increased by (a) diversifying both its energy mix and its sources of energy imports, and (b) seriously pursuing the overseas acquisition of energy assets as oil and gas are non-renewable and are in limited supply. So it is no surprise that energy cooperation is at the heart of India's engagement with Central Asia.

In the scenario of India's unprecedented energy requirement and stupendous foreign dependence, the energy resources of Central Asia including the Caspian Sea region certainly play an important role in India's energy strategy. Further, Central Asian oil and gas are of high quality, largely untapped, and the investment environment is open and very friendly. As the producing countries consume less, a major chunk of these resources is meant for export. Also, unlike the Middle East and African energy-rich countries, Central Asia is very stable and popular uprisings against outside power are seemingly absent there. The gas of Central Asia and the Caspian has less ash compared to other gas-producing regions of the world. All these happen to be the driving factor for resource scramble by major powers in general and India in particular to the Central Asian energy hub. However, the region does not give a free pass and comfortable access to its oil wells and gas fields as the competition over control and administration of energy resources and routes is intense and widespread. Therefore, it would be pertinent to discuss the energy geopolitics of Central Asia and India's position and strategies in the region amidst the new great game.

It is needless to say that, for the last several years, the region of Central Asia has been intensely discussed and widely debated over its possession and potentiality of energy resources. One thing that undoubtedly is true is that Central Asia has assumed a new role in the era of globalization. In the early 1990s, there were frequent discussions about the Central Asian region becoming another Middle East. Although this rhetoric has become relatively more sober, the Central Asian region (CAR) possesses 3 to 4 per cent of proven global oil and gas reserves. Moreover, production of oil and gas has increased in the last few years and there are prospects for more discoveries and growth in production output. The aggravated competition between nations in the grand chessboard of Central Asia further testifies the looming presence of energy in the heartland. With this premise, this book delves into the energy factor in the geopolitics of Central Asia and tries to figure out the position of India in the epic quest for oil in the traditional bastion of Russia, China and the United States. The study further investigates India's policy towards the region and examines the strategies put in place to acquire the much-needed energy resource to run its economic engine, feed the burgeoning population and fulfil the millennium development goals it has set forth to achieve by 2020.

This study is an extension of my PhD work on the Geopolitics of Energy in Central Asia and its implication for India. This book is an academic pursuit and written to share my research findings and personal insights. In addition to my research work, my academic visits to Central Asia especially to L. N. Gumilyov Eurasian National University, Nursultan, Kazakhstan as Visiting Professor, visits to Kazakhstan and Kyrgyzstan have helped in developing my understanding and shaped my ideas about the heartland region. The contacts I have developed in Central Asian countries and experts like Prof. Robert Cutler, Prof. Mizohid Rakhimov, Prof. Akbota Zholdasbekova, Prof. Sayit Ali, Prof. Yasar Sari and many others have helped in augmenting new horizons of ideas on assessing

Central Asian countries' perspective on India in the epic quest for energy in the grand chessboard of world politics. This book primarily aims at initiating debate and dialogue for opening up new directions to strengthen the relationship between India and the Central Asian Republics.

Disclaimer: *The maps and the graphics inserted in the book from several national and international sources are only visual depictions and not the actual boundaries. Therefore any inaccuracy and inconsistencies in demarcation and presentation of maps, routes and graphics in terms of their national boundaries are regrettable and unintentional.*

ACKNOWLEDGEMENTS

This book is based on research conducted on the geopolitics of energy in Central Asia and the implications for India. Many of the ideas of this book have been the thrust of my research and kept me engaged for years in developing them. Some parts of this book have appeared in article form in different journals such as *Fudan Journal of Humanities and Social Sciences*, *India Quarterly*, *Jadavpur Journal of International Relations*, *Central Asia and the Caucasus*, *Contemporary Central Asia*, *Asia Europe Journal*, *IUP Journal of International Relations*, *Mainstream*, *FPRC* and others. I am sincerely obliged to them for their cooperation.

In this journey of preparing this book, I have received encouragement to start the work, persevere with it and finally publish it from our friends and colleagues from both India and Central Asia. I remain grateful to them.

A special word of appreciation to the late Prof. Arun Mohanty for introducing me to this literary moonlight. I owe him a lot. My words may not match the spirit of the help and emotional support Prof. Mohanty extended to me during my research in JNU. I am indebted to Madam Namita Mohanty for her encouragement in my academic and research activities. Their help and cooperation during my JNU days is a memory to be cherished.

I am thankful to Prof. Phool Badan, my research guide during MPhil and Ph.D for boosting my spirit and developing my research domain. My sincere gratitude to him for his constant support and thorough guidance both in my professional and personal life.

I am indebted to the Vice-Chancellor of Fakir Mohan University Prof. Madhumita Das for her unconditional support, help and encouragement extended to me in academics and research.

I am thankful to Amb. Phunchok Stobdan, Prof. Nirmala Joshi, Prof. Asha Hans and Prof. Aswini Mohapatra for being my mentors and a major source of motivation.

My gratitude is also due to Dr Atanu Mohapatra, Dr Mahesh Ranjan Debata, Prof. Manish, Dr Siba Sankar Mohanty, Dr Sumanta Swain, Mr Adikanda Sahu and Mr Duryodhan Patra for their invaluable support and boosting my spirit in completion of the work.

My heartfelt thanks to my colleagues and friends Dr Sunil Kumar Padhi, Mr Sachita Nanda Sa and Miss Smruti Sikta Thapa for their invaluable help and support in editing, providing important information and materials throughout the research work and importantly being at my side during the rough days of my life.

I would like to thank my friends in Kazakhstan, Prof. Akbota Zholdasbekova, Vice-Rector, L. N. Gumilyov Eurasian National University and Prof. Sayet Ali Avcu for their help and academic support from time to time and in particular during my stay in Astana in 2018. I am also grateful to yet another friend from Turkey, Prof. Yasar Sari for his intellectual and philosophical inputs in the book.

Special mention for invaluable support provided by my dear student friends Mr Abhisekh Mohanty (Moscow), Miras (Moscow), Monalisha Das, and Makaranda from JNU.

I am grateful to my family members especially my elder brother Mr Prashant Kumar Pradhan who has been my source of strength all through. I am indeed fortunate to have his blessing whenever I require. I am thankful to *Nana* (father), *Bou* (mother) for their unconditional love and support.

I am grateful to my loving wife Mrs Punya Prabha Pradhan for her role and contribution in writing and shaping the book. Without her total dedication to domestic affairs and letting me stay away from home for days and weeks, this work would not have seen the light of day. My love is also due to Harshit (Badal), Varsha and Bristhi.

I owe sincere gratitude to Dr Shoma Choudhury, Commissioning Manager at Routledge for her constant support and help in publishing this book. I am also thankful to Miss Shloka Chauhan of Taylor & Francis Group for setting the deadlines and making me honour them, enabling the completion of the editing of the book on time. Big thanks to the editorial team of Routledge for their invaluable support in bringing the book to this form. I am thankful to Rennie Alphonsa and her team at Deanta Global for the invaluable service rendered in thorough editing of this manuscript.

My thanks are also due to many other unnamed friends and acquaintances whose help and influence helped me to develop the ideas in the book.

Ramakrushna Pradhan

ABBREVIATIONS

ADB	Asian Development Bank
AEC	Asian Energy Club
AFRICOM	African Command
AIDS	Acquired Immune Deficiency Syndrome
AIIB	Asian Infrastructure Investment Bank
AMOCO	American Oil Company
APPTA	Afghanistan–Pakistan Transit–Trade Agreement
ARAMCO	Arabian-American Oil Company
ASCOPE	Association of Southeast Asian Nations Council on Petroleum
ASEAN	Association of Southeast Asian Nations.
ASLS	Achhacarry Agreement
ATEC	Agreement on Trade and Economic Cooperation
BBC	British Broadcasting Company
BCF	billion cubic feet
BCM	billion cubic meters
BJP	Bhartiya Janata Party
BP	British Petroleum
BRI	Belt and Road Initiative
BTC	Baku–Tibilisi–Ceyhan
BTE	Baku–Tibilisi–Erzurum
CA	Central Asia
CAC	Central Asia Center
CACO	Central Asian Cooperation Organization
CAEC	Central Asian Economic Community
CAR	Central Asian Region
CAREC	Central Asia Regional Economic Cooperation
CARS	Central Asian Republics

CAS	Central Asian States
CASAREM	Central Asia–South Asia Regional Electricity Market
CASOC	California Arabian Standard Oil Company
CBTA	Cross-Border Transport Agreement
CCAP	Connect Central Asia Policy
CCC	Consolidated Construction Company
CEO	Chief Executive Officer
CFP	Companie Française de Petroles
CGNPC	China Guangdong Nuclear Power Co.
CHP	Combined Heat and Power plant
CICA	Conference on Interaction and Confidence Building Measures in Asia
CIS	Commonwealth of Independent States
CNOC	China National Oil Corporation
CNPC	Chinese National Petroleum Company
COM	Cabinet of Ministers
CPC	Caspian Pipeline Consortium
CSR	Corporate Social Responsibility
EAEU	Eurasian Economic Union
EBRD	European Bank for Reconstruction and Development
ECO	Economic Cooperation Organization
ECO	European Coal Organization
EEU	Eurasian Economic Union
EIA	Economists Intelligent Agency
EIA	Energy Information Administration
EIU	Economists Intelligent Unit
EU	European Union
EURASEC	Eurasian Economic Community
FAO	Food and Agriculture Organisation
FDI	Foreign Direct Investments
FSU	Former Soviet Union
GAIL	Gas Authority of India Limited
GDP	Gross Domestic Product
GHGS	Greenhouse Gases
GT	Gigatonnes
GW	Gigawatts
GWH	Gigawatt-hour
HIV	Human immunodeficiency virus
HPP	Hydro Power Plant
IAEA	International Atomic Energy Agency
ICG	International Crisis Group
IEA	International Energy Agency
IEA	International Energy Agency
IGC	Inter-Governmental Commission

IISS	International Institute of Strategic Studies
IMF	International Monetary Fund
IMF	International Monetary Fund
IMU	Islamic Movement of Uzbekistan
INOGATE	Interstate Oil and Gas Transport to Europe
INSTC	International North–South Transportation Corridor
IPC	Iran Petroleum Company
IPC	Iran Petroleum Company
IPI	Iran–Pakistan–India
ISI	Inter-Service Intelligence (Intelligence agency of Pakistan)
ISL	In situ leach
ITEC	Indian-Technical and Economic Cooperation
J&K	Jammu and Kashmir
KfW	Kreditanstalt fuer Wiederaufbau
KIO	Karachaganak Integrated Operation
KMG	KazMunaiGas
KNOC	Korean National Oil Company
KPO	Karachaganak Petroleum Operating
KWH	Kilowatt-hour
LNG	Liquefied Natural Gas
LNP	Look North Policy
LPG	Liquefied Petroleum Gas
MARAL	Market Allocation
MEA	Ministry of External Affairs
MNE	Multinational Enterprises
MOIP	Mandatory Oil Import Programme
MOU	Memorandum of Understanding
MT	Million Tonnes
MTOE	Million tonnes of oil equivalent
MW	Megawatt
NATO	North Atlantic Treaty Organization
NCOC	North Caspian Operating Company
NEP	National Energy Plan
NEPAD	New Partnership for Africa's Development
NIS	New Independent States
NOC	National Oil Company
NPCI	Nuclear Power Corporation of India
NPT	Non-Proliferation Treaty
NSG	Nuclear Supplier Group
OAPEC	Organization for Arab Petroleum Exporting Countries
OBOR	One Belt One Road
OECD	Organisation for Economic Cooperation and Development
OMEL	ONGC-Mittal Energy Limited
ONGC	Oil and Natural Gas Corporation

OPEC	Organization of Petroleum Exporting Countries
OSCE	Organization for Security and Cooperation in Europe
OVL	ONGC Videsh Limited
PL	Petroleum Law
PREMEX	Petromex Petroleos Mexiconos
PSA	Production Sharing Agreement
PTL	Power Transmission Line
SARDP	Special Accelerated Road Development Project
SCO	Shanghai Cooperation Organisation
TACIS	Technical Aid to the Commonwealth of Independent States
TAP	Trans-Afghan Pipeline
TAPI	Turkmenistan–Afghanistan–Pakistan–India
TCF	trillion cubic feet
TCGP	Trans-Caspian Gas Pipeline
TCM	Trillion Cubic Metres
TCO	Tengiz Chevro Oil
TCP	Trans Caspian pipeline
TERI	Tata Energy Research Institute
TKR	Turkmenistan–Kazakhstan–Russia
TPC	Turkish Petroleum Company
TPC	Turkish Petroleum Company
TPS	Thermal Power Station
TRACECA	Transport Corridor Europe-Caucasus-Asia
TU	tonnes of Uranium
UK	United Kingdom
UNCTAD	United Nations Conference on Trade and Development
UNDP	United Nations Development Programme
UNG	UzbekNeftGaz
UNO	United Nations Organization
UNSC	United Nations Security Council
UPA	United Progressive Alliance
US	United States
US DOE	United States Department of Energy
USAID	United States Agency for International Development
USGS	United States Gas Survey
USSR	United Soviet Socialist Republics
WCA	World Coal Organization
WMD	Weapons of Mass Destruction
XUAR	Xinjiang–Uighur Autonomous Region

INTRODUCTION

> *"Access to raw materials, especially access to energy is a top priority of international Political Relations."*
>
> – Melvin A. Conant and Fren Gold (1978)

Energy is what keeps the world going. History shows evidence that energy has been the driver of economic growth in all countries and through all ages. It has been the main source of military power and the sole determinant of people's welfare. It is the access to energy, whether human, animal or natural, that has primarily determined the scale and success of civilization or state. Given the impeccable importance of energy, it has rightly been said that energy is required not just for the survival of human life but for their civilized existence as well.

Moreover, in the 21st century energy has become a fundamental aspect of human life. This indeed has become the mainstay of modern life without which moving a step further becomes impossible. Energy has been the core of economic development for all countries as it powers the state and runs their offices, factories and government buildings, hospitals and schools. It runs the entire world transportation system, heats homes in chilly winter and preserves perishable foods in scorching summer. Its centrality explains its complexity. Energy is the source of wealth and competition, the basis of political controversy and technological innovation, and the core of an epochal challenge to our environment. The energy sector further in the contemporary world order has entered into an era of unprecedented transformation. Global demand for fossil fuel reserves is rising, energy price volatility is higher than ever, funding has become increasingly uncertain and climate change is firmly taking its place on the global political agenda.

Furthermore, in the age of globalization, the growing trends of liberalization and marketization along with modernization and industrialization have led to a highly materialistic pursuit of life. Competition among countries of the World to control and administer the energy resources has become the order of the day. Hence, capturing the nerves of the world has led to an unabated drive and quest for energy. Due to growing demands for energy, the priority focus of major energy-consuming countries has become to ensure secure, affordable, reliable and unrestricted flow of energy to maintain their energy security. For that, along with available domestic energy resources, having an unrestricted hold over the energy resources of foreign countries has become inevitable. On the other hand, the energy-producing countries have consequently developed monopoly following the remarkable rise in demand for energy all over the world. Since energy is their only resource, they have been trying their best to make the utmost possible utilization of this resource for their economic development and national growth.

Energy factor in geopolitics

Geopolitics in recent years has been revolving closely around energy and the geographical landmasses rich in sources of energy. Since energy has been the driver of economic growth, the source of military power and the main determinant of people's welfare, ensuring a timely, adequate, reliable and affordable, easily accessible and secure supply of energy has become imminent for all countries of the world. As most of the world's principal energy producers are not principal consumers, there is bound to be stiff competition in the resource scramble in the limited geological landscape blessed with energy. Hence, the structural dimensions of energy geopolitics can be seen from both the supply and demand sides. The supply side includes the volumes of global reserves, their distribution pattern, their longevity, the discoveries, capacity building and so on. On the demand front, the issues are related to the market size and its geography, logistics of transport and its delivery and others.

Although energy includes in its fold oil, gas, coal, hydel, uranium and others it is primarily around oil and natural gas that the geopolitics of energy revolves to a greater degree and towards uranium and hydel potentials to a lesser extent.

> Since the availability of hydrocarbons is determined by geology, the global politics of energy is, therefore, shaped mainly by the "arc of energy" stretching from the Gulf region to the Caspian Sea, through Siberia and the Arctic region to the Russian Far East, Alaska and Canada. In this regard, it can be said that nearly 80 per cent of the world's oil and gas including potential reserves are located in this region.
>
> *(Sikri 2008)*

Nevertheless, factors like economics, technology and politics have played a critical role in determining the supply and demand side of energy geopolitics. For the energy-producing countries, energy is not only a source of enormous power and wealth, it also constitutes leverage. Since energy is a strategic resource, denial of it to any rival or enemy increases the latter's vulnerability.

The political nature of energy linked to the sources of supply and demand comes to public attention at moments of crisis. But energy politics have become yet more complex as transport systems, particularly in the United States, Europe, China and India have become largely reliant on oil. Access to energy remains critical to sustaining growth in China and India – not just to keep pace with the burgeoning population. Failure to deliver on the hope of greater prosperity could unravel even authoritarian regimes and even more so democratic ones, as populations become more educated and demanding. And it is these very factors that have turned the market power of energy suppliers into political power. Importers have come to compete for supplies, driving up prices, suppliers' wealth and the capacity to play roles in regional and international politics.

The traditional geopolitical considerations have become even more complex with global climate change leading to environmental security concerns. Besides, the security of supply, i.e. the security of transit through chokepoints, is also critical to energy geopolitics. Because nearly 30 per cent of world oil exports pass through the Strait of Hormuz, nearly 16 per cent through the strait of Malacca, and nearly 5.5 per cent through Bab el-Mandeb, the narrow strait connecting the Red Sea and the Gulf of Aden.

In recent years there has been a growing debate over the running out of oil and other energy sources. It has been reiterated several times by the Peak Oil theory that Russia is producing at its peak and Saudi Arabia has limited additional short-term capacity. Due to commercial disputes, regional instability, civic unrest and political coups in the Persian Gulf, investors are thoroughly worried about their energy security concerns. In this scenario, the issues of energy security are now moving beyond the exclusive concerns of consumers. Producers too require a stable regime with a coherent demand and supply scenario. Although global reserves have been the principal factors in the influencing if not defining of the energy security debate, it may be recalled that the Club of Rome Thesis cautioned the world community about the limited span of non-renewable sources of energy in its paper "There Are Limits to Growth". That is why perhaps the global scramble for oil and energy has taken a fast track route all around geopolitical landscapes abundant with energy resources. No wonder the Central Asian geographical landscape in terms of its huge energy potentials and congenial investment environment invites global attention, thereby accentuating the competition over petro-politics and pipeline diplomacy in the region and beyond.

The Club of Rome Thesis is not the only one to predict the drying out of oil and energy; even *The Peak Oil Theory* advocated by King Hubbert (1956), a well-known geologist of the United States, in 1956 asserted that oil discovery, and therefore production, would follow a bell-shaped curve over its life. Peak-Oil is the point at which oil production will reach its maximum output, and thus begin a terminal decline – accompanied by an indefinite rise in price for the remaining supply.

Peak oil in simple terms = Limited Resources + Geometric Growth

The key message this theory delivers is that world oil has already reached its maximum and will decline to less than 39 million barrels per day. It also claims through the help of Hubbert methodology, with a collection of more recent data for oil reserves and production, that world oil will reach a peak in and around the year 2025. This theory tells us that any finite resource (including oil) will have a beginning, middle and an end of production, and at some point, it will reach a level of maximum output. It is here this theory helps us to understand why there is a scramble for oil and energy in the contemporary world energy market.

Concerning energy security, the *geopolitical theory* addresses the unbalance in the distribution of natural resources worldwide and struggle for their control and administration. It is indeed evident that energy resources are abundant in the poverty-stricken areas of third world countries such as the Middle East, Latin America and Africa. The Caspian and Central Asian region, though not belonging to the third world category, are also not clubbed among developed economies either. These regions for their development need economic resources, which they ensure by selling their energy resources to developed countries. Developed countries, on the other hand, need the energy to fuel their growth and sustain their civilized existence. As these resources are limited and demand is high, countries, in order to have access to and control over these resources, try to manipulate the producer countries in the lure of huge economic benefits. If this fails, they resort to war as well. There exists competition among the big powers to gain these resources either by outplaying the competitor or by granting huge economic concessions. The geopolitical theory here suggests that in international politics there is always a power play between two states concerning their geographical resources or possessions.

Energy security has also been articulately explained through various paradigms of international relations theory. And there seems to have been consensus on the issue of energy security achieving particular importance since the energy shocks of the 1970s when present asymmetries between the geographical distribution of resources and energy consumers was consolidated by oil shortages in the petroleum-dependent countries. Since then, energy security has been integrated into the debates of International Relations theories. An overview of existing International Relations theories demonstrates four important approaches. The first among these is the rational approach which focuses on international political relations, shaped by structural imbalances between energy-producing and energy-consuming regions. Oil supply has become a subject of vulnerability, either perceived or real. Since then, much analysis has been done on the growing rate of energy consumption and the energy import dependency of many industrialized states. Particular emphasis has been attributed to political conflicts in connection to natural resources. Failures of cross-border energy trade cast a sharp light on the efficacy of institutions governing and regulating this trade. Here, the second approach delves into analysing the efficiency of international economic institutions on enhancing security. The third approach can be defined from several recent assessments of the academic and business world of a "new political economy of energy" characterized by a growing diversity in energy technology, trends towards deregulation, foreign investments and interdependency in the sector. Energy becomes a complex system of trade transactions, where price formation becomes the major source of political vulnerabilities. The fourth approach is the international political economy (IPE) which stems from the points of view of S. Strange (1988); this theory criticizes the rationalist economic theories. The interest of the critical IPE theory consists of the importance accorded to economic values (nationalism, liberalism), which limit the rational approach of international regimes. All these approaches together strengthen the research theme concerned by enriching it through a contribution from various dimensions.

Setting the milieu

Energy is undoubtedly the most abundant and valuable natural resource in Central Asia. Although energy in its fold includes oil, natural gas, coal, hydroelectricity, uranium etc., today oil and gas have assumed greater importance in the world energy sector than any other variants. Hence, there is much political debate and economic interest in these two energy resources which Central Asia has in great quantity.

Central Asia as a single geographical entity consists of five "stans", namely Kazakhstan, Kyrgyzstan, Tajikistan, Turkmenistan and Uzbekistan. It spreads over an area of 1.5 million square miles in the heart of Eurasia, a region that once used to be called the "centre of Asia". Geopolitically, the region is the geographic hub of Asia and the heart of Eurasia. Located literally in the middle half of the Silk Route, Central Asia is strategically a vital region to almost every major country on earth. It shares a 6200 kilometre border with Russia in the north, a 3500 km long border with China in the east, approximately a border of more than 3500 km to the west with the Caspian Sea and a huge length of inland border with Iran and Afghanistan in the south-west and the south. At the crossroads of Europe and Asia, Central Asia has always been in the focus of world politics. Even today, it has enormous strategic as well as economic significance in international politics. Its abundance of energy resources and its geographic location has rightly placed Central Asia in the global limelight. In the 19th century, Central Asia was at the centre of the classical Great Game played out between the imperial Tsarist regime and colonial British empire. Later on, it became part of the former Soviet Union. However, the disintegration of the USSR in 1991 suddenly led to the independence of the Central Asian states. These Central Asian states have again become the centre of global attention and regional competition and rivalry due to their geographical location, strategic position and possession of valuable energy resources.

The Central Asian region is predominantly a gas-producing region with significant amounts of untapped oil resources (proved and probable). However, it also possesses huge reserves of uranium, coal mines and hydroelectricity resources as well. It has proven gas reserves of about 6.6 trillion cubic metres (tcm) of which approximately 2.9 tcm are found in Turkmenistan, 1.9 tcm in Uzbekistan and 1.8 tcm in Kazakhstan. The region represents about one-tenth of the known gas reserves of the Commonwealth of Independent States (CIS). Turkmenistan with 80 billion tcm per year and Uzbekistan with 50 billion tcm per year are the two leading gas producers, although Kazakhstan also produces a significant amount of gas in the region.

So far as oil is concerned, Central Asia has an estimated 200 billion barrels of hydrocarbon reserves. Kazakhstan, the main producer of oil in the region, is projected to have between 30 and 40 billion barrels of crude oil reserves. Turkmenistan, the most important producer of gas with 50.4 trillion cubic meters also had as many as 19 oil and 65 gas fields as of 2017. The fact of the matter is that Uzbekistan consumes more energy than any other country in the region. The Kyrgyz Republic and Tajikistan produce only small quantities of oil but have massive hydroelectric potentials.

In addition to Central Asia, the Caspian Sea region (of which Kazakhstan and Turkmenistan are littoral states) also possesses huge hydro-carbon resources, mainly oil and gas. Uzbekistan, although not a littoral state, is generally considered to be part of the Caspian Sea region. According to the July 2001 report of the US Energy Information Administration, "the Caspian Sea region possessed about 34 billion barrels of proven oil and 235 billion barrels of possible oil reserves". It is about one-fourth of that of the oil reserves of the Middle East. The proven natural gas reserves of the Caspian region including that of Uzbekistan were quoted at 243–248 trillion cubic feet (tcf). Thus, 88 per cent of Caspian oil reserves are located in the states of Azerbaijan, Kazakhstan and Turkmenistan. Turkmenistan and Uzbekistan have the majority portions of gas reserves in the region. Therefore, it becomes essential to study the Caspian region while dealing with the energy sectors of Central Asian states.

Moreover, Central Asia is home to huge stocks of uranium. Among the Central Asian states, Kazakhstan and Uzbekistan have a fair amount of uranium deposits. They are the two important states in the region to have strategic uranium reserves in large quantities. According to the estimates of the World Nuclear Association, Kazakhstan, possessing about 12 per cent of world uranium resources, produces around 41 per cent of world Uranium, making the country the leading uranium producer in the world, surpassing Canada and Australia. In 2019 Kazakhstan produced about 22,800 tonnes of uranium. Besides, Uzbekistan has the second-largest uranium reserves in Central Asia after Kazakhstan with a production capacity of 2404 tonnes of uranium for the year 2018. As of February 2020, Uzbekistan ranks as the seventh-largest uranium supplier of the world. Tajikistan has significant amounts of uranium reserves with the capability of enrichment. Kyrgyzstan has also a lot of nuclear waste left over as a legacy of the former Soviet Union.

It is crystal clear from the above discussion that the regional political vacuum created by the sudden demise of the Soviet Union – the largest geopolitical landscape in the world map – was filled by the entry of the United States, China, the European Union, Russia and regional powers such as Iran and Turkey among others. The motivating factors for global as well as regional powers to explain their serious interests in the region have been as follows.

1. The oil of the region is considered to be of good quality.
2. The region represents one of the world's last great frontiers for geological survey and analysis offering opportunities for the discovery, production, transportation and refining of enormous quantities of oil and gas and other energy resources.
3. The Central Asian energy market seems more promising as most of its reserves are unexplored and underdeveloped.
4. Although the Central Asian republics have physical possession of the energy resources, they don't have the capital and technology to go into production. This, therefore, offers opportunities for foreign companies to invest and acquire a share in the energy markets.
5. Since the domestic necessities of the producing countries are relatively low and expected to be low, the biggest part of Central Asian oil is meant for export.
6. Importantly, Central Asia is relatively a stable region in contrast to other energy-rich destinations.

Compounded with the world energy crises in 1973 and the 1990s and the commencement of globalization, the huge reserves of oil, gas, hydel, uranium and other energy resources of Central Asia along with the Caspian region has indeed attracted the attention of major energy-consuming countries of the world. Energy-consuming countries have accordingly formulated their policies towards the Central Asian region. Consequently, growing engagement, intense competition and mutual interests among the major regional and extra-regional countries have increased over the region. The big powers have brought in major changes in their policy procedures and efforts are made to remain more dynamic and proactive in the region. This, in turn, has led to greater engagement and counter engagement of the big powers, leading to more frequent, complex and often conflicting situations. However, this growing engagement is not one-sided; unlike the great game, Central Asian states are equal partners in the new great game. However, the countries of Asia, particularly China and India being proximate players, have assumed a larger role in the geopolitical region of Central Asia.

India – a geographical landmass to the south of Central Asia – covering an area of approximately 3.28 million sq. km (2.4 per cent of the world's total land surface) ranks as the seventh-largest country in the world. It is also the second most populous country on earth with a population of 1.26 billion as of 2011. The main challenge before India, therefore, is to maintain sustainable growth at a rate of 8 per cent Gross Domestic Product (GDP) over the next quarter-century to meet its Millennium Development Goals of poverty eradication, education and health facilities for all, water and sanitation services, and, most importantly, ensuring energy security and food security. India had an average growth rate of GDP of 7 per cent in the last decade of the twentieth century and attained a growth rate of 9.2 per cent up to September 2008, which then slowed down due to the global financial crisis. To maintain this pace, the country will have to increase its energy consumption by at least 4 per cent annually. To catch this relentless demand for energy, India will have to import energy from external sources as its domestic sources are not sufficient to meet India's energy needs in the long term.

Although India is the eleventh largest producer of energy in the world with 2.4 per cent of energy production, simultaneously she is the fifth largest energy consumer of the world as well. With 3.5 per cent of global energy consumption, she is projected to surpass Japan and Russia to take third place by 2030. Domestic coal reserves account for 70 per cent of India's energy needs. The remaining 30 per cent is met by oil, with more than 65 per cent of that being imported. Due to the high rise in consumption on the domestic front and necessitating stability for economic growth at a sustainable rate, India's demand for energy is expected to double by 2025. It is projected that, by 2025, India will have to import 90 per cent of its petroleum from abroad. This is an uphill task for India, given its contiguous limitations.

From the climate change standpoint, coal is the dirtiest and most unpurified among all fuels. Hence, coal though abundant in India cannot meet her energy needs in the days to come. Further, India's oil and gas reserves are not sufficient to convene its rapidly growing energy needs. In addition to this, India's energy sector which is dominated by the public sector is thoroughly lacking in coordination and competition, adding to its already concerning issues.

As a result, India has timely opened up its external wings to acquire oil and gas from the external sources. In this context, India's basic approach to energy diplomacy of both oil and gas primarily has been to develop as many potential supply arrangements, with as many potential suppliers as possible. India currently imports around 65–72 per cent of its oil needs mainly from the Middle East. As the Middle East has always been the centre of a political hotbed, civil strife, regional instability and insecurity, Central Asia as an energy hub provides an opportunity for India. India as an extended neighbour of the Central Asian region, therefore, has major geostrategic and economic stakes and interests, particularly in the field of energy, i.e. oil, gas, hydel and uranium. This is because energy security is the basic requirement of India today.

However, the passage for India is not free of problems. The growing presence of big powers in the Central Asian region to control its huge reserves of oil, gas and other resources, in addition to its strategic position, somewhat restrict India in playing a significant role in this region. In addition to this, India in its energy endeavour has to encounter many more challenges, mainly from the geographical front. The great Himalayas in particular stand as a major constraint for India in any further endeavour towards her northern neighbours. Further, the often hostile attitude of her neighbours certainly impacts its energy security issues to a large extent. The steep competition from China, pursuing a similar strategy of diversifying its sources of supply through energetic business and political diplomacy also stands as a stumbling block in the way of India. Given the geopolitical position, at the moment China is well ahead of India in acquiring new sources of energy. Similarly, the competition between India and China for new energy sources in Central Asia is also clearly well in favour of China. So far, the collaborative efforts between India and China regarding new energy sources have been minimal. Given the South China Sea energy confrontation between India and China, it is fair to assume that, as far as energy is concerned, Sino-Indian relations will continue to be competitive in Central Asia as well.

With energy increasingly being viewed as a vital component of what is now broadly defined as "national security", cultivating alternative sources of energy and reducing dependence on the volatile Middle-Eastern region has become a vital concern for India. Further, for keeping India's economic engine in motion, an assured and uninterrupted supply of energy is critical. India's strategic interests at stake in the region make it imperative for the country to evolve a clear policy, capable of addressing the existing as well as potential challenges that may arise in the future. Therefore, notwithstanding any of the above impediments, this study focuses on the central problems in the way of Central Asia–India energy relations. Does this also examine in detail what significant role Central Asia can play in meeting India's energy needs? What would be the major implications on India of the growing energy diplomacy in Central Asia? And what approach should India follow to connect transit routes for the supply of gas and oil from the Central Asian Republics to India? Most importantly, in what way would China implicate India's interests in Central Asia?

The book vividly discusses India's virtuous objectives in her epic quest for energy in the traditional bastions of Russia, the United States and China as explained as follows:

- As a short-term objective India is aiming at the construction of a cheaper, shorter and quicker route to connect with Central Asia. The International North–South Transportation Corridor (INSTC) proposed in 2002 by India, Russia and Iran and joined by other Eurasian countries offers India bounties of opportunities to sideline Islamabad by working out the INSTC option through the Bandar Abbas and Chabahar port of Iran to Mumbai through the Arabian Sea. Also from the cost–benefit analysis point of view, this has been seen as less expensive than other available routes and importantly it is secure and free from any sort of hostages.

  Recently good news has come from the International North–South Transportation Corridor (INSTC) that India and Russia have agreed to bolster their mutual trade by overcoming their geographical distance via the INSTC through Iran despite the United States warning against trade activities with Iran. If things go well then it is just a matter of time that India will overcome the greatest geographical barrier that has posed a challenge for New Delhi.

- The medium-term objective is that New Delhi is closely working to pursue the connectivity front through Iran and Afghanistan with Central Asia. The trilateral transit agreement proposed during the visit of Indian Prime Minister Shri Narendra Modi to all the Central Asian countries in 2015 and subsequently to Iran in May 2016 opened up a window of opportunity to develop a deal towards the construction of Chabahar Port in Iran and to build a transit corridor through Afghanistan that could help India to halve its costs in doing business with the Eurasian region.
- The long-term objective of India has been to create a stable and cost-effective energy supply network bypassing any sort of competition in Central Asia.

As such, energy cooperation forms an important component of India's Central Asian Policy. Importantly, this will allow India to lessen its growing dependence on the Gulf energy. Politically, the Gulf energy trade has been full of risk and unreliable. The countries of the Middle East themselves are a great stumbling block in the way of the supply of energy. Economically, importing oil from the Gulf is also very expensive. Following the oil crisis of the 1970s, oil prices became high which forced consumer countries to search for viable alternatives. Thus, the emergence of Central Asia as an energy hub undoubtedly provides India with an immense opportunity to ensure its energy needs.

In the backdrop of such developments, this book focuses on a balanced study of the energy politics in Central Asia and maps India's policy strategies, overriding the predominantly historical and cultural narratives emphasized so far in New Delhi's engagement with Central Asian republics. This book is unique and adds value to the knowledge domain of academic and research realms as India has been understudied in several available sources. Either India is avoided as a potential player in the region or considered an unrelated and underrated player in Central Asia. This book, therefore, is a deviation from the past and sets the trend in focusing India's growing energy needs and claims Central Asia as an alternative and viable source of energy supply with ample justification. With energy requirements skyrocketing, India's attention is now focused on tapping the energy resources of the Central Asian region including the Caspian. This book is an extension of the author's PhD thesis which largely exhibits a balanced study of India's needs and interests in terms of energy in Central Asia. It offers the single most extensive analysis of India's energy security strategy towards the region with updated data representation, and comprehensively examines the comparative energy policies of other similar countries that significantly clash with India's interests in Central Asia and the Caspian Region.

This book has been categorized into eight chapters excluding the introduction. The first chapter of this book deals with energy security and world politics. It offers a vivid account of world energy politics and the military and strategic power play associated around it. It elaborates in detail the conceptual understanding of energy security and the growing mismatch between energy demand and supply. As the global energy scenario after the 1970s with the world oil crisis was transformed thoroughly, the geopolitical aspects of world energy security discourse became intricately connected with international political deliberation which consequently resulted in the formulation of country-specific energy security strategies and policy formulations for the energy quest.

The second chapter explains the geopolitics of energy in Central Asia. It provides a detailed account of the geopolitics of energy in Central Asia. The objective of this chapter revolves around examining the multifaceted nature of Central Asian energy geopolitics and the global competition for its energy resources. In pursuit of this object, this chapter provides a quantitative analysis of the Central Asian energy potential, and offers an understanding of the unique position that each republic occupies in the geopolitics of oil and energy in Central Asia. It also examines the geopolitical pluralism of the region that not only attracts the outside powers but also significantly enhances the economic status of the countries and bestows them with international recognition. However, for the lucidity of the study and theoretical understanding of the themes, the chapter attempts to start with the theoretical background of geopolitics and its growing attachment with energy in contemporary times.

The third chapter illustrates India–Central Asia relations and endeavours to know the strategic interests of India in Central Asia in terms of geo-economics and geopolitics and to investigate what policies India needs to follow to strive for and secure its interests in the region. This chapter tries to objectify why India seeks to reconnect with Central Asia and lays emphasis on the geostrategic and geo-economic perspectives for the attempted re-engagement with the region, with due weight on the geopolitical significance of the region for New Delhi.

The fourth chapter depicts India's energy trajectory. It broadly emphasizes India's energy profile and the dilemma it faces to meet its burgeoning demands. It critically evaluates the four major challenges that India's National Energy Policy faces in ensuring access to energy at affordable prices, improved security and energy independence, greater sustainability, and economic growth to support the demands of the burgeoning population and maintain the growth trajectory. Then the chapter evaluates India's energy demand and supply scenario and establishes the relevance of Central Asia in India's energy quest, given its huge resource base and affordable prices, as New Delhi's overdependence on the Middle East causes energy monopoly, therefore, a price hike of exorbitant scale.

The fifth chapter deals with the issue of India–Central Asia and the energy quest. This chapter makes an effort to study the brand new avatar of Central Asia in its reordered geopolitical form that has emerged as a continuous field of interest and concern for countries around the region and world over. This chapter contends with the issue of India's energy security with the help of Central Asian energy resources. It elaborates the energy engagements of India with the Central Asian states. It also discusses the status of various bilateral and multilateral energy projects New Delhi has been pursuing in the heartland region.

The sixth chapter depicts the energy great game in Central Asia and presents the case of India in this epic quest for oil and energy in the region. It explains that the heartland region has witnessed a new great game through the scramble for resources. This has further accentuated the struggle for oil and energy in the region and led to aggressive foreign policy formulations and strategic calculation by countries such as the United States, China, the European Union, Japan, Israel, Iran, Pakistan and India which many now refer to as the new great game for not just controlling but administering the energy resources of the region. The bottom line of the new great game, unlike the previous version, is essentially played out around petropolitics and pipeline diplomacy. In this scramble for resources this chapter tries to figure out the position of India in the epic quest for oil in the traditional bastion of Russia and the new grand chessboard of China and the United States.

Chapter 7 examines the various transit route options between India and Central Asia. It describes various existing routes as well as several projected routes that would connect India with Central Asia to import oil and gas through pipelines. While defining the importance of these transit pipelines for India's energy security, this chapter highlights the problems and challenges New Delhi is facing from transit issues. Apart from the discussion of the International North–South Transportation Corridor (INSTC), Turkmenistan–Afghanistan–Pakistan–India (TAPI) and Iran–Pakistan–India (IPI), it also looks into the cost–benefit analysis of the projects to ascertain the benefits they will offer to India in terms of its economy and the feasibility of the pipeline.

Finally, the concluding chapter presents the current dynamics in India–Central Asia relations, highlighting the problems New Delhi is facing in its energy quest, and offers various dimensions to overcome the immediate concerns and recommends certain feasible solutions to enable India to deepen its ties with all the Central Asian republics to achieve its long-term interests in the region.

Reference

Strange, Susan (1988), *States and Markets*, London/New York: Pinter.

FIGURE I.1 Geographical Map of Central Asia.

Source: Author

1

GEOPOLITICS OF ENERGY AND ENERGY SECURITY

The politics of the state is in its geography.

– *Napoleon* (Kaplan 2012)

Geopolitics is a complex concept and earns a variety of definitions depending upon the nature of the subject under analysis. The study of geopolitics like any other subject of inquiry deals with geographical variables like location, size, resources, population, technological development and so on. It plays an important role in national political decision making and strategy building. While performing its role, generally geopolitics delves into analysing the link between geography and politics. In a nutshell, it affirms that every political decision of the state is influenced by its spatial conditions. It means national policies and political decisions are intricately influenced by the geographical elements that a state possesses. As thus, it establishes a well-knit connection between national interest, power politics, strategic thinking, and decision making with geographic space. It is therefore vital to understand that the very essence of geopolitics is revolving around power and space. It means geography and national political interests are the central parameters to understand the meaning of geopolitics. It thus implies that geography does play an important role in both national and foreign policymaking process and it cannot be ignored while analysing a country's international relations.

Similarly, another key concept, energy security, is the driver of growth and tool for social change as an important element in the geography of a state undoubtedly influences its decision-making abilities. Since energy resources have been the propeller of the world economy and the key to national and global security and stability, it has assumed the role of a decisive public, economic, social and environmental issue of high importance. Given its centrality, a constant flow of energy, therefore, has remained at the heart of maintaining this order. Referring to the seminal importance of energy for the individual and society at large, Nobel Laureate Richard Smalley (2005) prioritized ten problems in the context of the world's quest for sustainability. "These precedence problems are energy, water, food, environment, poverty, terrorism and war, disease, education, democracy and population. He accorded the highest priority to energy among all the chronic problems the world has been facing in contemporary times" (Randolph and Masters 2008: 4).

Energy from the above understanding is certainly the keystone of nature and society. Besides Smalley's observation, revelations of history reflect the resultant use of energy in the advancement of human society and civilization. Energy has freed people from slave and animal labour, from an agrarian society and the constraints of space. Energy is fundamental to economic development. Without energy resources,

> business would not be able to light their stores; people and goods would not be able to reach markets on the other side of the world; homes and schools would be more difficult to heat, and manufacturing sector would not be able to produce any products used daily.
>
> *(Ibid)*

In short, the world economy depends on energy and the largest economies of the world rely on cheap and abundant supplies of energy. Historically speaking, each phase of development of civilization was triggered by changes in patterns of energy use for the growth of human populations and economic systems. In fact, since the mid-19th-century, use of diverse sources of energy has enabled unprecedented fourfold growth of the human population and a forty-fold increase in the global economy. Its rate is even higher in the 21st century. In global terms, the US Geological Survey in its study has shown that "compared with 60 years ago, the planet is consuming today, in percentage terms, 618 times more oil, 1000 times more gas, 756 times more nickel, 1500 times more bauxite" (Klare 2012).

Faced with the growing increase of global demand for energy, imbalances in energy supply and monopoly in the world energy market, claims by the Club of Rome thesis and Peak Oil theory regarding the drying up of world oil coupled with the unequal distribution of energy resources, the energy consuming countries of the world have developed protective economic policies to ensure their energy security through domestic means and diversify their sources of supply to meet the demands. This sudden rise in demand for fossil fuels and the monopoly of supply has led to increasing geopolitical tensions and international competition among the world's countries to acquire, control and administer these scarce resources. Further, the threats to energy supply, instability in the producing countries, vulnerability of supply routes, piracy, terrorism and even the fear of climate change have drawn the attention of states and world governments to develop short- and long-term strategies to address the concerns leading to the formulation of energy policies. This is how the spatial resource (energy) remained critically linked to the political decisions (foreign policy) of nations worldwide which has opened up a genuine debate to understand the anatomy of the geopolitics of energy and energy security.

Geopolitics: a conceptual understanding

Geopolitics is a word as well as a set of associated ideas. A much-debated term among scholars and in popular writings, geopolitics is etymological, a combination of geography and politics. In this capacity, it refers to "the relation of international political power to the geographical setting" (Cohen 1964). It is a philosophy which "seeks to understand, explain and predict international political behaviour, primarily in terms of geographical variables, such as location, size, climate, topography, demography, natural resources and technological development and potential" (Penguin Dictionary 1998; Leigh 2014).

It denotes the impact of geography on politics, particularly as it pertains to relations between states. In this sense, it would be quite accurate to denote geopolitics as a combination of geography and foreign policy. Thus, geopolitics is a scientific way to understand the relationship between states, their history and politics and their geographical settings. It is also said to be a combination of geography and politics, which views a state's political position in the world based on its geographical resources. It is a philosophy launched as a scientific approach to the understanding of global relationships. No two states have identical geographical conditions nor identical geopolitics. Each state must develop its geopolitics based on its knowledge of geography and political conditions to give direction to its relationships with other nation-states of the world.

Geopolitics did not begin as objective science, although it was promoted as a scientific approach to the analysis of the space, location, size and resources of nation-states. The term geopolitics is more than hundred years old and was first coined in 1899 by the Swedish Political Scientist, Rudolf J. Kjellen as "science of the state" in his book *Foundations for a System of Politics* (Muir 1997). He has described geopolitics as "the theory of the state as a geographical organism or phenomenon in Space" (Cohen 2003). Kjellen was interested in the geographical attributes of states and in the implications those features related to their spatial location had for political power.

Towards the end of the 19th century, "classical geopolitical theories were developed when the supremacy of the British Empire was challenged by other countries to expand their colonial presence across the globe" (Flint 2017). Geographers such as Halford Mackinder, Alfred Thayer Mahan, Nicholas J. Spykman and Giulio Douhet have developed geopolitical theories based on land, maritime and air power respectively (Campos and Fernandes 2017). As a subfield of political science and geography, geopolitics focuses on the relationship between territory and power, particularly the influence of geography on state behaviour (Sullivan 1986: 7; Stogiannos 2019). The fundamental concern of geopolitics, at the height of the imperial age, was the struggle between sea and land power. It was exemplified by the raging confrontations between Britain and Germany, and Britain and Russia. US Admiral Alfred Thayer Mahan believed in the superiority of sea power over land power, while the British geographer Sir Halford Mackinder saw land power as crucial in determining the outcome of the struggle (Mahan 1897: 29). Mackinder's geopolitical thought is particularly relevant to the Caspian/Central Asian region, which constituted an integral part of his "Heartland" theory. He defines "the Heartland" as the core of the Eurasian landmass, inaccessible by sea, and considered it the "pivot" area of world politics. Around the Heartland, there is an "inner crescent", consisting of China, India, Turkey and Germany, which is circumscribed by the 'outer crescent' of Britain, Japan and Southern Africa (Mackinder 1962: 150).

Mackinder's hypothesis gained considerable relevance in the Second World War and the Cold War in the context of the German–Soviet struggle to control the Heartland, followed by the US containment policy towards the USSR. In a later revision of his theory, Mackinder saw the Atlantic Alliance as capable of countering Soviet land power. In a reformulation of Mackinder's theory, Nicholas Spykman (1893–1943) proposed a geopolitical model centred on the "World Island". It comprised the core of the Heartland and the inner crescent, surrounded by a "rimland" which coincided with Mackinder's outer crescent. As a realist thinker, Spykman viewed international politics as a struggle for power in which American and British security necessitated control of the rimland as a means of blocking the expansion of the World Island (Spykman 1944: 39–44). A century after the acme of the Great Game between Russia and Britain, which centred on Mackinder's Heartland and inner crescent, a new contest was triggered in the far more complex milieu of the 1990s. Yet, in contrast to the territorial imperative of nineteenth-century imperial rivalries, the new Great Game is ostensibly a power struggle for the Heartland's energy resources. This situation, in reality, constitutes the signposts and stepping-stones of clashing hegemonic interests (Dekmejian and Simonain 2001: 6).

However, it was only in Germany that geopolitics was widely used to promote German nationalism under the leadership of Adolf Hitler. German *Geopolitik* (replaced by geopolitics after the Second World War), a loose translation of geopolitics, necessarily meant the exploitation of knowledge to serve the purpose of a national state or regime. The introduction of geopolitics as a deterministic field of study and a recipe for statecraft was first offered as a set of geographically determined laws governing a state's strategic destinies and evolved as the geographical underpinning of realpolitik. This identification of geopolitics, associated with the aggressive and expansionist Nazi Germany has had an unfortunate effect on the study of the subject, largely confining it to the military field. Therefore it is not wrong when many concluded that the study of geography in conjunction with politics means an obsession with strategy, which in turn means a predilection for war and conquest. This study of geopolitics as pseudoscience is associated with the works of Karl Haushofer (the father of German *Geopolitik*) – a soldier turned academician – and the Institute of Geopolitik set up in Munich in 1924 (Norris and Lloyd 1980). He started a journal named *Zeitschrift Für Geopolitik*, which was exclusively devoted to various kinds of geopolitical research having strong links to the development of Germany. For Karl Haushofer, "Geopolitics is the new national science of the state ... a doctrine on the spatial determinism of all political processes, based on the broad foundations of geography, especially of political geography" (Cohen 2003). It was not surprising that he exploited the geographical concepts for the specific power-political purposes of Germany and particularly in support of the expansionist policy of Hitler. Whatever may have been the design of the Germans behind using the term *Geopolitik*, the outline of the practice remained at the heart of the geographical factors determining their domestic and foreign policy objectives.

However, the military dimension of classical geopolitics inherited from German nationalism in the 1970s took a new form with its involvements in "the study of the evolution of power relations between different political poles considering their geographical characteristics and finding nodes that condition them, restricting or enhancing their capacity of affirmation" (Campos and Fernandes 2017: 25). Geopolitical theorists and diplomats of the highest order such as Raymond Aron, Zbigniew Brzezinski, Henry Kissinger, Paul Kennedy and Samuel P. Huntington were the proponents of this sort of multidisciplinary approach of geopolitics.

Modern geopolitics, while describing the broad relationship between, geography, states and world politics, delves into including global issues such as economy, geo-economics and energy security at large. In simple terms, modern geopolitics was

> dominated by a panoptic form of power or knowledge that sought to analyze the conditions of World powers to aid the practice of statecraft by the great powers. Embedded within the imperialist projects of various states throughout the century, geopolitics generated comprehensive visions of World politics while also proposing particular strategies of states to pursue against their rivals.
>
> *(Pradhan 2010: 16–17)*

Development of this new trend of geopolitics largely helped to include economy and natural resources like oil, gas and coal in its fold as they can lead to social transformation and the economic developments of states. The natural resources are essential conditions and therefore an indispensable part of national and global security, given their capacity to influence foreign policy and regulate its outcomes. Given the impeccable utility of geopolitics for the state in its policy and decision-making process, assertions on states' emphasis on geopolitical factors has been greatly highlighted from time to time. For Geoffrey Parker, "Geopolitics is the study of international relations from a spatial or geographical perspective" (Cohen 2003). John Agnew defined the field as "examination of the geographical assumptions, designations and understandings that enter into the making of World politics" (Ibid). Saul Cohen defines geopolitics as,

> an analysis of the interaction between, on the one hand, geographical settings and perspectives and, on the other, political process. Both geopolitical settings and political processes are dynamics, and each influence and is influenced by the other. Geopolitics addresses the consequences of this interaction.
>
> *(Campos and Fernandes 2017: 25)*

For Colin Flint, "Geopolitics is the struggle over the control of geographical entities with an international and global dimension and the use of such geographical entities for political advantage" (Flint 2017; Campos and Fernandes 2017: 25). However, Gearoid O. Tauthail, an exponent of critical geopolitics, believes that "geopolitics does not have a singular, all-encompassing meaning or identity … It is a discourse, a culturally and politically varied way about geography and international politics" (Pradhan 2010: 3).

Geopolitics as such straddles two disciplines – Geography and Politics. Therefore, it is defined as the analysis of the interaction between on the one hand geographical settings and perspectives and, on the other political processes. The political processes include forces that operated at the international level and those on the domestic scene that influence international behaviour. Both geographical settings and political processes are dynamic, and each influences and is influenced by the other. Geopolitics addresses the consequences of this interaction as well.

Energy security: concept and character

Energy security, a term that is mentioned in every policy formulation, both in national and international forums, in contemporary times. But what does it mean? Does it mean national security? Well, sort of. Does it mean energy independence? Well, sort of that too. Does it mean economic security? Yes, all of the above.

"Energy Security" is probably best understood when taken literally. Energy needs to be secured in terms of the sources, i.e., where it comes from, control of the flow and distribution of that energy, and having alternatives in place to allow the countries of the world to withstand the highs and lows associated with any commodity (EAA 2005: 1).

Second only to national defence, energy plays a crucial role in the survival and well-being of all countries, both developing and developed. It determines whether our lights will go on or off, our agriculture and industry will go forwards or backwards. The specific policies a country chooses to make up its overall energy policy comprise "a subset of economic policy, foreign policy, and national and international security policy". These are how the country's concerns seek to achieve the end or ultimate goal of energy security. In its most fundamental sense, therefore, "energy security" means having the "assurance of the ability to access the energy resources required for the continued development of national power" (Hill 2003: 132). In more specific terms, it is the provision of affordable, reliable, diverse and ample supplies of oil and gas (and their future equivalents) and adequate infrastructure to deliver these supplies to the market (Kalick and Goldwyn 2005: 9). Energy security thus became a question of national strategy. As Churchill said, "safety and certainty in oil lie in variety and variety alone" (Yergin 2006: 69). Moreover, it must be recognized that energy security does not stand by itself but is lodged in the larger relations among nations and how they interact with one another.

Defining energy security

Energy security is an umbrella term that covers many concerns linking energy, economic growth and political power. The energy security perspective varies depending upon one's position in the value chain. Consumers and energy-intensive industries desire reasonably priced energy on demand and worry about disruptions. Major oil-producing countries consider the security of revenue and demand integral parts of any energy security discussion. Oil and gas companies consider access to new reserves, the ability to develop new infrastructure, and stable investment regimes to be critical to ensuring energy security.

Developing countries are concerned about the ability to pay for resources to drive their economies and fear the balance of payment shocks. Power companies are concerned with the integrity of the entire network. Policymakers focus on the risks of supply disruption and the security of infrastructure due to terrorism, war or natural disaster. They also consider the volumes of security margins – the amount of excess capacity, strategic reserves, and infrastructure redundancy. Throughout the value chain, prices and supply diversity are critical components of energy security.

The ideas of energy policy, foreign policy and national security are all linked together and are not new. Over the years, however, conceptions of "energy security" have evolved and grown rather more complicated. After the oil crisis of the 1970s, prices rose and a scarcity of affordable supplies became a real and pressing concern for countries in different parts of the world. Ensuring energy supplies has become a constant concern for all governments. Since then, energy security has been seen primarily as a problem of supplies and costs. In 1999, the United Nations defined energy security as ensuring "the continuous availability of energy in various forms and sufficient quantities at reasonable prices" (Noronha and Sudarshan 2009: 5).

The establishment of the International Energy Agency (IEA), pertaining to the main objective underpinning "energy security" with special emphasis on oil security, describes energy security as, "the uninterrupted physical availability at a price which is affordable while respecting environment concerns" (IEA 2010). Many other organizations such as the US Energy Information Administration, World Coal Institute as well as IEA use supply centric definitions of energy security (USEIA 2010, WCA 2010). Along with an emphasis on supplies and costs are debates on issues such as the geopolitics of energy, the links between energy and foreign policy, maritime safety of energy supplies, play-offs between strategic energy investments and the development of free global energy markets, the nationalization of energy resources and the value of increased self-sufficiency.

While all of these issues are certainly important, it has become increasingly clear in the last ten years that they provide only part of the picture. If the "security" in energy security is understood in the context of protection from energy-related threats, then the issues relevant to energy security suddenly appear much broader. One way to understand this is to look at threats due to energy use as falling into the two categories mentioned above – those affecting economic growth and those that are unique to conditions of poverty. The traditional threats that form a part of energy security definitions – supply constraints, costs, import dependency, geopolitical tensions – all of these may be called energy and growth threats because they directly affect economic growth and the normal functioning of the economy. Other problems such as energy inequity and the use of dirty, traditional biomass fuels with their associated health risks could be treated as energy poverty threats (Noronha and Sudarshan 2009: 6).

The definition of energy security is variable, meaning something different for each country. For the United States, energy security means "producing energy at home and relying less on foreigners"; for China, it means "buying stakes in foreign oil fields"; for Russia, it is wrapped up in "restrictions on foreign investment in domestic oil and natural gas" while for Japan the focus is on "offsetting its scarcity of domestic resources through diversification, trade, and investment" (Matthew 2009). It is natural for each country to give priority to its own energy needs, but all of these needs must be reconciled if true energy security is to be attained. It is in this context that India's Integrated Energy Policy Report 2006 defines energy security as:

> The country is energy secure when we can supply lifeline energy to all our citizens as well as meet their effective demand for safe and convenient energy to satisfy various needs at affordable costs at all times with a prescribed confidence level considering shocks and disruptions that can be reasonably expected.
>
> *(Planning Commission 2006)*

The traditional areas of concern – supply sources, demand centres, geopolitics, market structures and responsiveness of related institutions – form the core of discussions about the best way to ensure that economies have sufficient energy to meet their needs. However, the energy security paradigm has shifted and become larger since the major supply disruptions of the 1970s and even the early 1990s. The risks are different, the considerations for the best response have changed, and the implications for solutions are far more complex. The 1970s model is no longer sufficient and a more expanded concept now seems necessary. In this context, the Indian definition of energy security seems to be quite satisfactory as it not only talks about energy security revolving around national economic growth but also covers energy poverty broadly in its fold.

The renewed focus on energy security is driven in part by an exceedingly tight oil market and by high oil prices, which have doubled over the past few years. But it is also fuelled by the threat of terrorism, instability in some exporting nations, a nationalist backlash and fears of a scramble for supplies and geopolitical rivalries, and countries' fundamental need for energy to power their economic growth. In the background – but not too far back – is renewed anxiety over whether there will be sufficient resources to meet the world's energy requirements in the decades ahead.

Concerns over energy security are not limited only to oil. Power blackouts on both the East and West Coasts of the United States, in Europe and Russia, as well as chronic shortages of electric power in China, India and other developing countries, have raised worries about the reliability of electricity supply systems. When it comes to natural gas, rising demand and constrained supplies, followed by an unprecedented monopoly on the prices' regulation front, have caused worries in the minds of energy-consuming countries.

On top of this, another problem raised its ugly head in the form of terrorism. It is a new range of vulnerability that has caused serious concerns for countries around the world. Al-Qaeda, then led by Osama bin Laden, threatened to attack what he called the "hinges" of the world economy, that is, its critical infrastructure of which energy is among the most crucial elements (Yergin 2006: 70). And the vulnerabilities are not limited to threats of terrorism in Africa and Asia, political turmoil in the Middle East, armed conflict and piracy in the Gulf of Aden and the Black Sea. Natural disasters like the tsunami in Japan, Hurricanes Katrina and Rita in the United States, cyclones and floods in India, earthquakes in China also greatly contribute towards energy shock by disrupting flows of oil, natural gas and electric power.

The Russian–Ukrainian natural gas dispute at the beginning of the years 2006 and 2009 temporarily cut supplies to Europe. Rising tensions over Tehran's nuclear programme brought threats from Iran, the second-largest OPEC producer, to "unleash an oil crisis". And scattered attacks on some oil facilities reduced exports from Nigeria, which is a major supplier to the United States (Yergin 2006). Political tension between Russia and Georgia, involving the United States and Europe created a situation that led to gas supply disruption from the Russian side. Recently, the downfall of the Hosni Mubarak regime in Egypt and political turmoil in Libya has resulted in oil and gas supply disruptions in the Red Sea leading to a manifold rise in oil prices in the world market. Likewise, piracy and sea crimes in the Arabian sea have raised serious concern on the Indian side to ensure its energy security, as 85 per cent of its oil imports are through the sea routes.

The key to these energy security problems perhaps lies in their diversification. This remains true, but a wider approach is now required that takes into account the rapid evolution of the global energy trade, supply-chain vulnerabilities, terrorism and the integration of major new economies into the world market.

Although in the developed world

> the usual definition of energy security is simply the availability of sufficient supplies at affordable prices, different countries interpret what the concept means for them differently. Energy exporting countries focus on maintaining the "security of demand" for their exports, which after all generate the overwhelming share of their government revenues. For Russia, the aim is to reassert state control over "strategic resources" and gain primacy over the main pipelines and market channels through which it ships its hydrocarbons to international markets. The concern for developing countries is how changes in energy prices affect their balance of payments. For China and India, energy security now lies in their ability to rapidly adjust to their new dependence on global markets, which represents a major shift away from their former commitments to self-sufficiency. For Japan, it means offsetting its stark scarcity of domestic resources through diversification, trade, and investment.
>
> *(Yergin 2006: 71)*

In Europe, the major debate centres on how to manage dependence on imported natural gas – and in most countries, aside from France and Finland, whether to build new nuclear power plants and perhaps to return to clean coal. And the United States must be sitting comfortably as its goal of "energy independence" – a phrase that has become a keyword since it was first articulated by Richard Nixon four weeks after the 1973 embargo was put in place – has become a reality under the presidency of Barack Obama (Silva 2017).

Although it is difficult to find an agreed and consensus definition of energy security, yet most of the concepts issued from the traditional school of energy security point to one other feature: the overwhelming prominence of the state as the main actor in charge and the chief receptor of energy security (Fernandes 2017).

Finally, it is worth noting one last issue regarding the definition of energy security. The broad term "energy security" risks obscuring the fact that contemporary economies employ energy in distinct forms for different purposes. The transportation sector relies heavily on petroleum in the form of gasoline, diesel fuel, jet fuel, and other petroleum-based products. Some substitution by other fuels is possible in the case of some automobiles, but almost all vehicles currently run on liquid fuels, most frequently petroleum-based fuels (Ibid: 130). Because of the particular demands of the transportation sector, the security of supply for oil and refined oil products is a key aspect of overall energy security for almost all countries of the world.

Geopolitics and energy security: from security to survival

Geopolitics in recent years has been revolving closely around energy and the geographical landmasses rich in energy. Energy is what keeps the world going. All through history, around the world and throughout all ages, energy has been the driver of economic growth, the source of military power and the main determinant of people's welfare. It is access to energy, whether human, animal or natural, that has primarily determined the scale and success of a civilization or state.

In a world of rapid progress and fast-paced industrialization, energy occupies the top priority. Therefore, to ensure timely, adequate, reliable and cheap energy, its secure and easy availability is of the utmost importance. Only this can enable the country to sustain its economic growth, maintain its society's lifestyle and feed its military needs. For that, competition plays a major role, because most of the world's principal energy producers are not principal consumers. For them, the concept of the geopolitics of energy arises, revolving around who supplies it, as securing reliable access to those supplies has been a driving factor in global prosperity and security. The structural dimensions of energy geopolitics can be seen from both the supply and demand sides. The supply side includes the volumes of global reserves, their distribution patterns, their longevity, the discoveries, capacity building and so on. On the demand front, the issues are related to the market size and its geography, logistics of transport and its delivery and others.

The geopolitics of energy in today's world principally revolves around oil and gas and to a lesser degree around nuclear and hydroelectricity sources, of which oil and gas are essentially geopolitical commodities. Since the availability of hydrocarbons is determined by geology, the global politics of energy is shaped mainly by the "arc of energy", stretching from the Gulf region to the Caspian Sea, through Siberia and the Arctic region to the Russian Far East, Alaska and Canada. In this regard, it can be said that nearly 80 per cent of the world's oil and gas including potential reserves are located in this region (Sikri 2008: 2).

Nevertheless, factors like economics, technology and politics played critical roles in determining the supply and demand side of the energy geopolitics. For the energy-producing countries, energy is not only a source of enormous power and wealth, it also constitutes leverage. Since energy is a strategic resource, denial of it to any rival or enemy increases the latter's vulnerability.

The political nature of energy linked to the sources of supply and demand comes to public attention at moments of crisis. But energy politics has become yet more complex as transport systems particularly in the United States, Europe, China and India have become largely reliant on oil. Access to energy remains critical to sustaining growth in China and India – not just to keep pace with the burgeoning population. Failure to deliver on the hope of greater prosperity could unravel authoritarian regimes and even democratic ones, as the populace becomes more educated and demanding. And it is these very factors that have turned the market power of energy suppliers into political power. Importers have come to compete for supplies, driving up prices, suppliers' wealth and the capacity to play roles in regional and international politics.

The traditional geopolitical considerations have become even more complex with global climate change leading to environmental security concerns. Besides, the security of supply, i.e. the security of transit through chokepoints, is also critical to energy geopolitics. This is because nearly 25 per cent of total world oil exports pass through the Strait of Hormuz, nearly 15 per cent through the strait of Malacca and nearly 5 per cent through Bab el-Mandeb, the narrow strait connecting the Red Sea and the Gulf of Aden (Pascual 2008: 3).

No other element has shaped the history of the past one hundred years as much as the fight to secure and control the world's reserves of petroleum and gas. It became further complicated with the involvement of the great powers of the world aiming at controlling and influencing regional affairs and resources. It seems a majority of the oil-producing nations are politically unstable or at serious odds with the external actors, especially the United States.

In the modern era, the geopolitics of energy operates on similar principles, with the difference that in today's interdependent world the matrix is more complex and sophisticated. Most countries, the industrialized ones in particular, have become unprecedentedly energy-dependent not just for their continued prosperity but even for their very survival. Whenever a country needs and consumes energy in large quantities, this leads to a shortfall of energy and all the major powers today fall within this category.

The 20th century was truly the "century of oil" since the geopolitics of energy in the contemporary world order is unprecedentedly in favour of oil and to a certain extent gas. The extraordinary technological advancements, the transportation revolution that unified countries and regions, have created an interdependent globalized economy. The agricultural revolution which freed up a huge labour force from the agricultural to the manufacturing and services sectors; the thriving sustainable concentrated urban conglomerations; the lifestyle facilitated by the petrochemical industries etc. are some of the developments that were achieved. The ability to amass these developments that have made the 20th century unique would not have been possible without access to plentiful and cheap oil. Oil constitutes the critical energy source of today's industrialized economies as well as for the developing economies. Without oil, the world as known to us would not exist. Disruptions in production and supply could bring the industrialized economies to a grinding halt.

Gas, increasingly being used as a substitute for coal in power generation and heating and as a substitute for oil in the transportation sector has of late acquired more salience in energy security. Nuclear energy is deeply mired in geopolitics. This is because the fuel and technology used to produce nuclear power can also produce nuclear weapons. That is why the global trade in nuclear materials and fuels is controlled by the cartel of the Nuclear Supplier Group (NSG).

Even though coal is and will remain for some time the most important fuel in the overall energy mix of most developing and industrializing economies, the geopolitics of coal is limited for several reasons:

a) Coal is so far available in adequate quantities within most countries that need it and international trading in coal is relatively restricted;
b) The sheer bulk of coal creates some constraints in transportation in very large quantities; and
c) Environmental considerations have to be kept in mind in expanding the use of coal which leaves a dirty footprint on the planet's eco-system and climate (Sikri 2008: 6).

As far as hydropower is concerned, it is quite important from a geopolitical standpoint. But it is strictly confined in a regional context and that too only in some parts of the world like South Asia and Central Asia. Given the changing nature of energy geopolitics, it is often referred to as the New Geopolitics of Energy.

Nevertheless, there is a growing debate over the impending exhaustion of oil and other energy sources. It has been reiterated several times by the Peak Oil theory that Russia is producing at its peak and Saudi Arabia has limited additional short-term capacity. Due to commercial disputes, regional instability, civic unrest and political coups in the Persian Gulf, investors are thoroughly worried about their energy security concerns. In this scenario, the issues of energy security are now moving beyond the exclusive concerns of consumers. Producers too require a stable regime with a coherent demand and supply scenario. Although global reserves have been the principal factors in the influencing, if not defining, the energy security debate, it may be recalled that the Club of Rome Thesis cautioned the world community about the limited span of non-renewable sources of energy in its paper "There are Limits to Growth" (Club of Rome, 2011). That is why perhaps the global scramble for oil and energy has taken a fast track route all around geopolitical landscapes abundant in energy resources. It is in this context that the Central Asian geographical landscape has been dealt with specifically in terms of its energy potentials and capacity to meet world energy demand in general, implicating Indian energy security in particular.

Geopolitics of oil and gas: strategic resources for power and security

The struggle for the control of energy sources, especially oil and gas, has been central to international politics since the early 20th century. The politics of energy involves stiff competition, dynamic foreign policy formulation and decision making; unprecedented power play and struggle for control, wars, coups and assassinations; fall of governments, economic crises, environmental disasters and corrupt governance as well as sustainable growth, technological innovation and social welfare. This section elaborates by introducing the contemporary politics of energy and attempts to discuss the causes, dynamics and implications of the global quest for energy. It especially focuses on the dynamics of oil politics and offers an introduction to the intricate and often misunderstood world of oil. For that purpose, strategic interests based on access to oil, big oil corporations, international cartels, the economics of the oil market, environmental risks and policies to generate alternative sources of energy are covered at some length. Some of the questions covered in this section are: Why is oil central to international politics? What factors cause wild fluctuations in oil prices? How viable are alternative energy sources? Does greater energy consumption inevitably lead to irreversible environmental costs? What are the prospects for energy scarcity?

Cheap oil and gas provided much of the energy that drove the prosperity of the 20th century. The world has now entered the 21st century knowing that deposits of these resources are going to dry up by the end of this century. Natural, renewable sources of energy have long been exploited by man. The sun, water, wind, wood, vegetable oil and peat fire – all are energy resources that man exploited through his muscle and animal power to energize his society for millennia. Until the 17th century man didn't know about the properties of steam as an agent of energy. However, with the invention of steam power in the 19th century as an energy resource, the pattern of energy uses for powering the Industrial Revolution changed society in Britain and the world forever.

The sudden rise of Britain and America as great powers in international politics around 1800–03 is no coincidence. Perhaps they found a reliable source of energy as a means to energize their expansion, economically, industrially and commercially.

> The most amazing fact of all history is this sudden skyrocketing from virtual obscurity of two nations to the most fabulous wealth and economic power ever possessed by the people. Britain became Great Britain – a gigantic, stupendously wealthy commonwealth of nations – the United States, the greatest nation of history.
>
> *(Fraser 2001)*

Incredibly,

> during the 19th century, steam power energized the most rapid expansion of industry, trade and transport ever in mankind's history. The growth of factories in the towns and cities, the development of vast rail networks, the leap from sail to steam-powered shipping, this all contributed to the British empire and the United States leading the world in the creation and movement of goods more rapidly and freely than ever before.
>
> *(Ibid)*

One hundred years on from that time, in 1898, the first oil well, at Titusville, Pennsylvania, was drilled. Just three years earlier, in 1895,

> a Parisian of Bavarian parentage, Rudolph Diesel, perfected his four-stroke cycle, oil-fuelled internal combustion engine. Both of those seminal events led to the explosion of exploration, extraction, and processing of liquid fossil fuel throughout the 20th century. Since then it became the prime energy source driving the unfettered expansion of the world economy.
>
> *(Fraser 2001)*

Through boom and bust, cycle after cycle, oil has filled the energy thirst of burgeoning national economies. Now it has reached such a point that, at the dawn of a new century, the prospect of exhaustion of the world's supply of this energy source is now seen as a foreseeable reality. "Coal was king in 1800; coal was still king in 1900; coal is a dethroned monarch in 2000. Oil is king in 2000; oil will have abdicated before 2100" (*The Times* 1999).

The International Energy Agency (IEA) publicized its findings in November 1998 that growth in oil output could not be expected to continue beyond about 2001. Although it has been recognized for at least 25 years that known resources of oil as a finite, limited source of energy, would run out in the present century, little or nothing has yet been done to deal with this prospect (Fraser 2001). Policy analyst David Fleming states, "The essential problem has been known for a long time. It is a fact, written up exhaustively in the literature, that the period around the turn of the millennium marks the end of growth in the world production of oil and the start of its long decline toward depletion" (Ibid).

In 1956, the geologist King Hubbert accurately forecast that the United States' oil production would peak in 1970. In 1970, Esso forecast that global production would peak in about 2000 (Ibid). Far from seeking to reduce our global dependence on oil as our prime energy source, during the past two decades or so the world went on an oil binge that increased consumption by 9 million barrels a day. Christopher Flavin, acting president of World Watch Institute, declared in 1999, "Unless we use the current crisis as an opportunity to improve fuel economy and diversify energy supplies, we will put the health of both the world economy and the global environment at risk" (Flavin 2000).

Although the search for oil continues, industry experts admit that they do not realistically expect to find another Saudi Arabia or Alaska. Extensive exploration indicates that the largest reserves of accessible oil have been found already. Those which yet remain to be developed are largely sited in territory that is located within countries that are either politically unstable, trouble-torn or have tenuous or hostile relationships with the major oil-consuming nations of the world.

Of the world's total proved reserves of oil, over 75 per cent lie underground or offshore of territory controlled by a cartel of 11 nations which comprise the Organization of Petroleum Exporting Countries (OPEC) (Fraser 2001). These countries are all developing nations having a heavy dependency on oil export revenues to sustain their economies. Collectively they produce about 40 per cent of the world's oil. Other than OPEC's reserves, much has been made of the prospect of developing flows of the black gold from the emerging oil region of Central Asia and the Caucasus. However, the landlocked Caspian will supply only 3 to 4 per cent of the world's oil supply by 2010–15 (Ibid). This is important for the fact that the Caspian oil will feed Asia and Europe and is highly unlikely to flow to the US markets.

Russia is touted as another alternative source of supply to OPEC. Forecasts indicate that oil production in Russia was estimated to increase between 410 and 450 million tonnes per year by 2005 (Fraser 2001). The EU has ensured a prime call on Russia as a principal supplier to its burgeoning energy needs. "Exports of Russian oil to Europe may amount to 210 million to 250 million metric tonnes per annum by 2005, which accounts for 30 per cent of European consumption, Yukos CEO Mikhail Khodorkovsky said in Moscow" (Ibid).

In May, Interfax reported that Gazprom which yields 98 per cent of Russia's gas production was gearing up to meet Europe's growing demand for natural gas. Germany was by far the largest buyer of Russian gas (Ibid). The EU and Russia are forging an increasing alliance against the United States; therefore, it is highly unlikely that American companies will be allowed to have their footholds in the region at least for the foreseeable future. However, given the Indo-Russian relations, it is believed that India may get greater access to Russian energy through pipelines. There is also a growing engagement between Russia–China and India to develop and construct pipelines through the South China Sea for the transit of gas from Russia. And India and Russia have also jointly participated in the Sakhalin III project.

North African oil is also coming into the picture, with south-western Chad oil fields being developed by consortia led by Exxon Mobil. Slated to begin operation in 2004, oil from the south-western Chad basin will be piped 663 miles to offshore loading facilities on the Cameroon coast of West Africa. This places the point of dispatch for export midway between Spain and Southern Africa with the EU and South Africa probably becoming the principal importers (Fraser 2001).

To compound the problem of supply, China and India ended decades of energy self-sufficiency when they became net importers of oil in the mid-1990s. Jaffe and Manning's report claims that "China's rising hunger for oil imports means that it will depend more on the same energy resources and sea transportation lanes shared by the United States, Japan, and other industrialized countries" (Jaffe and Manning 2000: 16–29). Which brings us to the question of future power plays, by not only the United States but all other major oil-consuming nations, looming large on the horizon and OPEC holding the whip hand.

However, not since the Suez Crisis or the torched oil wells at the climax of the first Gulf War have energy imperatives and national security concerns so manifestly intersected. Due to the rise of instability throughout the Middle East; the increase of gas prices at the pump; assertive new players on the global energy scene (producer and consumer alike) represented by China, India, Russia and

Venezuela, in addition to the already existing energy players like the United States and Europe; and the increasing alarm associated with carbon triggered global climate change, the global politics of energy now occupy centre stage among a broader set of foreign policy and national security concerns. Its weigh in global politics has been such that, the Centre for Strategic and International Studies (CSIS) in its Energy Report released in 2001 concluded that,

> one of the ironies of the turn of the century is that, in an age when the pace of technological change is almost overwhelming, the world will remain dependent out to the year 2020 at least essentially on the same source of energy – oil, natural gas and coal – that prevailed in the twentieth century.
> *(CSIS 2001)*

Energy security is one of the defining policy issues of the day. Dwindling low-cost hydrocarbon reserves, the rise of new and spectacularly hungry energy consumers such as China and India, and the spectre of climate change highlight that a fundamental reordering of the global energy system is in the works. That reordering raises many fears and concerns. Unfortunately, so far most policy debates on energy security issues take on a rather myopic character. The predominant focus in policy debates on energy is on "security of supply", suggesting that states around the world are locked into a competition over access to crucial energy resources that provide the key to continued prosperity and state power. This zero-sum perspective on energy security is certainly not new. Ever since Great Britain led the way in opening the Middle East for oil production in the early 20th century, energy security has been understood as an exercise in geopolitical scheming and competition. This paradigm stands to this day and defines analytical foci and policy prescriptions.

Energy use: a historical account of energy transition

Human history has generally been characterized by an increasing level of use of energy and natural resources. Humans depend on this transformation for their survival and much more energy flows for their civilized existence.

The evolution of human societies has been dependent upon the conversion of ever-larger amounts of ever more concentrated and more versatile forms of energy. From the perspective of natural science, both pre-historic human evolution and the course of history may be seen fundamentally as the quest for controlling greater energy stores and flows. This endeavour has brought about the expansion of human populations and allowed for increasingly complex social and productive arrangements. Neither the growth of technical capabilities nor a deeper understanding of the surrounding world or the efforts to secure a better quality of life would have been successful without innovations in energy.

The discovery of fire by striking stones for thermal uses about 100,000 years ago appears to be the first conscious human-engineered energy conversion

(Randolph and Masters 2008: 5). The invention of the wheel and stone tools and the domestication of working animals extended mechanical energy uses in the period from 8000 BC to 4000 BC. As of 4000 BC to 1000 BC, thermal energy from wood fires, then coal, not only provided warmth and cooking but also was essential in developing both ceramic and metal materials such as pottery (4000 BC), bronze (2500 BC) and iron (1500 BC) (Ibid: 5).

With the start of the first century AD, devices to harness water and wind power extended human ability to use mechanical power for grist milling and water pumping. The first wind-sail driven boats were used by the Egyptians about 2000 BC (Ibid: 6). But, advanced sailing took place only after 1250 AD. This enabled the ushering in of the age of trade and exploration (Ibid).

Coal and certain oils have been used for heat and illumination since AD 100. Coal and oil were later put to a different use as fuel for the newly developed steam engine of the 1800s. Later on, other heat and mechanical engines which revolutionized industry, transportation and mechanized agriculture were developed. The first commercial oil well (1859, Pennsylvania) in the invention of the internal combustion engine (1877), oil discoveries in Texas (1901) and Iran (1908), the invention of the aeroplane (1903) and the Model T and assembly production (1908) ushered in the age of petroleum, the automobile and air transport (Ibid).

The electrical age had its founding in the invention of the generator and motor (1831) but waited for further inventions of the electrical light (1879), refrigeration (1891) and air conditioning (1902), and development of electric companies and transmission (1891) before taking off after 1920 and revolutionizing living standards (Ibid).

After 1950, further growth of fossil fuels, electricity (including nuclear power) and related technologies for electronics and telecommunications, agriculture, manufacturing and transportation set the stage for global expansion and unprecedented population and economic growth.

Human population had been constrained to 1 billion people by 1800 by limits on energy use and technology. Before 1850, society had to rely on human and animal labour to plough fields, harvest crops, chop firewood, mine and haul coal, and transport people and materials. But after 1950, the advances in industry, agriculture, transportation and communication brought about by new energy technologies freed society from the constraints of slave and animal labour and expanded agricultural and industrial productivity. Human population ascended to 2 billion by 1927, 4 billion by 1974, 6 billion by 1999 and 6.6 billion by 2007 (Ibid: 6). So as energy supply and demand increased during these years as our reliance on fossil fuels has grown, so has the disparity of use between industrialized and developing countries. Given the fast pace of industrialization, heavy dependence on technology, transportation and communication, the demand for commercial energy has grown tremendously since 1860. The demand has grown manifold especially since 1940. Consumption of energy started massively and, in fact, doubled from 1970 to 2005. It was growing at 2 per cent per year until 2002 and 4.5 per cent per year from 2003 to 2005. This rate of growth is likely to continue, because of the expected demand by developing countries like China and India for energy (Ibid: 8).

Thus, the continued dependence on oil as the largest energy source poses special geologic, geographic and political problems. The supply is limited by geological conditions but the demand for it beyond the borders and barriers has given rise to energy price volatility, energy crises (1973, 1980 and 1991), political turmoil and lately climate change. Competition for oil started between developed and developing countries. As the supply remains concentrated in a few geographic locations of the world, countries formulate their foreign policy and direct them with a vision to acquire and control the resources for meeting their energy security needs. The more powerful the country, the more the influence it could inflict on these oil-producing countries, given the rise in intense competition for oil and gas. This consequently has led to the rise of an international dimension to the politics of energy.

Energy factor in geopolitics

Energy – the driver of national development, economic growth and effective tool of social change is essentially a significant resource for every country. But ironically the resources are scarce, expensive and unevenly distributed. Therefore, it is used as a handy weapon with significant repercussions in the perspective of world growth and the geopolitical interplay among the energy-producing and consuming countries and between the former and the latter.

The use of energy as a strategic weapon can be done through the least means: "by creating a surplus in the production or by decreasing that production with an aim either to attack the economy of the competing countries that are heavily dependent on energy exports or to cause market prices to soar" (Moreira 2017: 44).

World energy crisis, 1970s

The energy crisis that emerged during the 1970s was due to the conflict between Israel and the Arab world. Throughout the 1960s, the Middle East was the lifeline of world energy supply accounting for 38 per cent of world oil production and 90 per cent of international trade (Melosi 1985: 249). The Yom Kippur war of 1973 provided the catalyst for OPEC's emergence as the leader in oil production and pricing. When Egypt and Syria launched a surprise attack on Israel in October 1973, the United States airlifted weapons to aid the Israeli defence. In response, members of the Organization of Arab Petroleum Exporting Countries (OAPEC) initiated an oil embargo against the United States and other allies of Israel. Saudi Arabia participated in the embargo and ARAMCO was ordered to cut production by 25 per cent and cease shipments to the United States. Additionally, OPEC increased world prices of oil from $3.00 per barrel to $11.65 per barrel (Hatch 1986: 32). Although the major oil-producing companies responded by increasing production in other countries, shipments of crude to the United States dropped from 6 million to 5 million barrels per day; and the country experienced the worst energy crisis in its history (Melosi 1985: 238).

The embargo ended in March 1974, six months after it had been initiated. It was largely aimed at the United States and allies of Israel. Moreover, the action by OPEC had resulted in a drastic price increase in crude oil. Although a global recession resulted in a decrease in demand for OPEC oil, the cartel maintained its pricing power and the oil market remained stable between 1974 and 1978. In 1978, tensions in the Middle East again demonstrated the volatility of the oil market when the Iranian Revolution raised the price of oil in the market to as high as $45 per barrel (Ibid: 282).

Global response to the embargo

In 1974, the International Energy Agency (IEA) was established within the framework of the OECD as a direct response to the embargo. Its mission was to develop strategies for energy security during emergencies and to reduce member countries' dependence on oil (IEA 2005). Non-OECD countries also developed strategies for oil emergencies. The Association of Southeast Asian Nations (ASEAN) developed a council on Petroleum (ASCOPE). The main purpose of ASCOPE is to coordinate the management of energy resources in member countries in the event of shortages or oversupply of petroleum (Karki and Salehfar 2005: 499).

Many countries implemented national energy policies to address the concern over energy security. In Europe, France, Germany and the Netherlands began to expand their nuclear programmes. Great Britain continued to diversify its oil imports, exploiting resources in the North Sea and Algeria. Europe also began to increase oil imports from the Soviet Union.

The oil glut, 1980

In 1980, following the Iraqi invasion of Iran, oil production in Iran nearly stopped, and Iraq's oil production was severely cut as well. After 1980, oil prices began a six-year decline that culminated with a 46 per cent price drop in 1986 (Scribd 2009: 22). This was due to reduced demand and overproduction, which caused OPEC to lose its unity. Oil exporters such as Mexico, Nigeria and Venezuela expanded production. The ending of price controls allowed the United States and Europe to get more oil from Prudhoe Bay and the North Sea.

The 1980s oil glut was a surplus of crude oil caused by falling demand following the 1973 and 1979 energy crises. The world price of oil, which had peaked in 1979 at over $35 per barrel, collapsed in 1986 from $27 to below $10 (Ibid). The glut began in the early 1980s as a result of slowed economic activity in industrial countries (due to the 1973 and 1979 energy crises) and the energy conservation spurred by high fuel prices. The inflation-adjusted real 2004 dollar value of oil fell from an average of $78.2 in 1981 to an average of $26.8 per barrel in 1986 (Ibid: 22).

On June 15, 1981, *The New York Times* stated that "the world temporarily floats in a glut of oil", though the next week a *New York Times* article warned that the word "glut" was misleading and that in reality, while temporary surpluses had brought down prices somewhat, prices were still well above pre-energy crisis levels (*New York Times* 1981). This sentiment was echoed in November 1981, when the CEO of Exxon Corp also characterized the glut as a temporary surplus, and that the word "gluts" was an example of "American penchant for exaggerated language". He wrote that the main cause of the glut was declining consumption. In the United States, Europe and Japan, oil consumption had fallen 13% from 1979 to 1981, due to "in part, in reaction to the very large increases in oil prices by the Organization of Petroleum Exporting Countries and other oil exporters", continuing a trend begun during the 1973 price increases (Scribd 2009: 22–23).

After 1980, reduced demand and overproduction produced a glut on the world market, causing a six-year-long decline in oil prices, culminating with a 46 per cent price drop in 1986.

Iran–Kuwait War 1990 and the Gulf War 1990

The invasion of Kuwait in 1990 is also famously known as the Iraq–Kuwait War. It was a major conflict between the Republic of Iraq and the State of Kuwait. It resulted in the seven-month-long Iraqi occupation of Kuwait, and subsequently led to direct military intervention by United States-led forces in the Persian Gulf War.

Kuwait was a close ally of Iraq during the Iraq–Iran war. However, after the war ended, the friendly relations between the two neighbouring Arab countries turned bitter. The Iraqi–Kuwait relations became dampened for several economic and diplomatic reasons. In 1990, Iraq accused Kuwait of stealing Iraq's oil through slant drilling and the invasion started on August 2, 1990 (2009: 23). This finally culminated in full-fledged war in the Middle East starting with the Iraqi invasion of Kuwait.

Kuwait had heavily funded the 8-year-long Iraqi war against Iran and, as a result, had gone bankrupt. By the time the war ended, Iraq was not in a financial position to repay the $40 billion which it had borrowed from Kuwait to finance its war (Ibid). Iraq indeed argued that the war had prevented the rise of Iranian influence in the Arab world. However, Kuwait's reluctance to pardon the debt created strains in the relationship between the two Arab countries. This seems to be the main reason behind the Iraq–Kuwait war of 1990.

Whatever the nature of the Iraq–Kuwait war, it has had implications and effects that have reached far beyond what was thought. Given the geopolitical significance of the region, its consequences have resulted in a global problem. Iraq tried to repay its debts by raising the price of oil through OPEC's oil production cuts. However, Kuwait, a member of OPEC, prevented a global increase in petroleum prices by increasing its petroleum production. This lowering of price from the Kuwait side prevented Iraq from recovering its war-crippled economy. This was seen by many in Iraq as an act of aggression, further aggravating the discord between the two countries. The collapse in oil prices had a catastrophic impact on the Iraqi economy. According to former Iraqi Foreign Minister Tariq Aziz, "every US $1 drop in the price of a barrel of oil caused a US $1 billion drop in Iraq's annual revenues triggering an acute financial crisis in Baghdad". It was estimated that Iraq lost US $14 billion a year due to Kuwait's oil price strategy (Ibid: 24).

After the Iran–Iraq war and the Iraq–Kuwait war, the Iraqi economy was struggling to recover. Iraq's civil and military expenditure was higher than its state budget. Most of its ports were destroyed, oil fields were mined, and traditional oil customers were lost. The case with Kuwait and Iran though were not similar but suffered heavy losses. To revive their dying economy, these oil-producing countries raised their oil prices which consequently helped in triggering oil prices the world over.

The Persian Gulf War started on August 2, 1990 and continued until February 28, 1991. It was a United Nations authorized military conflict between Iraq and a coalition force from 34 nations commissioned for expelling Iraqi forces from Kuwait after Iraq's invasion, occupation and annexation of Kuwait in August 1990 (Ibid: 28). This resulted in further deteriorating the regional stability, peace and order in the region and above all fuelled the oil crisis in the gulf.

United States' invasion of Iraq, 2003

The United States' invasion of Iraq in 2003 is also known as the Second Gulf War or the Occupation of Iraq. It was an ongoing military campaign that began on March 20, 2003, with the invasion of Iraq by multinational forces. The multinational forces were led by and composed almost entirely of troops from the United States and United Kingdom. The pretext of the invasion was a ploy on the part of the United States, United Kingdom and Spain who claimed that Iraq possessed Weapons of Mass Destruction (WMD) posing a serious and imminent threat to their security and that of their coalition allies. Within a few weeks Iraq was tumbled into dust. One of the ancient civilizations of human history had been mutilated. More than this, the cause of concern was the rising price of oil in the aftermath of the war, as oil wells were burnt and damaged resulting in a shortage of oil in the world market. It is also widely discussed in several quarters that the real motive behind the United States invasion of Iraq was to acquire and control its oil wells.

Global financial crisis, 2009

The world's dependence on energy supply continues to grow manifold, making energy security a strategic priority. The 2009 economic crisis may have driven down prices and slowed down economic growth, but this was nothing more than a pause. Resource-rich countries continued to use their assets to advance their interests, broaden their areas of influence and create alliances with like-minded partners. Similarly, energy transiting and importing countries also attempted to leverage their positions. These forces were about to change the nature of international affairs which would have some adverse implications on global energy security.

Russia, Iran and Venezuela, all resource-rich nations in terms of energy, seemed to have been hit hard by the financial crisis. This provoked certain oil-rich countries to nationalize their energy resources, to exercise a monopoly over price and control. Some observers believed that "energy nationalism" had been tempered. Others argued that whatever price concessions such countries accepted would be short term and tactical in nature. Besides, several analysts pointed to the growing number of unemployed migrant workers due to investment cut-backs, particularly in the energy sector. This was predicted to become a source of social unrest in Central Asia and certain Gulf states.

The crisis had mixed consequences for energy companies. On the one hand, increasing capital costs made investments more difficult. This was a problem for the renewable energy industry because investment costs were higher than in other energy sectors. Higher capital costs were also a problem for transmission and pipeline companies, which needed long-term financing for infrastructures, and oilfield services companies. On the other hand, energy-supplying countries tended to become more open towards multinational companies, as they needed partners to help shoulder the high costs of energy projects. This enabled new opportunities to open for cooperation.

Major events occurring in 2011

In 2011 four major events occurred that shaped the evolution of the Middle East: the withdrawal of American troops from Iraq; the death of Osama Bin Laden; the eclosion of the Arab Spring and the beginning of the Syrian Civil war (Silva 2017: 53). The turmoil in the Middle East caused serious concerns for the energy consumers of the world regarding the security of supply and uncertain future of the energy fields in the trouble-hit region.

Trade war between the United States and China, 2019

Given the nature and risks of the ongoing trade war between the United States and China and the opposition of Beijing to the ban imposed on ZTE and Huwei by Washington, it can't be ignored that this trade war wouldn't be extended to the much critical energy sector as well. Although, China doesn't directly depend on US oil, this doesn't discount the implications of US policy on China. One mustn't overlook the recent US blacklisting of dozens of tankers operated by Cosco that resulted not only in a spike in very large crude carriers (VLCC) rates but also created a logistic nightmare for Chinese oil traders. Energy matters most

TABLE 1.1 Summary of events and their impact (Prices represented in $ per barrel)

Year	*Event*	*Impact*
1956	Suez Crisis	• Altered the regional balance of power • Nasser status grew as a defender of Arab nationalism • Britain and France lost influence in the region • The US improved its relation with Egypt.
1960	OPEC Formation	• The cartelization of oil reach countries • Introduction of production quotas • Oil emerged as a weapon of geopolitics.
1971	End of Bretton Woods	• Value of currencies depreciated • Less real income realized for the same price • Oil was priced against gold • This led to the oil shock of the 1970s.
1973	Yom Kippur War	• As a punishment to the US for helping Israel, Arab Oil Embargo was imposed.
1973	Arab Oil Embargo	• Price of crude increased from $3 to $12 • Massive shortage in the US • Paved the way for the energy crisis.
1973	Energy crisis	• World economies went into recession • Inflation skyrocketed • Targeted countries responded with initiatives to contain dependency.
1977	The Iranian Revolution	• Shah left Iran and Khumayani returned to power • Declared the establishment of a new fundamentalist Islamic Republic • A drastic decline in production by British Petroleum • Paved the way for another oil crisis.
1979	Oil crisis	• Prices went very high from 13$ to 32$.
1980	The oil glut	• Oil prices fell from 78$ to 26$ • The lowest price was below 10$.
1980	Iran–Iraq war	• Iran emerged victoriously • Killed millions of people • Borders remained unchanged • Financial losses of 1.2 trillion US$ • Oil sector suffered huge production and monetary losses.
1990	Iran–Kuwait war	• Kuwait's oil production came down as many wells were set on fire by Iraq • Drew America and allies into the war • Heavy ground and air offensive by the Allies against Iraq.
1990	Gulf war	• Sanctions levied on Iraq oil exports • Saddam was allowed to remain in power • Prices rose from $21 per barrel at the end of July to $28 on August 6, reaching $46 by mid-October in 1990 • (Considered to be a milder Oil Shock).

Continued

TABLE 1.1 (*Continued*) Summary of events and their impact (Prices represented in $ per barrel)

Year	*Event*	*Impact*
1990–91	The disintegration of the USSR	• Birth of the Commonwealth of Independent States (CIS) • Central Asia and the Caucasus aroused as energy-rich hubs, possibly providing alternatives for energy consumers for diversification.
2003	US invasion of Iraq	• End of Saddam's regime • Formation of a new democratic government backed by the US.
2009–2010	Global financial crisis	• World oil and natural gas prices have gone up.
2011	Smooth disengagement of the US from the Middle East	• Withdrawal of American troops from Iraq • Death of Osama Bin Laden • Domino effect of the Arab Spring • The civil war in Syria.
2014	Shale revolution in the US	• The US declared itself as energy independent • From net importer, American now became an exporter of oil • The rise of China and Indi as energy importers • The decline of world oil price because of increasing production from shale companies in the US.
2019–20	Corona pandemic	• The complete shutdown of markets worldwide • Economic slowdown worldwide • The demand for energy except gas has slowed down • Yet a "Suez Scenario" remains plausible given the ongoing US–China trade war.

Source: (2009), The Oil World, A Geopolitical Warfield, pp. 32–33.

as it underpins China's economic rise and the United States won't hesitate to strike it the most (Beveridge 2019).

The outbreak of the corona pandemic (COVID-19)

The coronavirus outbreak worldwide known as the COVID-19 pandemic has caused a global energy demand shock that coincided with a supply shock in the oil and gas markets. The worldwide lockdown has resulted in a global economic downturn that has led to a reduction in the demand for oil and gas, but this seems only temporary. Once the world starts recovering from the effects of the pandemic there will be serious competition to raise the economy to the level it was before the pandemic, which would once again invite competition in the energy sector.

> Meanwhile, the geopolitics of crisis, whether that be Chinese efforts to lead the global response to the pandemic, the Trump administration's delayed and insular approach to the first global crisis of the decade, or the

outcome of an ongoing price war between Saudi Arabia and Russia amidst a fracturing of OPEC+, will shape trade relationships as the global economy recovers. The effects of these events are uncertain and have a long arc, but the odds of a return to the geopolitical status-quo after the trauma of COVID-19 are wildly slim.

(*Gordon 2020*)

Global energy use

Global energy consumption has increased steadily for much of the twentieth century, particularly since 1950. In 2008, the world consumed 11,294.9 million tonnes (mtoe) of oil in total energy (including hydroelectric and nuclear power). That amount corresponds to over 82 billion barrels of crude oil burned in 2007 (Matthew 2009: 4). Total energy consumption has increased by 27 per cent globally since 1998 (Ibid).

In addition to its economic side of growth and development, world energy demand continues to rise as more developing countries become industrialized. Increasing along with the demand is the scarcity of fossil fuel resources and the consequences of fossil fuel reliance. One of the most notable developments in recent years has been the explosion of growth in energy demand from Asia and it is expected to experience the largest increase in energy demand over the next 20 years. This region with over 50 per cent of the global population eclipsed North America for the first time in 2003 as the world's most energy-hungry region. (Manning 2000: 59). As of 2015, Asia Pacific was by far the largest regional consumer with 42 percent – this was about the same as North America, Europe and Eurasia combined (at 43 per cent). The Middle East, Latin America and Africa account for around seven, five and three per cent, respectively (Ritchie and Roser 2015).

Much of this increase in demand came from China and India. As China is rapidly industrializing, its need for energy is constantly growing. In the last few years, China has catapulted itself into second place for energy consumption behind the United States in global rankings. India, though a late starter, is also not lagging in this scramble for oil and energy.

This flow of increasing consumption in China and India reflects a larger trend of energy demand emerging from Asia. Energy consumption in South Korea and Indonesia has drastically increased and Japan continues to import the majority of its energy resources. It is important to note here that, the energy resources used to support the growth and development of these countries are non-renewable fuels: i.e., coal, petroleum, natural gas and nuclear sources. In China, 97.5 per cent of energy is derived from these resources (Manning 2000: 93). In the case of India, they account for about 92 per cent (Ibid: 125) and in the case of the United States, it is 85 per cent (Randolph and Masters 2008: 13).

Energy security debate and country specific analysis

This section aims to analyse the energy crisis in the current international system, which influences directly the actions adopted by many governments. It is necessary to understand how the dimension represented by energy, especially by oil, can influence a state's foreign policy and define its role within the system. The main purpose here is to develop a study on countries and regions that can directly interfere in energy security, as well as to analyse the scenario of competition by the acquisition of energy resources within the context characterized by growing demand and decrease of the offer. In the same way, it tries to understand the link established between economic development and the international energy crisis, emphasizing the energy security problem and the possibility of armed conflict caused by ownership of the resources. The current dependence of the present model of economic development on energy resources, particularly fossil fuels, has generated a scenario characterized by risks and vulnerabilities, caused by the difficulties of resource access and the intense demand. The main focus is to understand how energy matters can drive actions and redefine the position of the state on the system.

I. United States of America

At present, the United States of America consumes 25 per cent of the energy produced in the world. It is also expected that its energy consumption would increase manifold in the foreseeable future. As the country is not self-sufficient and independent in terms of energy, it ventures into faraway places like the Middle East, Caspian and Central Asian region, Africa and Latin America. It needs a massive energy supply to sustain its economic development. Therefore, it proceeds by seeking sources externally of what they do not own in their territory, even using its military capacity to achieve this:

> The need for a vigorous US military role in protecting energy assets abroad has been a major theme in American foreign policy since 1945 when President Roosevelt met with King Abdul Aziz of Saudi Arabia and promised to protect the kingdom in return for privileged access to Saudi oil. In the most famous expression of this linkage, President Carter affirmed in January 1980 that the unimpeded flow of Persian Gulf oil is among this country's vital interests and that to protect this interest, the United States will employ "any means necessary, including military force." This principle was later cited by President Reagan as the rationale for "reflagging" Kuwaiti oil tankers with the American ensign during the Iran–Iraq War of 1980–88 and protecting them with US warships a stance that led to sporadic clashes with Iran. The same principle was subsequently invoked by George H.W. Bush as a justification for the Gulf War of 1991.
>
> *(Klare 2007)*

The current scenario of this external search is characterized by the attempt to have access to oil, to keep United States supremacy in the international system. This way, the energy politics of this country is linked to its security and foreign policy, with the object of guaranteeing the energy safety of the country. The United States Energy Strategic Plan was elaborated in 2006. This plan strategizes everything about the energy imports of the United States and the necessary actions needed thereof.

The Unites States is very dependent on the import of oil. It imports more than 60% of what is consumed by the country. Among the dependence areas, the Middle East has always remained a core area. The main partner of the United States in this trouble-torn region is Saudi Arabia. In the western hemisphere, the main partners are Canada (18.2%), Mexico (11.4%) and Venezuela (10.1%) (US DOE 2009). Even with the difficult relations with Hugo Chavez, America has relied heavily on the Latin American country for meeting its massively increasing energy consumption. Even the administration of President Barack Obama for accomplishing a more affirmative politics regarding oil dependence reduction said that:

> the energy challenges our country faces are severe and have gone unaddressed for far too long. Our addiction to foreign oil doesn't just undermine our national security and wreak havoc on our environment – it cripples our economy and strains the budgets of working families all across America.
>
> *(US DOE 2009)*

II. China

Energy is critical in ensuring the sustainable development of China. Its consumption in 2000 represented 10 per cent of the world's search for energy and is consuming 24 per cent of the global energy as of 2018 (Medeiros 2009: 11; BP 2019). This energy utilization in China is justified not only by the needs of country industries but also by the rural exodus that has been carrying the population to the urban zones and intensifying consumption. Besides, the construction of the urban infrastructure of transportation to sustain economic growth reinforces internal consumption. Given China's challenge, the country needs to guarantee its energy supply and to create infrastructure in terms of propelling its economy.

China invests heavily in other energy resources such as the nuclear and hydropower sectors. But these are not sufficient to support the country's needs. So, the focus on the acquisition of hydrocarbons from external sources has remained one of the core Chinese foreign policy issues in recent times. For that, China has been undertaking a stupendous agreement with several countries, especially in Africa and Asia to secure its supply. The International Energy Agency affirms that if China keeps up this rhythm, in 2025 it is going to need to import 82 per cent of its oil used (IEA 2007). That context makes China seek oil outside its territory.

China is determined in its search and production of oil in all continents, especially in Asia, Africa, South America and the Middle East. That context demonstrates the form by which China comes to undertake an expansion of its presence in several countries, even in those with some military instability, like Sudan. The Chinese presence in Africa has been being more and more intense: China's drive to gain access to foreign supplies is most evident in Africa, where Beijing has established ties with the oil-producing governments of Algeria, Angola, Chad, Equatorial Guinea, Nigeria and Sudan (Klare 2007).

In South America, the main partners of China are Brazil and Venezuela. There is an agreement in which Venezuela pledges to help China in the formation of its strategic reserves of oil in exchange for Chinese investment in the agriculture of the country (Medeiros 2009: 12). Venezuela exports 300,000 barrels of oil a day for China and the goal is to reach 1 million daily barrels until 2013 (IEA 2009). In 2019, China became the no. 1 importer of Venezuelan oil and only in the first six months despite the U.S sanctions on Venezuela, Beijing has imported an average of 350,000 barrels per day (Reuters 2020). Regarding Brazil, it signed an agreement with China in May 2009 for promoting cooperation between *Petrobras* and the petroliferous sector (IEA 2009).

The Chinese established goals with regard to energy security that stand out: to enlarge the external supply; to reduce coal dependence; to build more hydroelectric plants and to expand transmission lines; to increase the production of natural gas; to encourage alternative energy; and the installation of more 31 nuclear reactors. China has been making efforts to increase the participation of renewable energies in its energy matrix, besides diversifying partners for oil purchase.

III. Russia

Russia is a strategically important country for world energy geopolitics. One cannot accomplish a study concerning energy without taking account of the Russian potentiality and its political relations with several countries, especially in Europe. Russia is not part of OPEC, but it has been a great competitor in the oil market in a different trend. Russia uses the hydrocarbons, depending on the deliberations and needs of the Kremlin. Despite Russia's existing occupation of the considerable oil and gas market, this country has been undertaking projects to diversify its partners and to conquer new markets in face of the strong demand context that is configured in the international system. Besides seeking to increase the volume of its commerce of energy resources with Europe, Russia also intends to expand sales to China and the United States.

For Clifford Gaddy, possible scenarios for the use of Russia's energy are both the physical product and the rents that flow from it. Russia's fundamental goal now is not to allow anyone else to be able to determine how Russia's greatest asset, its oil and gas, is used. And so, the goal is to control overproduction, transportation, distribution, and choice of customers (Gaddy 2007: 6–14). This is how Russian energy plays a role in shaping and securing its sovereignty.

The debate is not, therefore, in the Russian interest of being or not being an energy power, but in the direction of internal policies and the maintenance of its sovereignty. For a lot of states, the Russian resources are strategic, because of the need to keep up the production of their industries. For Russia, this enables the possibility of imposing its own rules in the international context, within a scenario characterized by the dependence of these other states regarding what Russia owns in abundance.

IV. Middle East

Blessed with a massive chunk of natural resources concerning oil and natural gas, the region of the Middle East has been deeply suffering from its resource curse. The region is constantly a highlight in the international agenda, given the political instability of the armed conflicts and several problems that comprise their reality. However, the enormous potential of oil in the Middle East region has attracted global attention in the search to guarantee the supply.

The Middle East is a strategic region full of hydrocarbons. The region is responsible for the energy supply of several countries because of the widespread capacity of its field. The International Energy Agency esteems that the Middle East will continue to be an oil supplier in the years to come, and this affirmation can be proved by the fact that just five countries (Saudi Arabia, Iran, Iraq, Arab Emirates, Kuwait) retain about two-thirds (about 61 per cent) of the world's proved reserves of oil (Sebille-Lopez 2006: 307). It is still necessary to consider that Iran and Qatar have the second and third world highest reserves of gas (IEA 2009). However, the recent tension in the region, marred with political turmoil, civic unrest, regional instability and intra-state war, has concerned the countries of the world.

V. Asia and Africa

The contemporary world order is shifting towards Asia. The present century has been rightly regarded as the Asian century. Acknowledging the rising importance of Asia in the global order, Peter Evan, director of Cambridge Research Associates Global Oil Group once said that,

> there are important things that are happening in the United States and Europe, but Asia is the centre and the key driver and is what we need to understand the future of energy markets unfolding in the coming years. Asia's oil demand is overtaking Europe and North America. And this is a reflection of Asia becoming a global demand centre for oil.
>
> *(Evan 2007)*

When it comes to energy matters, besides a cluster of countries from East Asia, it is Japan, China and India that first come to mind. As these three giants of Asia are intensely dependent on oil, and importance has been attached to these countries in contemporary times. Japan, historically, has been the continent's main oil market. China only recently overtook Japan as the largest consumer market in Asia. The Indian scenario, though not similar to China and Japan, is also not far below. Due to its intense dependence on external sources of oil, energy security has been a fundamental topic of discussion and debate in the country. It also expected that the energy consumption of India will double in another 25 years (IEA 2009). In this scenario of limited oil reserves in its territory, India needs to import oil, mostly from the Persian Gulf. However, with the increasing regional instability, regime change, civic unrest and political crisis in the Persian Gulf, the Indian side is induced to look for an alternative which can ensure affordable, undisrupted, easy and accessible oil to this second most inhabited landmass on the earth. In this regard, Central Asia seems to be by far the best option it is left with.

Africa, on the other hand, possesses about 7.2 per cent of the world's oil reserves (BP 2019). Two countries of the "Dark Continent" have the largest concentration of about two-thirds of these riches, namely: Libya and Nigeria (Sebille-Lopez 2006: 119; BP 2019). It is important to stress that most of the wealth of this region is exported to feed the industries of other countries. Africa becomes attractive for those with difficulties in energy supply, especially the United States, China and lately India.

VI. Europe

With regard to Europe, what one can consider is its fragility regarding its energy supply because the region is very dependent on Russian resources. It has been a historical fact that European production is not enough to supply local demands. Concerning gas commerce relations between Russia and the European Union, it is necessary to stress a critical point that denotes the vulnerability that Europe is exposed to. Europe does not produce enough energy to supply its industries and to supply homes in the rigorous winters that devastate the continent. Europe needs to import 80 per cent of the gas used (EU 2006). In 2018, petroleum products only constituted two-third of EU's energy imports while the imports of gas was 24 per cent and solid fuels about 8 per cent. Russia all alone remained the dominant energy exporter to EU (Eurostat 2019). The dilemma is that this resource arrives on the European continent through Ukraine. The Russian gas flow that goes to Europe across Ukraine was interrupted in January 2009, leaving countries like France, Germany, Austria, Czech Republic, Poland, Romania and others with serious difficulties in the middle of winter as a result of a disagreement between Russia and Ukraine over prices of gas (IEA 2009). Thus, a great dependence context is observed, with vulnerabilities and risks, whereby the threat of cuts to the energy supply complicate the peaceful relations in a region.

About Latin America, it is important to say that the region is becoming more and more relevant for the international system because of its energy resources. Brazil, Mexico and Venezuela with about 75 per cent of the region's total output and ranking as the world's 10th, 11th, and 12th oil producers dominate the Lain American oil production (Carpenter 2019). From certain recent developments in the region, it is needful to emphasize that these fuel-rich nations use their lucrative resources as a political weapon to make their importance felt in the international arena.

From the above understanding, it is quite clear that all the energy-producing countries suffer from one or other problem. If the Middle East is suffering from regional instability and political turmoil, Africa is suffering from poverty, unemployment, human rights violation, disease and starvation. Latin America, though not volatile, is always vulnerable to conflicts. It is Central Asia according to the better part of research analysis that seems to be a viable region; a region with largely untapped huge hubs of natural resources concerning hydrocarbons, hydroelectricity, and uranium. Central Asia offers plenty of opportunities for the countries of the world looking for diversification. It is a relatively stable region, hence, the security of supply is ensured.

Running out of oil and energy: the final countdown

Opinions about the future of energy are divided. In the 1970s, estimates were that oil reserves would last for another 20–30 years and expectations were that it would last at best up to the year 2007 (Simmons 2000). In the early 1980s, the proven oil reserves were calculated at 636 billion barrels (Pant 2008: 4). However, in the last two decades, the statistics show that the world's proven reserves have risen by a little over 50 per cent (Sikri 2008: 7). OPEC estimates that oil reserves are over one trillion barrels to meet the need for 40 years at the current consumption rate. Added to that, the recoverable oil reserves would enhance another 40 years of lifespan (Pant 2008: 4).

The global proven natural gas reserves are put at around 15.9 trillion cubic meters, which is a 38 per cent increase over the 1988 estimates (Shikri 2008). In 2004, the International Energy Association (IEA) in its publication "Energy Security in a Dangerous World" pointed out that "the Earth's energy resources are more than adequate to meet demand until 2030 and well beyond" (IEA 2004).

While dismissing the "peak oil" propaganda, Saudi Aramco, the world's largest oil company, feels that in assessing the availability of oil reserves the world should consider not just conventional oil but all the liquid energy resources. As per Aramco, liquid energy sources include condensates, natural gas liquids, tar sands, bitumen, extra heavy oil, oil shale, gas to liquids and even bio-fuels which can substitute oil in many fields (Sikri 2008: 7). By this calculation, the total in-place conventional oil is about 5.7 trillion barrels and the total in-place liquids about 13–16 trillion barrels of which only 1.1 trillion barrels have been consumed so far (Ibid). Moreover, large areas of the world indeed remain unexplored for even conventional oil, possibly because it was not considered economical to risk huge sums of money in oil exploration when ample oil was more easily and cheaply available elsewhere.

The point, however, cannot be ignored that, given the accelerated pace of energy consumption despite the enhanced recovery, the crisis of reaching the stage of decline in supply continues to loom large. This perception is widely shared by many oil companies and openly expressed by many governments and sections of civil society, who continue to be deeply worried on this account. Among the major oil companies, while Exxon-Mobil takes an optimistic view, British Petroleum, or BP as it is commonly known, has significantly chosen to project itself today not as British Petroleum, its original name, but as "Beyond Petroleum" (Sikri 2008: 7). Shell, too, is significantly investing in research and development of non-conventional energy in anticipation of the day when the world will run out of oil.

In addition to this, the world economies are globalizing; over 3 billion people in Asia are entering the economy, and information technology has exploded around the world and is connecting billions of people and to all human knowledge. Vast quantities of energy consumption are required to fuel and power today's global standard of living. Also, for the first time in human history, the use of vast and increasing quantities of coal and oil is becoming globally unsustainable and is creating economic, environmental and geostrategic limits to growth. Global oil consumption is running at about 84 million barrels per day or 31 billion barrels per year (*Wall Street Journal* 2007). This equals nearly 1,000 barrels per second or one cubic mile of oil per year (Amory 2006), which releases about 12 billion metric tonnes of CO_2 into the atmosphere (Campbell and Price 2008: 152). Oil consumption in a "business as usual" scenario is estimated to be well over 100 million barrels per day by 2030, which would release about 17 billion metric tonnes of CO_2 into the atmosphere each year (Ibid).

Global coal consumption is about 16 million tonnes per day or 6 billion tons per year (Ibid), a cubic mile of dirty black rocks that release about 10.5 billion metric tonnes of CO_2 to the atmosphere each year. A "business as usual" coal scenario calls for the consumption of nearly 10 billion tonnes per year by 2030 which would release over 16 billion metric tonnes of CO_2 annually (Ibid). In 2007, the global economy consumed 2 cubic miles of coal and oil that released over 20 billion tonnes of CO_2 or nearly 80 per cent of the entire world's human-produced CO_2 emission (Ibid). Over the coming decades, the existing energy infrastructure and ageing technologies will not be able to sustain the economic growth that will be needed for the continuing development of our globalized economies and increasing standards of living required to give hope for a better future for the global society. In this scenario, energy security puts complex questions into context.

For quite some time now, the demand for energy has skyrocketed across the globe. This has resulted due to sustained economic growth in industrialized countries and accelerated growth in China, India and other emerging economic powers. The transportation sector, which depends heavily on petroleum-based fuels, has expanded especially rapidly in the latter countries. Past oil and gas development has depleted the relatively easy-to-access petroleum reserves; because of that, future oil and gas development will involve deposits that generally are: scarcer, with fewer super-giant fields being discovered; farther from existing demand centres; deeper and harder to extract, often involving deepwater locations, high pressure or high sulphur content; located in poorer countries, with risks of political instability and poor governance; and concentrated in areas where governments restrict access, whether as a matter of cartel membership, as in OPEC countries, or in response to other policy priorities, such as environmental concerns and cost of development (Elkind 2010: 123).

India's energy approach

India's overwhelming dependence on domestic unpurified energy resources is attributed to the long-held autarkic world views of non-alignment and opposition to liberalism as far as possible. India's ideological neutrality position didn't allow her in the past to play any significant role either in bilateral or multilateral discussions on issues of energy security. The situation then was not as demanding as in 2020 as almost 80 per cent of the country's population was dependent on cow dung and traditional biomass uses. However, the situation has slowly been changing since the 1990s with India's entry into globalization through its New Economic Policy inviting Liberalization, Privatization and Globalization (LPG) to its economy under the leadership of Prime Minister P.V. Narasimha Roa. India's economic boom attributed to globalization has rapidly developed its energy crunch. In the last 15 years at least, "India has heavily relied on coal with 41 per cent of the total energy mix, oil 23 per cent (85 per cent of them are from imported sources) and natural gas 8 per cent" (ISS Report 2018).

Energy trade plays an important role in India's international engagements. New Delhi has been negotiating several energy projects all over the world although many of them have slow progress and are yet to be operational. Its hydroelectricity project in Nepal is running very slow; the proposed Myanmar-Bangladesh-India (MBI) pipeline is yet to be initiated as Bangladesh has been reluctant to sell its limited gas reserves, preferring to develop them for domestic use; India's over-reliance on the Middle East marred with the Arab Spring and civil war poses serious challenges before India on the energy security front. In this scenario, the emergence of Central Asia as an energy hub in the neighbourhood offers immense opportunities to meet its energy demands through equity oil and gas.

Looked at in global terms, in the past, 80 per cent of world oil demand was driven by the United States, the European Union and Japan, but today the geopolitical implications of energy security are wide as the world's demands for oil, gas and other energy resources have become truly globalized. It is so globalized that, "today 85 per cent of the world oil demand is driven by China, India and other emerging economies" (Silva 2017). A recent study by the US Geological Survey has shown that "compared with 60 years ago, the planet is consuming today, in percentage terms 618 times more oil, 1000 times more gas, 756 times more nickel, 1500 times more bauxite" (US Geological Survey 2000; Klare 2012).

And that too at a time when the key world oil and gas supplier, the Middle East, has been witnessing the "Arab Spring", the collapse of order, an intensive increase in terrorist activities, ISIS taking firm control of certain regimes, a fierce regional competition for hegemony between Saudi Arabia and Iran, the emergence of failed states in Syria, Iraq, Yemen and Libya and importantly the United States policy of "smooth disengagement" from the Middle East under President Barack Obama with his famous statement "leading from Behind" pose serious concerns for the security of energy supply from the Middle East to the rest of the world (Silva 2017).

From the above it is crystal clear that both the geopolitics of energy consumption and production are transforming at a rapid rate. While the global consumption scale has increased with the rising demands from China and India, the rate of global energy production has not witnessed any upward turn with the exception of new energy-rich regions' entry into the world energy market while the old energy market is facing turmoil. The emergence of Central Asia and the Caucasus at this juncture as an energy hub provides India with an opportunity in its energy quest.

Thus, in this confusing scenario of growing world oil demands and depleting resources, one thing that is quite obvious is that the world will have to turn to the regions having significant shares of global oil, gas and other energy resources to meet their energy crunch. Central Asia along with the Caspian Sea region in the heart of the Eurasian landscape is such a region, considered important for the world energy market. This is not because of the scale of its reserves, or of its production, but because, unlike most other regions of the world, significant new reserves have been found there recently and prospects remain promising. Additionally, the oil is of high quality and free from pollutants. The regimes are more stable than any other oil-rich regions of the world. This has further enabled attracting outside consumer nations to exhibit their keen interests in the region's energy resources.

References

Amory, Lovins (2006), "Getting off oil," The Economist's The World, November 16. retrieved from: https://www.economist.com/news/2006/11/16/getting-off-oil.

Beveridge, Neil (2019), "The U.S–China Trade War May Escalate to Energy", *Petroleum Economist*, November 26, available at: www.petroleum-economist.com/articles/politics-economics/north-america/2019/the-us-china-trade-war-may-escalate-to-energy [accessed April 16, 2020].

BP (2019), Oil - BP Statistical Review of World Energy, British Petroleum, 68th Edition, retrieved from: https://www.bp.com/content/dam/bp/business-sites/en/global/corporate/pdfs/energy-economics/statistical-review/bp-stats-review-2019-oil.pdf.

Campbell, Kurt M. and Price, Jonathan (2008), *The Global Politics of Energy*, Washington, DC: Aspen Strategy Group.

Campos, Ana and Fernandes, Carla Patricio (2017), "The Geopolitics of Energy", in Carla Patricio Fernandes and Teresa Ferriera Rodrigues (eds), *Geopolitics of Energy and Energy Security*, Lisbon: Portuguese National Defence Institute (IDN).

Carpenter, William (2019), The Biggest Oil Producers in Latin America, Investopedia, December, 5, retrieved from: https://www.investopedia.com/articles/investing/101315/biggest-oil-producers-latin-america.asp.

Clifford, G. G. (2007), "The Future of Energy Security", The Brookings Institution, Washington, January 23, available at: www.brookings.edu/events/2007/0123global-environment.aspx [accessed January 23, 2011].

Club of Rome (2011), The Limits to Growth, A Potomac Associate Book, available at: https://clubofrome.org/publication/the-limits-to-growth/

Cohen, S. B. (1964), *Geography and Politics in a Divided World*, London: Methuen, p. 24.

Cohen, S. B. (2003), *Geopolitics of the World System*, London: Rowman & Littlefield, p. 11.

CSIS (2001), *Energy Policy and Energy Analysis: Flawed Analysis Means Flawed Policy*, Centre for Strategic and International Studies, April, 26, available at: http://csis.org/files/media/csis/pubs/energypolicy_analysis[1].pdf [accessed January 7, 2011].

Dekmejian, R. Hrair and Simonain, H. Hovann (2001), *Troubled Waters: The Geopolitics of the Caspian Region*, London: I. B. Tauris, p. 28.

EAA (2005), *Issue Brief: Energy Security*, Ethanol Across America, available at: www.ethanol.org/pdf/contentmgmt/Energy_Security_Issue_Brief.pdf, summer [accessed January 7, 2011].

Elkind, Jonathan (2010), "Energy Security: Call for a Broader Agenda", in Carlos Pascual and Jonathan Elkind (eds.), *Energy Security, Economics, Politics, Strategies and Implications*, Washington, DC: Brookings Institution Press.

Eurostat (2019), From where do we import energy and how dependent are we? Eurostat, European Union, retrieved from: https://ec.europa.eu/eurostat/cache/infographs/energy/bloc-2c.html.

Evan, Peter (2007), *The Future of Energy Security*, Washington, DC: The Brookings Institution, January 23, available at: www.brookings.edu/events/2007/0123global-environment.aspx [accessed January 10, 2010].

Fernandes, Carla Patricio (2017), "A Contribution to the Analysis of Energy Security", in Carla Patricio Fernandes and Teresa Ferriera Rodrigues (eds.), *Geopolitics of Energy and Energy Security*, Lisbon: Portuguese National Defence Institute (IDN).

Flavin, Christopher (2000), "It's Time to Quit Our Damaging Addiction to Oil", *The International Herald Tribune*, September 26, available at: www.nytimes.com/2000/09/26/opinion/26iht-edflavin.t.html?scp=1&sq=Christopher%20Flavin+%20September%2026,%202000&st=cse [accessed January 11, 2011].

Flint, C. (2017), *Introduction to Geopolitics*, New York: Routledge.

Fraser, Ron (2001), "The Politics of Energy", *Trumpet Print Edition*, July, available at: www.thetrumpet.com [accessed December 7, 2010].

Gordon, Jennifer (2020), "The Implications of the Corona Virus Crisis on the Global Energy Sector and the Environment", *Atlantic Council*, March 24, available at: https://atlanticcouncil.org/blogs/new-atlanticist/the-implications-of-the-coronavirus-crisis-on-the-global-energy-sector-and-the-environment/ [accessed April 16, 2020].

Hatch, M. T. (1986), *Politics and Nuclear Power: Energy Policy in Western Europe*, Lexington: University Press of Kentucky.

Hill, Christopher (2003), *The Changing Politics of Foreign Policy*, London: Palgrave Macmillan.

IEA (2004), *World Energy Outlook*, International Energy Agency, available at: http://library.iea.org/dbtw-wpd/textbase/npsum/WEO2004SUM.pdf [accessed January 11, 2011].

IEA (2005), *Introduction to the IEA*, International Energy Agency, available at: http://www.iea.org/about/index.asp [accessed December 2010].

IEA (2007), *World Energy Outlook 2007, China and India Insight*, International Energy Agency, available at: www.iea.org/textbase/nppdf/free/2007/weo_2007.pdf [accessed June 10, 2010].

IEA (2009), *World Energy Outlook 2009*, International Energy Agency, available at: http://www.iea.org/textbase/nppdf/free/2009/WEO2009.pdf [accessed June 10, 2010].

IEA (2010), *About the IEA*, International Energy Agency, available at: www.iea.org/about/index.asp [accessed August 2, 2011].

ISS Report (2018), "Energy Statistics," Indian Statistical System Report-2018, Ministry of Statistics and Programme Implementation, Government of India, 25th Issues, available at: http://mospi.nic.in/sites/default/files/publication_reports/Energy_Statistics_2018.pdf.

Jaffe, A. and Manning, R. (2000), "The Shocks of a World of Cheap Oil", *Foreign Affairs*, January-February.

Kalick, J. H. and Goldwyn, D. L (2005), "Introduction: The Need to Integrate Energy and Foreign Policy", in Kalick and Goldwyn (eds.), *Energy and Security: Toward a New Foreign Policy Strategy*, New York: Johns Hopkins University Press.

Kaplan, Robert (2012), *The Revenge of Geography*, New York: Random House.

Karki, Mann and Salehfar (2005), "Energy and Environment in the ASEAN: Challenges and Opportunities", *Energy Policy* 33(4), March 2005.

Klare, Michael T. (2007), "Preparing for Life after Oil", *The Nation*, November 8, available at: http://www.alternet.org/module/printversion/66625 [accessed September 10, 2010].

Klare, Michael T. (2012), *The Race for What's Left: The Global Scramble for the World's Last Resources*. London: Picador.

Leigh, M. (2014), "Energy: A Geopolitical Game Changer?", *The International Spectator: Italian Journal of International Affairs*, [e-journal] 49(2), pp. 1–10. doi: 10.1080/03932729.2014 [accessed September 9, 2018].

MacKinder, Halford (1962), *Democratic Ideals and Reality*, New York: Greenwood Press.

Mahan, Alfred (1897), *The Influence of Sea Power Upon History, 1660–1783*, Boston, MA: Little Brown.

Manning, R. A (2000), *The Asian Energy Factor: Myths and Dimensions of Energy*, Security and the Pacific Future, New York: Palgrave.

Medeiros, Daniela Marques (2009), "Energy and International Relations: The Problem to Conciliate Energy Security and Development", *Paper Presented in at the Annual Meeting of ISA-IBRI Joint International Meeting, Pontifical Catholic University*, Rio de Janeiro Campus (PUC-Rio), Rio de Janeiro, Brazil, available at: http://www.allacademic.com/meta/p381065_index.html [accessed January 10, 2011].

Melosi, V (1985), *Coping with Abundance Energy and Environment in Industrial America*, Colombous OH: McGraw-Hill College Press.

Moreira, Filipe Arnaut (2017), "Energy as Social, Strategic and Geopolitical Equation", in Carla Patricio Fernandes and Teresa Ferriera Rodrigues (eds), *Geopolitics of Energy and Energy Security*, Lisbon: Portuguese National Defence Institute (IDN).

Muir, Richard (1997), *Political Geography*, London: Macmillan Press Ltd.

New York Times (1981), *A oil Glut that Rises Prices*, June 15, available at: http://www.nytimes.com/1981/10/09/opinion/an-oil-glut-that-raises-prices.html [accessed 10 December 2010].

Noronha, Ligia, and Sudarshan, Anant (2009), *India's Energy Security*, Oxon: Routledge Contemporary South Asia.

Norris, R. and Lloyd, L. (1980), *Political Geography*, Columbus, OH: Charles E. Merrill Publishing Co. A Bell & Howell Company, p. 56.

Ocheltree, Matthew (2009), "Energy Issues Brief", *Carnage Endowment for International Peace*, A Project of the Levin Institute, available at: www.globalisation101.org [accessed January 11, 2011].

Pant, Girijesh (2008), *India: The Emerging Energy Player*, Delhi: Dorling Kindersley (India) Pvt. Ltd.

Pascual, C. (2008), *The Geopolitics of Energy: From Security to Survival*. Brooking Institutions. p. 3.

Planning Commission (2006), "Integrated Energy Policy: Report of the Expert Committee," *Planning Commission*, Government of India, New Delhi.

Pradhan, Ramakrushna (2010), Geopolitics of Central Asia: China-US Engagement, VDM Verlag-Muller, Germany.

Randolph, J. and G. M. Masters (2008), *Energy for Sustainability: Technology, Planning, Policy*, Island Press, London: Bloomsbury Publishing.

Reuters (2020), Special Report: How China got shipments of Venezuela oil despite the U.S sanctions, Reuters, June 12, retrieved from: https://www.reuters.com/article/us-venezuela-oil-deals-specialreport-idUSKBN23J1N1.

Ritchie, Hannah and Roser, Max (2015), Energy, Ourworldindata, retrieved from: https://ourworldindata.org/energy.

Scribd (2009), "The Oil World, A Geopolitical Warfield", April 21st, available at: www.scribd.com/doc/14472626/Geopolitics-Oil-Dilpomacy [accessed December 2010].

Sebille-Lopez, Philippe (2006), *The Geopolitics of Oil*, Perspectives géopolitiques series, Paris: Armanda Colin.

Sikri, Rajiv (2008), "The Geopolitics of Energy Security and Implications for South and Southeast Asia", *ISAS Working Paper*, National University of Singapore, Singapore, No. 37, February 11.

Silva, Antonio Costa (2017), "Energy: From Geopolitics to Security", in Carla Patricio Fernandes and Teresa Ferriera Rodrigues (eds.), *Geopolitics of Energy and Energy Security*, Lisbon: Portuguese National Defence Institute (IDN).

Simmons, R. Matthew (2000), "Revisiting the Limits to Growth: Could the Club of Rome Have Veen Correct, after All?", *Energy Bulletin*, October, available at: www.energybulletin.net/node/1512 [accessed December 10, 2010].

Smalley, R (2005), "Our energy challenge," 27th Illinois Junior Science & Humanities Symposium, Rice University, April 3.

Spykman, Nicholas (1944), *Geography of Peace and Foreign Policy of the United States*, New York: Harcourt Brace and Company.

Stogiannos, Alexandros (2019), *The Genesis of Geopolitics and Friedrich Ratzel*, Washington, DC: Springer.

Sullivan, Patrick (1986), *Geopolitics*, New York: Routledge.

The Times (1999), "Strategic Gloom and Doom: Rees-Mogg on Oil and Islam", *The Times*, London, August 30, available at: www.the-times.co.uk/news/pages/tim/99/08/30/timopnope01004.html?999 [accessed January 11, 2011].

US DOE (2009), *Energy Situation Analysis Report*, US Department of Energy, available at: www.energy.gov [accessed September 10, 2010].

USEIA (2010), *Energy Situation Analysis Report*, US Energy Information Administration, available at: www.eia.gov/emeu/security/esar/esar.html [accessed December 2010].

US Geological Survey (2000), *Minerals Year Book, Meals and Minerals 200*, US Geological Survey, July 25, Vol. 1.

Wall Street Journal (2007), "Energy Demand Will Outstrip Supply, Oil Industry Says", July 16, available at: http://india.wsj.com/search/term.html?KEYWORDS=Energy%20Demand%20will%20outstrip%20supply&mod=DNH_S [accessed January 11, 2011].

WCA (2010), *Coal: Secure Energy*, World Coal Association, available at: www.worldcoal.org/bin/pdf/original_pdf_file/coal_energy_security_report(03_06_2009).pdf [accessed January 11, 2011].

Yergin, Daniel (2006), "Ensuring Energy Security", *Foreign Affairs*, 85(2), March/April.

2

GEOPOLITICS OF ENERGY IN CENTRAL ASIA

Who rules the World-Island commands the World.
Who rules East Europe commands the Heartland;
Who rules the Heartland commands the World-Island;

(Halford Mackinder 1919: 194)

Before the Mackinder thesis of "he who controls the heartland controls the world" (Mackinder 1904), Central Asia remained an unknown landmass to the rest of the world. The geographical pivot of history thereafter started to attract the imperial attention of some mighty empires, given its geostrategic importance to control over Europe and subsequently the world over. Its internal dynamism coupled with hydrocarbon resources and geostrategic significance holds the heartland important to those around it and beyond. More and more attention is being focused on redefining the importance of Central Asian in the changing regional and international context. Since its reappearance, many suitors have been seeking affinity, proximity and legitimacy with the region on political, strategic, cultural and economic grounds. The internal dynamics of Central Asia and the prolonged zero-sum game that has been occurring with the persistent rhetoric of controlling the region at present has more far-reaching implications than would have been imagined decades ago. One may call it the "Great Game", round three. The first such contest, famously chronicled by Rudyard Kipling, involved the 19th-century struggle for dominance between the British and Russian empires over access to India and its lucrative trading routes. The second centred on the post-Soviet scramble for resources and influence in energy-rich Central Asia. Today, a third such round of geopolitical competition is emerging in Central Asia, spurred on by the vast energy potential of the post-Soviet space and the uncertain political disposition of Afghanistan (Smith and Berman 2011).

It is with this objective that this chapter examines the multifaceted nature of Central Asian energy geopolitics and the global competition that its energy resources have accentuated. In pursuit of this objective, this section provides a quantitative analysis of the Central Asian energy potential and offers an understanding of the unique position that each republic occupies in the geopolitics of oil and energy in Central Asia. It also examines the geopolitical pluralism of the region that not only attracts outside powers but also significantly enhances the economic status of the countries and bestows on them international recognition.

Geopolitics of Central Asia

Central Asia, strictly speaking, has remained a term without a clear-cut definition. It has always been used at random to refer to the whole or any part of an area that extends from the Kipchak steppes of Central Russia to the Great Wall of China (Kaushik 1970: 12–13). The name Central Asia, as an indicator of a particular region, is not an indigenous term. It was imposed on the region by 19th-century Europeans in a vain attempt to establish at least a territorial identity for this protean, tantalizing stretch of land that had for so long survived uneasily in the interstices of great empires.

Central Asia geographically situates at the crossroads of Russia, the People's Republic of China and the Islamic world. It is an entity of five former Soviet republics of Kazakhstan, Uzbekistan, Turkmenistan, Kyrgyzstan and Tajikistan. It covers a vast area of approximately 4 million square kilometres, almost one-sixth of the size of the former Soviet Union (Kaushik 1970: 13). It stretches from the seashores of the Caspian Sea and River Volga in the west to China in the east and Russia in the north to Afghanistan and Iran in the south. Because of this unique geographical location, Central Asia after its independence both literally and figuratively changed the map of Asia and subsequently redefined the world politically.

Location-wise, Central Asia is the geographic hub of Asia. It is situated at the heart of Eurasia. Located literally on the middle half of the Silk Route, the region is strategically vital to almost every major country on the planet. Central Asia shares a long, 6200 kilometres border with Russia in the north, 3500 km long border with China in the east, approximately a border of more than 3500 km to the west with the Caspian Sea and a huge length of inland border with Iran and Afghanistan in the south-west and the south respectively (Akiner 1994: 5–7).

However, until 1991 the region of Central Asia was the least known to the outside world. The unilateral declaration of three Slavic states – Russia, Ukraine and Belarus on December 8, 1991 at Malta, formally marked the disintegration of the Union of the Soviet Socialist Republics (Banuazizi and Weiner 1994). As a result of the disintegration of the USSR – the largest political landmass of the World was divided into 15 new, independent sovereign states. A massive chunk of its territory was torn away from the biggest geographical landmass of the world into diverse directions only to be territorially demarcated into several, unique, political units. Out of which, a vast area one-sixth the size of the former Soviet Union, turned towards the south and was distributed and categorized into eight new states with unfamiliar names in world politics. Five among them are collectively known as Central Asia.

Historical background

The history of Central Asia is long and exceedingly complex from the geopolitical point of view. It has experienced waves of migrations from various directions and later on settled down in the three Khanates of Khiva, Kokand and the Emirate of Bukhara. Though Russia had dominated the region for several centuries before Central Asian independence, Russia was not the only power to control and administer the region. The people of Central Asia were not Russians, and long before the Tsarist Russian Empire would hold their land, these people felt the power of mighty Chinese dynasties (Bulger 2005: 1).

It was only after the 1700s that Russia started impressing upon the Central Asian states. The Tsars began to start expanding their empire in the eastward direction. By the 19th century, Central Asia had turned into a grand chessboard for a power struggle between Russia and Britain. This situation was referred to as the Great Game by many people. However, it was British Lieutenant Arthur Conolly who used the famous phrase "Great Game" in his official letter (Hopkirk 1990: 124). As the British Empire expanded its borders northward through India, the Tsarist Russian Empire moved south-east across modern-day Kazakhstan. Russia captured the major city of Tashkent and then conquered the Turkmen tribes soon. Only Afghanistan remained as a stumbling block between the Russian frontier and British India (Alaolmolki 2001: 19).

Under the Tsarist Russian Empire, Central Asia had to endure lasting colonial exploitation. But, during the Soviet rein Central Asia was most profoundly shaped. However, the region failed to escape the grip of Russia after the Bolshevik revolution and was forcefully incorporated into the Soviet Union in 1917. Under Stalin, Central Asians were forced to abandon their native languages. They were compelled to learn Russian, and the practice of their native religion was aggressively attacked (Ibid: 22–23). Central Asia's borders, governing elites and energy infrastructures were all engineered by Soviet Russia for administrative convenience especially during Stalin's regime. The political and economic integration has been such that even after Central Asia returned to its former role as a crossroads for global powers, the Soviet legacy has remained intact. This started haunting the Central Asian states (CAS) in their relations with outside powers in terms of energy.

As a single entity

Although often lumped together by outsiders as a single entity, the five states of Central Asia are anything but homogeneous.

> Their boundaries are the product of a drive by the Russian states in the nineteenth century to the south-east compounded later by arbitrary territorial divisions in the Soviet era. Borders arbitrarily traversed ethnic enclaves, turning Central Asia into a patchwork quilt rend by complex disputes (ethnic, regional, tribal) over land, water and natural resources. The veneer of a common religion and to some extent Turkic language only conceals the deep divisions below territorial conflicts, interethnic tensions, clan rivalries and class antagonism.
>
> *(Rumer 1996: 40)*

These otherwise nomadic peoples are now divided into separate states and have come to see themselves as Kazakhs, Uzbeks, Tajik, Turkmen and Kyrgyz after being ruled under imperial Tsarist regimes and subsequently by Soviet Russia for generations. Later on, the region was divided and redrawn into various provinces for administrative convenience. Through

> the territorial economic planning of Moscow, Stalin divided the entire territory into eighteen economic regions. The four Central Asian republics – Uzbekistan, Tajikistan, Turkmenistan and Kyrgyzstan are being combined into a single Central Asian economic region. Kazakhstan was not treated as part of Central Asia then because of its climatic, topographic and economic uniqueness in contrast to the rest of the countries of the region.
>
> *(Ibid: 41–42)*

The centrality of Central Asia

Central Asia from independence was an isolated and unwanted landmass to its neighbours. It was struggling with the economic crisis, political instability, ethnic strife and civic unrest. Its security problem was even greater than the political and economic ones. It was in the initial years that the region was held unwanted and considered a burden on its immediate neighbours. For Russia, the region is no longer its hinterland in the aftermath of the disintegration of the USSR. The new Russian federation used a novel term called "the Near Abroad" to indicate Central Asia in its foreign policy objectives. Once regarded as the backyard of Russia, Central Asia hardly got any attention from Moscow in its policy initiatives for quite some time. Until 1994, not only Russia, but all the major countries of the world seemed not to be interested in the region historically expressed as the heartland. Central Asia was then central to none. However, the proximate players such as Russia, China, Iran, Turkey, Saudi Arabia, India and Pakistan attempted hard to influence the region; their line of thought was to take advantage of its geopolitical significances. Nevertheless, they treated this region as everything central to their national interests.

Despite its name and geopolitical location, Central Asia was not central to any of the regional and extra-regional countries. For Turkey, the European Union remains the primary object and vector of its foreign policy, while for Iran the Persian Gulf is still paramount in its orientation and security concern. It is beset with its domestic problems and the US hegemonic attitude pointing towards it. China's security lies to the east, with the Taiwan and Hongkong issues looming large over its foreign policy and relations to the Korean Peninsula and Japan following closely. In addition to this, China no more considers itself as a mere regional power. Particularly after the disintegration of the USSR, the role and importance of China have increased manifold. Hence it is obvious to note that China's focus should be all-pervasive rather than particularistic. India and Pakistan focus primarily on their bilateral relationships. Kashmir stood as a bone of contention in the domestic developments and bilateral and international relations of the two countries right after their independence in 1947. Russia, despite its historical influence and interests in Central Asia, was preoccupied with the Caucasus and its relations with the West. The Chechnya problem is no less perplexing to Russia in the realm of international relations. Finally, the United States, though no way near the region, is considered to be a significant proximate player in the area. It has no central role to play in the region except to gain some significant hold on the oil, gas and geostrategy.

It would, therefore, be quite interesting to note that an impoverished region suddenly became the focal point of regional politics and global economics. It is the oil and energy reserves and promising potentials of Central Asia and the Caspian Sea region that brought it into the global limelight.

There is little doubt that Central Asian oil and natural gas infrastructure and reserves have come to be regarded as strategic assets, and are the object of rising political and economic rivalry. Today, China, Russia, India, and the United States (among others) are competing for influence and market shares of Central Asian energy. Many observers of Central Asia, as well as policymakers, are beginning to believe that it is only a matter of time before the region experiences an intense struggle over energy resources. Central Asian governments, for their part, have sought to mitigate the influence of the major consumer states in the region, while profiting from their need, to pursue their agendas. In this context, the present chapter tries to know the actual energy share of the region in the global context. It also seeks to look into the objectives behind the rapidly increasing global attraction towards the region. Finally, efforts are made to examine the profits the region is gaining and losses it has to bear.

Energy and Central Asia

Central Asia today represents one of the world's last great frontiers of geological survey and analysis. It offers opportunities for the discovery, production, transportation and refining of enormous quantities of oil, gas and other energy resources. The region is rich in hydrocarbons with gas being the predominant energy fuel. While Kazakhstan is especially known for its large reserves of oil and coal and some significant amount of uranium deposits, Turkmenistan and Uzbekistan are noted for their gas reserves. Kyrgyzstan and Tajikistan produce a significant amount of hydroelectricity power. With proven oil reserves estimated to range from 9 to 40 billion barrels and natural gas reserves possibly exceeding 131 trillion cubic feet (tcf) (Patnaik 2016), Central Asia is poised to become a major world supplier of energy, especially in the oil and gas sectors. Since most of its reserves are undeveloped and promising, it is no wonder Central Asian energy excites international interests.

a) Oil

Oil, the most valuable traded energy commodity in the world, is only second in rank after gas among the energy resources of Central Asia. The oil reserves of the region in 2017 were pegged at almost 3 per cent (38.284 billion barrels) of the world oil reserves (ENI 2018). As of 2018 as shown in Tables 2.2 and 2.3, Kazakhstan is the main producer of oil in the region with proven reserves of 31.2 thousand million barrels with the production capacity of 1835 thousand million barrels per day (BP 2018). Turkmenistan has proven oil reserves of roughly 0.6 thousand million barrels based on estimates by British Petroleum (BP 2018). It has a production capacity of 258 thousand million barrels per day (BP 2018).

The *Oil and Gas Journal* estimates that Uzbekistan has 594 million barrels of proven oil reserves with 171 discovered oil and natural gas fields in the country (*Oil and Gas Journal* 2008). However, in 2015 Uzbekistan had 0.6 thousand million barrels of proven oil with the production capacity of 54 thousand barrels per day (BP 2016). Unlike some of their Central Asian neighbours, Kyrgyzstan and Tajikistan produce only undersized quantities of oil.

b) Gas

Central Asia is predominantly a gas-producing region. In 1997, the region had proven gas reserves amounting to 6.6 trillion cubic meters – 2.9 trillion cubic meters in Turkmenistan, 1.9 tcm in Uzbekistan and 1.8 tcm in Kazakhstan (BP 1997). This then represented about one-tenth of the known gas reserves of the CIS. In 2007 as per the International Crisis Group Report, Central Asia was home to an estimated 4 per cent (270–360 trillion cubic feet) of world gas reserves (ICG 2007).

Turkmenistan and Uzbekistan are the two leading gas producers, although Kazakhstan has significant deposits. As shown in Tables 2.4, 2.5, 2.6 and 2.7, at the end of 2015 Turkmenistan had 17.5 tcm of proven reserves with a production capacity of 72.4 billion cubic meters; Uzbekistan is home to 1.1 tcm gas reserves with a production potential of 57.7 bcm, and Kazakhstan has 0.9 tcm of gas

TABLE 2.1 Primary energy resources in Central Asia

Primary energy resources in Central Asia

Fossil fuel reserves	Unit	Kazakhstan	Kyrgyzstan	Tajikistan	Turkmenistan	Uzbekistan	Total
Crude oil	MTOE	1100	5.5	1.7	75	82	1264.20
Natural gas	MTOE	1500	5	5	2252	1476	5238
Coal	MTOE	24,300	580	500	Insignificant	2851	28,231
Total	MTOE	26,900	591	507	2327	4409	34,734
% of Total		77.4	1.7	1.5	6.7	12.7	100
Hydro potential	GWh/Year	27,000	163,000	317,000	2000	15,000	524,000
	MTOE/Year	2.3	14	27.3	0.2	1.3	45.1
% of the Total		5.2	31.1	60.5	0.4	2.9	1000

Source: Asian Development Bank (2004), Central Asia: Regional Electricity Export Potential Study, December, www.adb.org/Documents/Reports/CAREC/Energy/CA-REEPS.pdf.

TABLE 2.2 Total oil proved reserves (thousand million barrels)

Country name	*1995*	*2005*	*2007*	*2014*	*2015*	*2017/18*
Kazakhstan	5.3	9.0	30.0	30.0	30.0	31.2
Turkmenistan	0.5	0.5	0.6	0.6	0.6	0.6
Uzbekistan	0.3	0.6	0.6	0.6	0.6	0.6
Kyrgyzstan	40.0[a]		NSR	NSR	NSR	NSR
Tajikistan	12.0[a]		NSR	NSR	NSR	NSR

Source: BP Statistical Review of World Energy, 2018.
NSR: Not Separately Reported
★BP Statistical Review of World Energy, 2007, 2009 and *Oil and Gas Journal* 2007 and 2009. It represents the data of 1995.

TABLE 2.3 Oil production in Central Asia (thousand million barrels per day)

Country name	*2007*	*2008*	*2009*	*2010*	*2011*	*2012*	*2013*	*2014*	*2015*	*2016*	*2017*
Kazakhstan	1415	1485	1609	1676	1684	1664	1737	1710	1695	655	1835
Turkmenistan	204	222	218	212	215	225	232	241	261	253	258
Uzbekistan	104	102	95	78	77	68	63	61	59	58	54
Tajikistan★	NSR	NSR	NSR	NSR	NSR	NSR	NSR	NSR	NSR	NSR	NSR
Kyrgyzstan★	NSR	NSR	NSR	NSR	NSR	NSR	NSR	NSR	NSR	NSR	NSR
Other CIS	135	131	126	117	111	111	105	97	91	89	90

Source: BP Statistical Review of World Energy, 2018.
NSR: Not Separately Reported
★BP Statistical Review of World Energy, 2007, 2009 and *Oil and Gas Journal* 2007 and 2009.

reserves with a production capacity of 27.1 bcm (BP 2018). However, gas from the region is generally high in sulphur, containing corrosive properties as is the case of oil from Kazakhstan and other parts of Central Asia. The pipelines have to be adjusted accordingly and insulated.

Tables 2.4–2.7 are testimony to the fact that natural gas is abundant in Central Asia and holds the possibility of the discovery of even more gas fields in the near future given technological assistance from outside and logistic help through manpower, money and materials. What seems to be the stumbling block again is the transportation problem. Shortages and difficulties in the trade of natural gas reflect deficiencies in transportation, pricing and the payment system. Geologically, valuable resources are one thing, economic resources are another. It does not matter if the resources exist geologically, the key is to develop and move them to the market place. The transportation network for Central Asian gas was established during the Soviet era and reflected the priorities of the Soviet Union. The value of gas and oil here depends on getting those resources to the markets in Europe, Asia and the Middle East areas. Therefore, for Central Asia, obtaining access to markets that do not require using the Russian Federation's pipelines is an important objective.

TABLE 2.4 Total proved reserves of natural gas in Central Asia, 2018 (trillion cubic metres)

Country name	*1997*	*2007*	*2015*
Kazakhstan	1.8	1.5	0.9
Turkmenistan	2.9	0.8	17.5
Uzbekistan	1.9	1.3	1.1
Tajikistan*	0.2	0.2	NSR
Kyrgyzstan*	0.2	0.2	NSR
Other CIS	–	–	1.2

Source: BP Statistical Review of World Energy, 2018.
NSR: Not Separately Reported
*BP Statistical Review of World Energy, 2007, 2009 and *Oil and Gas Journal* 2007 and 2009.

TABLE 2.5 Total natural gas production in Central Asia 2018 (billion cubic metres)

Country name	*2007*	*2008*	*2009*	*2010*	*2011*	*2012*	*2013*	*2014*	*2015*	*2016*	*2017*
Kazakhstan	15.8	18.3	19.0	20.4	20.1	19.8	21.4	21.7	22.0	22.9	27.1
Turkmenistan	68.4	69.1	38.0	44.3	62.3	65.1	65.2	70.2	72.4	66.9	62.0
Uzbekistan	60.9	60.4	58.1	56.9	53.9	53.9	53.9	54.2	54.6	53.1	57.7
Tajikistan*	0.2	0.2	0.2	NSR	NSR	NSR	NSR	NSR	NSR	NSR	NSR
Kyrgyzstan*	0.2	0.2	0.2	NSR	NSR	NSR	NSR	NSR	NSR	NSR	NSR
Other CIS	0.2	0.2	0.2	0.2	0.2	0.2	0.2	0.2	0.2	0.2	0.2

Source: BP Statistical Review of World Energy, 2018.
NSR: Not Separately Reported
*BP Statistical Review of World Energy, 2007, 2009 and *Oil and Gas Journal* 2007 and 2009.

TABLE 2.6 Natural gas production (million tonnes oil equivalent)

Country name	*2007*	*2008*	*2009*	*2010*	*2011*	*2012*	*2013*	*2014*	*2015*	*2016*	*2017*
Kazakhstan	13.6	15.7	16.3	17.6	17.3	17.1	18.4	18.6	18.9	19.7	23.3
Turkmenistan	59.8	59.4	32.7	38.1	53.5	56.0	56.1	60.3	62.6	57.6	53.3
Uzbekistan	52.3	51.9	50.0	48.9	46.4	46.3	46.3	46.6	47.0	45.7	45.9
Tajikistan*	0.2	0.2	0.2	NSR	NSR	NSR	NSR	NSR	NSR	NSR	NSR
Kyrgyzstan*	0.2	0.2	0.2	NSR	NSR	NSR	NSR	NSR	NSR	NSR	NSR
Other CIS	0.2	0.2	0.2	0.2	0.2	0.2	0.2	0.2	0.2	0.2	0.2

Source: BP Statistical Review of World Energy, 2018.
NSR: Not Separately Reported
*BP Statistical Review of World Energy, 2007, 2009 and *Oil and Gas Journal* 2007 and 2009.

Compounding these problems are the distances involved. The gas fields in Kazakhstan, Turkmenistan and Uzbekistan are a considerable distance from major consumers. With exports having to pass through bordering countries, they are subjects to political risks.

TABLE 2.7 Reserves, production, exports and consumption of natural gas in the Central Asian region

Country	*Reserves bcm 2008*	*Production bcm 2007*	*Exports bcm 2005*	*Production/ consumption 2006*	*Reserves in 2015/ TCM*	*Production in 2015/ TCM*
Kazakhstan	1900.0	25.7	15.4	1.18	0.9[a]	12.4[a]
Kyrgyzstan	10.0	0.0		0.03	n/a	n/a
Tajikistan	10.0	0.0		0.05	n/a	n/a
Turkmenistan	2860.0	64.8	46.6	3.89	17.5[a]	72.4[a]
Uzbekistan	1870.0	56.2	12.0	1.26	1.1[a]	57.7[a]
5 Stans	6650.0	146.7	74.0		–	
Central Asia*	8226.0	152.9	74.1		–	
World total	181,945.5	2,929.1	953.7			
Percentage of 5 stans	3.60%	5.00%	8.70%		–	
Percentage world's first 5	62.50%	52.19%	59.52%		–	
Percentage world's first 10	76.07%	65.53%	76.41%		–	

Source: ENI (2008), World Oil and Gas Review.
Central Asia* includes Armenia, Azerbaijan and Georgia
[a] BP Statistical Review of World Energy, 2018.

The other major problem that affects the intra-regional trade of gas is payments. Insolvency and large outstanding inter-republic debts have led to the suspension of trade on numerous occasions. Barter trade arrangements sometimes substitute for cash payments, especially between Kazakhstan and Uzbekistan, but these transactions have not been stable or fully satisfying to the parties involved.

Finally, the pricing of natural gas in the subregion has the effect of suppressing gas supplies and gas trade in the evolving market economies of Central Asia. All of the countries subsidize gas prices; this artificially inflates demand and makes it difficult for the governments to pay for imported gas (Figure 2.1).

c) Coal

Despite the importance of oil and gas to the region's export economy, coal remains the most common source of energy. It is the primary source of electricity in Kazakhstan and a major source of heat in Kazakhstan and Kyrgyzstan.

Kazakhstan is the biggest coal producer in Central Asia with an estimated 33,600 million tonness of coal in Karaganda and other areas; Uzbekistan also has 1900 MT of coal to its credit as well (BP 2018). Kyrgyzstan is reported to have substantial coal reserves. But these are located in an inaccessible part of the country with no railroad to transport the coal to market. Notwithstanding

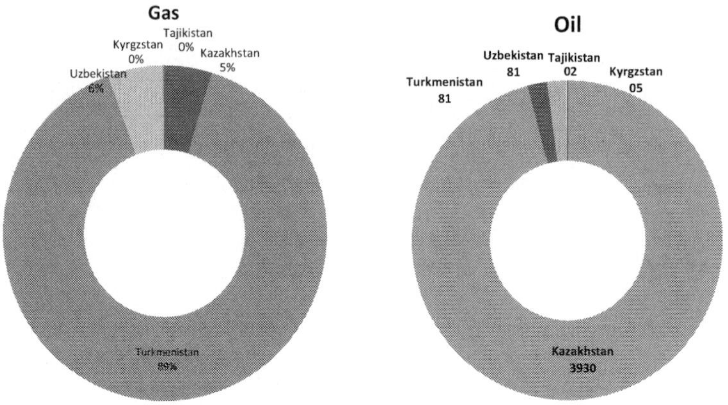

FIGURE 2.1 Energy resources of Central Asian states in mtoe.

Source: UNESCAP, 2018

limited coal reserves in Uzbekistan and Kyrgyzstan and the low quality of coal in Kazakhstan, coal is an important energy source in Central Asia. Kazakh coal is regularly exchanged for Kyrgyz electricity and the coal industry is a major employer in Kazakhstan (Dorian 2006).

d) Electricity

Central Asia has tremendous potential as an electricity generation hub. The region is rich in both thermal and Hydel resources. Among the Central Asian republics, Tajikistan and Kyrgyzstan have more hydropower potential. While Tajikistan has the largest hydroelectricity potential with an installed capacity of 5.19 GW (with annual total hydropower potential of 527 billion kWh) the Kyrgyz republic has the 3.09 GW and Kazakhstan and Uzbekistan have 2.26 GW and 1.73 GW respectively (EIU 2017). Uzbekistan relies primarily on thermal power stations fuelled by natural gas, although cheaper energy from hydropower electric plants exists. The country also draws significantly on hydropower produced from power stations in Kyrgyzstan and Tajikistan. Kazakhstan depends primarily on coal to generate electricity

Tajikistan occupies the second-largest producer of hydroelectricity in the Commonwealth of Independent States (CIS) and more than half of hydropower resources in Central Asia. Tajikistan has about 4 per cent of world hydroelectricity potential and occupies eight ranks in the world. Kyrgyzstan is also the third-largest in CIS countries after Russia and Tajikistan in Hydel power. It produces 80 per cent of electricity by hydropower plant (Ministry of Energy and Industry 2015). Kyrgyzstan and Tajikistan have intensified their electricity transmission

TABLE 2.8 Energy resources of Central Asia (mtoe)

Countries	*Oil*	*Gas*	*Coal*	*Uranium*	*Hydel/GW*
Kazakhstan	3930	842	23,500	22,800	2.26
Turkmenistan	81	15,700	na	na	na
Uzbekistan	81	977	1330	2404	1.73
Kyrgyzstan	5	5	na	na	3.09
Tajikistan	2	5	na	na	5.19

Source: UNESCAP, 2017; World Nuclear Association 2020; EIU 2017.

to South Asia (Afghanistan and Pakistan) through a visionary concept of Central Asia–South Asia Regional Electricity Market (CASAREM).

e) Uranium

Central Asia has a fairly considerable amount of uranium deposits. Among the Central Asian states, Kazakhstan and Uzbekistan have a fair amount of uranium deposits. They are the two important states in the region to have strategic uranium reserves of a larger quantity. According to the estimates of World Nuclear Association, Kazakhstan possessing about 12 per cent of world uranium resources produces around 41 per cent of world uranium making the country the leading uranium producer of the world surpassing Canada and Australia. In 2019, Kazakhstan produced about 22,800 tonnes of uranium (WNA 2020). Besides, Uzbekistan has the second-largest uranium reserves in Central Asia after Kazakhstan with a production capacity of 2404 tonnes of uranium per year in 2018. As of February 2020, Uzbekistan ranks as the seventh-largest uranium supplier of the world (WNA 2020a). Tajikistan too holds a fairly sizeable amount of uranium ore and the potential for its enrichment. To its credit, Kyrgyzstan has also some huge amounts of uranium, which is obtained from the erstwhile Soviet Union. Thus, the Central Asian region can be tapped by any country as a potential source of direly needed uranium to sustain their civil nuclear programs (Table 2.8).

f) Non-traditional energy resources

Some of the countries in Central Asia have made substantial commitments to supporting the development of non-traditional or renewable energy. In Kyrgyzstan, the Kyun government agency is devoted entirely to examining alternative energy supplies, notably solar, wind, geothermal and coal bed methane gas (Dorian 2006: 550). Likewise, in Kazakhstan, government officials have mapped alternative energy resources across the country to determine the feasibility of developing these resources. Kazakhstan's southern and northern tiers receive an abundance of sunshine annually and possess significant potential for solar energy. Potential wind and biogas resources have been identified in the west. Both southern and north-eastern regions of Kazakhstan have the potential for tapping geothermal energy. This alternative source of energy would not only help the countries of Central Asia but also greatly benefit the countries that are dependent upon the region for their energy consumption.

Within this framework, it can be said that in the regional political vacuum left by the sudden demise of the Soviet Union, the United States, the European Union, Russia and the Peoples Republic of China have been approaching new levels of engagement in Central Asia. There is one common interest that all of these powers share and that is the energy resources available in the region. There are certain motivating factors that the global powers view seriously and explain their interests in Central Asian energy resources despite the presence of already mentioned difficulties. These are:

1. The oil of the region is considered to be of good quality.
2. Central Asia represents one of the world's last great frontiers for geological survey and analysis offering opportunities for the discovery, production, transportation and refining of enormous quantities of oil and gas and other energy resources.
3. Since most of its reserves are unexplored and undeveloped, its contribution to world energy market seems quite promising.
4. While the Central Asian states have physical possession of their oil and gas reserves, they do not possess the capital and technology that would allow them to go into production alone, a fact which offers an opportunity to the foreign company to invest and brings along with it a share in production and revenues.
5. More importantly, the biggest part of the Central Asian oil refined is intended for export, since the needs for producing countries are relatively low and are expected to remain low.
6. Finally, Central Asia is a relatively stable region in contrast to other energy-rich destinations.

Compounding these, two other major factors motivate the global powers to expand their interests in Central Asian energy sectors: First, countries of the world strive to secure energy to meet the demands of their domestic consumption. Domestic concerns exert a pounding influence on the foreign policymaking of a country, which James Rosenau refers to as "Linkage Politics" (Rosenau 1969: 12). Second, energy today is something beyond just a natural resource. It is, in fact, a strategic commodity that allows the state to enhance their own economic and political power at the cost of its competitors.

The first factor speaks volumes about the natural resources of Central Asian states especially its energy potentials. On the one hand, it would help in meeting domestic demands of energy consumers and on the other hand, it would bring adequate economic benefits and international significance to the exporting countries of the region. The second factor talks of a diplomatic rivalry and power play resulting out of the intense competition for greater access and control over energy. For a comprehensive understanding of the regional dynamics and external power play, this section clearly articulates the energy geopolitics in Central Asian states on the one hand and the role of major external players in Central Asian geopolitics on the other.

Central Asian energy resources in each country

After the collapse of the Soviet Union, the Central Asian countries were plunged into a deep economic depression. Its magnitude and duration were such that their plight far exceeded that of the United States Depression of the 1930s (Mahnovski, Akramov et al. 2007: 4–5). Like most of the former Soviet republics, Central Asia initially turned to the West for direction and aid. As it turned Westward, Central Asia found international interests in its oil and gas reserves. This allowed them to harness the fullest potential of their natural resources. It has brought in some dramatic improvements in the economic conditions of Kazakhstan, Turkmenistan and Uzbekistan, leaving behind Kyrgyzstan and Tajikistan. Although global interest in the region's energy holds economic promise, at the same time it creates certain geopolitical complications. Therefore, it is on the onus of the young independent states of Central Asia to delicately chart out a course between the West, Russia and China while maintaining their importance in international politics.

Kazakhstan

Geographically, Kazakhstan is the largest among the Central Asian countries and the largest landlocked country in the world as well. It has made the most impressive economic advances among all the Central Asian Countries since independence. Its economy has accounted for roughly 50 per cent of the region's total Gross Domestic Product (GDP) and 85 per cent of its cumulative Foreign Direct Investment (FDI) since independence (Mahnovski, Akramov et' al. 2007: XIV). This may be attributed to Kazakhstan's immense energy resources and its geographical position atop Central Asia. This allows Kazakhstan a great range of potential export routes while making it a transit state for other Central Asian energy sectors. Kazakhstan's economy had grown to 80 billion dollars by 2007 (Dave 2008: 46) and jumped to 179.34 billion dollars in 2018 (The World Bank 2020). Its per capita GDP as of 2016 was estimated to be around $10,589 (UNESCAP 2017). And the reason for its phenomenal growth in the region as the most economically advanced country is attributed to its huge base of natural resources that include petroleum, natural gas, coal, iron ore, manganese, uranium and others (Map 2.1).

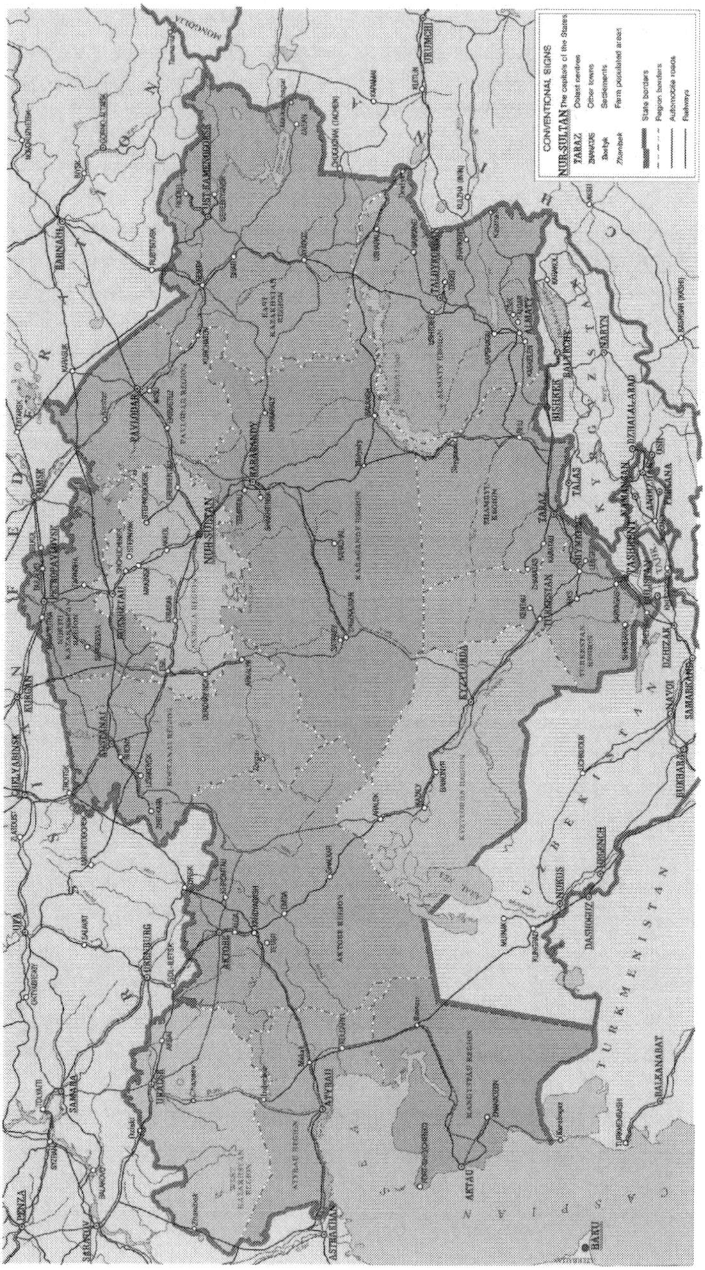

MAP 2.1 Map of Kazakhstan.

Source: Wikimedia.org

Energy profile of Kazakhstan

I. Oil

Kazakhstan is the main oil producer in the Central Asia region. An oil producer since 1991 the country has the reputation of having the second-largest reserves and second-largest oil production among the former Soviet states except for Russia (EIA 2018). It is estimated to have between 30 and 40 billion barrels of crude oil reserves (O&G 2017). Its oil potential is about half of Russia and 11 per cent of Saudi Arabia. It ranks 12th in the world, between Nigeria and the United States in terms of oil (EIA 2018). In 2016 the country's estimated total petroleum and other liquids production was about 1.698 million barrels per day (EIA 2018). However, in January to May 2018, "Kazakhstan has increased production of oil and gas condensate by 6.4 per cent to 37.7 million tons" (The Embassy of the Kingdom of the Netherlands 2018).

> The unprecedented increase in oil production in the first quarter of 2018 is attributed to the increasing production level in the three major oil fields amounted to 22.7 million tons including 5 million tons at Kashagan field, 12.5 million tons at Tengiz field and 5.2 million tons at Karachaganak field.
>
> *(Ibid)*

Additionally, the Tengizchevroil consortium decided to proceed with expansion plans that will increase liquid production in Tengiz by about 260,000 billion barrels per day by the beginning of 2022 (EIA 2018).

Kazakhstan's hydrocarbon reserves are contained in 153 occurrences, including 80 petroleum, 24 gas-petroleum, 21 petroleum-gas condensate, 5 gas condensate and 19 gas fields (EIA 2018). The main hydrocarbon reserve base is concentrated in western Kazakhstan's Guryev, Mangistu, Uralsk and Aktubinsk regions. The hydrocarbon resources of these regions are almost equivalent to those of western Siberia within Russia in terms of explored and extrapolated petroleum and gas reserves (Ibid). Most of Kazakhstan's oil growth in petroleum, however, comes from four large oil fields. These are (Table 2.9).

i. The Tengiz Field

This field was discovered in Atyrau province in 1979. This field is regarded as the largest source of oil and substantial source of gas production started its operation first in 1993 under the joint venture of Tenizneftgas and Chevron Tengizchevroil (TCO). Ranked as the world's sixth-largest oil reserve (International Crisis Group 2007: 7), this oil field is located in the northwestern part of Kazakhstan. Tengiz is a unique petroleum and gas deposit, unrivalled in the size of its reserves by any other known deposits in the world. Even though the deposit has been explored to a depth of only 5500 metres, its

TABLE 2.9 Kazakhstan's major oil and gas fields

Field name	*Companies*	*Start year*	*Liquids production*	*Natural gas production*
Tengiz & Korolev	Chevron, ExxonMobil, KazMunaiGaz and Lukoil	1991	570,000 bl/d petroleum and other liquids production in 2016 Expansion projects to add 260,000 bl/d of crude production beginning in 2022	274 bcf dry marketed gas production in 2016
Karachaganak	BG, Eni, Chevron, Lukoil, KazMunaiGaz	1984	206,000 bl/d total liquids production in 2016 An expansion project is under consideration, but potential production volumes are uncertain	About 300 bcf we marketed gas production in 2016
Kashagan	KazMunaiGaz, Eni, ExxonMobil, Shell, Total, CNPC, Inpex	2016	370,000 bl/d liquids processing capacity with current developments	Over 100 bcf gas production capacity

Source: EIA (2019), based on TengizCheroil, Chevron, Karachaganak Petroleum Operating (KPO) and Eni.

potential recoverable reserves are estimated at 6–9 billion barrels of petroleum by consortium member Chevron Texaco (Zhanseitov and Asanov 1993: 388). "The size of the Tengiz reservoir is 21 km long and 19 km wide. All transportation of Tengiz oil field is carried out through Atyrau situated in the North of Tengiz about 350 km away from Tengiz" (Javaid and Rashid 2015). For production purpose from Tengiz oil field

> there is a 40 years joint venture agreement of Chevron having 50% of shares, Kazakhstan Petroleum with 20%, Exxon Mobil 25% and LUKOIL with 5% production shares working under the umbrella of Tengizchevroil Consortium. A 1505 km long CPC has constructed with US 2.7 billion investment and with a maximum capacity of 1.5 million barrels per day oil exports from Tengiz oil field to the Novorossiysk Russian port of Black sea in 2001.
>
> *(Ibid)*

In 2007 Chevron was the leading partner (50 per cent) in the Tengiz Chevron Oil (TCO) consortium that has developed the field since 1993 and operates at 50/50 production sharing with the government (International Crisis Group 2007: 7).

In 2016, Tengiz contributed about 35 per cent of the country's oil production (EIA 2018). Besides, it has decided to partner with the Future Growth Project in a bid to expand its productions. It is expected that the expansion project would complete by 2022 accounting to about 260,000 billion barrels of additional oil from Tengiz (EIA 2018).

ii. The Kashagan Field

Discovered in the northern Caspian Sea basin in 2000, the Kashagan is the largest oil field outside the Middle East and is the fifth largest oil field in the world in terms of reserves (EIA 2018). Kashagan is spread over an 80×25 km field, the oil field is located off the northern shore of the Caspian Sea near Atyrau. Its recoverable reserves are estimated to be around 7 to 13 billion barrels of crude oil. As of January 2017, the field was producing more than 100,000 billion barrels per day (EIA 2018).

The North Caspian operating company consortium (NCOC) has developed and is operating this oil field.

> This consortium contains ExxonMobil, Shell, Total, Eni and KMG having 16.8% of shares each. Kashagan area includes Kairan, Kalamkas, Kashagan, Kashagan Southwest and Aktoty fields. Reservoirs of Kashagan oil field are located 13,000 feet below the Seabed with the pressure level of 770 psi.
>
> *(Javaid and Rashid 2015)*

Conventional production technologies cannot be used due to the cold climate and shallow water.

With a record investment of $116 billion, this is the world's most expensive and largest oil field discovery constructed during the last 30 years. The Kashagan oil field started its commercial production of oil in 2013. This oil field project has been the most challenging project due to territorial disputes, high levels of hydrogen sulphide and shallow water. The main oil companies indulging in the exploration work of the field are Royal Dutch Shell, Total, Eni, BP Statoil, Mobil and BG group, working under Kazakhstancaspishelf. In 2001 Eni became the operator of the Kashagan oil field project which was renamed as Agip KCO (Agip Kazakhstan North Caspian Operating Company NV). In 2007 the parliament of Kazakhstan approved a law making the Government empowered to cancel the contract of foreign oil companies if they should violate the national interests of the country (Javaid and Rashid 2015).

KazMunayGas state-owned company authorities and Agip KCO with a joint venture under NCPSA (North Caspian Purchase and Sales Agreement) transferred into North Caspian Operating Company BV (NCOC). Oil production was started in 2013 and oil companies ConocoPhillips and ExxonMobil with the help of Kazakhstan Government estimated that the oil production in 2014 from Kashagan oil field would be 8 million tonnes (Javaid and Rashid 2015).

iii. The Karachaganak Field

The Karachaganak field was discovered in 1979. It is an oil and natural gas and condensate field located in Western Kazakhstan province (International Crisis Group 2007: 7). According to the estimate of Karachaganak Petroleum Operating (KPO), the reserve of the oil field is about 1.2 billion tonnes and condensate of approximately 8.76 billion barrels (Ibid). It, however, has significant growth potential as certain deep geological structures are not even included in the current reserve estimates.

This oil field in 2009 went gone on to produce a record production of 139.5 million barrels of oil. After this record, the Kaz Munai Gas joined the Karachaganak field venture in an official capacity in 2012 for the development of phase three of Karachaganak. The Karachaganak field venture utilizes the knowledge and expertise of the BG group 29.25 per cent shares, Kaz Munai Gas 10 per cent, LUKOIL 13.5 per cent, Eni. 29.25 per cent and Chevron 18 per cent. At the end of 2012, the production of the Karachaganak field was 139.5 million barrels of oil (Javaid and Rashid 2015).

iv. The Kurmangazy Field

This field, in the earliest stage of development of the four, is located in the Caspian Sea, on the maritime border with Russia (Ibid). A 1998 agreement and a 2002 protocol granted Kazakhstan sovereignty over it, while Russia obtained two nearby fields (Ibid). The Kurgmengazy partners, Kazmunai Gas (KMG)

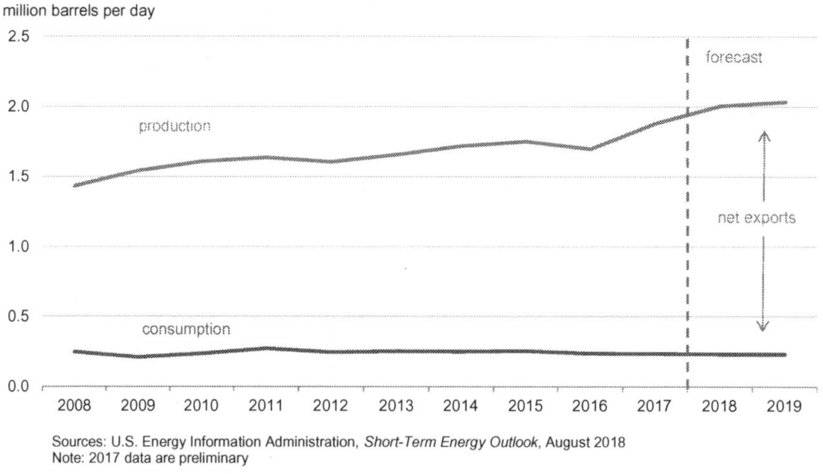

FIGURE 2.2 Kazakhstan's petroleum and other liquid production and consumption (million barrels/day).

Source: US Energy Information Administration

and Rosneft, are supposed to develop under 50:50 PSAs (Ibid). The reserves of the field are estimated to be around one billion tonnes. The first well started operating in 2006 (Ibid). The successful development of this field and realization of the others' full potential is essential if Kazakhstan is to become one among the eight non-OPEC countries with daily production of over 2 million barrels (Ibid).

Kazakhstan operates three oil refineries: Pavlodar, Shymkent (formerly Chymkent), and Atyrau located in the northern, southern and western regions of Kazakhstan respectively (Dorian 2006: 546). As of 2004, the refineries had a combined total crude oil refining capacity of 427,000 barrels per day (bl/d) (20 million metric tonnes per year) and capacity utilization of 95 per cent (EIA 2004). In 2006, Kazakhstan used about 10 million metric tonnes of domestic crude oil annually in three refineries. But the import was relatively small amounts of product to make up for slightly inadequate domestic refinery output, notably at harvest time (International Crisis Group 2007: 8). Given the crude oil production of 54 million metric tonnes in 2016, net crude oil export was set to be about 41 million metric tonnes (about 820, 000 billion barrels per day (bbl/d) (Ibid). Outside OPEC, only Russia, Norway and Mexico export more (EIA 2016).

The country has the greatest conventional oil production growth potential of any non-OPEC country. Of course, domestic oil consumption will grow in the future. But, given the small population and the large addition expected in production, most of the increase will translate to exports as long as the means are there to get the hydrocarbons to market. Kazakhstan is an exporter of light and sweet crude oil. In 2016 it exported about 1.3 trillion barrels per day as per the estimate of EIA (2018). Most of Kazakhstan's crude export travels across the Caspian Sea and to the European Countries. However, since 2009 Kazakh oil started going eastward to China. Although a significant portion of oil exports transits through Italy and the Netherlands, an additional 5 per cent of Kazakh crude oil also goes to China (EIA 2018).

Export routes

Since Kazakhstan is a landlocked country, supply of oil through the pipeline has always been a formidable challenge for the Eurasian country. The state-run KazakhTransOil, a subsidiary of KazMunaiGas, is in charge of operating the pipelines that transport Kazakh crude oil. As noted above, due to its geographical compulsions it has either to depend on the Soviet-era infrastructure or the major Caspian oil and natural gas export routes for transportation of its oil and gas (EIA 2018). The major crude oil export pipelines include the Caspian pipeline Consortium to the Black Sea port of Novorossiysk, the Kazakh–China pipeline and the Uzen–Atyrau Samara pipeline to Russia as shown in Figure 2.3 (Ibid).

Kazakhstan also exports oil via the Caspian Sea and by train. At Aktau and Atyrau oil is loaded into tankers and then shipped across the Caspian Sea, where it is loaded onto the Baku–Tbilisi–Ceyhan (BTC) pipeline or the Northern Route pipeline (Baku–Novorossysk) for onward transportation (EIA 2018). Apart from the rail networks through which Kazakhstan transports its oil to other neighbouring countries, one such potential route like the BTC pipeline exports to Iran via the Caspian Sea port of Neku (Ibid). Although, no such swap had been operationalized as of 2016, since 2013 Kazakhstan and Iran have been discussing the resumption of the swap arrangement. If this starts operating, Kazakh oil will have access to the South Asian and African Market. Importantly, the recent modalities reached by Iran and India on Chabahar port will allow India to have access to Central Asian oil which it can then load onto the tankers to India via the Arabian Sea.

Besides, Kazakhstan has a built-in facility for refining its crude oil before it is loaded for transportation. According to *Oil and Gas Journal* (2017) as of January, the country had three major oil refineries with a crude oil capacity of 340,000 barrels per day. Pavlodar, Atyrau and Shymkent are the three major oil refineries in the country (EIA 2018). The Pavlodar refinery is in north-central Kazakhstan and is supplied mainly by a crude oil pipeline from western Siberia because Russian supplies are well placed geographically to serve that refinery. The Atyrau refinery uses only domestic crude oil from north-west Kazakhstan,

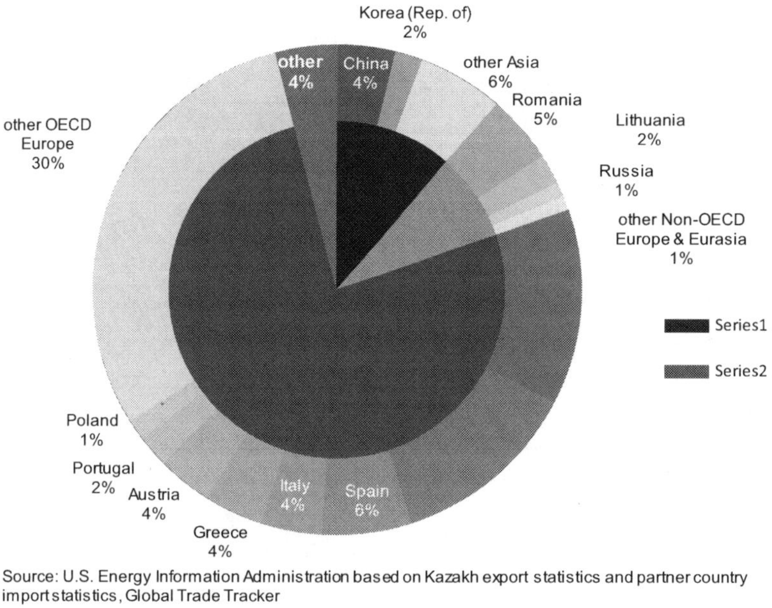

FIGURE 2.3 Kazakhstan's crude oil exports by destination, 2017.

Source: US Energy Information Administration

and the Shymkent refinery currently uses crude from the oil fields at Kumkol and the nearby area in central Kazakhstan. There is also a smaller refinery at Aktau that processes heavy crude oil produced at a nearby field to make bitumen for road construction (Ibid).

II. Natural gas

Kazakhstan with proven natural gas reserves of around 85 tcm, ranks eleventh in the world (*Oil and Gas Journal* 2017). In 2007, however, its reserves were the same as those of Turkmenistan and Indonesia (International Crisis Group 2007: 12). Kazakhstan has 83 deposits in total containing natural gas. Only 17 of those are exclusive gas reserves and the remaining are oil and associated gas reserves (Dorian 2006: 546). Natural gas is unevenly distributed throughout the country. More than 40 per cent of Kazakhstan's gas reserves are located in one field – the huge Karachaganak and Tengiz fields in the north-west part of the country (EIA 2018).

Kazakhstan has two distinct gas distribution networks. One is in the west, which services the nations producing natural gas fields, and the other in the south which primarily delivers imported natural gas to the southern consuming regions (EIA 2018). Natural gas output has risen steadily since 2000 with

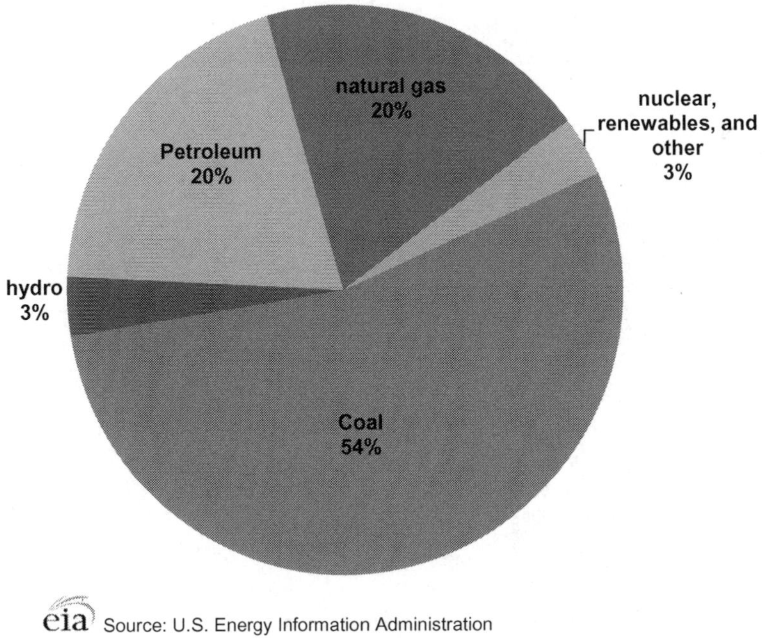

FIGURE 2.4 Kazakhstan energy consumption by fuel, 2015.

Source: US Energy Information Administration, 2017, Available at: http://www.ieee.es/en/Galerias/fichero/OtrasPublicaciones/Internacional/2017/EIA_Country_Aanlysis_Kazakhstan_10may2017.pdf output in 2015 1.5 tcf from 25.65 bcm in 2007 (Russia/CIS Energy Digest 2007, Reuters 2006, Kazakh Ministry of Energy and Mineral Resources 2007, Dorian 2006: 546, EIA 2018).

Kazakhstan's primary oil pipelines with a total length of 3384 km were constructed at the end of the 1960s and have now deteriorated (Dorian 2006: 546). Until 2003, Kazakh crude oil was refined in Russian refineries and exported via the Abut Volga and Black Sea pipelines. But in 2004, additional pipelines were built, which allowed Kazakh oil to be exported in three directions. These are northward (via the Russian pipeline system and rail network), westward (via the Caspian Pipeline Consortium (CPC), project and barge to Azerbaijan), and southward (via swaps with Iran) (EIA 2018). Since October 2001, the CPC has transported roughly 250,000 barrels per day (b/d), or one-third of Kazakhstan's exports (Dorian 2006: 546). Most of this oil came from the Tengiz field.

In 2016 alone, Kazakhstan exported natural gas of approximately $22.3 billion in comparison to its 2007 estimate of about 408 tbl/d northward via Russian pipelines and rail; 620 tbl/d westward via the CPC; 70–80 tbl/d southward via an oil swap with Iran; and 85 tbl/d eastward via the Atasu–Alashankou pipeline (EIA 2009, UNESCAP 2018). The CPC pipeline was Kazakhstan's main line for exporting Caspian Sea oil in 2007. There are further plans to increase its carrying capacity. The other manner through which Kazakhstan exports its Caspian oil is by barge to Baku, Azerbaijan, Neka and Iran. It is still looking to increase pipeline and rail shipments to China or shipments to Baku for transportation on the BTC pipeline.

Kazakhstan currently serves as a transit state for natural gas exports from U zbekistan and Turkmenistan to Russia and onward. The two branches of the Central Asia-Center (CAC) gas pipeline, controlled by Gazprom, meet in the south-western Kazakh city of Beyneu. Then it crosses into Russia at Alexandrov Gay and feeds into the Russian pipeline system. Almost all Uzbek and Turkmen natural gas is exported through this pipeline along with some Kazakh gas produced from Karachaganak and Tengiz. Several new natural gas export pipelines from the Caspian Sea region are also in development or under consideration, potentially opening up new markets for Kazakh natural gas.

III. Coal

With 28,225 million short tonnes (MMst) of total recoverable coal reserves as of 2014, Kazakhstan is in the top ten countries in the world in terms of coal reserves, coal production and coal exports. It is also in the top 15 countries in the world in terms of coal consumption. Despite being among the top coal countries, Kazakhstan is a relatively small contributor to global coal volumes. The top four countries globally account for disproportionate shares of total global coal reserves, production, consumption and exports (between 65 and 75 per cent combined), while Kazakhstan accounts for between 1 and 4 per cent (EIA 2018).

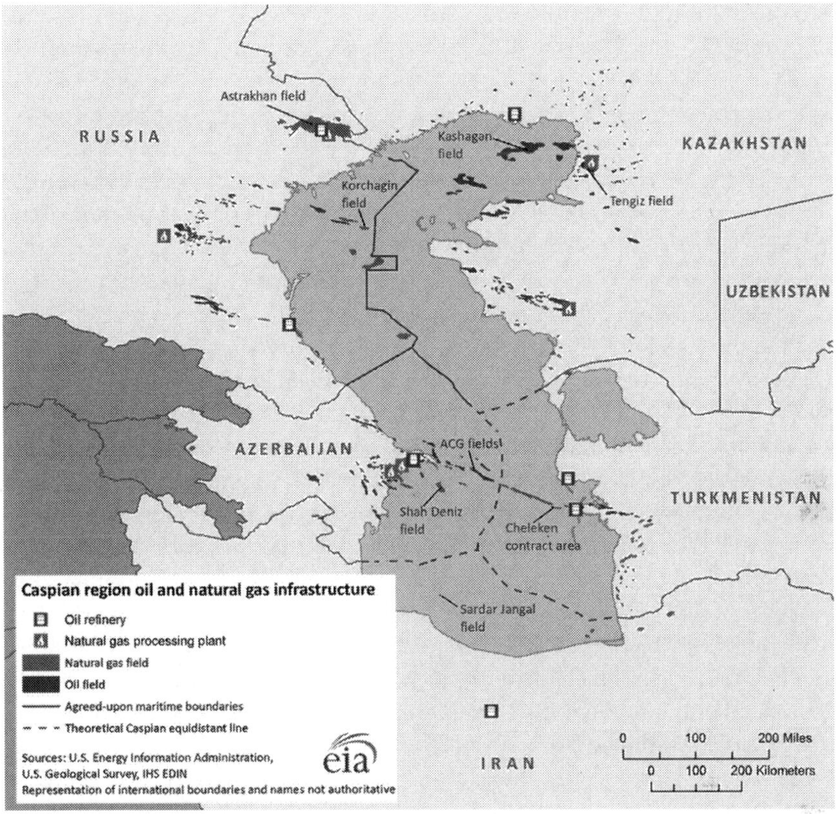

FIGURE 2.5 Oil and gas fields in the Caspian Sea region.

Source: US Energy Information Administration, 2013, August 26

IV. Uranium

Kazakhstan's only nuclear power plant, a BN-350 nuclear reactor at Aktau, was shut down in 1999. Kazakhstan has some of the largest uranium deposits in the world and is the world's largest uranium producer (EIA 2018). Kazakhstan has been an important source of uranium for more than 50 years. From 2001 to 2013 production of uranium rose from 2022 to 22,550 tonnes per year.

Of its 17 mine projects, five are wholly owned by Kazatomprom and 12 are joint ventures with foreign equity holders, some of which are producing under nominal capacity. In 2016, 12,986 tU was attributable to Kazatomprom itself – 21 per cent of world production – putting it ahead of Cameco, followed by Areva and ARMZ-Uranium One. The country's total production in 2016 was 24,575 tU, and in 2017 it was 23,600 tU. In January 2017 Kazatomprom said that production would be reduced by about 10 per cent due to low prices; in December 2017 Kazatomprom announced that the reduction would be 20 per cent from 2017 levels, enacted for three years. The announced cuts amounting to a production deferral of 11,000 tonnes of natural uranium. In May 2018 the country's energy minister announced that the production target for 2018 was set at 21,600 tU (WNA 2018), 15 per cent of the world's uranium resources (WNA 2010; KazAtomprom 2010). Kazatomprom is the national atomic company set up in 1997 and owned by the government. It controls all uranium exploration and mining as well as other nuclear-related activities, including imports and exports of nuclear materials. It announced in 2008 it would supply 30 per cent of world uranium by 2015 and it produced 39 per cent and through joint ventures: 12 per cent of the uranium conversion market, 6 per cent of enrichment and 30 per cent of the fuel fabrication market by then (WNA 2018).

Uranium exploration started in 1948 and economic mineralization was found in several parts of the country and this supported various mines exploiting hard rock deposits. Some 50 uranium deposits are known to exist in six uranium provinces. Reasonably Assured Resources plus Inferred Resources to $130/kgU were 816,000 tU in 2005. In 1970, tests on in situ leach (ISL) mining commenced and was successful, which led to further exploration being focused on two sedimentary basins with ISL potential. Up to the year 2000, twice as much uranium had been mined in hard rock deposits than sedimentary ISL. But almost all production is now from ISL. Uranium production dropped to one-quarter of its previous level from 1991 to 1997 (Ibid).

All except one of the operating and planned ISL mine groups are in the central south of the country and controlled by the state corporation Kazatomprom. Mines in the Stepnoye area have been operating since 1978. Some in the Tsentralnoye area has been operational since 1982. Both these sites are in the Chu-Sarysu basin/province, which has more than half the country's known resources. Mines in the Western area of the Syr Darya basin/province have operated since 1985. All have substantial resources (Ibid).

Since it has massive uranium deposits and potential of production, Kazatomprom has forged major strategic links with Russia, Japan and China. It is also taking a significant share in the international nuclear company Westinghouse. Canadian and French companies are involved with uranium mining and other aspects of the fuel cycle. A country like India is also stepping into the shoes of other actors in the region for gaining access to the uranium resources of Kazakhstan.

Kazakhstan in Central Asian energy geopolitics

Kazakhstan possesses the most advantageous geopolitical position among all Central Asian states, placing it in a position to be courted by the West, Russia and China. It has taken advantage of its location by adopting a "multi-vector" foreign policy, pursuing friendly relations with all and playing each against the other (Hanks 2008). Though Kazakhstan is most clearly tied to Russia in its energy sector, the former has cautiously sought out deals with the EU and China without alienating Russia.

The United States and the EU have been pushing plans for a trans-Caspian pipeline for quite some time, but Kazakhstan and Turkmenistan have thus far refused to bite. To so blatantly bypass Russia could be politically costly. Instead, Kazakhstan has pursued options that allow it to increase its exports to Europe while cooperating with Russia. This includes Kazakhstan's agreement to expand the CAC gas pipeline. The CPC pipeline also has a planned second phase that Kazakhstan could use to boost carrying capacity to 67 MT/y (Dave 2008: 54). While that route would still pass through Russia, it bypasses the Ukraine–Russian chokepoint. Now that Kazakhstan's new oil pipeline to China is up and running and will be joined by the Turkmen–China gas pipeline, Kazakhstan has a very strong position in Central Asian energy geopolitics. Shrewd planning has mitigated Kazakhstan's dependence on Russia, strengthening its already attractive bargaining position with its regional and global neighbours.

Importance of oil and gas to Kazakhstan

In the age of globalization and information, the importance of energy especially oil and natural gas in the prosperity and security of the state is difficult to overstate. But one can understand their importance from the estimation of Energy Information Administration (EIA) in 2012 as it mentions that oil amounts to 41.2 per cent and gas 15.2 per cent of global energy consumption. Combined, these fuels constitute 54.6 per cent of the total world energy consumption with oil being the dominating fuel type. Kazakhstan, having huge bases of oil and gas, of course, has a vital source to develop its economy. The oil sector has been dominating the Kazakh economy since independence by contributing more than 25 per cent to its GDP; it comprised 65 per cent of total exports and more than 40 per cent of the total budget revenue in 2012 (Cummings 2012: 128). It is also a fact that the Kazakh economy, despite the hardships in the early 1990s after the disintegration, has bounced back and emerged as the leading economy in Central Asia, which is largely attributed to the Foreign Direct Investments (FDI) it has invited, mainly in the oil and gas sector. Table 2.10 shows the way energy, especially oil has been the defining factor in the economic development of Kazakhstan. Many such major oil and gas projects have contributed to the socio-economic development of Kazakhstan and made it stand as one and unique among the Central Asian countries in terms of developmental indicators, as can be seen in Table 2.11 and Table 2.12 as well.

TABLE 2.10 Natural gas reserves, production, consumption and export trend of Kazakhstan (in billion cubic feet)

Category	*1992*	*2002*	*2010*	*2011*	*2012*	*2013*	*2014*	*2015*	*2016*
Reserves	NA	65	85	85	85	85	85	85	85
Productions (bcf)	286.05	462.6265	1238.85	1308.421	1334.907	1387.88	1430.258	1515.014	1638.602
Consumption	709.83	526.1935	411.0666	459.095	437.5529	477.812	463.686	480.6372	511.9966
Exports	257.8	226.016	410.7135	396.9406	389.5245	402.591	418.8359	434.0214	460.8605

Source: EIA 2020 (Uranium Deposits of Kazakhstan, map from KazAtomProm 2007. Scale: Kyzlorda to Shieli/ Kokzhoky is about 100km).

TABLE 2.11 Total coal reserves, production, consumption and export scenario of Kazakhstan (in mst)

Kazakhstan's total primary coal in mst	*1992*	*2002*	*2003*	*2004*	*2005*	*2006*	*2007*	*2008*	*2009*	*2010*	*2011*	*2012*	*2013*	*2014*	*2015*	*2016*
Production	139481.9	78264.01	89074.36	91563.38	91258.04	106554.8	107836.8	109118.8	111172.4	122278.1	128364	132858.1	131807.6	125646.8	118298.8	113619.5
Consumption	97374.76	55116.6	61939.9	68504.16	70291	75657.05	80189.75	93502.34	83975.08	90875.54	97718.68	99173.73	98450.61	91382.6	84313.49	87226.89
Exports	46802.98	25474.86	30665.99	26890.99	27301.6	31636.48	29218.05	37345.05	29438.51	20863.14	7318.461	8335.034	6043.439	6510.662	6932.105	4273.196
Reserves	NA	NA	NA	NA	NA	NA	NA	20885.46757	20668.31	20668.31	19006.03	28224.65	28224.65	28224.65	28224.65	28224.65

Source: EIA, 2020.

TABLE 2.12 Economic data on Kazakhstan, 2007–17

Economic variable	*2007*	*2008*	*2009*	*2010*	*2011*	*2012*	*2013*	*2014*	*2015*	*2016*	*2017*
GDP growth (annual %)	8.9	3.3	1.2	7.3	7.4	4.8	6	4.2	1.2	1.1	4.1
Oil rents (% of GDP)	18.43	21.52	14.20	16.60	19.42	17.25	14.28	13.62	6.74	7.14	10.19
Natural gas rents (% of GDP)	1.21	1.89	2.08	1.22	1.45	1.45	1.29	1.01	0.94	0.82	1.18
Foreign direct investment, net inflows (% of GDP)	11.41	12.60	12.38	5.037	7.14	6.56	4.23	3.30	3.56	12.54	2.82

Source: World Bank (2020), World Development Indicators-Kazakhstan, available at: https://databank.worldbank.org/reports.aspx?source=2&series=BX.KLT.DINV.WD.GD.ZS&country=KAZ#.

Export of energy: pipelines and transportation

Kazakhstan, as we know, is the biggest landlocked country in the world. Despite Kazakhstan's vast hydrocarbon endowment, there are many challenges and limitations to adequate production. As it doesn't have any access to the sea, transit has been its central problem in exporting oil and gas. Astana is heavily dependent on pipeline networks for transportation of its oil and gas. And exporting through a pipeline requires huge investment and planning. Importantly, the pipeline once constructed can't be shifted, therefore it requires long-term vision and strategy to build those pipelines. Until the independence of Kazakhstan, the pipeline networks of the USSR were controlled from Moscow under the aegis of the Russian Federation. Russia is still largely able to control Kazakhstan's access to its pipeline network. In June 2002, Kazakhstan signed a 15-year oil transit agreement with Russia, under which Kazakhstan undertook to export at least 17.4 million tonnes per year (350,000 barrels per day) of crude oil using a pipeline system owned by the Russian state monopoly Transneft (KazMunaygaz; 2008). Previously, the Russian monopoly had allowed Kazakhstan to transit only 2 million tonnes of oil per year via the Transneft system, and KazMunayGaz had to fight for any increases in quotas (Sieff, 2004). Kazakhstan has been engaged in talks with Russia to expand the CPC capacity to 67–70 million tonnes a year from the current 28 million, 20 million tonnes of which comes from Kazakhstan (Cohen 2008: 126).

That is why Kazakhstan has been in favour of diversification of export routes to lessen its overdependence on Russia for energy transportation. As of 2020, most of Kazakhstan's oil is exported through three main pipelines (see Table 2.15), where the largest part goes through the Russian pipelines. Oil is also exported by tanker from the maritime terminal at Aktau to Makhachkala in Russia, Baku in Azerbaijan and Neka in Iran.

TABLE 2.13 Major onshore oil and natural gas projects in Kazakhstan

Name of the project/field	*Project partner*	*Estimated reserves*	*Project status*
Aktobe ZhanazholKenkiyak	–CNPC Aktobemunaigaz – 85% In the block ADA: –KNOC (South Korea) –LGIC –Vertom	1.17 billion barrels of oil (2007)	Produced 116,660 bbl/d of oil, and 69.6 bcf a year of gas (1.948 bcm) in 2005
Alibekmola and Kozhasai	–KMG – 50% –Caspian Investments Resources – 50%	Proven reserves of 102 million barrels of oil (2011)	Produced 1.14 million tonnes of oil (22,891 bbl/d) in 2011
Amangeldy	–Amangeldy Gas (KazTransGaz subsidiary)	22–25 bcm of gas (2008)	Produced 0.32 bcm of gas in 2007
Arman	–Caspian Investments Resources – 50% –Shell – 50%	Proven reserves of 2.8 million barrels of oil (2011)	Produced 76,500 tonnes (1536 bbl/d) of oil in 2011
Emba	–KMG – 51% –MOL Rt. Vegypszer (Hungary) – 49%	500 million barrels of oil (2007)	Produced 57,700 bbl/d of oil in 2004, 3.1 bcf of gas (0.086 bcm) in 2004
Karachaganak	–BG Group (UK) (joint operator) – 29.25% –ENI (joint operator) – 29.25% –Chevron – 18% –Lukoil – 13.5% –KMG – 10%	Gross reserves of 2.4 billion barrels of condensate, 16 Tcf of gas (2013)	Producing 202 900 bbl/d, 1.1 mmcf/d natural gas (2005). 244,000 bbl/d of condensate in first half of 2012. 70% of oil is exported through CPC pipeline
Karakuduk	Caspian Investments Resources: –Lukoil (Russia) – 50% –Sinopec (China) – 50%	Proven reserves of 56.6 million barrels of oil, 22.7 bcf of gas (0.635 bcm) (2011)	Produced 1.4 million tonnes of oil (28,112 bbl/d) and 120 mcm of gas in 2011

(*Continued*)

TABLE 2.13 (Continued) Major onshore oil and natural gas projects in Kazakhstan

Name of the project/field	*Project partner*	*Estimated reserves*	*Project status*
Karazhanbas	Karazhanbasmunai: –Citic Resources Holdings (China) – 50% –KMG – 50%	286 million barrels of oil (2011)	Produced 36,200 bbl/d in 2011
KazgerMunai	–KMG – 50% –PetroKazakhstan (China) – 50%	100 million barrels of oil (2007)	Produced 3.0 million tonnes of oil (60,240 bbl/d) in 2011.
Kumkol North	Turgai Petroleum: –Lukoil – 5% –PetroKazakhstan – 50%	Proved reserves of 86 million barrels of oil, 29.7 bcf of gas (0.83 bcm) (2011)	Producing 2.5 million tonnes of oil (50,200 bbl/d) in 2011
North Buzachi	–CNPC – 50% –Caspian Investments Resources (Russia/China) – 50%	Proved reserves of 134 million barrels of oil (2011)	Produced 1.97 million tonnes of oil (39,558 bbl/d) in 2011
Tengiz	TengizChevroil: –Chevron (US) – 50% –ExxonMobil (US) – 25% –KMG – 20% –LukArco (Russia) – 5%	6–9 billion barrels of oil (2013)	Produced 25.8 mill tonnes of oil (579,000 bbl/d), 1.3 million tonnes of LPG and 6.9 bcm in 2011 The majority of oil is exported through CPC
Uzen	Uzenmunaigaz (KMG subsidiary) – 100%	Proved and probable reserves of 166 million tonnes of oil (1.2 billion barrels) (2011)	Produced 5.1 million tonnes of oil (102,409 bbl/d) in 2011

Modified from the following sources: Olcott 2007; Yenikeyeff 2008, 32, 78-80; Ekspert Kazakhstan 2010; CITIC Resources Holdings 2011; KazMunaiGaz 2011; KazMunaiGaz 2011; EIA 2012; Lukoil 2012; PetroKazakhstan 2012a; PetroKazakhstan 2012b; BG Group 2013; CNPC 2013; KMG EP 2013; KPO 2013; Lukoil 2013; TCO 2013.

TABLE 2.14 Major oil and natural gas projects of Kazakhstan in the Caspian Sea region

Name of field/project	*Project partners*	*Estimated reserves*	*Project status*
Kashagan: **Kashagan E** **Kashagan W** **Kairan** **Aktoty** **Kalamkas**	North Caspian Operating Company (NCOC): ENI (Italy) – 16.81% KMG – 16.81% Total (France) – 16.81% Shell (UK/Nederland) – 16.81% ExxonMobil (US) – 16.8% ConocoPhillips (US) – 8.40% Inpex (Japan) – 7.56%	9 to 13 billion bbl of oil recoverable (2007)	PSA.20 Production is estimated to start in the first half of 2013. Initial production of 75,000 bbl/d, and max of 1.2 million bbl/d
Kurmangazy	KMG – 50% Rosneft (Russia) – 50%	550 to 1800 million tonnes of oil recoverable (4 to 13 billion barrels) (2013)	PSA. Exploration
Tyub–Karagan	KMG – 50% Lukoil (Russia) – 50%	N/A	PSA. Exploration. Lukoil financing 100% of the exploration
Atash	KMG – 50% Lukoil (Russia) – 50%	N/A	Exploration contract. Exploration. Lukoil financing 100% of the exploration
Zhemchuzhiny (“Pearls Block”)	Shell (UK and Netherlands) – 55% KMG – 25% Oman Oil Company (Oman) – 20%	N/A	PSA. Exploration. Shell and Oman Oil Company financing 100% of the exploration

(*Continued*)

TABLE 2.14 (Continued) Major oil and natural gas projects of Kazakhstan in the Caspian Sea region

Name of field/project	*Project partners*	*Estimated reserves*	*Project status*
Makhambet	Atyraumunaigaz (KMG subsidiary)	N/A	PSA. Exploration
Bobek	Atyraumunaigaz (KMG subsidiary)	N/A	PSA
Imashevskoe	–KMG –Gazprom (Russia)	Over 100 bcm of gas (2011)	Joint Russian–Kazakh agreement on exploration
Khvalynskoe	–Lukoil – 50% –KMG – 25% –Total (France) – 17% –GDF Suez (France) – 8%	N/A	Negotiations. Russia's jurisdiction
Tsentralnoe	–KMG – 50% –TsentrCaspNeftegas (Gazprom/Lukoil) – 50%	N/A	Negotiations. Russia's jurisdiction
Abai	–KMG –Statoil (Norway)	N/A	Negotiations
Isatai	–KMG –ENI (Italy)	N/A	Negotiations
Darkhan	–KMG –Chinese consortium headed by CNOOC	N/A	Negotiations

Modified from the following sources: Olcott 2007; Yenikeyeff 2008, 32, 78-80; Ekspert Kazakhstan 2010; CITIC Resources Holdings 2011; KazMunaiGaz 2011; KazMunaiGaz 2011; EIA 2012; Lukoil 2012; PetroKazakhstan 2012a; PetroKazakhstan 2012b; BG Group 2013; CNPC 2013; KMG EP 2013; KPO 2013; Lukoil 2013; TCO 2013.

As shown in Table 2.13 and Table 2.14, Kazakhstan and Western companies have been rather successful in the development of onshore and offshore oil fields. In 2008 the Baku–Tbilisi–Ceyhan (BTC) pipeline project was developed to export oil and gas to Europe from Baku (Azerbaijan) through Tbilisi (Georgia) to Ceyhan (Turkey).

Nevertheless, Kazakhstan's companies are anxious to get their oil to the market separately from the Russian Urals brand, which has a high sulphur content. Currently, this issue is in limbo due to the insufficient capacity of quality banks (these are facilities for separating oil with different chemical parameters, particularly sulphur content). While the Chevron-dominated Caspian Pipeline Consortium (CPC) built a quality bank, thus resolving the issue for its exports, the Russian pipeline monopoly Transneft stubbornly refuse to do so, denying Kazakhstan hundreds of millions of dollars in revenue.

In recent years China has made a massive inroad into the oil and gas sectors of Central Asia especially Kazakhstan and has built the southern energy corridor of the China–Central Asia pipeline for transportation of gas and oil from the region. This has led to the lessening of Kazakhstan's dependence on Russia for energy transportation.

Like oil pipelines, Kazakhstan also has four main gas pipelines such as the Central Asia Center pipeline, the Bukhara-Ural pipeline, Bukhara-Tashkent-Bishkek-Almaty pipeline and the Turkmen-China pipeline (EIA 2012). It is controlled and administered by KazTransGaz – a KMG subsidiary. Initially, Kazakhstan had to import gas from Uzbekistan, Russia and Turkmenistan to meet its domestic demands but due to exploration of more gas fields and an increase in production, it has been exporting gases to outside markets since 2009. The main gas pipelines of Kazakhstan are mentioned in Table 2.16.

Refineries

Kazakhstan currently has three major oil refineries: Atyrau, Pavlodar and Shymkent. These refineries are from the Soviet era and were being upgraded and modernized until 2014 (KazMunaiGaz 2011). These refineries supply most of Kazakhstan's domestic fuel (Olcott 2007: 18). Most of Kazakhstan's oil and gas production facilities are located far away from these refineries, which can be problematic for Kazakhstan. The Pavlodar refinery, in the eastern part of the country, receives oil supplies from Russia, while Kazakh oil is being exported in the western part. The refinery still depends on the old soviet pipeline system for supplies, since the pipeline infrastructure is not fully developed. This fact of being dependent on Russian supplies can be seen as a risk, which the Kazakh government recognizes. In addition, the Karachaganak field, close to the Russian border, is dependent on the Russian refinery in Orenburg for processing and keeping up production. Kazakhstan is planning to build a refinery to handle production from the Karachaganak field, as a response to this situation (Bloomberg 2012; Nazarbaev 2012).

TABLE 2.15 Main oil export pipelines

Pipeline	*Ownership*	*Length/Capacity*	*Notes*
CPC pipeline: (Tengiz–Novorossiisk pipeline)	Caspian Pipeline Consortium (CPC): –Russia/Transneft – 31% –KMG – 19% –Chevron (US) – 15% –LUKARCO B.V. (Russia) – 12.5% –ExxonMobil (US) – 7.5% –Rosneft–Shell (Russia/UK/Nederland) – 7.5% –BG Group (UK) – 2% –ENI (Italy) – 2% –Kazakhstan Pipeline Ventures (Kazakh) – 1.75% –Oryx – 1.75%	1511 km from Tengiz field to the port of Novorossiisk in Russia, Black Sea. Phase I capacity of 565,000 bbl/d; Phase II capacity of 1.3 million bbl/d (2015)	First tanker loaded in 2001. Transported about 670,000 bbl/d in 2012
UAS pipeline (Atyrau, Samara; Connecting with the Russian pipeline system)	KazTransOil (KMG Subsidiary) – 100% on Kazakh side of the border	From Uzen via Atyrau to Samara in Russia and linking up with the Russian pipeline system. Capacity of about 300,000 bbl/d	Old pipeline built in 1970s. Upgraded in 2002 to about 300,000 bbl/d, and are in discussions to expand further. Transported 15.4 million tonnes (309,000 bbl/d) of oil in 2011.

China pipeline (Atasu–Alashankou or KCP)	KMG/KazTransOil – 50% CNPC (China) – 50%	Initially 7 million tonnes of oil, then upgraded to 10 million from 2008. From 2011, a capacity of 12 million tonnes a year (240,000 bbl/d)	First oil reached China in 2006. Plan to expand capacity to 20 million tonnes a year (400,000 bbl/d) in 2013
BTC (Baku–Tbilisi–Ceyhan pipeline)		The Baku–Tbilisi–Ceyhan Pipeline Company: BP (UK) – 30.1% SOCAR (Azerbaijan) – 25% Chevron – 8.9% Statoil (Norway) – 8.7% TAPO (Turkey) – 6.5% ENI – 5% Total (France) – 5% Itochu (Japan) – 3.4% Inpex (Japan) – 2.5% ConocoPhillips – 2.5% Hess Corp. (US) – 2.4%	

Sources: Olcott 2007; Upstream 2008; Babali 2009; International Energy Agency 2010; Trend 2011; EIA 2012; KazMunaiGaz 2012; BP 2013a; CPC 2013a; KazTransOil 2013a.

TABLE 2.16 Main gas pipeline of Kazakhstan

Pipeline	*Direction/Capacity*	*Notes*
Central Asia Centre (CAC)	The eastern part origins from south-eastern Turkmenistan (2.2 tcf), western part from Turkmen Caspian coast (120 bcf). They link up at Beineu in Kazakhstan and go to Alexandrov Gai in Russia	Two branches controlled by Gazprom. Exports gas from Central Asia to the Russian gas system
Bukhara – Ural	Uzbekistan via Kazakhstan to Russia. Capacity of 706 bcf	Transit pipeline through Kazakhstan
Bukhara Gas Region – Tashkent–Bishkek–Almaty (BGR-TBA)	From the Bukhara area in Uzbekistan to Kazakhstan with a link to Kyrgyzstan. Capacity of 160 bcf	Supply southern Kazakhstan with gas
Kazakhstan–China (also known as Turkmenistan–China gas pipeline)	From Turkmenistan, along BGR–TBA to Almaty and China. Export capacity of 30 bcm to China, 10 bcm for domestic use	First line commissioned in 2009. Supply China with Turkmen gas, and can supply China with Kazakh. Expansion is planned. Section two, Beineu-Shymkent is expected finished in 2015, with a capacity of 10 bcm. Development financed by China

Sources: Yenikeyeff 2008, 33-36; KazMunaiGaz 2011; EIA 2012; Pirani 2012; KazTransGaz 2013b; KazTransGaz 2013a.

Energy policy of the Republic of Kazakhstan

Kazakhstan is a major oil and gas producing economy. Exports went up from 1 million barrels/day (mb/d) in 2005 to 1.3 mb/d in 2017 (Cohen, Ariel 2008: 117; IEA 2019), putting Kazakhstan in the same category of oil exporters as Kuwait, Iran and Iraq. Besides, it has large reserves of coal, uranium, gold and other precious metals.

Kazakhstan has declared a policy of openness to foreign investment and its assurances of political support for pipeline routes. This didn't have an instant effect as international oil companies wanted firm guarantees for their investments, demanded protection from nationalization and introduced taxation stability clauses into their contracts.

During the early years of Kazakhstan's independence, the country worked to establish a balance between its geopolitical vectors to protect its national interests. At the same time, Kazakhstan was implementing an integrated development strategy, which at times may have deviated from its strategic partners' agendas. The Kazakh government has sought to ensure the proper pace of development of the country's Caspian hydrocarbon reserves, while simultaneously implementing tax reforms and claiming preferential rights to the largest fields.

In the early years of independence, the newly born nation had to face several alternatives in the energy policymaking field: the road to full nationalization and transfer of some energy to private sectors. In his 1997 annual State of the Nation address, Nazarbayev emphasized that the opportunities offered by Caspian mineral wealth included potential dangers:

> Our natural resources are an enormous wealth. Ironically, world experience shows that many countries with natural resources were not able to dispose of them properly and never came out of poverty. The East Asian countries, poor in natural resources, have demonstrated the most dynamic development. These examples highlight that the people, their will, motivation, persistence and wisdom, primarily determine the development outcome.
>
> *(Nazarbayev 2008)*

Ultimately, Kazakhstan opted for a balanced approach, with proper consideration for the interests of all the world powers involved in the region, by opening access to the international oil companies. The Kazakhstani leadership considered this strategy to be consistent with the country's foreign policy priorities, believing that Kazakhstan would be able to maintain partnerships with key players in the region and utilize oil revenues towards achieving sustainable economic development.

In deciding in favour of foreign direct investment, "Kazakhstan was becoming one of the few oil-rich countries that are open to foreign companies" (Cohen, Ariel 2008: 118). In a short time, Kazakhstan undertook a series of legislative initiatives and became the most attractive CIS country for foreign investment (Shiells 2003). Interestingly, the country did not apply the model that is used in opening the energy sector to foreign capital to other sectors of the economy. Thus, protectionism and reliance on internal resources dominated the financial sector, the media and other markets (The Heritage Foundation 2008).

Despite its declared policy of limiting government interference in the economy, transnational corporations contending for a slice of the "Caspian cake" had to undergo rigid screening. The Kazakh government gave preference to internationally recognized companies interested in developing long-term projects and ready to take into account the country's domestic interests. They had to emphasize environmental safety programmes, train local staff and exercise corporate social responsibility. Transnational companies, such as ChevronTexaco, ExxonMobil, Agip/Eni, Royal Dutch Shell, British Group, TotalFinaElf, Impex and others emerged as the winners in this race.

Second-wave investors – Canadian, Middle Eastern and Russian companies – have been rapidly establishing their presence in the Caspian region. China's desire to strengthen its role became more obvious in 2005 and 2006, with Russia's presence on the increase and American influence on the wane. With Chinese and Indian extractive and financial corporations entering the scene, the interests of all major world players were represented in the Caspian region.

The arrival of foreign corporations demanded the construction of a system of export oil and gas pipelines. To realize the full potential of its oil fields, Kazakhstan had to assure export routes that would guarantee its ability to fill the demand for "black gold", particularly to the West, South Asia and China. Nazarbayev was also aware that respecting the interests of all the major players in the Caspian region, namely the West, Russia and China would enhance the stability of the energy sector in Kazakhstan. This approach would facilitate a balance of power in the region, keeping major players in check.

Despite its strategic partnership with Russia, Kazakhstan has actively promoted economic ties with Ukraine, Georgia and Kyrgyzstan, particularly in the area of energy supply, transit and investment. Thus, in late 2006, KazTransOil, a subsidiary of the national oil and gas operator KazMunayGaz, signed a joint venture deal with the Batumi oil terminal in Georgia (2006). The newly established Batumi Terminals JV, in which Kazakhstan owns a 50 per cent stake, exports Kazakh oil via the Black Sea route. Considering Washington's close attention to the Kazakh–Iranian relationship, Astana has taken a wait-and-see position on the development of any large-scale energy projects with Teheran.

The role of Kazakhstan as a reliable supplier of hydrocarbons to the global market has greatly increased since the beginning of the 21st century. The attacks of September 11, 2001, growing destabilization in the Middle East, and increased demand for energy throughout the world, especially in China and India, have all led to an insatiable thirst for oil, especially non-Middle Eastern oil.

Control over natural resources

Over the years, as oil prices went up, so did Kazakhstan's attractiveness as an investment destination. As a result, its perceived need for unrestricted Western investment has declined and the country has started to develop policies to retain its strategic control over oil resources and improve its position vis-à-vis Western companies. The government aspires to increase its mineral resources revenues, ensure cash flow in the event of a global economic crisis and diversify sources of investment.

There is a sentiment among Kazakh political and intellectual elites that in the early and mid-1990s, the country entered into agreements with international oil companies that benefited the foreign investors to a much greater degree than they did the people of Kazakhstan. As the country has become stronger economically, the government has moved to change its oil and gas legislation in ways that boost the role of the state in the vital energy sector. However, those who emphasize the sanctity of contract view the issue differently. They stress Kazakhstan's financial needs that the earlier investors satisfied, and the high degree of political risk international oil companies took on when very few people were willing to invest there on a large scale.

Reasserting the state's role in the energy sector has taken place gradually. In 2004, the Kazakh Majilis adopted a law giving the state priority rights to acquire fields or shares in various energy projects that are up for sale. Western business interests protested. A managing partner at Denton Wilde Sapte in Almaty, a law firm specializing in oil issues, Marla Valdez, called this legislation "virtually unprecedented in other jurisdictions" (*The New York Times* 2004). The state-owned KazMunayGaz has already secured its legal right to acquire a 50 per cent stake in the Karazhanbas field.

In the same year, Kazakhstan also amended its Tax Code to increase the income tax imposed on oil companies from 25–30 per cent to 60–85 per cent. This same amendment also precluded the state from freezing tax rates on energy companies for signed deals. A year later, in 2005, the Kazakh government adopted restrictions on transfers of subsoil use rights and interests in mining companies. Article 71 of the Subsoil Law gives the state the "the right of first refusal" for the acquisition of energy assets, and prevents investors from transferring their mining rights for two years after signing a contract (Kenjebayeva 2005).

In late 2006, the government established a special department to work with major subsoil users. Its main task is to "restore the balance of interests between the state and subsoil users who initially entered into long-term lucrative contracts with substantial preferences for themselves" (Cohen 2008: 122). Although these steps were not even close to the Venezuelan-style radical nationalization programme, the most recent round of amendments, put forward in 2007, raised fears of a possible turn toward Russian style "resource nationalism" (Cutler 2007).

In July 2007, the Kazakh parliament adopted legislative amendments to enhance the state's role in the economy and ensure effective state control over industrial assets deemed vital to national security and other interests (*Kazakhstan Today* 2007). In October 2007, Nazarbayev approved changes to Kazakhstan's Law on Subsoil Resources, allowing the state to reconsider, review and revise contracts with subsoil users in a unilateral manner. Under these amendments, the Kazakh government can revoke any contract considered a threat to the country's national security or detrimental to its economic interests.

The business community, unsurprisingly, opposed these new regulations. As a practical step toward bringing subsoil users into better compliance with the terms of their contracts, the Kazakh Ministry of Energy and Mineral Resources (MEMR) reportedly compiled a list of current hydrocarbon development licences in the country, ranked according to the degree to which the licensees met their contract obligations (Cohen 2008: 123).

Prime Minister Karim Massimov was enthusiastic in defending the interests of the state vis-à-vis foreign investors. Just one week after his appointment as head of the government in 2007 he made the following statement at a MEMR board meeting:

> Contract terms implementation by the natural resource users is generally unsatisfactory … In this matter, we should be more rigorous and clear, and should further advance the national interest within the legal framework ... We, as a state, must carry out our tasks and obligations.
>
> *(Kazakhstan Today 2007)*

Nevertheless, Caspian energy deposits are still attractive to foreign investors. To date, high demand and high prices for oil have mitigated the recent moves by the Kazakh government. Tighter regulations and increasing state involvement in the oil sector have not stopped the flow of investment. However, if an oil glut develops and energy prices decline, these policies may prompt oil companies to decrease their appetite for Kazakh crude. While it may be possible to introduce more stringent conditions for new contracts as the market for oil tightens, it is detrimental to revise existing agreements. As the Roman legal dictum goes, "agreements are there to fulfil" (Zimmerman 1996: 539–544). The recent Russian experience shows that overtaxing oil production leads to output declines. The Kazakh case is symbolic of a larger trend – the rise of state power in regulating hydrocarbon wealth and access to it. When markets are tight, it is easier for governments to direct revenue to their coffers.

Foreign direct investments in the energy sector

Foreign direct investments in Kazakhstan have been largely driven by two important factors: *economic growth* in the early years of independence and *resource nationalism* as the price of oil and gas goes up. Astana in the early 1990s developed a favourable attitude towards the Multinational Enterprises (MNE) inviting massive Foreign Direct Investments (FDI) yielding economic growth in the newly independent Central Asian state. However, with the rise of world oil prices, Astana desired to extract high rent from MNE through fiscal regulation and nationalization of natural resources.

The increasing state intervention in the energy sector, demand for greater Corporate Social Responsibility (CSR) and participation of government in energy projects have frustrated the big oil corporations, leading to criticism of the Kazakh policy of resource nationalism which has also prompted the consumer countries to impose pressure on the leadership in Astana.

Moreover, the existing legislation of Kazakhstan vests the national oil companies (NOCs) with a right to acquire at least 50 per cent stake in any new hydrocarbon development project. In conformity with this objective, the state bound NOCs to enter into the "strategic partnership" with Kazmunaigas. Thus, any foreign investor in Kazakhstan's oil and gas sector was "forced to work in one way or another" with the NOC (Olcott 2007: 2). By doing this, the government facilitated the "forced cooperation" of the company with foreign multinationals. Furthermore, Kazmunaigas' role with MNEs is not univocal since it cooperates and at the same time competes with them (Orazgaliyev 2018).

Energy and Kazakhstan's legal framework

Mainly there are two important pieces of legislation regulating foreign investment into Kazakhstan's energy sector (Griffin 2008). The first is the "Republic of Kazakhstan Law on Petroleum", originally passed in June 1995. The other is the "Law on the Subsurface", passed in January 1996 (Ibid). Both laws, however, have undergone tremendous change since their original introduction.

The Subsurface Law has a wider scope of the two pieces of legislation. It outlines the rules and regulations for an investor to acquire a "subsurface-use right". In Kazakhstan, the subsurface use right is the equivalent to a licence or a concession in other jurisdictions. In oil and gas projects, it is granted upon the execution of a "Hydrocarbon Contract" between the "Competent Body", i.e., the Kazakhstan Ministry of Energy and Mineral Resources and the producer, known in Kazakhstan typically as the "Contractor" (Griffin 2008). The Petroleum Law is in some ways an addendum to the Subsurface Law in that it regulates petroleum and gas projects.

One important feature of Kazakhstan's energy law is the government's preemptive purchase right to produce hydrocarbons. Previously, the Petroleum Law required the Kazakh Government to pay "world-market price" for any hydrocarbons that it received from producers. The 2007 Amendments provided that petroleum acquired by the government under pre-emptive right from the Contractor be compensated "at prices not exceeding world-market prices" (Barry, P. Michael; 2009: 46). This is significant because it means that the Kazakh Government now has the choice of negotiating down the price, instead of automatically paying the world market price.

To conclude, Kazakhstan's overall potential is immense. Its territory is four times that of France. It currently surpasses Kuwait in its oil production and expects to export 3 million barrels of oil a day by 2015, more than Iran currently provides. Kazakhstan also has some of the largest reserves of uranium on the planet and is a major exporter of grain. Kazakhstan's economic and political reform agenda is largely on track, despite setbacks caused by the spread of global financial instability.

Kyrgyzstan

Kyrgyzstan – a small Central Asia country of roughly 200,000 sq kilometres in the area is a landlocked and mountainous region packed with natural beauty and abundant natural resources. Kyrgyzstan has gorgeous mountain ranges and hundreds and hundreds of rivers and exquisite lakes. Over 90 per cent of Kyrgyzstan is blanketed by mountains with the Tien Shan range being the largest, covering almost 80 per cent of the country (Begaliev 2016). Interspersed with mountains, Kyrgyzstan is blessed with over 4000 rivers and almost 2000 lakes (Ibid). The world's second largest alpine lake, Issyk Kul, is also located in this country. As such, water constitutes an extremely rich resource for Kyrgyzstan among the Central Asian countries in terms of energy resources.

Energy profile

Unlike its neighbours, Kyrgyzstan has no significant exploited reserves of oil or natural gas. In 1994, petroleum production was 88,000 tonnes, and natural gas production was 39 million cubic metres (Curtis 1996). Although substantial coal deposits are present, in the mid-1990s experts described Kyrgyzstan's coal industry as in a state of collapse. In the early 1990s, only four of the 14 state-owned coal mines were considered economically viable, and only a little coal came from privately owned mines. Between 1991 and 1993, brown coal production decreased by 50 per cent (to 959,000 tonnes), and black coal production decreased by 53 per cent (to 712,000 tonnes). The domestic price of conventional fuels rose slightly above world levels after the much cheaper energy-sharing arrangements of the Soviet era ended. In 1992 oil and gas import costs were 50 per cent of the total state budget, compared with 10 per cent in 1991. In 1994 some 39 per cent of Kyrgyzstan's total import expenditures went for the purchase of conventional fuels, contributing an estimated $100 million to the country's trade imbalance. Energy consumption, meanwhile, has declined sharply since 1991, and experts do not expect it to return to its 1990 level (Ibid).

Kyrgyzstan has a proven oil reserve of around 0.04 billion barrels and produces roughly 0.96 tbl/d (2007). Domestic consumption is 13 tbl/d. Kyrgyzstan possesses 200 bcf of proven natural gas reserves. It has yet to significantly tap those reserves, producing only 1 bcf/y in 2006 (EIA 2009A).

It is to be noted that,

> Kyrgyzstan's coal reserves are at about 27 billion tons, of which the majority remained entirely unexploited in the mid-1990s. About 3 billion tons of that amount is judged to be of the highest quality. This coal has proven difficult to exploit, however, because most of it is in small deposits deep in the mountains. Kyrgyzstan also has oil resources; small deposits of oil-bearing shale have been located in southern Kyrgyzstan, and part of the Fergana oil and natural gas complex lies in Kyrgyzstani territory. In the Osh region, four pools of oil, four of natural gas, and four mixed pools have been exploited since the 1950s; however, the yield of all of them is falling in the 1990s. In 1992 their combined output was 112,000 tons of oil and 65 million cubic meters of natural gas, compared with the republic's

> annual consumption of 2.5 million tons of oil and 3 billion cubic meters of natural gas.
>
> *(Begaliev 2016)*

Kyrgyzstan contains seven developed oil-fields and two oil/gas fields (Dorian 2006: 548). Exploration continues in the favourable Naryn oblast area of eastern Kyrgyzstan, situated just across the border from China's Tarim Basin. Current crude oil production levels in Kyrgyzstan are at 972 barrels per day; consumption is 40,000 b/d (Worldometer 2016). In October 1996, Kyrgyzstan's first and only oil refinery Jalalabad, opened with a capacity of 10,000 b/d (Dorian 2006: 548). However, it remains mostly underused.

In addition to oil, with a domestic gas consumption of 27 bcf/y, Kyrgyzstan has to rely on gas imports as well (EIA 2009A). However, Kyrgyzstan has enormous hydro-electricity production potential. It is the Kyrgyz Republic delegation's view that water is a commodity, like energy, and can be traded as such. Any problem should be seen less as a deficit of energy but as a deficit of capacity. It is planned that the Kambarata power stations I and II would greatly alleviate many problems concerning electricity generation. It is expected to help expand and increase the reliability of power in the interconnected power grid. The average annual energy production of Kambatara I as of 1997 (a 1,900 MW plant) was 5, 164 Giga Watt-hours (GWh). Kambarata II (a 360 MW plant) would produce 148 GWh for a total of 6, 312 GWh (ADB 1997: 36). The delegation pointed out that, the region had all the resources, the only problem was to determine the perfect balance that would be acceptable to all the countries in the region. Since then many agreements, both bilateral and multilateral, have been signed between the neighbouring countries of the region. This has helped in bringing major changes in the energy mix of the region.

As per the data of EIA, in 2017 Kyrgyzstan produced total energy of around 0.16 quadrillion Btu while consuming 0.243 quadrillion Btu (2020). In the case of oil, its consumption rate is 32 times more than its production rate. So Kyrgyzstan is a net importer of oil and gas as far as its domestic requirements are concerned.

Water and energy in Kyrgyzstan

Kyrgyzstan is located in the high mountains of Pamir and Tien Shan, whose many glaciers supply the water which is the main energy resource in this country. Hydropower provides over 90 per cent of its energy supply (Roul 2010). In the former Soviet space, after Russia, Kyrgyzstan was only second to Tajikistan with the third-highest water resource potential of 142 billion kWh/year. However, most of the experts and government agencies are of the view that Kyrgyzstan exploits less than 9 per cent of its hydroelectric potential. The annual hydropower potential of the smaller rivers is between 5 and 8 billion kWh, but only 3 per cent has been utilized so far. Its rich water resources consist of 50 cubic kilometres of surface runoff a year, 13 km^3 of potential groundwater resources, 1,745 km^3 of lake water and 650 km^3 of glaciers. The region's largest rivers (the Naryn, 807 km; the Chu, 380 km; Talas, 200 km; Saryjaz, Kara Darya, Chatkal, and others that belong to the Syr Darya and Amu Darya basins) find their headwaters in Kyrgyzstan (Ibid).

There are 20 major power plants with a total installed capacity of 3680 MW in the country. There is conflicting information about the total number of large hydropower and combined heat and power plants (CHP) in the Republic. It is commonly accepted that 2950 MW comes from 18 hydropower plants and approximately 725 MW comes from two heat and power plants (Ministry of Industry, Energy and Fuel Resources, Kyrgyzstan 2006).

According to the National Energy Program (NEP) of the Kyrgyz Republic for 2006–2010 and the Strategy of the Fuel and Energy Complex until 2025 (NEP), there will be an addition of 3960 MW from several hydropower stations by 2025 (See Tables 2.17, 2.18 and 2.19). However, this ambitious programme needs sufficient investment. The NEP also envisages to commission a 1200 MW Kavak state district heating power station by 2015. During the same period, the NEP will add to the hydropower generation from small hydropower stations amounting 178 MW (NEP 2010). Kyrgyz Republic has 3.09 GW and Kazakhstan and Uzbekistan have 2.26 GW and 1.73 GW respectively (EIU 2017). Total hydropower potential and export trend of Kyrgyzstan between 2017—2017 has been mentioned in Table 2.17 while Table 2.20 mentions the ongoing and proposed hydropower plants in the Republic of Kyrgyzstan.

Most of the existing hydropower plants were constructed in Soviet times entirely along a single river – the Naryn. Before 1991, Toktogul Reservoir was operated in "irrigation mode", with large summer releases to satisfy irrigation demands in Uzbekistan and Kazakhstan, and low winter releases. Surplus hydropower in summer produced by the Naryn Cascade was transmitted to the downstream Republics. During the winter, the Kyrgyz Republic received sufficient fuel to operate its combined heat and power plants. After 1991, fuel deliveries did not fully satisfy Kyrgyzstan's needs. Therefore, the Kyrgyz Republic increased releases from the Toktogul Reservoir during winter. As a result, the reservoir

TABLE 2.17 Hydel power in Kyrgyzstan

Hydel power	*2007*	*2008*	*2009*	*2010*	*2011*	*2012*	*2013*	*2014*	*2015*	*2016*	*2017*
Generation (billion Kwh)	14.57	11.58	10.92	11.92	14.95	14.96	13.85	14.36	12.80	13.04	15.29
Hydroelectricity (billion Kwh)	12.60	10.02	10.11	10.99	13.99	14.03	12.99	13.16	10.98	11.37	14.06
Capacity (million Kwh)	3.73	3.74	3.74	3.76	3.76	3.86	3.86	3.86	4.04	4.04	4.04
Exports (billion Kwh)	2.37	0.86	1.25	1.82	2.84	1.84	0.37	0.07	0.18	0.19	1.21

Source: Ministry of Industry, Energy and Fuel Resources, Kyrgyz Republic; UNCTAD 2013.

TABLE 2.18 Existing power plants in Kyrgyzstan

Name of the power plant	*Categories*	*Installed capacity (in MW)*	*River*
Biskek Heating Plant	Thermal	678	
Osh Heating Plant	Hydro	50	
Toktogul HPS	Hydro	1200	Naryn Lower
Kurpsai HPS	Hydro	800	Naryn Lower
Tashkumyr HPS	Hydro	450	Naryn Lower
Shamaldysai HPS	Hydro	240	Naryn Lower
Uchkurgan HPS	Hydro	180	Naryn Lower
Karabulak HPS	Hydro	149	Naryn Lower
Karabulun HPS	Hydro	163	Naryn Lower
At-Bashy HPS	Hydro	40	Naryn Lower

Source: Ministry of Industry, Energy and Fuel Resources, Kyrgyz Republic. World Bank 2017; UNCTAD 2013.

TABLE 2.19 Small hydropower plants on the Naryn River

Name of the SHP	*Installed capacity (MW)*
Bystrovka HPS	8.7
Lebedinov	7.6
Kalinin	1.48
Alamedin N1	2.2
Alamedin N2	2.5
Alamedin N3	2.14
Alamedin N4	6.42
Alamedin N5	6.42
Alamedin N6	6.42
Small Alamedin HPS	0.41
Kalinin HPS	1.5

Source: Ministry of Industry, Energy and Fuel Resources, Kyrgyz Republic. World Bank 2017; UNCTAD 2013.

TABLE 2.20 Hydropower plants proposed or under construction

Name	*Installed capacity (in MW)*	*Probable construction timeline*
Kambarata-1	1900	2010–20
Kambarata-2	360	2007–12
DJilanaryk-1	100	2007–10
DJilanryk-2	100	2007–10
Akbulun	200	2010–14
Saryjaz	1200	2010–25

Source: Ministry of Industry, Energy and Fuel Resources, Kyrgyz Republic. World Bank 2017; UNCTAD 2013.

operation shifted to "power mode" with large winter releases and lower summer releases. However, to address growing problems in the first half of the 1990s, the Basin States entered into annual agreements on water allocation energy exchanges. This was an attempt to re-establish the pre-1991 operating regime. The 1998 Framework Agreement on the joint use of water and energy resources in the Syr Darya Basin between the five states placed these agreements on a more formal footing. However, the implementation of the yearly basis negotiation outcome of the 1998 agreement is always questionable (Roul 2009).

i. Oil

Kyrgyzstan contains seven developed oil fields and two oil/gas fields (Global Security 2010: 1). Kyrgyzneftgaz is the state-owned joint-stock company responsible for the production of oil and gas. It is presently looking for a foreign partner to introduce modern methods of oil and gas drilling. During the year 2000, Kyrgyzstan had oil field surveys by a team of specialists which, in November 2000, forecasted that Kyrgyzstan could become self-sufficient in oil by exploiting various reserves (Ibid).

In the Fergana Valley, there is an estimated reserve of over 700 million barrels, and the combined reserves of depressions at Chuy, Alay, Issyk-Kul and At-Bashi could be as much as 1.5 to 2.2 billion barrels. These are not yet proved, however. Kyrgyzstan's known proved crude oil reserves are presently only 40 million barrels (Global Security 2010).

In the Soviet days, Kyrgyzstan had not fully exploited its domestic reserves, since it depended on Russia, Kazakhstan, and Uzbekistan for oil and gas imports. However, these neighbouring countries are now increasingly exporting to world markets, where they can get higher prices. In this new environment, Kyrgyzstan is planning for increased reliance on domestic fuels. The Kyrgyz government launched an initiative to begin large-scale domestic oil extraction in the 2006 to 2007 time frame, with the first well anticipated by the end of 2001. It costs as much as $120,000 to drill a single well, so Kyrgyzstan sought investors for this venture, as well as multilateral development bank financing. A Dutch–Kyrgyz joint venture has been exploring for oil and gas since 1998 (Ibid).

There is one oil refinery in Kyrgyzstan, at Dzhalalabad, approximately 150 miles south of Bishkek. It was built in 1997 with a capacity of 10,000 bl/d and is now operated by the Kyrgyz Petroleum Company (KPC), a joint venture of the British firm Petrofac Resources International, Ltd and Kyrgyzneftgaz, the state-owned oil company. Petrofac Resources acquired its interest in the refinery from the Canadian firm Kyrgoil in June 2000 (Ibid). The KPC Dzhalalabad refinery has had problems in obtaining sufficient crude from neighbouring countries, especially Kazakhstan. This has led to reduced outputs of heavy fuel, diesel and gasoline. Two plants for converting condensed gas into gasoline were constructed in the 1990s, in the Chui oblast of Kyrgyzstan, by the Kyrgyz–American company Vostok. These plants can supply approximately 40 per cent of Kyrgyzstan's gasoline needs. There is currently a monopoly in petroleum products for the state-owned enterprise Munay. It was created by a presidential edict on March 9, 1999, which stated that only Munay can import or sell petroleum products in Kyrgyzstan. Munay is also responsible for licensing other companies for importing petroleum products and selling them wholesale. There are approximately 60 companies distributing petroleum products in Kyrgyzstan (Ibid).

ii. Natural gas

Natural gas accounts for almost 30 per cent of Kyrgyzstan's total energy consumption (Global Security 2010: 2). Kyrgyzstan consumed 67 billion cubic feet (Bcf) of natural gas in 1999, almost all of which came from imports; Kyrgyzstan's natural gas production in 1999 was 0.35 Bcf. Kyrgyzstan has estimated natural gas reserves of about 200 Bcf, but these reserves are hard to exploit (Ibid). At present, Kyrgyzstan does not have the infrastructure for increased natural gas operations nor the capital to exploit these reserves.

Kyrgyzstan imports most of its natural gas from Uzbekistan. This commercial relationship has been difficult for both countries, with Kyrgyzstan often paying late and Uzbekistan frequently cutting off the supply. This has caused problems for Kyrgyzstan in the winters when imported natural gas is used for both heating and electricity production. The officials of Kyrgyzstan and Uzbekistan have inked several natural gas supply contracts, usually involving barter.

None of these deals has worked in the long run, however. In the round of negotiations which concluded in October 2000, an agreement was reached where Kyrgyzstan would cover 50 per cent of its natural gas purchases with hard currency and barter electricity and water for the remaining 50 per cent (Ibid). However, starting on December 25, 2000, Uzbekistan cut off natural gas to Kyrgyzstan for several days, due to slow repayment of the debt, which had reached $1.6 million by the beginning of December 2000. The cut-off occurred when Uzbekistan requested that Kyrgyzstan speed up payment; 33% of the gas already delivered had not yet been paid for. Kyrgyzstan again lost its gas supply in January 2001, when an accident disrupted the pipeline in the Bukhara region of Uzbekistan. A dispute between Uzbekistan and Kyrgyzstan in October 2001 over Kyrgyzstan's slow payment of back debts from gas purchases resulted in yet another cut-off of gas supply for several days (Ibid).

In July 2000, the World Bank gave Kyrgyzstan $5 million in credit under a technical assistance project; the purpose of the project was to reform Kyrgyzstan's energy sector, especially Kyrgyzgaz, the state-owned joint-stock natural gas company (Ibid). The money strengthened the financial position of Kyrgyzgaz, allowing them to buy gas meters, spare parts and other equipment.

Despite abundant energy potentials, Kyrgyzstan suffered a massive energy crisis in the winter of 2007–08. The imminent energy crisis became evident to the public as the level of water in Toktogul reservoir, the country's main water source, dropped critically by early spring 2008. This threatened the operation of the major hydropower plants of the country, which are located below the reservoir. The Kyrgyz government introduced severe restrictions on energy consumption both for industry and the population and announced an increase in electricity tariffs. Despite these measures, by November 2008 and the beginning of winter, the water level in Toktogul reservoir remained at about 70 per cent of the previous year's, auguring an even worse electricity supply situation for the winter of 2008–09 (Juraev 2009: 1).

Energy policy of Kyrgyzstan

Management of national energy and fuel policy is distributed among several ministries and other state agencies – an arrangement that has hindered efficient acquisition and distribution. Distribution of heat and electricity is the responsibility of the state-run Kyrgyzstan National Energy Holding Company, and natural gas purchases are managed by the Kyrgyzstan Natural Gas Administration (Kyrgyzgas). Oil, gas and coal exploration is the responsibility of the State Geological Commission (Goskomgeologiya). Natural gas, provided by the Republic of Turkmenistan in the Soviet era, now comes mainly from neighbouring Uzbekistan. Coal, used to heat households and to fuel some thermoelectric plants, is mainly received from Kazakhstan in a barter arrangement for electrical power. Kazakhstan's coal is preferred because the heaviest demand in Kyrgyzstan is concentrated in the north, and Kyrgyzstan's remaining coal mines are in the south, from which transportation is problematic (Curtis 1996).

For these reasons, existing thermoelectric stations were de-emphasized in the 1990s in favour of expanded hydroelectric production. Thus, in 1994 thermoelectric power production dropped by 46 per cent while hydroelectric production rose by 30 per cent (Curtis 1996). These statistics enabled the national energy sector to show a modest drop of 4 per cent in total power generation in 1994, but district heating, which comes from coal and gas, powered by combined heat and power plants, suffered heavily from the transition. Meanwhile, government promotion of electricity brought an increase of 117 per cent in household power use between 1991 and 1994, although overall household energy consumption declined by 36 per cent during that period (Ibid). Some aspects of the promotion plan have been criticized, including the large-scale promotion of electric heat in a country with poorly insulated houses.

Emphasis on electricity is backed by abundant water power, mainly from the country's location at the mountain headwaters of the Syrdariya, one of the two largest rivers in Central Asia. On the Naryn River, the chief tributary of the Syrdariya, a series of hydroelectric stations was built, the largest of which is the Kürp-Say Hydroelectric Plant, fed by the Toktogol Reservoir in central Kyrgyzstan. Other major hydroelectric plants are located at Atabashin, Alamedin, and Uchkorgon. Such stations have made possible the net export of electric power, worth an estimated $100 million in 1994 (Curtis 1996). That figure was only about half the value of Kyrgyzstan's 1990 exports, however, because demand in neighbouring republics dropped considerably in the early 1990s. The main customer is Kazakhstan, with which power is exchanged through the Central Asian Integrated System (Ibid).

Only about 10 per cent of Kyrgyzstan's hydroelectric power potential and only about 3 per cent of the potential of its smaller streams are currently being exploited. The Naryn River is estimated to afford an additional 2200 megawatts of easily accessible rated capacity. Meanwhile, the Fergana Valley, the only working oil field in the country, has remaining reserves of 14 million tonnes of oil that require expensive recovery technology. No serious oil exploration has been done elsewhere, although the Chu and Aksay valleys are believed to be promising (Curtis 1996).

On the other end, Kyrgyzstan has been negotiating with Gazprom and Itera of Russia to supply natural gas from Turkmenistan via the Uzbek pipeline. Two additional pipelines which were started several years ago but had never been completed are also under consideration as potential projects. One of these uncompleted pipelines is a second branch of the Uzbek pipeline which was begun in Soviet times, but was suspended because of lack of money; about $16 million in construction funding is still needed. There is also a second partially completed pipeline from Russia to Kyrgyzstan, which has had no construction activity since 1991. Kyrgyzstan is in talks with Russia and Kazakhstan about completing this pipeline, which would require an additional $60 million (Global Security 2010: 2).

The Kyrgyzstan electricity grid consists of more than 10,000 kilometres of power transmission lines of 35 kilovolts or greater and more than 58,000 kilometres of high voltage lines of 0.4–10 kilovolts. There are more than 500 operating substations of 35–500 kilovolt capacity. Kyrgyzstan has identified construction of a new 500 kilovolt (kV) transmission line from Frunzenskaya to Kemin as a strategic need for the country (Ibid). Implementation would help improve the reliability of electricity supply to the northern part of the country. The German bank KfW (Kreditanstalt fuer Wiederaufbau) has financed a feasibility study for the project and might be one of the financiers.

Kyrgyzstan's electricity distribution grid is presently in need of rehabilitation, as not enough resources have been allocated in previous years for maintenance. As much as $180 million could be required for this upgrade. The result of these years of neglect is that there are substantial electricity losses of up to 25 per cent that occur during transmission through the grid. Grid management is also in need of improvement; non-payment of electricity is common (especially in Bishkek), and there are payment privileges for certain customers. Overall, almost half of all electricity generated does not produce any revenue.

Kyrgyzstan exports over 10 per cent of the electricity it produces and increased exports are planned. However, Kyrgyzstan currently lacks the transmission lines to implement this. The possibilities for constructing transmission lines to China are being studied. Kyrgyzstan has tried to improve its electric system. In July

2000, the Ala–Archa substation on the outskirts of Bishkek was opened, an $11 million project partly funded by the Asian Development Bank. The substation is intended to prevent interruption of service to people in Bishkek and northern Kyrgyzstan.

Four regional electricity distribution companies are coming into existence (as independent joint-stock companies). Vostokelectoset will serve the eastern part of Kyrgyzstan and will incorporate the distribution grids of the Naryn and Issyk-Kul regions. Oshelectro will service the Osh region of the country, Djalal-Abadelectro will service the southern Djalal-Abad region, and Sevelectro will service the Bishkek, Chu and Talas regions (Global Security 2010: 2).

The energy crisis in Kyrgyzstan is more than just a shortage of water and electricity. The energy sector does not attract significant investment and is plagued by poor governance. Improvements in accountability and transparency are required to overcome the major problems facing this sector. A collapse of the energy sector would have far-reaching consequences in Kyrgyzstan and could become the catalyst for widespread social unrest, which would, in all likelihood, harm the wider region, reflecting the complex upstream–downstream dependencies of Central Asia.

Tajikistan

Tajikistan – smallest among the Central Asian states – occupies an area of about 140,000 sq kilometres. Like Kyrgyzstan, Tajikistan is also a country with 93 per cent covered by mountains (IHA 2019) and 73 per cent out of the total population of 1.7 million live in rural areas and have no or little access to adequate energy supply, particularly in winter (UNDP 2010). Today over 95 per cent of Tajikistan's power generation capacity is based on hydroelectricity. However, the infrastructure is old and no significant investments have been made in the sector over the past two decades. Almost every winter the country is faced with an energy crisis and is dependent on unreliable electricity imports from neighbouring countries (Ibid). The absence of reliable electricity supply has forced large parts of the rural population to increasingly turn to the burning of conventional biomass and fossil fuels to meet their energy needs. This has compelled Tajikistan to look for reform in the energy sector with strategic priority in 2018.

Energy profile

The energy sector of Tajikistan includes several entities. The electric power is the responsibility of the state-owned joint-stock company Barqi Tojik, which entirely controls production, transportation and distribution of electricity in Tajikistan. Oil and gas production and development of oil and gas deposits are the responsibility of the State Committee for Oil and Gas. Distribution of natural and liquefied gas in Tajikistan is carried out by the national gas company

TajikGas, while import and distribution of oil products are carried out by the State Company Tajiknefteproduct. The coal-mining sector is controlled by the State Committee for Industry.

Tajikistan has 4.4 gigawatts (GW) of generating capacity, about 90 per cent of which is hydroelectric. A major portion of this hydroelectric capacity is used in aluminium production, which consumes 40 per cent of all the country's electric power. Tajikistan produces practically no oil, gas or coal of its own. However, Tajikistan imports 43 billion cubic feet of natural gas per year, mostly from Uzbekistan (Global Security 2010a: 1).

i. Oil

Tajikistan has proven reserves of 12 million barrels of oil. Most of them are located in the northern part of the country in the Leninobod Soghd Region. The national oil company is Tajikneftegaz, which handles oil exploration, drilling and production. In 2001, Tajik oil production was only 350 bl/d. There was a long period of production decline since Tajikistan produced 1311 b/d in 1992. This decrease has been attributed to the 1992–97 civil war, economic troubles, and lack of investment in the oil infrastructure (Ibid).

Tajikistan consumes 29,000 bl/d of oil products, almost all of which are imported. The main source is Uzbekistan, which provides 70 per cent of Tajikistan's oil product imports. In July 2001, Tajikistan brought its first small oil refinery online at Konibodom. The refinery has a capacity of 400 b/d and produces gasoline, diesel fuel, kerosene and fuel oil. The production is far too small for the country's needs; however; Tajikistan still imports almost all its oil as refined petroleum products (Ibid).

ii. Natural gas

Tajikistan has 200 billion cubic feet (bcf) of natural gas reserves, comprised of several fields. In 2000, Tajikistan began operations in the Khoja Sartez field in the southern Khatlon region and also increased its activity in the Qizil Tumshuq deposit in the Kolkhozobod district of the southern Khatlon region. Tajikistan also tried to increase its gas production in 2000, by exploratory drilling in the Khatlon region. Some of the drillings were successful enough to interest China in future drilling activities. The total natural gas production for Tajikistan in 2000 was 1.4 bcf. With its small domestic production, Tajikistan must rely on imports for 95 per cent of the natural gas it consumes (Global Security 2010a: 1).

Tajikistan has had continuing problems in paying for the gas it imports. There is an intergovernmental agreement with Uzbekistan for a fixed annual quantity, but consumption has been running ahead of schedule. An additional problem is that only 18 per cent of the gas consumed in 2001 was paid for by users. As a result of these issues, Tajikistan has had to cut off non-paying customers and negotiate with suppliers for more gas (Global Security 2010a: 1).

iii. Hydroelectricity

A mountainous country, Tajikistan hosts 55 per cent of the Aral Sea basin's hydraulic resources, from which much of the water furnished to the five Central Asian republics comes. In terms of hydraulic resources per capita, Tajikistan holds first and third place in Central Asia and globally respectively (Guerin 2007).

The major river system in Tajikistan is the Amudarya watershed (Global Security 2010a: 2). The Amudarya River itself only forms a relatively small portion of Tajikistan's southern border with Afghanistan as it flows westward then north-west toward the Aral Sea. Its major tributaries within Tajikistan include the Panj River along the southern border of Tajikistan with Afghanistan, the Gunt and Bartango rivers in the eastern part of the country, and the Kafirnigan and Vakhsh rivers in central and western Tajikistan. Of these, the Vakhsh is the most important, in terms of power production potential (Ibid).

There is a greater hydroelectric power capacity in Tajikistan than any other country in Central Asia. Tajikistan has the potential to produce more than 300 billion kilowatt-hours of electricity per year but currently produces only 16.5 billion kilowatt-hours. The majority of Tajikistan's hydroelectric energy is produced by the hydroelectric stations on the Vakhsh River, with a total capacity of about 3800 megawatts (MW), producing 14 billion kilowatt-hours annually (Ibid). The largest of these is the Nurek hydroelectric facility, which is rated at 3000 MW. An even larger facility at Roghun (which at 335 metres height will be the tallest dam in the world) is under construction and will have a capacity of 3600 MW (Ibid). But little is being done at present, partly because of security problems in the area. There are also concerns about the relatively high seismic activity of the area, which presents engineering as well as safety issues.

Tajikistan currently has a moderately large hydropower plant under construction at Sangtuda. The Khatlon dam for this power plant (also referred to as the Sangtuda 1 and 2 power stations) is being built with Russian and Iranian financing. Overall, the two Sangtuda power stations are expected to generate nearly 900 MW of electricity (Ibid). This has been a very long-duration project which was started back in the Soviet days but has sat in limbo for many years because of lack of funding. The government of Tajikistan now considers Sangtuda 2 to be a priority and is willing to commit state resources toward its completion. An even larger hydroelectric facility is in the planning stages for Shurob, which could have a generating capacity of about 750 MW. A similar-sized facility is planned for Kaphtarguzar, on the Obikhingou River in the Garm Valley, while a truly mammoth hydroelectric facility of about 4000 MW capacity is being planned for Dashtijum, on the Panj River along the Afghan border (Ibid).

In 2018,

> Tajik President Emomali Rahmon inaugurated the first of six turbines at the 3,600 MW Rogun hydropower scheme, which began operations in

2018, adding a much needed 600 MW of capacity to the grid. The dam height was reported to reach 75 metres at the end of 2018 and will be the world's tallest at 335 metres upon completion in 2032.

(IHA 2019)

CASA 1000

Alongside hydropower, development of the grid network is a focus for the government. With diplomatic relations much improved in recent years, Tajik–Uzbek transmission lines were restored in April 2018 allowing annual export of up to 1.5 TWh to Uzbekistan. Also, the CASA 1000 project is progressing and will bolster regional trading opportunities with Afghanistan and Pakistan once completed (IHA 2019).

The Central Asia–South Asia Regional Electricity Market (CASAREM) is based on the vision of a Greater Central Asia. This, in turn, is based on the premise that Central and South Asia are, or can become, a single integrated unit committed to economic activity and growth.

Energy policy

Despite existing reserves of different fuel and energy resources, Tajikistan needs to import them all. The problem of provision with power resources is very acute. Analysis of fuel and energy resources in the Republic of Tajikistan shows that extraction decreased twofold in 2001 in comparison with the extraction in 1990; oil plus gas condensate decreased by 8.8 times; power output by 14 per cent; coal extraction by more than by 28.6 times. At one time, the consumption level of natural gas decreased by 4–5 times, petroleum and oil products by 6 times, coal by more than 70 times. Imports of fuel and energy complex products to the republic were reduced, on petroleum and oil products by 1.5 million tonnes, on natural gas by 1.6 billion tonnes, on gas liquids by 100,000 tonnes, whilst coal was supplied in insignificant volumes (Ministry of Energy and Industry of the Republic of Tajikistan 2010).

In these hard times, the requirement of a well-versed energy policy becomes highly evident. Although Tajikistan has an official energy policy, as such, however, it has certain aims and objectives in the sphere of energy production, consumption and investment. Energy policy, which follows in the republic, is providing a rise in the integration of energetic systems.

The primary regulatory–legal base for the collaboration of the republic with other countries in the area of fuel and energy complex must be based on the Law of the Republic of Tajikistan "about energy". Similarly, interstate bilateral and multilateral agreements and contracts should also toe the lines of the law of the land.

Formulation of policies based on the regulatory and legal framework of the republic keeping in mind the main purpose of this policy will yield results as follow:

- the perfection of the regulatory–legal base must aim towards the free movement of capital, labour resources and manufacturing equipment between fuel and energy complex state-partners;
- making and mechanism conservation rapport on the market of states, adjusted for mutual interests of state-partners;
- assistance for making and stimulation activities of interstate fuel and energy companies, interest, consortium;
- Working of mechanism problem-solving of mutual non-payments in the energetic, including on the basis of clearing, bill agreements, interests, and nettings, agreements with joint ownership (Ministry of Energy and Industry of the Republic of Tajikistan 2010).

The main aim in the sphere of development of fuel and energy complex is well-balanced usage of fuel-energy and water resources and insurance of stable fuel and energy provision in the republic. It was necessary to solve the following objectives for reliable provision with fuel and energy resources between 2003 and 2015:

- development of perspective prognosis of needs of the Republic of Tajikistan in energy resources and possible ways of its provision;
- fuel-energy and water resource development, creation of appropriate infrastructure with attracting state and international investments;
- at the base of perspective prognosis, the conclusion of long-term bilateral and multilateral intergovernmental agreements between producing countries and consuming countries for energy resources supply with mutual responsibility of sides on respecting these agreements;
- rehabilitation of economic relations in spheres of fuel and energy complex, power-plant industry, power equipment and combined branches at the base of development of intergovernmental scientific–technical programmes between Eurasian region countries and staff preparation for its realization;
- rehabilitation of the functioning process of unified gas, petroleum, coal and electricity provision systems;
- raising of work reliability and technical security of pipeline transport, higher voltage lines and other equipment;
- active usage of ecologically poor and safety power-supply apparatus and untraditional types of energy (Ministry of Energy and Industry of the Republic of Tajikistan 2010).

Turkmenistan

Turkmenistan is one of the five Caspian Sea littoral states with large volumes of oil and natural gas deposits. It has vast reserves of oil and gas. Its proven hydrocarbon reserves run from offshore Caspian fields to the Darya Basin reserves bordering Uzbekistan. Although natural gas is Turkmenistan's most important export resource, it also produces significant quantities of oil and has about 600 million barrels of proven reserves (*Oil and Gas Journal* 2016). The country's estimated total petroleum and other liquids production in 2015 was 261,000 barrels per day an increase from 2014, which averaged 249,000 bl/d (BP 2016). It has two oil refineries in Sheidi and Turkmenbashi with a total crude oil distillation capacity of almost 237,000 bl/d (EIA 2018).

Energy profile

Turkmenistan is an energy leader in Central Asia. The country with the lowest population in the region has the fourth-largest estimated gas reserves of the world. It exports about 65 bcm gas to China, around 10 bcm gas to Russia and more than 50 bcm gas to Iran. With the operationalization of the Turkmenistan–Afghanistan–Pakistan–India pipeline (TAPI), it would export up to 33 bcm and the Turkmenistan–Europe gas pipeline exports 30 bcm through the Trans-Caspian Gas pipeline (Khan 2016). Besides,

> Turkmenistan has ambitious plans to bring power generation capacity to about 26 billion kWh by 2020 and to 35 billion kWh by 2030 by upgrading existing power stations and building new ones. The country has announced plans to build 14 new gas turbine power stations with a total capacity of 4,000 megawatts by 2020.
>
> *(Ibid)*

i. Natural gas

Turkmenistan is known for its enormous gas deposits. It is credited to be the sixth-largest natural gas reserve holder in the world and placed among the top 15 natural gas producers of the world with estimated proven gas reserves of 265 trillion cubic feet (*Oil and Gas Journal* 2016). In 2015 two new gas fields, namely Garakel and Bagli, were discovered near the Galkynysh field. These fields are estimated to hold around 42 tcf of recoverable resources (EIA 2018). Apart from this, the country is blessed with several of the world's largest natural gas fields including ten with over 10.5 tcf of reserves. These fields are located primarily in the Amu Darya basin in the south-east, Muga basin in the south, and the South Caspian basin in the western part of the country (Ibid).

As far as production of gas is concerned, Turkmenistan as of 2015 produced more than 2.5 tcf of dry natural gas. The Galkynysh gas field – the second-largest gas field in the world started its production in 2013. In the first year, the gas field produced 1 tcf in full capacity while in 2014 it increased its capacity to 1.2 tcf and the Turkmen energy ministry plans to produce 3.3 tcf gas from this field annually (EIA 2018).

As of 2018, Turkmenistan was the leading gas exporter among the Caspian and Central Asian countries. It had exported 1.3 tcf via pipeline in 2015 itself.

Most of its gases went to China, Russia and Iran. It entered into several natural gas contracts with China in 2013 and is stated to supply 2.3 tcf of natural gas to China by 2020 through the Central Asia–China Pipeline (CACP) (EIA 2018). In December 2015 Turkmenistan began construction of its part of the TAPI pipeline project. This pipeline starts from Galkynysh in Turkmenistan and ends in north India and has a proposed capacity of more than 1 tcf per year.

ii. Oil

Unlike gas, when it comes to oil, Turkmenistan also lacks any international export pipelines, with a single import line running from Kazakhstan. As a result, Turkmenistan exports all of its oil by barge across the Caspian. A small amount is shipped north to the Russian port of Makhachkala. The rest is shipped to Baku in Azerbaijan, for transportation on the BTC (Baku–Tbilisi–Ceyhan pipeline), or is swapped in Neka, Iran for revenues from Iranian oil exported through the Persian Gulf (Ibid).

Turkmenistan is the largest Central Asian producer of natural gas. It has been counted among the world's top 15 producers (Ibid). Major Turkmen gas fields include the Amu Darya in the east, the Murgab Basin, and the south Caspian Basin in the west. As far as oil is concerned, Turkmenistan has both onshore and offshore fields. In 2017, Turkmenistan's oil production capacity including all liquids was about 200,000 bbl/d (EIA 2018).

Turkmenistan in Central Asian energy geopolitics

The death of Turkmen President Saparmurat Niyazov in 2006 led to a shift in political relations among the Central Asia states and has created an opportunity for foreign investment in the country. Under President Gurbangugly Berdmuhammedov, Turkmenistan promises to be a more stable legal environment. Because of its large gas reserves, Turkmenistan remains an area of interest to the EU, though Russia has tried to lock up Turkmenistan's onshore fields. Yet, there is still room for European companies to develop Turkmenistan's offshore reserves. Turkmenistan's disagreement with Azerbaijan over the ownership of the Kyapaz/Serdar field in the Caspian Sea, however, is an obstacle to a greater Western orientation of Turkmen energy exports. Settlement of this dispute would speed up the development of offshore fields. This would likely feed the BTC and Baku–Tbilisi–Erzurum (BTE) pipelines and might even make a trans-Caspian pipeline more viable (Denison 2008: 97-98).

Energy policy of Turkmenistan

Turkmenistan has the world's fourth-largest estimated reserves of natural gas. The country, in pursuit of diversifying its energy supplies in order to avoid overdependence on Russia or China, and to develop its economy and sell its rich natural resources both to the Western and Eastern markets has developed its own energy policy.

According to Turkmenistan's president, diversification of oil and gas pipelines transit and various hydrocarbon projects has created appropriate conditions for prioritizing Turkmenistan's international economic and investment relations with energy-consuming countries. Moreover, Turkmenistan has strategic priorities, due to its hydrocarbon resources reserves, diversification of energy transits pipelines and geopolitical condition. As part of its energy diversification strategy apart from the China–Turkmenistan gas pipeline projects, Ashgabat is pushing forward with two main projects trying to diversify its energy supply routes in order to decrease its dependency on China. One of the projects is the Trans-Caspian pipeline to deliver Turkmen gas to Europe. Another is the TAPI pipeline, which will deliver Turkmen gas to Pakistan and India via Afghanistan.

Furthermore, Turkmenistan pursues the politics of a "balanced policy" to reduce its dependence on "Gazprom"; but at the same time, this does not damage the Russian gas monopoly policy. As a result, Turkmenistan has built relations with Russia, China and other countries interested in Turkmen gas, as well as the implementation of various pipeline projects involving Turkmenistan. It is obvious that Turkmenistan prioritizes its own national interests, and only then the interests of Russia, China and other countries. This could be a reason why each of these countries tries to offer better terms and conditions to Turkmenistan.

> Energy policy of Turkmenistan is based on diversified operationalization and channelization of energy resources, efficiency and saving of energy, optimal use of energy resources, energy security, investments, energy diplomacy, innovations and the last but not the least development of renewable or green energy resources. Moreover, increasing internal/national production capacity to meet external demands, diversifying energy export routes, increasing export capacity, securing energy transportation and networks to external markets are also salient features of its energy policy.
>
> *(Khan 2016)*

Uzbekistan

Located in the heart of Central Asia, Uzbekistan is a double landlocked country with desert covering 80 per cent and mountains in the east reaching over 4500 metres high. The most populated country in the region, the country is blessed with natural resources including natural gas, petroleum and coal. Its energy sectors are well developed and modern. It is among the top ten gas producers of the world. Among the primary energy resources, natural gas is the main source and constitutes nearly 85 per cent of the total amount of energy it produces.

Energy Profile

Uzbekistan is currently the second-largest producer of Central Asian gas. Because of larger domestic demand, it exports much less of its gas than Turkmenistan. As it is not a littoral state, lack of direct access to the Caspian Sea compels Uzbekistan to rely on overland export routes. The lack of economic and political reforms though has stifled the necessary FDI (Mahnovski 2007: xiv–xv). The *Oil and Gas Journal* in 2016 estimated that Uzbekistan had 594 million barrels of proven oil reserves, with 171 discovered oil and natural gas fields in the country (*Oil and Gas Journal* 2016). The majority of the known oil fields in Uzbekistan are in the Bukhara–Khiva region, including the Kokdumalak field, which accounts for about 70 per cent of the country's oil production. The country also has oil fields in the Ferghana Valley region in the northeast, the Ustyurt plateau and the Aral Sea (Ibid). The Ferghana basin bridging Uzbekistan, Kyrgyzstan and Tajikistan contains huge reserves according to the USGS. Most of Uzbekistan's petroleum production consists of about 60 per cent high sulphur crude and 40 per cent gas condensate (Ibid). Existing fields are depleting faster than new discoveries coming on line, spurring the need for further investment. Despite having reserve levels similar to those of Turkmenistan, Uzbekistan produces significantly less oil due to a decade without significant investment in the upstream sector (Ibid).

In contrast to oil production, Uzbekistan's gas production is much stronger with around 2 tcf in 2016. Even though its domestic consumption is high at 1766 bcf per year, Uzbekistan has still maintained its position as a net exporter of gas. Its reserves of 65 tcf may allow it to continue to be a net exporter for some time (EIA 2018).

Uzbekistan's natural gas production comes from 52 different fields and 12 major regions. The Shurtan, Kokdumalak, Gazli, Pamuk and Khauzak regions account for 95 per cent of gas production (Ibid). Many of its oil fields are old, prompting Uzbekistan to urgently seek the development of new fields. While Uzbekistan consumes much of its gas production, it managed to expand exports by 10 per cent between 2015 and 2016. Over half of its exports are sent to Russia and the rest are sold to Central Asian neighbours like Kazakhstan. Uzbekistan currently serves as a transit point for Turkmen gas travelling to Russia via Kazakhstan. When the Turkmen–China line is completed, Uzbekistan may use that as an additional export route (Ibid). Besides, Uzbekistan has significant coal reserves and hydro-electricity potentials.

Uzbekistan in Central Asian energy geopolitics

After signs that its oil and gas production was slowing in 2005, Uzbekistan actively sought to attract foreign investment for exploration and additional production. It primarily formed new contracts with Russian and Asian companies. The main companies now operating in Uzbekistan are Russia's Gazprom,

Soyuzneftegaz and Lukoil; China's CNPC; Malaysia's Petronas; and Korea's KNOC (IEA 2018).

Uzbekistan's ability to serve customers like the European Union is currently very limited. Its gas networks are inefficient and dominated by Russia's Gazprom. To maintain steady exports, Uzbekistan sometimes has to cut gas to its domestic consumers, causing anger among its citizens (Hall 2008: 73). This instability in supply, coupled with Uzbekistan's human rights violations have created uncertainty on the future of its relationship with the West. In the short run, China poses a great opportunity for export of any additional gas, and Russia tends to be less critical than the West.

Energy policy

Uzbekistan adopted its energy policy in the early years of its independence intending to maintain its energy security by using energy resources for the socio-economic development of Uzbekistan. Government policy has focused on achieving its main energy strategy priorities, namely, to:

- achieve fuel independence by increasing petroleum and natural gas condensate output;
- create a reliable raw materials base for the energy sector;
- maximize the public's access to natural and liquefied gas, electricity and the latest types of fuels;
- promote the financial stability of and attract more investments in the energy sector;
- develop the energy sector's legal framework and improve its financial–taxation system, taking into account the peculiarities of price formation and how the energy sector interacts with closely allied sectors;
- use energy resources more efficiently; and
- promote competition in the energy sector by consistently establishing entities that are genuine market entities and consistently building an economic infrastructure that is a genuine market economy infrastructure (UNDP 2007).

The Caspian Sea in the energy geopolitics

The Caspian is the world's largest inland sea. It has a sea basin of around 700 miles. It is surrounded by the five riparian states of Azerbaijan, Turkmenistan, Kazakhstan, Russia and some part of Iran and adjacent countries of Central Asia and the Caucasus (Dekmejian and Simonian 2001: 3). Iran is a member of the Organization of Petroleum Exporting countries (OPEC) and the rest form a part of the Former Soviet Union (FSU), since the split in 1991. Russia, Kazakhstan, Azerbaijan form a part of the Non-OPEC and Non-Organisation for Economic Co-operation and Development (OECD) group along with Latin America,

Africa and China. FSU contributes 11.60 million barrels per day of crude oil production in the group (2009: 76).

The primary factor that brought world attention towards the Caspian Basin was the prospect of its large oil and gas deposits found in this region. Consisting of five littoral states, namely, Russia, Iran, Azerbaijan, Kazakhstan and Turkmenistan, it accounts for 7 per cent of the total world gas production (Patnaik 2016, Dekmejian and Simonain 2001). This is much higher than its oil share in total world oil output. Although the Caspian region has a huge energy resource base, there is hardly any consensus among littoral states and outside powers about the exact energy potential of the basin. In the mid-1970s, the Soviet estimates were around 35 billion barrels (Dekmejian and Simonian: 29, Patnaik 2016). However, a decade later other estimates stated that it had around 10–11 bn barrels. Nevertheless, in 1994 when the "Contract of the Century" was signed between Azerbaijan and a Consortium of eight oil companies in September, the energy resources of the Caspian littoral states were said to be comparable to those of the Emirates of Kuwait (Pradhan 2010). Other estimates, on the other hand, placed Caspian reserves on a par with the massive energy wealth of the Persian Gulf.

In 1997, the US government stepped in and announced that the Caspian Region possessed around 15.6 billion proven and 163 billion possible barrels of oil (Dekmejian and Simonian: 30). However, the first credible study on Caspian energy potential was done by Wood Mackenzie, a Scottish consulting company in 1998. It revealed that the combined proven oil and gas reserves of Azerbaijan, Kazakhstan, Turkmenistan and Uzbekistan were 68 billion oil barrels equivalent. Of this amount, the total for oil was 25.2 billion barrels, 65 per cent of which belonged to Kazakhstan (16.43 bn), and the rest to Azerbaijan (6.5 bn), Turkmenistan (0.91 bn) and Uzbekistan (1.34 bn) (Ibid). Two further studies published in April 1998 by Rice University's Baker Institute and the International Institute of Strategic Studies of London (Ibid) confirmed Wood Mackenzie's figures. Even with this energy potential, the Caspian seemed important for energy-consuming countries. Given India's healthy and cordial relations with all littoral states, it needs to step ahead with massive economic investments backed with political willpower to ensure its energy security.

Caught in the throes of the restructuring of global power relations after the Soviet demise, the Caspian has emerged as a focal point of world attention. The situation is reminiscent of the 19th century's great game between the clashing imperial ambitions of Great Britain and Russia. However, the new Great Game over the Caspian and Central Asian region is more complex than the old in its scope, determinants and implications. But the main concern is why did the Caspian become a centre of international attention in the last decade of the 20th century? Why was it accorded such a prominent position in the crowded policy agenda of the United States, the West vis-à-vis the Russian Federation, China, Japan, India and Pakistan and so on?

History of the Caspian

The Caspian Sea has had a history of oil production right from the start. It was perceived as a modern El Dorado with the discovery of oil reserves. Oil, as early as 2600 years ago, was used to scare the enemy fleets. The record of oil being extracted dates back to the 7th century. Way back, primary methods were used to extol the western shores of the Caspian (Baku), with the first well being drilled at Bibi-Aybat in 1846. During the period between 1850 and 1891, the production of oil rose to 22.5 billion tonnes from 300 million tonnes. This enhancement in the activity of the Black Gold increased the inflow of expertise and labour into the Caspian countries. The oil industry had begun to develop, with the entrance of players like the Nobel Brothers starting the Nobel Oil Extraction Company in 1873. The year 1877 saw the launch of the first oil tanker, *The Zoroaster.* After that, pipelines were laid for the transport of oil to Western markets which cut down costs to about one-fifth of the earlier total. New players like Rothschild Company and Shell had entered the market in the Caspian. They altered the face of the oil industry by the introduction of transportation means like railways and the construction of more major pipelines (Ibid: 76–77).

As a block stone, the Russian revolution nationalized the oil industry in 1920. Owing to the Communist protests, Shell and Rothschild retreated from the countries, draining the aid to the industry. However, due to the discovery of oil in Russia, it became the second-largest oil-producing nation in the world. This facilitated a flow of cheap oil in the world, thus lowering fuel prices. OPEC was formed by the Middle East as a revolt against Soviet expansion. In response to this formation, the Soviet oil industry started its downfall. With the short-term accomplishment of objectives leading to an improperly planned utilization of reserves and mindless drilling of wells slowly terminated the chances of the Soviet Union to achieve and be successful in the long run. Later, the collapse of the Soviet Union led to an extended decline owing to the drop in the economy of the region (Ibid: 76–77).

Although the Caspian Basin is one of the earliest sources of oil production in the world, significant extraction of the resources began only in the nineteenth century. Today, despite years of under-investment, engineering difficulties and the problem of piping the oil and gas to markets outside of the region, the Central Asian and Caspian fields are emerging as some of the most important in the world. This importance is not just based on the physical volume of oil and gas, estimated at 48 billion barrels of oil and 292 trillion cubic feet of gas (EIA 2013). It is based on the fact that the flow of Central Asian hydrocarbons could help to meet the burgeoning world demand and provide a surplus that would help regulate world prices in times of temporary shortage (Johnson 2007: 198). The offshore fields of the CSR account for 41 per cent of the total Caspian crude oil and lease condensate and 36 per cent of natural gas. In addition to this, the US Geological Survey (EIA 2013) estimated another 20 billion barrels of oil and 243 trillion cubic feet of natural gas is yet to be recovered from the sea basin.

For decades, Saudi-based oil companies generated sufficient reserves to assist in the regulation of prices. They poured more oil into the markets if prices increased or reduced their production when more oil was being sold from other areas such as Nigeria, Russia or South America. However, the rapid growth in consumption in the Asia–Pacific region in the last years of the 20th and early years of the 21st centuries, and conflicts in Southwest Asia, all but eliminated the surplus reserves available in the Middle East. Attention has therefore been focused on processing more oil but also on developing new fields for extraction, and Central Asia and the Caspian Basin region are under the spotlight. This is why the region has been in the limelight of great power politics extending for years, decades and centuries.

Legal status of the Caspian Sea

The Caspian Sea littoral states, including Russia, Azerbaijan, Iran, Kazakhstan and Turkmenistan, on August 12, 2018 signed the Convention on the Legal Status of the Caspian Sea pending for last three decades (CMS 2018). The Convention, which agreed to be operational for unlimited duration, has the following key features:

1. It establishes a 15-mile wide sovereign water zone, plus an additional 10 nautical miles of exclusive fishing zones followed by common waters;
2. The construction of underwater pipelines doesn't require parties' unanimity. A party proposing to construct a pipeline only needs to agree (on a bilateral basis) with the party through whose territory the pipeline will cross. However, the route of the pipeline must be communicated to the remaining signatories;
3. The key conditions for the construction of pipelines are compliance with environmental standards and requirements including compliance with the Framework Convention for the protection of the Marine Environment of the Caspian Sea; and
4. The Caspian Sea is declared a zone of peace and only signatories can deploy military assets in the Caspian Sea (CMS 2018).

The dilemma on whether the Caspian Sea is a "sea" or a lake and which international law should regulate its delineation, going on since the 1990s, ended for all practical purposes with the signing of the much needed Convention. However, one of the most controversial issues – the sectoral division of the hydrocarbon-rich seabed has been left for further multilateral discussions. Although commercial challenges to pipeline projects will persist for a while, the convention definitely will provide an impetus towards the realization of the Trans-Caspian pipeline effectively in a time-bound manner. The legal status of the Caspian Sea is well depicted in Table 2.21.

TABLE 2.21 Caspian legal status alternatives

Classification	*Applicable regime*	*Effect*
Sea	United Nations Convention on Law of the Sea (UNCLOS, 1982)	– Coastal states have "territorial sea", breadth not exceeding 12 miles, and continental shelf – Territorial seas do not extend "beyond the median line every point of which is equidistant from the nearest points on the baselines from which the breadth of the territorial seas of each of the two states is measured" – Land-locked states (Azerbaijan, Kazakhstan, Turkmenistan) can claim right of access to high seas
Lake	Customary international law governing border lakes	– Border states regulate use of water through international agreements – Each state has exclusive rights over resources and water surface in its national sector – Lakes can be delimited several different ways, such as by coastal line or median line

Source: EIA, 2013, August 26.

Distribution of the Caspian reserves

The Caspian Basin has a potential of huge reserves. Much of the reserves have not yet been explored and those are predicted to be much larger than the amount estimated. It is said that an additional 184 million barrels of oil are possible from the basin. The gas to oil ratio for the Caspian is much higher as compared to the Middle East. As far as projections go, it was estimated that by 2010, the oil production would double and the gas reserves would be twice that of Saudi Arabia. However, owing to the economic scene, the ability of the region to develop those reserves depends on how well they develop relations with the energy companies.

The Caspian is in a dilemma of being classified as a lake or a sea. But this might seem small in front of the issue of dividing the reserves, both on the seabed and the shore, among the surrounding countries. Efforts to reach a multilateral agreement have failed, leading to the formation of a Special Working Committee to help reach an agreement over the sea. Russia seems to have taken the lead in forging individual agreements, in the absence of a multilateral agreement. Russia, Kazakhstan and Azerbaijan have signed an agreement among themselves in order to divide the resources as per the agreement. The hydrocarbon fields falling on the line of the divide (Median delimitation line) is the distinct line that divides the Caspian into the Northern, Middle, and Southern region. These are settled between the concerned nations based on mutual decisions (three disputed fields between Russia and Kazakhstan). However, the lines of the agreement are only applicable to the seabed resources (2009: 76–78).

Due to the energy resources that Central Asia boasts, this region has once again assumed a pivotal position in international affairs. Like the United States, the European Union, Russia and China pursue access to the region's energy; they must not only engage each other but must also court each newly independent state. For the Central Asian states, this international interest offers both opportunity and threat. New export routes promise greater economic reward and less dependency, but with each new pipeline new enemies are created and the weight of the global powers in the region threatens to undermine political autonomy.

In the immediate post-Cold War, the advantage shifted to the West in the new geopolitics of Central Asian energy. Russia was preoccupied with its internal turmoil and China was slower to significantly engage the region. Today, however, Russia has awoken to the economic and political gains that it might secure by reasserting its influence over the whole of Central Asia. United States actions may be interpreted as primarily driven by strategic aims to discourage the monopolization of Central Asian energy by any one state and prevent any state that it identifies as a threat from realizing economic gains from energy export. Practically, this means encouraging pipeline routes that directly undermine Russian influence in Central Asia, and continuing the economic isolation of Iran. The European Union has both domestic level motivation and strategic international motivations. Its domestic energy demands drive it to import Central Asian energy, which in turn make it dependent upon pipelines travelling through Russia. The European Union has a strategic interest, therefore, to enhance its energy security by developing new pipelines outside of Russian control. The Nabucco project is a specific example of the ongoing attempt to circumvent Russian territory.

Russia does not possess a domestic demand for more energy, but its economy would benefit from transit fees gained from increasing transportation of Central Asian energy. It could also realize economic gains if it can develop a monopoly over Central Asian gas. And it would allow Russia to dictate the price at which Central Asian states sell their energy and the price at which Europe and China must buy their energy. Additional pipelines passing through Russian territory serve a dual purpose. Building capacity to export rising Central Asian production brings economic benefits, and simultaneously, these pipelines secure energy that might have flowed directly to the West, Iran or China. The Russian South Stream pipeline proposal may be seen as a direct counter to the Nabucco pipeline. These pipelines serve the same market and cannot both be economically viable, so there is a race to see which may be activated first.

China, like the European Union, is driven to engage Central Asian energy geopolitics because of its domestic demands for additional energy consumption. It too possesses strategic motivations to enhance its energy security. In the pipeline deal with Kazakhstan, China secured its first international pipeline, and it now anticipates complementing this oil pipeline with a gas pipeline very soon. Though China and Russia have been cooperative in Central Asia, Chinese unwillingness to remain dependent on Russia for overland energy

TABLE 2.22 Caspian basins proved and probable reserves

Caspian basins proved and probable reserves		
Country	*Crude oil and lease condensate (billion bbl)*	*Natural gas (Tcf)*
Azerbaijan	**8.5**	**51**
Offshore Caspian	6.8	46
Onshore Caspian	1.7	5
Iran	**0.5**	**2**
Offshore Caspian	0.5	1
Onshore Caspian	(s)	1
Kazakhstan	**31.2**	**104**
Offshore Caspian	15.7	36
Onshore Caspian	15.5	68
Russia	**6.1**	**109**
Offshore Caspian	1.6	14
Onshore Caspian	4.5	95
Turkmenistan	**1.9**	**19**
Offshore Caspian	1.1	9
Onshore Caspian	0.8	10
Uzbekistan	**(s)**	**7**
Offshore Caspian	0	0
Onshore Caspian	(s)	7
TOTAL CASPIAN	**48.2**	**292**
Offshore Caspian	19.6	106
Onshore Caspian	28.6	186

Source: EIA, 2013, August 26.

supplies demonstrates that it is not blind to the potential threat of a Russian energy monopoly.

At the global level of energy geopolitics in the region, then, the struggle for control of energy production and pipelines appears to often be a zero-sum game. With each new pipeline proposal, there arise clear losers and winners. The question has never been which route is the most efficient. Otherwise, Iran would currently have a greater role in the export of Central Asian energy.

For the Central Asian states, however, regional energy geopolitics is not as clearly a zero-sum game. Kazakhstan has most clearly demonstrated how state energy resources may be utilized to establish positive relationships with each of the global powers while playing these powers against each other to avoid one power gaining economic or political leverage that is too great. This so-called "multi-vector approach", offers a model to the other Central Asian states that have significant energy reserves. Turkmenistan and Uzbekistan, though, do not occupy the same central geographical position occupied by Kazakhstan; their ability to deal directly with the global powers is degraded because of their position deep in the heart of Asia. Any pipelines from these states must pass through other transit states, and development of their energy sectors has lagged behind Kazakhstan. Finally, Tajikistan and Kyrgyzstan, though they have little to offer in this game of energy geopolitics, also immensely benefited.

References

ADB (1997), Energy and Cooperation in Central Asia, Challenges and Opportunities in Energy, Asian Development Bank, available at: www.adb.org/carec/energy.asp.

Akiner, Shirin (1994), "Post-Soviet Central Asia: Past is Prologue", in Peter Ferdinand (ed.), *The New Central Asia and Its Neighbours*, The Royal Institute of International Affairs, London: Pinter Publishers.

Alaolmolki, Nozar (2001), *Life after the Soviet Union*, New York: State University of New York Press.

Banuazizi, Ali and Weiner, Myron (1994), *The New Geopolitics of Central Asia and Its Borderlands*, Colombia: Indiana University Press.

Barry, Michael P. (2009), "Foreign Direct Investments in Central Asian Energy: A CGE Model", *Eurasian Journal of Business and Economics*, 2(3), pp. 35–54.

Begaliev, Mirlan (2016), "Natural Resources of Kyrgyzstan that Will Surprise You", *Prezi*, November 20, available at: https://prezi.com/6qwuvs0qxu2n/natural-resources-of-kyrgyzstan-that-will-surprise-you/ [accessed on April 18, 2020].

BG Group (2013), "Kazakhstan" Available at: http://www.bggroup.com/OurBusiness/WhereWeOperate/Pages/Kazakhstan.aspx [accessed February 26, 2013].

Bloomberg (2012), "Kazakhstan May Limit Borrowings from State Companies", *Bloomberg Business*, May 21, available at: https://www.bloomberg.com/news/articles/2012-05-21/kazakhstan-may-limit-borrowing-by-state-companies-zamishev-says [accessed February 16, 2015].

BP (1997), *BP Statistical Review of World Energy 1997*, British Petroleum, June, available at: http://www.bp.com/liveassets/bp_internet/globalbp/STAGING/global_assets/downloads/S/Stats_Review:1997_slide_pack.pdf [accessed June 10, 2010].

BP (2016), *BP Statistical Review of World Energy*, British Petroleum, March, available at: www.bp.com [accessed on September 11, 2018].

BP (2018), *BP Statistical Review of World Energy*, British Petroleum, March, available at: www.bp.com [accessed on April 14, 2019].

Bulger, Demetrius Charles de Kavanagh (2005), *Central Asian Questions: Essays on Afghanistan, China and Central Asia*, London: Adamant Media Corporation.

CITIC Resources Holdings (2011), "Oil: Karazhanbas Oilfield, Kazakhstan", April 11, Retrieved from: http://www.citicresources.com/eng/business/oil.htm [accessed April 12, 2014].

CMS (2018), "Convention on the Legal Status of the Caspian Sea: Implications for Oil and Gas Companies", *CMS Law Now*, August 22. Retrieved from: www.cms-lawnow.com/ealerts/2018/08/convention-on-the-legal-status-of-the-caspian-sea-implications-for-oil-gas-companies?cc_lang=en [accessed on April 7, 2019].

CNPC (2013), "CNPC in Kazakhstan," China National Petroleum Corporation, Available at: http://www.cnpc.com.cn/en/cnpcworldwide/kazakhstan/?COLLCC=775047979&CO LLCC=1232181519& [accessed February 27, 2014].

Cohen, Ariel (2008), "Kazakhstan: The Road to Independence, Energy Policy and the Birth of a Nation", Central Asia-Caucasus Institute & Silk Road Studies Program Joint Center, Washington, DC: Johns Hopkins University.

Cummings, N. Sally (2012), *Understanding Central Asia: Politics and Contested Transformations*, New York: Routledge.

Curtis, Glenn E (1996), "Kyrgyzstan: A Country Study, Washington: GPO for the Library of Congress", available at: http://www.loc.gov/index.html [accessed on February 20, 2008].

Cutler, M. Robert (2007), "Kazakhstan's Foreign Investment Law Changes Again", *CACI Analyst*, December 12, available at: http://www.cacianalyst.org/?q=node/4754 [accessed on February 20, 2008].

Dave, Bhavna (2008), "The E.U and Kazakhstan: Is the Pursuit of Energy and Security Cooperation Compatible with Promotion of Human Rights and Democratic Reforms?", in Neil J. Melvin (ed.), *Engaging Central Asia: The European Union's New Strategy in the Heart of Eurasia*, Brussels: Centre for European Studies.

Dekmejian, R. Hrair and Simonain, H. Hovann (2001), *Troubled Waters, The Geopolitics of the Caspian Region*. London: I. B. Tauris, p. 28.

Denison, Michael (2008), "Turkmenistan and the EU: Contexts and Possibilities for Greater Engagement", in Neil J. Melvin (ed.), *Engaging Central Asia: The European Union's New Strategy in the Heart of Eurasia*, Brussels: Centre for European Studies.

Dorian, J. P (2002), "Turkmenistan's Future on Gas and Oil Hinges on Certainty for Export Options", *Oil and Gas Journal*, 7 October.

Dorian, J. P. (2006), "Central Asia: A Major Emerging Energy Player in the 21st Century", *Energy Policy*, Vol. 34, December 27, pp. 544–555.

EIA (2004), *International Energy Outlook*, Energy Information Administration, available at: ftp://ftp.eia.doe.gov/forecasting/0484(2004).pdf [accessed on February 2008].

EIA (2009), "Kazakhstan Energy Profile", Energy Information Agency, available at: http://www.eia.doe.gov [accessed on March 12, 2010].

EIA (2009a), "Kyrgyzstan Energy Profile", Energy Information Administration, available at: http://www.tonto.eia.doe.gov/country_energy_data_cfm?fips=kg [accessed on March 12, 2010].

EIA (2012), "Kazakhstan-Country Specific Analysis", U.S. Energy Information Administration, September 2012, available at: https://www.eia.gov/outlooks/aeo/assumptions/pdf/055(2012).pdf [accessed August 15 2017].

EIA (2013), "Oil and Natural Gas Production is Growing in the Caspian Sea Region", Energy Information Administration, September 11, available at: https://www.eia.gov/todayinenergy/detail.php?id=12911 [accessed August 15 2017].

EIA (2016), "The Assumption to the Annual Energy Outlook", U.S. Energy Information Administration, September 2016, available at: https://www.eia.gov/outlooks/aeo/assumptions/pdf/0554(2016).pdf [accessed on August 15 2017].

EIA (2018), "World Oil Transit Chokepoints", U.S Energy Information Administration, July 25 [accessed August 15 2019].

EIA (2019), "Background Reference: Kazakhstan", US Energy Information Administration, January 7, retrieved from: https://www.eia.gov/international/content/analysis/countries_long/Kazakhstan/pdf/kazakhstan_bkgd.pdf

EIU (2017), "Central Asia Falling Short of Power Generation Potential, Energy", *The Economist Intelligence Unit*, December 15, available at: www.eiu.com/industry/article/806239664/central-asia-falling-short-of-power-generation-potential/2017-12-15 [accessed April 14, 2019].

Ekspert Kazakhstan (2010), "Tovarishchi po kazakhstanskoi nefti,"[translated into English: Friends in Kazakh Oil], Ekspert Kazakhstan 39(4), p. 8.

ENI (2018), "World Oil Review", Vol. 1, available at: https://www.eni.com/docs/en_IT/enicom/company/fuel-cafe/WORLD-OIL-REVIEW-2018-Volume-1.pdf [accessed April 19, 2019].

Global Security (2010), "Kyrgyzstan: Energy", available at: www.globalsecurity.org/.../kyrgyz-energy.htm [accessed September 25, 2010].

Global Security (2010a), "Tajikistan: Energy", available at: www.globalsecurity.org/.../tajik-energy.htm [accessed January 11, 2011].

Griffin, T. Andrew (2008), "The January 2007 Amendments of Kazakhstan's Petroleum and Subsoil Use Laws", *DL Piper LLP*, April.

Guerin, Frederique (2007), "Tajikistan's Energy Ambitions", *Caucaz Europe News*, February 8, available at: www.caucaz.com [accessed September 25, 2010].

Hall, Michael (2008), "The EU and Uzbekistan: Where to Go from Here?", in Neil J. Melvin (ed.), *Engaging Central Asia: The European Union's New Strategy in the Heart of Eurasia*, Brussels: Centre for European Studies.

Hanks, Ruel (2008), "'Multi-Vector Politics' and Kazakhstan's Emerging Role as a Geo-Strategic Player in Central Asia", *49th Meeting of the International Studies Association*, San Francisco, CA, March 26.

Hopkirk, Peter (1990), *The Great Game: On Secret Service in High Asia*, London: John Murray Publishers Ltd.

ICG (2007), "Central Asia's Energy Risks, Asia Report", International Crisis Group, Bishkek, No. 133, May 24, p. 12.

IEA (2018), "World Energy Outlook 2018", International Energy Agency, available at: https://webstore.iea.org/world-energy-outlook-2018 [accessed March 8, 2019].

IEA (2019), Kazakhstan - Countries and Regions, International Energy Agency, May, retrieved from: https://www.iea.org/countries/kazakhstan.

IHA (2019), "Tajikistan", International Hydropower Association, May, available at: https://www.hydropower.org/country-profiles/tajikistan [accessed April 18, 2020].

Javaid, Umbreen and Rashid, Azhar (2015), "Oil and Gas Potential of Central Asian Republics and Relations with Pakistan", *Journal of South Asian Studies*, 30(1), pp. 127–148.

Johnson, Rob (2007), *Oil, Islam and Conflict, Central Asia Since 1945*, London: Reaktion Books.

Juraev, Shairbek (2009), "Energy Emergency in Kyrgyzstan: Causes and Consequences", Policy Brief, EU-Central Asia Monitoring, No. 5, February.

Kaushik, Devendra (1970), *Central Asia in Modern Times*, Moscow: Progress Publishers.

Kazakh Ministry of Energy and Mineral Resources (2007), "CIOC Unveils 2007 Work Plan for North-West ZheTybai", Kazakh Ministry of Energy and Mineral Resources, Republic of Kazakhstan.

Kazakhstan Today (2007), "The Senate Approved the First Reading of Amendments to the Law on the Interests of the State in the Economic Sphere", July 10, available at: www.kz-today.kz [accessed July 10, 2009].

KazAtomoprom (2010), National Atomic Company, Kazakhstan, available at: http://www.kazatomprom.kz/en/ [accessed December 10, 2010].

KazMunaiGaz (2006), "Kazakh Company KazTransOil and Batumi Oil Terminal Have Formed a JV", nregion.com, December 23, 2006, available at: www.nregion.com/pringt.php?i=7873 [accessed December 20, 2007].

KazMunaiGaz (2011), "Oil Refining and Marketing", KazMunaiGaz, available at: http://www.kmg.kz/eng/refining/investment/prm/ [accessed January 11, 2011].

KazMunaiGaz (2012), "Oil transportation", available at: http://www.kmg.kz/manufacturing/oil/ [accessed December 13, 2012].

KazMunaygaz (2008), "Kazakhstan's Oil and Gas Sector", February 18, available at: http://www.kmgep.kz/eng/kazakhstan/kazakhstan_oil_and_gas_sector/ [accessed November 2008].

Khan, Mehmood Ul Hasan (2016), "SD Analysis-National Energy Policy of Turkmenistan", Institute of Strategic Thinking, available at: https://www.sde.org.tr/analysis/sd-analysis-national-energy-policy-of-turkmenistan-analizi-7304 [accessed April 15, 2020].

Kenjebayeva, Aigoul (2005), "Transfer of Subsoil Use Rights in Kazakhstan: New Rules", American Chamber of Commerce in Kazakhstan, 2005", available at: http://www.amcham.kz/article.php?article_id=442&PHPSESSID=1ff0de31b8a327d9af5da2317d873096 [accessed March 12, 2008].

KPO (2013), "About the company," Karachaganak Petroleum Operating, available at: http://www.kpo.kz/about-kpo.html?&L=1.

KMGEP (2013), "Oil and Gas Sector", KazMunaiGaz, retrieved from: http://kmgep.kz/eng/about_kazakhstan/oil_and_gas_sector/.

Lukoil (2013), "Kazakhstan," Lukoil, retrieved from: http://www.lukoiloverseas.com/projects/kazakhstan/.

Mackinder, Halford (1904), "The Geographical Pivot of History", *The Geographical Journal*, 170(4), December.

Mackinder, Halford (1919), *Democratic Ideals and Reality*, New York: Greenwood Press.

Mahan, Alfred (1897), *The Influence of Sea Power Upon History, 1660–1783*, Boston, MA: Little Brown.

Mahnovski, Sergei, Akramov, Kamil and Karasik, Theodore (2007), *Economic Dimensions of Security in Central Asia*, Santa Monica, CA: RAND Corporation.

Ministry for Energy and Industry (2015), "Tajikistan towards Development Sustainable Energy, Energy Charter, Regional Energy Cooperation in Central and South Asia meeting", *Ministry for Energy and Industry of the Republic of Tajikistan*, Astana, 7 October.

Ministry of Energy and Industry of the Republic of Tajikistan (2010), "The Concept of Fuel and Energy Complex Spheres of the Republic of Tajikistan during 2003–2015", availableat:http://minenergoprom.tj/index.php?lng=en&id=4&PHPSESSID=276a7597c140d5c48baf92be1ca60aac [accessed September 26, 2010].

Ministry of Industry, Energy and Fuel Resources of the Kyrgyz Republic (2006), available at: http://www.mpe.gov.kg/ru/?d=branchs/energy [accessed September 10, 2010].

Ministry of Industry, Energy and Fuel Resources of the Kyrgyz Republic (2006), "Hydroelectricity Power Stations of Kyrgyzstan," Ministry of Industry, Energy and Fuel Resources, Republic of Kyrgyzstan, available at: http://www.mpe.gov.kg/ru/?d=branchs/energy [accessed September 10, 2010].

Nazarbauev, Nursultan (2008), "Address at the ceremonial meeting dedicated to the 15th Anniversary of Kazakhstan's independence," Economist Intelligence Unit, February 6.

NEP (2010), "The National Energy Programme of the Kyrgyz Republic for 2008-2010 and the Strategy of Fuel and Energy Complex Development until 2025", National Energy Programme, Decree of the Government of the Kyrgyz Republic, No. 47.

Oil and Gas Journal (2008), "Uzbekistan's Energy Profile", *Oil and Gas Journal*. September, available at: http://www.ogj.com/index/search.html?q=Uzbekistan%2527s+energy+profile+2008&sort=rel&type=all [accessed January 9, 2010].

Oil and Gas Journal (2016), "Oil and Gas Profile of CIS Countries", *Oil and Gas Journal*, September, available at: https://www.ogj.com/index.html [accessed September 8, 2018].

Oil and Gas Journal (2017), "Kazakhstan's Energy Profile", *Oil and Gas Journal*. September, available at: http://www.ogj.com/index/search.html?q=Kazakhstan%2527s+energy+profile+2008&sort=rel&type=all [accessed June 10, 2018].

Olcott, Martha-Brill (2007), "KazMunaiGaz: Kazakhstan's National Oil and Gas Company", Carnegie Endowment for International Peace, March.

Orazgaliyev, Serik (2018), "State Intervention in Kazakhstan's Energy Sector: Nationalization or Participation", *Journal of Eurasian Studies*, 9(2), pp. 143–151.

Patnaik, Ajay (2016), *Central Asia: Geopolitics, Security and Stability*, New Delhi: Routledge.

Pradhan, Ramakrushna (2010), *Geopolitics of Central Asia: China-US Engagement*, Germany: VDM Verlag-Muller.

Reuters (2006), "Russia Rejects Expansion of Chevron Oil Link – Paper", *Reuters*, 13 November.

Rosenau, James (1969), *Linkage Politics*, New York: The Free Press, p. 12.

Roul, Avilas (2010), "The Elusive Yet Abundant Hydropower in the Kyrgyz Republic, 2010", *ECO World*, January 15, available at: http://www.ecoworld.com/energy-fuels/the-elusive-yet-abundant-hydropower-in-the-kyrgyz-republic.html [accessed January 11, 2011].

Rumer, Boris (1996), "Disintegration and Reintegration in Central Asia: Dynamics and Prospects", in Boris Rumer (ed.), *Central Asia in Transition: Dilemmas of Political and Economic Development*, New York: M. E. Sharpe.

Russia/CIS Energy Digest (2007), "Oil Production in Kazakhstan Grows to 54.3 Mln T, that of Gas - 25.65 BCM", *Russia/CIS Energy Digest*, 15 January.

Scribd (2009), "The Oil World, a Geopolitical War Field", available at: http://www.scribd.com/doc/14472626/Geopolitics-Oil-Diplomacy [accessed October 18, 2009].

Shiells, R. Clinton (2003), Presentation "FDI and the Investment Climate in the CIS Countries", *IMF*, November 2003, available at: http://www.imf.org/external/pubs/ft/pdp/2003/pdp05.pdf [accessed February 22, 2007].

Sieff, Martin (2004), "Interview: Kazakhstan's Oil Company Chief", *United Press International*, June 28, available at: http://agonist.org/story/2004/6/28/82714/7966 [accessed February 22, 2007].

Smith, Jeff and Berman, Ilan (2011), "Central Asia's Energy Bazaar", *The Wall Street Journal*, January 27, available at: https://www.wsj.com/articles/SB10001424052748703398504576101063649062424 [accessed January 11, 2011].

TCO (2013), "About TCO," Tengizchevroil, available at: http://www.tengizchevroil.com/en/about/ [accessed May 25, 2013].

The Heritage Foundation (2008), "Index of Economic Freedom", available at: http://www.heritage.org/research/features/index/country.cfm?id=Kazakhstan [accessed January 12, 2008].

The New York Times (2004), "Investors Recoil from Oil Terms in Kazakhstan", October 27, available at: http://www.nytimes.com/2004/10/27/business/worldbusiness/27kazakh.html [accessed February 10, 2008].

The New York Times (2004), "Amid Growing Wealth, Nepotism and Nationalism in Kazakhstan", December, 23, available at: http://www.nytimes.com/2004/12/23/business/worldbusiness/23kazakh.html?pagewanted=print [accessed February 10, 2008].

UNDP (2007), "Uzbekistan's Energy Sector", United Nations Development Programme, available at: https://www.undp.org/content/dam/uzbekistan/docs/Publications/environmentandenergy/The_Outlook_for_the_Development_of_Renewable_Energy_in_Uzbekistan/uzb_un_1_The_Outlook_for_the_Development_of_Renewable_Energy_in_Uzbekistan.pdf [accessed April 19, 2019].

UNDP (2010), United Nations Development Programme, "Tajikistan: Energy and Environment", available at: http://www.undp.tj/index.php?option=com_content&task=blogcategory&id=85&Itemid=129 [accessed September 26, 2010].

UNESCAP (2018), "Energy and Development in Central Asia, A Statistical overview of energy sectors in Kazakhstan, Kyrgyzstan, Tajikistan, Turkmenistan and Uzbekistan," *United Nations Economic and Social Council for Asia and the Pacific*, available at: https://www.unescap.org/sites/default/files/Central%20Asia%20Statistical%20 Perspective%202018_WEB.pdf, [accessed December 14, 2018].

WNA (2018), Uranium and Nuclear Power in Kazakhstan, World Nuclear Association, October 31, available at: http://www.world-nuclear.org/information-library/country -profiles/countries-g-n/kazakhstan.aspx [accessed April 9, 2020].

WNA (2020), "Uranium and Nuclear Power in Kazakhstan", World Nuclear Association, April, available at: https://www.world-nuclear.org/information-library/country-pr ofiles/countries-g-n/kazakhstan.aspx [accessed April 9, 2020].

WNA (2020a), "Uranium in Uzbekistan", World Nuclear Association, June, available at: https://www.world-nuclear.org/information-library/country-profiles/countries-t-z/ uzbekistan.aspx [accessed April 9, 2020].

World Bank (2017), "Small Hydropower Plant in the Kyrgyz Republic: Assessment of Potentials and Development Challenges," World Bank, Final Report, June, available at: http://documents1.worldbank.org/curated/en/274331513353253592/pdf/116656-REVISED-WP-PUBLIC-FinalreportSHPPDevelopmentinKYREngSept.pdf [accessed September 12, 2018].

Worldometer (2016), "Kyrgyzstan Oil," Worldometer, retrieved from: https://www. worldometers.info/oil/kyrgyzstan-oil/.

Yenikeyeff, Shamil M (2008), Kazakhstan's Gas: Export Markets and Export Routes, Oxford Institute for Energy Studies, NG 25, November, retrieved from: https:// www.oxfordenergy.org/wpcms/wp-content/uploads/2010/11/NG25-Kazakhstansg asExportMarketsandExportRoutes-ShamilYenikeyeff-2008.pdf.

Zhanseitov S. F and Asanov M. A (1993), "Kazkhstan's mineral raw materials industry and its potential" in James P Dorian, P. A. Minakir and V. T. Borisovich (eds), *CIS Energy and Mineral Development: Prospects, Problems and Opportunities for international cooperation*, Dordrecht: Kluwer Academic Publishers, the Netherlands.

Zimmerman, Reinhardt (1996), *The Law of Obligations: Roman Foundations of the Civilian Tradition*, London: Oxford University Press.

3

INDIA–CENTRAL ASIA RELATIONS

Looking back and looking ahead

> *For India, Central Asia is an area "of high priority, where we aim to stay engaged far into the future. We are independent partners with no selfish motives. We only desire honest and open friendship and to promote stability and cooperation without causing harm to any third country".*
>
> – *Shri P. V. Narasimha Rao* (Muni 2003)

India and Central Asia constitute strategic neighbours and natural allies. Both regions are geographically proximate, sharing a common history and cultural affinity. Notwithstanding the great historical linkages, New Delhi's presence in and policies towards Central Asian countries over the past decades have demonstrated the challenges of competing with China on energy issues, with Russia on matters of regional security, with Pakistan on issues of Islam and secularism and with the United States on matters of regional influence. India so far has managed to secure only a tenuous foothold in Central Asia with the tag of a latecomer. When considered alongside other major players, India has yet to translate the aspirations of its recent "Connect Central Asia Policy" into reality with strategic and sustainable policy action. As we look back we derive the impression of strong bonding between India and the Central Asian Republics but when we look ahead the road looks patchy with a lack of clarity and vision in their relationship. Nevertheless, with the recent emphasis accorded to Central Asian Republics by Indian Prime Minister Mr Modi, terming their relationship as that of a "Partnership for Prosperity", New Delhi perhaps has signalled its arrival in the heartland region. However, this is just a drop in the entire ocean. With this premise, this chapter explores the great historical relations established over the years and emphasizes India's need for stronger and active engagement with all the Central Asian states, given their strategic leverages for India in terms of geo-economics and geopolitical interests.

Historical background

India and Central Asia had been enjoying civilizational and historical relations since millennia. Both regions are geographically proximate, and share a common history and cultural affinity. Historically, both these Asian neighbours share an exceedingly superb bonding and thorough friendship through the ages (Joshi 2010; Kumar 2007). The region as such is an extended and strategic neighbour of India and undeniably constitutes a natural ally. Until the Sovietization of Central Asia, India's relations with the countries of the region were positive and relatively uncomplicated. There were no major issues of dispute between India and the Central Asian khanates. Traditionally, India's relations with the Central Asian Republics have always been close (Kaushik 1970). However, between 1917 and 1991, India's contacts with Central Asian states were largely mediated through Russia. Although India during this period had maintained certain privileged links with Central Asia, those too were filtered through Moscow. Even in the 1971 Indo-Russian Treaty of Peace, Friendship and Cooperation, India was the junior partner. With the dissolution of the Soviet Union, five new independent entities commonly known as Central Asia emerged onto the world scene. Due to the strategic significance and geopolitical virtues of the Central Asian states located at the heart of Asia, this attracted tremendous global attention. Even during this period, there was a rising presence in Central Asia of countries such as the United States, Europe and China, as well as Japan and Korea, but not India. India to date is a low profile country in the region with the tag of a latecomer. Historically, deep-rooted civilizational linkages, thorough friendship, cultural affinity, and economic bonding largely remained disconnected throughout the years between these two Asian neighbours until recently. Neither the Central Asian countries nor India felt any compelling need to include each other in their geopolitical calculus. Despite the seminal importance of Central Asia for New Delhi, India time and again failed to concretize its relations with the region even in the changing geostrategic environment of post-cold war world politics. At a time when the Silk Road Foreign Policy discourse is being adopted by the United States, China and Russia with their strategic agendas in mind, India cannot afford to be a fence sitter. This chapter argues for a growing and active India–Central Asia relationship and establishes the assertion to develop a comprehensive, long-term strategy to protect and promote its geopolitical interest in this region.

Looking back: historical contacts and cultural affinity

India's relations with the countries of the region are positive and relatively uncomplicated. There are no major issues of dispute between India and the Central Asian republics. India's relations with the countries of Central Asia have always been close. The revelation of history also shows that much of India's political history was shaped by events in Central Asia. Two important aspects that need to be underlined here are: first, Central Asia was a staging ground for invasions into India. The description of the region in the military context is found amply in our history textbooks. Indian strategic thought, propounded in Kautilya's *Arthashastra*, had its genesis in Central Asian dynamics. Second, Central Asia was a bridge for promoting Indian commerce and culture across Asia (Stobdan 2004: 55). India was part of the Silk Route dynamics, something that has been grossly ignored in history.

In the past, India has been closely linked to Central Asia through the famous Silk Route. Vivid impressions of this interaction are also visible in classical Indian literature, poetry and the Sufi strand of Islam. Periodic spurts of invasions from the region over the ages have resulted in unleashing the movement of people, goods and culture to India and vice versa. Following the consolidation of the British Colonial Empire in the Indian subcontinent, relations between India and Central Asia took different transformations. Let's discuss in detail the prehistoric and historical roots of India–Central Asia closeness.

It is widely believed that India's interaction with Central Asia dates back several millennia. The prehistoric interactions of India with CAR are evident from the excavations of the Takmak region of Kyrgyzstan, Amu Darya Valley in Southern Uzbekistan, the northeast of Samarkand and several other places in Turkmenistan and Kazakhstan (Kumar 2007: 4; Singh 2015: 62). India's ancient connections with CA were further reinforced with the remarkable findings in places like Kara Tepa, Isykata, Kranayerzka, A.K Beshin, Yer Kurgan, Dalvergin Tepa, Fayaz Tepa and many others, indicating deep cross-cultural links among them. Similarly, in India, the earliest and most direct evidence of mutual links was found in the excavation of Harappa sites (Joshi 2010: 21). The ruins of Afrasiab in Uzbekistan and Nakichikan in Azerbaijan exhibiting a cultural diffusion during the Paleolithic Age to the Bronze Age known as Sohan culture further confirm the rooting of India–Central Asia historical relations. Historian Ronov indicates the Sohan culture popular across the terrains of the Pamir and the Hindukush in the Oxus Valley was witnessed during the first stage of Paleolithic culture, which strikes close similarities with the Neolithic culture of India prevalent in the Indus valley civilization (Singh 2015: 63). Depending upon the historical evidence, it can be believed that India's cultural and historical connections with CAR have taken shape during the Paleolithic age. However, renowned historian T. Shrinov has factually established that the relations between both regions were much closer, intermingled and deeper in the 3rd and 4th centuries BC (Shrinov 2000). This is further confirmed with new research findings showing the Indus Valley's close trade and cultural contacts with Altyn Depe – an ancient civilization of Turkmenistan (Joshi 2010: 21). Amiya Chandra supports the claim, indicating the close contacts Indus Valley Civilization had with the Bronze Age people of Bactriana–Margiana Archaeological Complex (BMAC) covering parts of Central Asia around the 3rd century BC (2017: 17). Roy and Kumar have corroborated the fact that the evidence of remains of camels and horses found in Harappan spots establish direct proof of Central Asian caravans coming to the Indus valley (2007: 44).

The interactions since then continued relentlessly until the British arrived here in India. Bal provides an account of such interaction with the Aryans coming to India from Central Asia in the 2nd century BC (2004: 5). The findings of Bal Gangadhar Tilak also establish the fact that the Aryans came to India from outside (Singh 2015: 61). A milestone development that took place in the life of the people of India as a result of this migration of Aryans was the introduction of the horse (Joshi 2010: 21). Depicting the importance of the horse, Ahmad Hasan Dani of Pakistan writes, "it was the horse brought by the Aryans that changed the whole perspective of life in South Asia including political, social and cultural aspects" (Dani 1999: 6). The introduction of the horse has significantly motivated the trade relations between both regions leading to increasing caravans from both sides. And with trade came cultural interaction between India and CAR (Joshi 2015: 21).

Silk Route and caravan trade

The economic dimensions of India–Central Asia relations were stimulated by the emergence of the Great Silk Route connecting Asia with Europe in a diverse way. However, the oasis of Bukhara and Samarkand in Central Asia were the centres from which feeder routes to north, south and central directions branched out (Joshi 2010: 23). It was the southern branch of the Silk Route that passed through Afghanistan near the Hindukush that connected India with Central Asia and China on the one side and Persia on the other (Chandra 2017: 18). Takshashila (now in Pakistan) was strategically located on the river Indus and the city of Puruspura (near Peshawar in Pakistan) former major centres of Indian land routes to Central Asia and beyond (Joshi 2010: 23). Along with the caravan route and camel trade, the opening up of the Silk Route has provided a powerful incentive to trade. Among the prized commodities in great demand were Chinese silk, Indian ivory, Syrian glass and Roman metalware. From the Indian side, Kashmir Shawls and wooden and silk carpets were in great demand in Central Asia. Prominent goods transported from India through the Silk Route were sugar, cotton cloth and dyes while items imported were horses, sheep, gold, silver, precious stones, metals and fruits (Joshi 2015). The expansion and diversification of the caravan trade led to the travel of Indian merchants to distance places via Turkmenistan and the Caspian region to reach Kolkheti on the Black Sea (now in Georgia) and consequently to the emergence of Indian diaspora in Central Asia.

Indian diaspora in Central Asia

As already stated, Bukhara and Samarkand were the centres of the Great Silk Route. As such Bukhara was the commercial hub on the Silk Route with more than 200 caravanserais. Indians were allotted one such caravanserai for their use. Continuous trading activities and long routes motivated several Indians to settle down there instead of coming back to their homeland and many hundreds of people settled in different cities and towns of Central Asia. Alexander Burnes in 1832 noted that about 300 Hindus were living in Bukhara. They were chiefly natives of Shikharpoor in Sindh (Pakistan) and their number as of late has increased (Burnes 1834: 286; Joshi 2015: 24). Besides trading activities, Indians were also engaged in money lending and exchanging. Apart from Bukhara, a large number of Indians lived in Andijon, Fergana, Namangan as well as in small towns and villages of Central Asia. "The Guide Book of Turkistan published in 1903 mentions the name of ten main trading firms of Andijon – two of which Ramby Pasha and Ramsu Sufa – were Indians engaged in silk trade" (Joshi 2015). According to archival materials,

> there were six Indians engaged in the bread and fruit business in Khodzhent in Tajikistan. There were nearly forty Indians in Tashkent actively engaged in trade. In 1901 around fifty-two Indians in Kokand while in Namangan and Osh there were twenty-eight and four Indians respectively.
>
> *(Rasulzade 1968: 40)*

Many of the Indians were owners of land, horses, caravans and gardens. It is estimated that around the second half of the 19th century there were approximately 8000 Indians settled in CAR. However, India's trading activities which started in the prehistoric age suffered a setback with the expansion of British colonialism to India.

Mutual influence of monarchy

After religion, the single most influencing factor between India and CAR was the monarchies of both regions. Central Asian dynasties like Huna, Kushanas and Saka ruled India while Indian dynasties ruled Khotan and elsewhere in Central Asia. The small and sporadic kingdoms of India were united under one administrative and monetary system under the Kushan rule in India. The Kushan king gave importance to irrigation, handicrafts, trade and commerce, and architecture and brought dramatic transformations in the life of the people and society in India. Evidence of the influence of Kaniska is still found in India and Central Asia in the form of his currency from Bihar to the Aral Sea.

Indian medical studies and research have been the other area of interaction between India and Central Asia. Indian texts on medicine by Charak and Susrat were translated into Arabic and local language. A famous physician from Hazrat Abu Mansur Muwaffaq confessed having adopted the Indian way of learning as Indians were more sharp-sighted in medical sciences and more accurate in their research (Joshi 2010: 26).

Religious influences on bilateral relations

Another milestone that led to the development of relations between India and Central Asia was religious transactions. It is believed that religious interactions have been there since the Paleolithic age. It was only during the Kushan dynasty for the first time in history that religious transactions became more visible with Buddhism, Jainism, Jorashtrianism etc. thriving together (Singh 2015: 65). However, Prof. Nirmala Joshi establishes the fact that "Vairochana – a Kashmir Buddhist scholar – was the first missionary to introduce Buddhism into Central Asia and in due course, CAR served as a transit route for Buddhism to China" (Joshi 2010: 21). According to Chinese sources, Buddhism came to China around 217 BC. Indian emperor Ashok in 203 BC and King Kanishka of the Kushan empire of Central Asian origin were mainly credited for spreading Buddhism in the region (Gafurov 1974: 74). Another account suggests that evidence of the first Buddhist monastery dates back to 211 BC and Fae-han and Huen-Tsang were described as significant Buddhist influences in CAR.

Buddhism in Central Asia was spread in two different strands: the *Mahayana* which stressed selfless service to the poor, tolerance etc, and the *Hinayana* which emphasized only the monastic order. In CAR the Mahayana sect of Buddhism received wider acceptability. The monks working as missionaries travelled immensely as a result viharas were built prominently along the Silk Route. The Gandhara School of Arts was developed under the influence of Buddhism. A 12-metre-long sleeping statue of Buddha in Tajikistan and the massive statue in Bamiyan in Central Afghanistan or the various historical sites discovered in the North-West Frontier Province of Pakistan are part of the priceless heritage of mankind (Joshi 2010: 22).

In west Central Asia, Vedic traditional funeral rites were in practice in Sogdiana. Brahma as Ravan, Indra as Adbad and Shiva as Vishparkar were worshipped in Sogdiana. Durga is worshipped with a new incarnation of four arms. The worship of water deities like Gandharvas and Vishwakarma was also practised in CAR. These all show close and intricate religious connections between India and Central Asia (Singh 2015: 66). Scholars also relate Kank with Ganga. Paintings and idols of Narayana, Shiva, Ganesh, Kartikeya, Mahakala, Digpals, Krishna are being found in various places, showing strong Hindu linking.

Buddhism was the medium of cultural and religious exchange of India and CAR and was later replaced by Sufism. Apart from Buddhism as we know it, Central Asia was also influenced by Lamaism – a Tibetan version of Buddhism. The evidence of Lamaism can be found in the MANAS epic. The flourishing Buddhism since ancient days practised with fervour and devotion was later dominated by Islam in the 8th century with the advent of Arabs in Central Asia defeating the Chinese in the battle of Talas River in 751 AD (Singh 2015).

Like Buddhism, Sufism was an equally significant source of religious interaction between India and Central Asia. Sufism is a liberal strand of Islam that promotes benevolence and tolerance. Although Islam in the Indian subcontinent was introduced by the Arabs in the 7th century AD, it was the Sufis who came from Bukhara, Samarkand and other cities of Central Asia who popularized the religion of India (Joshi 2010: 23).

In addition to Buddhism and Sufism, Christianity has helped religious transactions between India and CAR. It is believed by some tribes in CAR that Jesus was not dead when he was crucified and instead was rescued by one of his female disciples Mary Magdalene after three days of crucifixion. She brought him to Kashmir safely as she was living in a Kashmiri village Pahalgam. The story seems true as there is a Christian shrine believed to be the grave of Jesus worshipped by people all around the world. The shrine place in Kashmir is called "Takht-e-Suleman" and a place in similar name and shrine located in Osh city of Kyrgyzstan vindicates it.

Islam was also an important connecting link between India and Central Asia. The Islamic history of India started with the penetration of Islam to India with the invasion of Mahmud Ghazni in (998–1030) and was consolidated with the beginning of the Delhi Sultanate phase under the Khiljis. The founder of the Khilji dynasty owed their origin to Turkmen tribes. In 1526, Babur hailing from Fergana laid the foundation of Mughal rule in India. The consolidation of Islam, however, attributed to the secular and tolerant leadership of Akabar. During this period, cultural interaction grew manifold between the two regions. Travellers like Al Beruni and Abdurazzak Samakandi of Khworezm visited India in the 11th and 15th centuries respectively. Al Beruni stayed in India for 15 years, studied Sanskrit and translated valuable treatises on Mathematics and Astronomy into Arabic. He penned his memoir "Tarrik-i-Hind" depicting his impression on India. The Tajik poet Bedil and Turkmen poet Magtymguly Pyragy wrote passionately about India. Magtymguly described his travel to India as "Here and There, all the ways in Turkmenistan go to my Hindustan" (Joshi 2010: 26). Poet Bedil lived and died in India. The mighty Mughal Empire ruled India from the 16th century until 1857 when it finally crumbled under the onslaught of British colonial empire.

However, the interests of the British over Central Asia inspired Mackinder's Heartland thesis and the Russian advancement into the Central Asian khanates and their aggressive positioning against each other led to a Great Game in the second half of the 19th century (Hopkirk 1990). Moreover, the independence of Afghanistan and the establishment of the Durand Line between Afghanistan and British India radically changed the scenario between Russia and Britain. The British oriented Indian trade on sea lanes of communication while the Russians controlled the Central Asian activities through a northern-oriented approach which posed as a stumbling block between India and Central Asia. With the closing of land route trade and caravans along the Silk Route, the glory of cross-cultural connections and economic activities waned over the years.

India and Central Asia during the Soviet era

India and Central Asian states entered into a testing time in their relationship with the Sovietization of Central Asia and subsequent territorial divisions of the khanates into five autonomous countries for political and administrative convenience and the partition of India into two dominions: India and Pakistan. While erstwhile India was bordering Central Asia under the new geopolitical situation, Pakistan became the new neighbour of India and Central Asia.

Even though relations were revived in the years following independence, they failed to acquire any depth or intensity. Indian presence in Central Asia was characterized by its closeness to the Kremlin following the Sino-Indian border conflict of 1962 (Sharma 2009: 3). It was further strengthened by the Sino-Soviet schism in the years that followed. India, anyhow, managed to get a cultural anchor in the region under the Indo-Soviet Friendship Treaty of 1971 (Ibid). However, its presence in the region nevertheless remained "muted" and constrained by its ties to the Kremlin (Blank 2004: 7). Although, the politics of Central Asia was then controlled from Moscow, India was among the few countries to interact with Central Asia. As in the other parts of the Soviet Union, Indian films, epics and music were extremely popular in Central Asia.

The contemporary period

The end of the Cold War brought the world to a standstill with the collapse of the great USSR. The sudden disintegration of the USSR led to a fundamental change in the geopolitical situation in Eurasia and opened up Central Asia to the rest of the world. Like any other neighbour, India too recognized the newly independent states at the earliest and established diplomatic relations with them. New Delhi India acknowledged Central Asia as an area of strategic importance. The "Look North Policy" of India is a standing example of this shift. During a visit to Turkmenistan in September 1995, the then Prime Minister P.V. Narasimha Rao made it amply clear that "for India", Central Asia was an area

> of high priority, where we aim to stay engaged far into the future. We are independent partners with no selfish motives. We only desire honest and open friendship and to promote stability and cooperation without causing harm to any third country.
>
> *(Muni 2003: 110)*

Such a proclamation offers a glimpse into the discursive genesis of the Look North Policy, that India is less likely to fight a war in its neighbourhood. The country will quite simply be too engaged with trade and business. Moreover, the propositions of the Look North Policy point to "secularism", "democracy" and "literacy" as national strength, an outlook that both India and Central Asia share. This is an assumption that underpins the myth-making that both of the Asian neighbours are "once again poised for greatness" (Sinha 2004: 6, Pradhan 2015: 3).

The trend of pragmatic engagement with CAR was again well reflected in India's foreign policy doctrine of 1997 popularly known as "Gujral Doctrine". It is here that Central Asia got referred to as "India's near abroad". Public rhetoric to the effect also gained momentum, especially with the coming to power of the Bhartiya Janata Party (BJP) and its proclaimed ambition to make India occupy the global political centre stage. New Delhi is making a concerted effort to cement its existing ties with these republics, intending to establish a peaceful and cooperative framework in the region. These efforts were strengthened by the visit of Prime Minister Vajpayee to Almaty in June 2002 for the 16 nation Conference on Interaction and Confidence Building Measures in Asia (CICA) (The Hindu 2013).

In tune with that, the bilateral and multilateral relationships between India and Central Asia have been oriented over time. The United Progressive Alliance (UPA) government led by Dr Man Mohan Singh also cultivated cordial and close relations with all the countries of Central Asia. The Annual Report of India's Ministry of Defence stressed Central Asia as an area of vital importance to India, not only on account of its geographical proximity and India's historical and cultural links with the region but also because of the common challenge they all faced from extremism and terrorism. Prime Minister Manmohan Singh, addressing the Combined Commanders Conference in October 2006, observed:

> When we look at our extended neighbourhood we cannot but be struck by the fact that India is the only open pluralistic democratic society and rapidly modernizing market economy between the Mediterranean and the Pacific. This places a special responsibility upon us not only in the defence of our values but also in the search for a peaceful periphery. We have traditionally conceived our security in extending circles of engagement. Today, whether it is West Asia, the Gulf, Central Asia or the Indian Ocean region, there is an increasing demand for our political, economic and defence engagement.
>
> *(The Indian Express 2006)*

Central Asia in its new avatar offered immense geopolitical and geostrategic interests and at the same time challenges to New Delhi. The discovery of large reserves of hydrocarbons and other resources in the Central Asian region off course offers attractive opportunities for India in her energy quest but threats to its security emanating from Islamic fundamentalism in Pakistan, drug trafficking and smuggling of illegal arms and weapons in Pakistan and Afghanistan brings India and Central Asia further together. The unabated support of Pakistan for Islamic fundamentalist movements in the region served to push the secular-minded countries of the CAR closer to India (Lal 2006: 29). The current security imperatives facing India are common with those of the Central Asian states. This is true for Russia, China and Iran as well. This, however, implies that greater security and economic cooperation in the region is certainly probable.

India's growing interest in the region came to the forefront when the Kazakh President Mr Nursultan Narzbayev was invited as a Chief Guest on the occasion of India's Republic Day in 2009. This close friendship and cordial relations with the region led to the formation of India's "Connect Central Asia" policy 2012 at the first India–Central Asia dialogue. Representing India, Mr E. Ahamed, the then Minister of State for External Affairs emphasized growing closeness between India and the Central Asian States. He underlined the following channels for strengthening the relationship between the two regions:

> First, a strategic and security cooperation including coordination in the arena of counter-terrorism was proposed. Second, enhancing bilateral trade flows through entering into a Comprehensive Economic Cooperation Agreement (CECA), covering trade in merchandise products and services as well as investment provisions, was recommended. Third, deepening cooperation in energy and natural resources products was proposed. Fourth, the possibility of cooperation in key services sectors, namely, medical, higher education, construction etc., where India has improved its global foothold over the last decade, was noted. Finally, the need for creating road transportation connectivity by bridging the missing links in the International North-South Transport Corridor (INSTC) was highlighted.
> *(MEA 2012)*

The visit of the Indian Prime Minister to the landlocked region on July 6–13, 2015, further leased a new life to the relationship between New Delhi and the CAR. His five-nation tour preceding the Ufa Summit was designed to create India's regional influence in the inner Asian countries through a partnership for prosperity. Modi's Central Asian engagement for the first time covered a broad area including everything from energy ties, pipeline politics, trade and commerce, transportation, security and counterterrorism, and cooperation in healthcare and pharmaceuticals. He went on to reiterate that "India is the new frontier of opportunities for the world while Central Asia represents a vast region of immense resources" (Eurasianet 2015). India's reengagement with Central Asia and the rising profile in the past few decades has been spurred on by its soft power image in contrast to the hard power positioning of the regional players including Russia, China and Pakistan. Importantly, the countries of the region have also been seriously interested in remaining engaged with New Delhi as their search for a Chinese alternative ends here.

India's deepening engagement with the region was further buttressed when full membership in the Shanghai Cooperation Organization (SCO) regional grouping was accorded for India at the Astana Summit of June 8–9, 2017 (Desai 2017). Prominent members of the organization from the CAS such as Uzbekistan, Kyrgyzstan, Tajikistan and Kazakhstan have always indicated their support for India joining the organization. Kazakhstan and Tajikistan have also stated their support for India's bid for a seat on the UN Security Council (Pradhan 2015).

India as of 2020 has a very close and firm bonding with all the five Central Asian republics. Every country of the region looks up to India for its greater democratic values and secular credentials while India sees her future global role finding its place in wider engagement with the region. Positive relations with both regions have been further strengthened by forging bilateral and multilateral cooperation in the fields of security, economy, energy and strategy. The recent visit of the Tajik President to India and India's Foreign Minister to Tajikistan and Uzbekistan only show the desire for the respective sides to forge strong ties. The idea of "Connect Central Asia" as advanced by the Government of India is believed to usher in a new era and dynamic vision in the relationship between India and Central Asia.

The developments in both regions helped the modest relation between India and Central Asia to rise steadily for the last two decades or so. The driving force in this phase of relations between these two regions is primarily marked by two concerns: securing and diversifying India's energy security and keeping a check on the rise of Islamic groups that seriously threaten India's national security in the region. Also, with the intense power play taking place between Russia, China the United States and the Western countries in the strategic arena of Central Asia, India's emphasis on soft power strikes a positive chord among these nations.

India's interests in Central Asia

India's engagement in Central Asia since the early years of the 21st century has been marked with a need to realize Indian interests in four broad areas. First, to give India an entry into the hydrocarbon resources would enable the country to diversify and secure energy sources vital to her growth momentum. Second, following the Soviet collapse and because Pakistan pursued a strident Islamist agenda, India's security interests demanded a need to check the rise of radical Islam as a political force in Central Asia. Third, it is vital to keep a tab on drug trafficking and potential weapons proliferation in this geostrategically important region, and fourth, to promote interests in the commercial arena. Apart from the above-mentioned four significant areas of focus, India also sees the region as a geopolitically vital area for New Delhi in terms of fulfilling its fundamental interests critically connected with its national security. The entire gamut of India's interests is clubbed into two categories, namely geopolitical interests and geo-economic interests for lucid understanding and has been elaborated as follows.

Geopolitical interests

Geostrategy refers to India's long-term, strategic management of her geopolitical interests, influences and involvement in Central Asia – an area that separates vital centres of two nuclear powers – the Russian Federation (RF) and China – and the place of intersection of major geopolitical massifs – the Eurasian, Islamic, Chinese and Indian. Placed in the geographical centre of Asia as a mosaic between four world civilizations, namely Islam, Buddhism, Christianity and Hinduism, the Central Asian geographical setting critically links to the security of almost all the countries of the world and offers immense opportunities to all the regional and extra-regional players. India, being the strategic neighbour and natural ally, has profound interests more than any other regional player in the heartland region. Some of the areas concerning Indian critical interests in the region are broadly discussed in the following paragraphs (Patnaik 2016).

Security issues

Looking at the centrality of the region's location, in a changing strategic environment and security alignments, India's security is closely tied to the instability in the region between Afghanistan and Pakistan. An unholy alliance between the Taliban and Pakistan before September 11, 2001, has contributed to terrorist attacks against India on several occasions. It is now beyond doubt that many Pakistani militants received training in Pakistan and Afghanistan training camps to wage war against the Indian state. To mention a few, in 1999, terrorists hijacked Indian Airlines flight IC-814, departing from Kathmandu, landing the plane in Kandahar in Afghanistan (Sharma, Raghav 2009). Various Pakistan supported terrorist groups active in Kashmir, such as Lashkar-e-Toiba and Jaish-e-Mohammed, received military training in Afghan camps alongside Central Asian militant groups such as the Islamic Movement of Uzbekistan (IMU), as well as Tajik and Uighur militants (Rohde 2002). Attacks on the Indian Parliament, state legislative Assembly of Jammu and Kashmir, sporadic terror incidents in Indian cities and inciting recent cyberterror in India have an active Pakistani hand. Therefore, instability in Afghanistan and the often hostile attitude of Pakistan are intricately linked to the security, unity, and integrity of India; hence, the importance of forging strong ties with the states of Central Asia to counter such future confrontations. Above all, counterterrorism cooperation has been the main security concern for India concerning Central Asia. For that, cooperative security initiatives have already begun with Tajikistan, Uzbekistan, Kyrgyzstan and Kazakhstan (Pradhan 2010).

From the security point of view, the emergence of radical Islam in Central Asia in the shadow of the dramatic demise of the Soviet Union and its aggressive propagation of atheism generated a great degree of unease in Indian quarters. There was a feeling in New Delhi that the simmering rise of Islamic fundamentalism will eventually pose a serious threat to Indian security, especially in the state of Kashmir. Such fears have been accentuated in light of the increasingly close linkages that Islamist movements such as the IMU have forged with the Taliban and the ISI (Blank 2003). Such developments certainly do not augur well for India's security interests, given the ISI's history of flirtation with radical Islamist groups to prop them up against India. This analysis is vindicated in the UNI report of April 3, 2000, which states that "Afghan and Pakistan trained mercenaries are seeking fresh pastures to exploit their brand of fundamentalism with Tajikistan, Kazakhstan, and Kyrgyzstan emerging as their new hot spots". The doubt is further strengthened by the proven link between ISI and militant groups operating in Xinjiang resulting in civil riots in 2010. Thus, the security of the entire region is closely intertwined. Given the increasingly trans-national nature of linkages being forged by extremist groups, especially with the Taliban in Afghanistan and the ISI in Pakistan, these developments have potentially serious security ramifications for India. Thus, this makes it imperative for India to be more closely involved in Central Asia's regional security matrix and ensure that instability does not spill over into Central Asia (Campbell 2013).

Drug trafficking and weapons proliferation concerns

The Central Asian region is strategically located between two nuclear superpowers, Russia and China, as well as their nuclear-armed neighbours Pakistan and India. Central Asia previously served as a raw materials base for the Soviet weapons programme, with Kazakhstan holding large reserves of highly enriched uranium, while Kyrgyzstan has substantial amounts of nuclear waste scattered around. Uzbekistan and Tajikistan hold sizeable uranium reserves and the potential for its enrichment. This, coupled with the absence of special-detection equipment at border and customs checkpoints, rampant corruption and little political will, has the potential to render the region highly susceptible to and a lucrative route for smuggling fissile material. This has serious security implications as there is a potential danger of proliferation of lethal weapons technology and material into the hands of not just states hostile to India, but also non-state actors like the Taliban, Al-Qaeda, and groups such as the IMU linked to them. This assumes further significance in light of a resurgent Taliban that will not lose out on the opportunity to use to its advantage the porous Tajik–Afghan border. Drug trafficking potentially poses a major security threat to the region (Sharma 2009). The poor state of border management and rampant corruption, coupled with soaring opium production in neighbouring Afghanistan – all spell a dangerous trend. India needs to pay greater heed to drug trafficking since much of the money generated is used to fund activities of extremist Islamist terror networks that possess the ability to foment trouble for India in the long run. This is an area where India has a broad overlap of interests with three other key players in the region: the United States, Russia and China, with whom it could engage in multilateral cooperation (UNODC 2011).

CASAREM option

Growing relations and improved connectivity between Central Asia and India is a key element of the concept of a "Greater Central Asia", vision. This, in turn, is based on the premise that Central and South Asia are, or can become, a single integrated unit committed to economic activity and growth. Besides deep cultural and historic ties and the war on terrorism, the countries of the region and particularly India as the leading force of South Asia have many common concerns, such as finding outlets for energy supplies, achieving prosperity through economic cooperation, and moving towards enhanced security and stability. This concept further strengthens the spirit of regional security and inter-regional cooperation in the greater Central Asian region which also includes India, Pakistan and Afghanistan. This, in turn, boosts India's concerns about national security (CASAREM 2007).

SCO and India

The SCO has now emerged as a major geostrategic, security and economic initiative throughout Eurasia. India applied for full membership of SCO at its Dushanbe summit in 2014 and was included as a full member state at the Ufa Summit of 2015 in Russia (Ufa 2015). All the Central Asian Countries and Russia supported India's full membership of the SCO. China, though, was initially a bit reluctant but finally approved India's full membership of the organization along with Pakistan. Membership of the organization now will not merely help India in getting entry into the region but will also enable it to propel its interests vis-à-vis China in the region. It will also facilitate India in countering Pakistan's anti-India propaganda and ensure its economic participation with the greater Central Asian region while providing New Delhi a market in Central Asia as an alternative to Chinese goods. Importantly, the energy crunch of India will get a ray of hope with Central Asian oil and gas being imported to India through Iran's Chabahar port. The operation of the International North–South Transportation Corridor (INSTC) is a positive initiative that may encourage the partner country to strengthen it to the next level of construction of a pipeline with a win–win design for both the supplier and consumer countries (*Indian Express* 2015).

Support for UNSC reforms and permanent seat for India

In its bid to reform the United Nations Security Council India is garnering support from all the countries of the neighbourhood and extended neighbourhood. Mr Modi and his government, taking the initiative forward, seem to be working towards building global support for their push for reforms in the structure of the United Nations. There has been an effort to get as many countries as possible to endorse India's claim for a permanent seat in the UNSC. It is expected that these endorsements would help in at least initiating a larger multilateral dialogue on the agenda of UNSC reforms and could help in paving the way for India's entry in the future. The Central Asian countries have stated their support for a permanent seat for India (ET 2015).

Geo-economic interests

Economic relations

Economically, India has a growing presence in Central Asia in the energy and pharmaceutical sectors. Trade in consumer goods is increasing but is constrained by economic barriers, particularly in Turkmenistan and Uzbekistan. Trade with Uzbekistan amounted to more than $121 million in 2004 with more than 30 Uzbek–Indian joint ventures in Uzbekistan (MEA 2005, Uzbek Embassy 2015). A significant source of revenue for India is in pharmaceutical sales from Ajanta Pharma and Reddy Labs. The two countries are considering Indian gas exploration in Uzbekistan through India's public sector Oil and Natural Gas Commission (ONGC) and Gas Authority of India Limited (GAIL). ONGC has moved forward to stake claims in four of Kazakhstan's oil fields as well (MEA 2016). Both countries are developing bilateral trade in mechanical engineering and pharmaceuticals, and in the defence sectors; total bilateral trade in 2003 was at $79 million (Interfax 2005) and in 2015 it had grown to $311.76 million (MEA 2016).

Bilateral trade between India and Turkmenistan for 2003 was only $19.1 million (MEA 2005) which had grown manifold to $185 million in 2014 (MEA 2016a). The joint venture between the Indian company Ajanta Pharma and the Ministry of Health in Turkmenistan, named Turkmenderman Ajanta Pharma Limited (TDAPL), currently provides approximately half of the pharmaceutical needs of Turkmenistan. However, difficulty in converting currency has limited the joint venture's ability to procure raw materials and expand production. India has widened information exchange programmes with Turkmenistan, establishing the $0.5 million Turkmen–Indian Industrial Training Centre as a gift to train Turkmen in basic skills, in the manufacturing of tools and components, and business practices for small and medium enterprises, and to provide financial, computer and language training through its Indian Technical and Economic Cooperation (ITEC) programme (Lal 2006).

Development of a gas pipeline connecting India to Turkmenistan has been an issue of intense focus, though the viability of such a plan is as yet unclear. India remains concerned that such a pipeline would need to traverse both Afghanistan and Pakistan, thereby putting the pipeline at risk due to instability in Afghanistan and giving Pakistan the ability to threaten India's access to energy. However, recent positive trends in relations between India and Pakistan have improved the feasibility of this plan.

Central Asian countries also provide a convenient and low-cost hub for Indian travellers. Services in the form of flights from India to London, the United States and Europe provide a lucrative export for Uzbekistan. However, for commodity trade in other areas, Indian businesspeople note that currency conversion restrictions mean that repatriation of profits is a problem, hampering the expansion of economic ties.

Pharmaceuticals and healthcare sectors

Another key area of cooperation between India and Central Asia is pharmaceuticals and healthcare. Mainly due to its efficiency and cost advantage, India has a competitive advantage in the global market in this field. Some of the Indian companies exporting pharmaceutical products to Central Asia are Claris Life sciences, Ranbaxy, Dr Reddys Labs, Lupin Laboratories, Unique Laboratories and Aurobindo Pharma. Some of these companies are planning to set up manufacturing units in Central Asia. The pharmaceutical factory of the Kazakh–India joint venture Kazakhstanpharma is in the process of completion in Almaty (Sajjanhar 2016).

Trade relations

In the post-USSR period, economic relations with the Central Asian region and other former Soviet republics declined considerably. However, in the last few years, there has been an upward trend. A decade back, in 2010, the official two-way annual trade turnover between India and the Greater Central Asia region was about $700 million (with about $500 million of exports) (Sachdeva 2010) whereas in 2017 it had only grown to $934.57 (MEA 2017). Apart from Afghanistan and Kazakhstan, economic relations with other countries are minimal. This trade is also restricted mainly to traditional items. The main commodities being exported from India are pharmaceuticals, tea, ready-made garments, leather goods, jute manufactures, cosmetics, cotton yarn, machinery, machine tools, rice, plastic products, machinery and instruments, electronic goods and chemicals. Imports from Greater Central Asia are restricted to fruits and nuts, raw cotton, iron and steel. Uzbekistan and Kazakhstan also export zinc to India.

The Export–Import Bank of India has identified potential export items for this region. These include machinery and transport equipment, chemicals, food products, transport vehicles, agricultural machinery, and cement, etc. At present, India's trade with the Greater Central Asia region is rather insignificant (only 0.17 per cent of total Indian trade), hence it does not make any sense to use any model. The gravity models of international trade in which distance heavily influences the destination of trade have not worked even in the case of South Asia. In the case of India–Central Asian countries, the application of the gravity model is of little use due to data limitations. Even if there is a manifold increase in trade in the coming years, it will still constitute less than 1 per cent of total Indian trade. If all formalities regarding Afghanistan's membership of SAFTA are completed soon, trade could get a further boost. The earlier India–Afghanistan preferential trade agreement signed in 2003 was quite helpful in boosting bilateral trade. In fact, in 2007–08, India was Afghanistan's number one export market (MEA 2017).

Investment potentials

The countries of this region provide good investment opportunities for Indian businesses. This is clearly shown by London-based Indian steel tycoon Laxmi Mittal. He owns a 5.5 million ton capacity steel plant in Kazakhstan employing more than 50,000 people. From there he supplies the Chinese market. To facilitate trade and investment with this region, Indian policymakers during the last decade created an institutional framework. The Indian government set up bilateral Inter-Governmental Commissions for trade, economic, scientific and technical cooperation with all the Central Asian countries, which have been meeting regularly. These relations are further institutionalized through joint working groups in various fields, such as IT, science and technology, hydrocarbons, military–technical cooperation, etc. The Indian government also extends small lines of credit for the countries in the region to enable Indian exporters to export to these markets without repayment risk. In this scheme, around 15–20 per cent of the contract value is paid as advance by the importers; the balance contract value is disbursed by the Indian EXIM Bank to the exporters upon shipment of the goods. The recovery of credit extended to the overseas buyer is taken care of by the EXIM Bank, without recourse to the Indian exporter. To promote and facilitate trade, Double Taxation Avoidance Agreements have also been signed (MEA 2017).

There have also been improvements in the banking sector. The Punjab National Bank has a full-fledged branch in Kabul and many other Indian banks have inter-banking arrangements with countries in the region. Canara Bank has links with Commercial Bank for Foreign Economic Affairs of Tajikistan, the State Bank of India with Turan-Alem Bank of Kazakhstan, the Commercial Bank of Kyrgyzstan, the National Bank of Tajikistan, the State Bank for Foreign Economic Affairs of Turkmenistan and the National Bank for Foreign Economic Activity of Uzbekistan. In 2003, the Indian Ministry of Commerce launched a *Focus CIS* programme. The first phase focused on the five Central Asian countries plus Azerbaijan and Ukraine. Other CIS countries have also been included in the programme. The programme aims to promote business-to-business linkages, and support trade fairs and different promotional meetings and seminars (Sachdeva 2017).

India has also signed many agreements with these countries for technical–economic cooperation under ITEC. Thus far, thousands of candidates from Central Asia have come to India under the programme in such disciplines as diplomacy, banking, finance, trade, management, and small industry promotion. The highest number of seats allotted to Central Asia is for Uzbekistan, which sends about 120 candidates every year. Thousands of Afghan citizens have been able to participate in various short- and long-term study and training programmes in the last few years. The Federation of Indian Chambers of Commerce and Industry (FICCI) has set up Joint Business Councils with Kazakhstan, Uzbekistan and the Kyrgyz republic. Recently the governor of the West Kazakhstan region invited the Indian industry to invest in areas such as extraction of sunflower oil, wheat production, wool, leather, and the construction of elite housing complexes and five-star hotels (Sajjanhar 2013).

Many Indian business organizations and think-tanks have identified such areas of cooperation as energy, food processing, textiles, tourism, information technology, education, consultancy services, petrochemicals, and construction. Another area of major interest to Indian businesses would be to participate in the continuing privatization process in the region. Under an Uzbek privatization programme, India's Spentex Industries in 2006 acquired Tashkent-To'yetpa Tekstil, a state-owned spinning company, for $81 million. The transaction comprised the acquisition of two manufacturing facilities at Tashkent and Toyetpa that has a combined installed capacity of 220,000 spindles and a weaving capacity of 236 air-jet looms. Later, the company also acquired the assets to set up a dyeing facility there. The Vardhaman group is also planning to acquire a textile firm in Uzbekistan. Uzbekistan has announced many incentives to attract $300 million from Indian textile companies over the next three years. Uzbekistan and Kazakhstan are heavily marketing a bounty of fiscal sops to Indian textile firms. Some other Indian companies such as Punj Lloyd have also participated in oil pipeline projects in Kazakhstan. With offices in Almaty, Atyrau and Tengiz, Punj Lloyd has completed four engineering and construction projects in the Kazakh pipeline building (Ibid).

If the Central Asian countries can reform their land policies, there is a tremendous possibility of investment in the agricultural sector. Investment opportunities can be identified country-wide: for Kazakhstan, it could include oil and gas, power generation and distribution, telecommunication equipment, medical equipment and supplies, agricultural machinery, food processing and packaging, construction and engineering services and mining.

In Uzbekistan, the focus could be on energy, IT, mining, food processing and packaging, textile machinery and equipment and tourism infrastructure. For Tajikistan, investment opportunities are identified in mining and related equipment, medical and pharmaceutical supplies, textile machinery, telecommunications, agribusiness and related sectors. In Turkmenistan, potential areas for investment would include the oil and gas industry (exploration, development services, and equipment), electrical energy (equipment and services), chemical and mining industry, transportation, communications (equipment and services), environmental technology and services, and the healthcare and medical industry.

Promoting "Make in India"

The recent visits of the Indian Prime Minister are different from his other trips to the United States, China and Europe where he was essentially looking at attracting foreign investment and convincing companies to increase production in India with a focus on *Make in India* to succeed.

For that India will have to improve its freight connectivity with other countries and especially with Central Asia – the proximate neighbour of India. The planned route of the International North–South Transport Corridor (INSTC) is a ship, rail and road connectivity project for moving freight between India, Iran, Azerbaijan and Russia (Niti Central 2015). The route greatly reduces the time taken for moving freight between India and Central Asia. Expansion of the corridor is a key objective of the Prime Minister as it could greatly improve India's trade connectivity with Central Asia. There were discussions over Uzbekistan and Turkmenistan joining the INSTC. The PM also proposed that the Kazakhstan–Turkmenistan–Iran Rail Link could become a linked corridor to the INSTC. Discussions have also been initiated with Kazakhstan on a dedicated freight terminal (Ibid).

The Ashgabat Agreement is a transit pact established in 2011 between Uzbekistan, Iran, Turkmenistan and Oman (Das 2012). The Prime Minister sought Uzbekistan and Turkmenistan's support for India joining the agreement as it would massively improve connectivity with Central Asia. During the visit of Cabinet Minister Nitin Gadkari to Iran, both countries signed a pact on developing the Chabahar port (Ibid). Through the Iran route, the time taken for transporting goods between India and Central Asia would be reduced immensely. For this, efforts need to continue on improving the linkage between Central Asia and Iran.

In Tajikistan, Prime Minister Mr. Modi discussed the proposed Pakistan Afghanistan Tajikistan Trilateral Transit Trade Agreement (PATTTTA) (MEA 2015a). It was decided that further consultations would start on the inclusion of India in this pact as it would further strengthen trade between South Asia and Tajikistan. There were also discussions on building an alternate surface route along with other countries (DNA 2012).

Cooperation on agriculture

The recent tour of Mr Modi to Central Asia was marked with substantive development on the agriculture front. An important agreement was signed between the *Turkmenhimiya* and Indian PSU Rashtriya Chemicals and Fertilizers Limited for long-term sourcing of urea from Turkmenistan in July 2015. India proposed to set up a Urea production facility in Turkmenistan (MEA 2015b). In the agriculture-dependent Kyrgyz Republic there were discussions over knowledge sharing and joint efforts in agricultural research (MEA 2015c). A plan of action was signed between the *KazAgroInnovation* and Indian Council of Agricultural Research for cooperation in the field of agriculture (MEA 2015d).

Other areas of cooperation

Information technology (IT) and technical training are the areas where India can make a substantial contribution to the Central Asian states. Already there are agreements in this regard with Uzbekistan, Kazakhstan and Kyrgyzstan. India is building a software technology park in Kazakhstan. A memorandum of understanding has been signed between Kyrgyzstan and the Indian company Edurite Technologies for cooperation in the field of IT education. Under the ITEC programme, India has allotted slots to all Central Asian countries for the training of their candidates in selected Indian institutes. Tourism, space-technology, defence cooperation, food and cotton processing, environment, disaster management and telecom are other emerging areas of cooperation (World Bank 2014).

Trade relations between India and Central Asian countries

The foundation of India–Central Asia relations has been laid on the issue of trade. Since the ancient Silk Route days, trade remains the vortex around all other relations. The historical and cultural connections are the results of trade transactions. As then, even today Central Asia holds significance as a market for Indian goods and can provide India with an opportunity to access the goods and services that Central Asia has in plenty.

The current analysis of India–Central Asian trade dynamics is arranged to provide a brief account of trade relations between both regions in macroeconomic perspective, to analyse India's export basket, to identify sectors with growing export inclination for selecting important trade indices and to identify important areas of trade between India and Central Asia.

India's trade relations with Central Asian countries in the export–import scenario have been discussed with the help of Table 3.1 to draw a picture of India's trade balance with the region. The annual average trade balance is calculated to understand the evolving trade relations during 2001–2015.

It is observed from Table 3.1 that over 2007–12 India witnessed a rising trade balance with the three economies, vis-à-vis the 2001–06 figures. Trade balance, though positive, declined for Kazakhstan and Kyrgyzstan. However, the import of mineral fuels from Kazakhstan and various primary and mineral products from other countries has increased significantly since 2013. As a result of sharply growing imports in these product groups, and moderately rising exports in comparison, an overall trade deficit concerning the Central Asian countries emerged during 2013–15. However, at the bilateral level, a trade deficit exists only against Kazakhstan, given the sharp rise in India's import of petroleum products from the country.

India's trade integration with the region was analysed with the help of Table 3.2 to summarize the share of the five countries in India's export and import baskets

TABLE 3.1 India–Central Asia average trade at a glance (in US$ million)

Country	*2001–06*	*2007–12*	*2013–15*
Kazakhstan	46	33	–341
Kyrgyzstan	28	27	33
Tajikistan	2	4	42
Turkmenistan	7	32	56
Uzbekistan	-10	26	88
Central Asia	73	122	–121

Source: Trade Map, ITC, 2016.

TABLE 3.2 Share of Central Asian countries in India's trade basket

Country	*Export share*			*Import share*		
	2001–05	*2006–10*	*2011–15*	*2001–05*	*2006–10*	*2011–15*
Kazakhstan	0.1021	0.0700	0.0782	0.0168	0.0447	0.0878
Kyrgyzstan	0.0413	0.0168	0.0109	0.0007	0.0004	0.0003
Tajikistan	0.0080	0.0078	0.0125	0.0033	0.0054	0.0016
Turkmenistan	0.0200	0.0200	0.0235	0.0089	0.0041	0.0044
Uzbekistan	0.0210	0.0256	0.0393	0.0300	0.0130	0.0095

Source: Trade Map, ITC, 2016.

TABLE 3.3 Major Indian exports to Central Asian countries (in %)

HScode	*Product description*	*Year*				
		2011	*2012*	*2013*	*2014*	*2015*
30	Pharmaceutical products	27.02	23.99	28.91	24.85	33.13
02	Meat and edible meat offal	3.48	2.57	5.68	11.38	13.06
61	Articles of apparel, accessories, knit or crochet	10.68	12.76	16.33	18.80	10.16
84	Machinery, nuclear reactors, boilers etc.	6.27	12.02	9.42	8.49	9.62
09	Coffee, tea mate and spices	15.15	9.65	7.57	6.93	8.92
62	Articles of apparel, accessories, not knit or crochet	6.57	6.04	5.31	7.44	6.88
85	Electrical, electronics equipment	10.06	11.61	6.84	1.88	2.53
87	Vehicles other than railway, tramway	2.21	6.85	3.29	3.73	1.68
90	Optical photo, technical, medical etc. apparatus	3.10	2.00	0.99	1.32	1.29
40	Rubber and articles thereof	1.07	0.86	1.67	1.09	1.24
Total		85.61	88.35	86.01	85.92	88.51

Source: Trade Map, ITC, 2016.

over 2001–05, 2006–10 and 2011–15. For the trade share analysis, the data is drawn from the Trade Map database maintained by the International Trade Centre.

Table 3.3 provides the list of top ten export items from India to Central Asia during 2011–15. As has been observed from the table, India has exported major items including primary (meat products; coffee, tea etc.), light manufacturing (apparels; pharmaceuticals; rubber products) as well as heavy engineering (machinery and equipment; electrical equipment; vehicles and automobile products) products. These top ten product groups cumulatively explain around 90 per cent of India's exports to the region. It is noted from the data that since 2012 the importance (i.e. share) of pharmaceutical and meat products in India's export basket to Central Asia has increased.

Similarly, Indian imports from Central Asia need to be discussed at length. For that matter, Table 3.4 mentions the share of India's top ten import items from Central Asia during 2011–15.

TABLE 3.4 Major Indian imports from Central Asian countries (in %)

HScode	*Product description*	*Year*				
		2011	*2012*	*2013*	*2014*	*2015*
27	Mineral fuels, mineral oils and products of their distillation	0.38	2.41	68.21	80.79	60.41
25	Salt; sulphur; earths and stone; plastering materials, lime and cement	19.53	33.32	10.75	4.87	13.71
31	Fertilizers	8.40	3.12	2.72	1.50	5.62
79	Zinc and articles thereof	18.20	13.39	3.34	2.17	4.11
71	Gems and jewellery	17.94	17.38	2.18	0.26	3.55
07	Edible vegetables and certain roots and tubers	1.26	3.70	2.24	1.48	3.07
26	Ores, slag and ash	0.47	0.04	0.00	3.91	2.15
72	Iron and steel	3.01	5.37	2.57	1.39	1.84
28	Inorganic chemicals	9.41	6.28	4.17	1.77	1.79
13	Lac, gum, resins and other vegetable saps and extracts	2.06	1.25	1.15	0.50	1.29
Total		80.66	86.25	97.34	98.64	97.53

Source: Trade Map, ITC, 2016.

India's Central Asia policy: looking ahead

The deep-rooted Nehruvian socialistic and idealistic international positioning of India's foreign policy has seen considerable recasting over the last two decades or so. The new-found pragmatism in India's foreign policy sidelining the historical and cultural silver lining has been widely acknowledged as the need of the time after the post-Cold War world order. In the post-1990 period, "India's foreign relations have been envisioned more in terms of widening circles around historical and cultural commonalities across the globe into categories viz. the immediate neighbourhood, the extended neighbourhood and the global powers" (Chandra 2017). In this framework, Central Asia has been described as India's "extended and strategic neighbour". Accordingly, India initiated policy process towards the region although this was not as robust as it ought to have been. Nevertheless, India took a firm stand towards the region to build its relationship in a greater way and started the initiative with the Look North Policy in the mid-1990s (Pradhan 2015).

Another significant transformation in India's foreign policy witnessed during the new world order was its shift from unilateralism to a proactive multilateral approach towards Central Asia. the increased bilateral exchanges and regular flow of high-level visits between India and Central Asian states have manifested in establishing meaningful and mutually beneficial ties, leading to enhanced footprints of India across various Central Asian republics. New Delhi has been actively pursuing several initiatives to enable her to attain a substantial position in the energy game of Central Asia. Some of these strategies are discussed below.

Look North Policy

The "Look North Policy" of India is an extension of India's cordial and superb bonding with the energy-rich nations of Central Asia. Going a step further, Shri P. V. Narasimha Rao, the then Prime Minister of India, in September 1995 during his visit to Turkmenistan made it aptly clear that Central Asia holds a region of high priority for India and would continue to do so in the future as well (Muni 2003: 110). In his address, he further emphasized that

> we aim to stay engaged far into the future with the Republics of Central Asia. We are an independent partner with no selfish motives. We only desire honest and open friendship and to promote stability and cooperation without causing harm to any third country.

This proclamation reflects the core of the genesis of the Look North Policy. Its vision of peaceful engagement with neighbours, extending that relationship in the context of trade and business, is at the heart of this policy. Moreover, the propositions of the Look North Policy point to "secularism", "democracy", and "literacy" as national strengths that India and Central Asia share (Blank 2003: 141) which together would further help in strengthening the bonding. Ironically, such a discourse didn't find its mention in the aftermath of Narasimha Rao's government in India. Although the Gujral Doctrine for several reasons is a positive step as far as India's relations with the neighbours is concerned, but ironically it is specifically confined to South Asia only. When it comes to Central Asia, the Gujral doctrine hardly offers anything new (Pradhan 2015). That is the reason why this policy of peaceful engagement with the energy-rich nations of Central Asia should be given due recognition in Modi's policy decisions as the region offers India much in return for what India offers to them.

Focus Commonwealth of Independence States (CIS) programme

"The Focus CIS programme was launched by the Ministry of Commerce & Industry of the Government of India in 2003 at the time of the announcement of the Exim Policy on March 31, 2003" (Chandra 2017). This programme aims at enhancing trade relationships with at least seven countries of the CIS region, namely Azerbaijan, Kazakhstan, Kyrgyzstan, Tajikistan, Turkmenistan, Ukraine and Uzbekistan. Since 2004, the programme has been further extended to the rest of the CIS countries including Russia, Armenia, Belarus, Georgia and Moldova. This initiative is indeed an encouraging step forward to boost bilateral and multilateral trade and economic relations with the partner countries which in turn helps India in attaining its energy quest.

Comprehensive Economic Partnership Agreement (CEPA)

CEPA is an omnibus free trade agreement between India and the member countries of the Eurasian Customs Union which aims at lowering tariffs on goods by both sides. This initiative was forwarded further by the UPA government during the visit of Dr Man Moha Singh to Russia in December 2011 (Chandra 2017). This agreement apart from sorting out trade issues with Russia is tailor-made to fit in the Eurasian Customs Union members' requirements, especially Kazakhstan and Belarus, to help Indian entrepreneurs enlarge their businesses.

India–EAEU FTA

India–Eurasian Economic Union (EAEU) has proposed to initiate a Free Trade Agreement (FTA) for expanding the trade and business interests of India and member countries of EAEU, largely dominated by Russia. Despite global economic recessions,

> the bilateral trade between India and EAEU in 2014 was at US$ 11.3 billion. India's total exports to the member states of EAEU stood at US$ 1.8 billion in 2016 while its imports from the EAEU are higher at US$ 5.1 billion in the same year.
>
> *(Chandra 2017)*

It can be seen that bilateral trade between India and members of EAEU is very weak except for Russia and Kazakhstan. The objectives of India has been to diversify its Russian dominated trade relationship and expand it to other members of EAEU so that bilateral trade would benefit the members and can be expanded to other sectors with mutual interests.

Indian-Technical and Economic Cooperation (ITEC)

Indian-Technical and Economic Cooperation (ITEC) has been a flagship programme since the 1990s between India and the Central Asian countries to exchange students and professionals for study and training in India. Since its inception, the programme has hosted more than 3000 people from Central Asia across the professions and streams. This is, in fact, a noble initiative through which people to people contact can be well developed between India and CAS and help strengthen ties between the two regions.

Despite all efforts, India's trade relationship with the Central Asian republics has been painful and discouraging. India's trade with CARs has grown sluggishly from $115 million in 1996 to $738 million in 2012 (Chandra 2017). India needs to address the low level of trade relations with Central Asia which indeed hampers India's larger energy interests in the region.

Connect Central Asia Policy

The Connect Central Asia Policy (CCAP) of India was first unveiled by the Minister of State for External Affairs, E. Ahmed in a keynote address at the first meeting of the India–Central Asia Dialogue, a Track II initiative organized on June 12–13, 2012, in Bishkek, Kyrgyzstan (Das 2012). The purpose of this policy is to fast track India's relations with Central Asian Republics. The policy calls for setting up universities, hospitals, information technology (IT) centres, an e-network in telemedicine connecting India to the CARs, joint commercial ventures, improving air connectivity to boost trade and tourism, joint scientific research and strategic partnerships in defence and security affairs. During S.M. Krishna's visit to Tajikistan on July 2–3, 2012, the former Foreign Minister expounded the unfolding policy under the rubric of "commerce, connectivity, consular and community" (Ibid). This policy initiative if properly channelized would enable India to attain centre stage in Central Asia which further would help India to attain its basic objectives of engagement in the greater Central Asian region.

Bilateral relations between India and Central Asian Republics

The historic Silk Route and the caravan trade since the 3rd century BC between the two regions are the testimony of their superb bonding and close friendship over the years. While India had very good and cordial overall relations with Central Asia, its relations with each country of the CAR need to be focused at length to understand India's country-specific engagements in the region.

India–Kazakhstan

The history of India and Kazakhstan dates back more than 2000 years. Apart from the cultural and philosophical interaction between India and Kazakhstan, regular exchanges of goods and services have been the defining characteristics of their friendship. It should be noted here that India was one among the first countries to recognize the independence of Kazakhstan. It set up its embassy in Almaty in 1992 to establish diplomatic relations with Kazakhstan while Kazakhstan opened up its embassy in New Delhi in 1993 which further brought them together.

Politically, both countries were friends even before their independence. The participation of Kazakhstan in the Asian Relations Conference in 1947 is a testimony to this. In 1955 India's first Prime Minister Pt. Jawaharlal Nehru visited Almaty along with his daughter Smt. Indira Gandhi. Dr S. Radha Krishnan visited Kazakhstan in his official capacity as Vice-President in 1956. Prime Minister of India Shri Narsimha Rao visited Kazakhstan in 1993, Prime Minister Shri Atal Bihari Vajpayee in June 2002, Dr Manmohan Singh in April 2011 and Shri Narendra Modi in July 2015 (bilateral visit) and June 2017 (Shanghai Cooperation Organization (SCO) summit). Vice-Presidents of India Shri K.R. Narayanan and Shri Hamid Ansari visited Kazakhstan in 1996 and 2008 respectively. Prime Minister Modi visited Astana on June 8–9, 2017 to participate in the 17th SCO Summit where India was admitted as a full member of SCO (MEA 2019).

Similarly, the President of Kazakhstan Mr Nursultan Nazarbayev visited India several times in 1992, 1993, 1996, 2002 and 2009. In 2009 he was invited as the Chief Guest of India's Republic Day Parade. H.E. Mr Askar Zhumagaliyev, Deputy Prime Minister of Kazakhstan visited India on September 20–22, 2018. Mr Kanat Bozymbayev, Minister of Energy accompanied by Mr Yermek Kosherbayev, Deputy Foreign Minister of Kazakhstan visited India to attend Petrotech-2019 on February 10–12, 2019, held in New Delhi. Mr Ilyin Yuri Viktorovich, Deputy Minister of Internal Affairs of Kazakhstan visited India to attend the 10th meeting of the Heads of Officers of the SCO member states on a joint urban earthquake search and rescue exercise held on November 4–7, 2019 in New Delhi (Embassy of India 2020).

India and Kazakhstan have been strategic partners since 2009. Also, both countries are actively cooperating under the aegis of multilateral fora including CICA (Conference on Interaction and Confidence-Building Measures in Asia), SCO and the UN organizations. Kazakhstan supports India's permanent membership in an expanded UNSC and has extended its support for India's non-permanent membership in 2021–22. India supported Kazakhstan's successful candidature for non-permanent membership of UNSC in 2017–18 (Embassy of India 2020). To further the close cooperation between both republics, institutional mechanisms were developed such as Foreign Office Consultant (FOC), Inter-Governmental Commission (IGC) and Joint Working Groups (JWG) in different fields of cooperation.

While cultural cooperation and consular services between both countries have been superb, the special focus of this section would be on the trade and economic relations between them. As such, Kazakhstan is the largest trade and investment partner of India in Central Asia. India's import from Kazakhstan amounted to $1299.1 million while exports to Kazakhstan were at $267.9 million in 2018, leading to total bilateral trade between them amounting to $1.56 billion as shown in Table 3.5 (Embassy of India 2020).

FICCI and the Chamber of International Commerce of Kazakhstan have set up a Joint Business Council (JBC) to promote bilateral trade, economic and investment cooperation. The Agricultural and Processed Food Products Export Development Authority (APEDA), responsible for promoting Indian agro-products, visited Almaty and Astana in June 2018 and conducted wet sampling of different varieties of Indian mangoes in prominent stores of Kazakhstan. Similarly, a Tea delegation visited Almaty in August 2018 and conducted tea promotion events and held B2B meetings. The Engineering Export Promotion Council of India (EEPC India) under the aegis of the Ministry of Commerce and Industry organized the India Pavilion at Kazbuild and Aquatherm 2019 which was held at Almaty on September 4–6, 2019. In the India Pavilion, around 30 Indian engineering companies participated in showcasing their product and capabilities in the areas of construction material and equipment, hardware and tools, roofing and technology, window décor, HVAC equipment and services, water purification, accessories and valves. A delegation led by CAPEXIL comprising 18 Indian

TABLE 3.5 Bilateral trade between India and Kazakhstan in last five years (in US$ millions)

Bilateral trade	*2014*	*% change over previous year*	*2015*	*% change over previous year*	*2016*	*% change over previous year*	*2017*	*% change over previous year*	*2018*	*% change over previous year*
Exports to Kazakhstan	260.50	–25.9	241.77	–7.2	203.81	–15.7	182.91	–10.25	242.78	+32.73
Imports from Kazakhstan	1083	+227.3	220.08	–79.68	414.61	+88.39	575.9	+38.9	954.08	+65.67
Total Trade	1343	+96.78	461.85	–65.61	618.42	+33.9	758.81	+22.7	1196.86	+57.73

Source: Embassy of India (2020), Bilateral Trade and Investment Statistics, Embassy of India, Nur-Sultan, Kazakhstan, March.

companies exhibited their products at the Kazcomak Expo held in Almaty on September 18–20, 2019, and also held B2B meetings with local businessmen. Ministries of Tourism from the states of Kerala, Rajasthan and delegates from Ministry of Tourism, Govt. of India and businessmen from the Indian tourism sector attended the PATA Travel Mart 2019 held in Nur-Sultan on September 18–20, 2019, to promote tourism in India (Embassy of India 2020).

India–Kyrgyzstan

In tune with its historical relations with Kyrgyzstan, India was among the first few countries to recognize Kyrgyzstan right after its independence in 1991. New Delhi established diplomatic relations with Bishkek on March 18, 1992, while the resident Mission was set up on May 23, 1994 (MEA 2019a). Since 1992 both countries have signed several framework agreements on different aspects including Culture, Trade and Economic Cooperation, Civil Aviation, Investment Promotion and Protection, Avoidance of Double Taxation, Consular Convention etc. President Jeenbekov visited India on a working visit on May 30, 2019, and attended the Swearing-in Ceremony of Prime Minister Narendra Modi and soon thereafter PM Modi visited the Kyrgyz Republic to attend the SCO Summit and for a bilateral visit on June 13–14, 2019 (MEA 2019a).

Bilateral trade and economic cooperation between the Kyrgyz Republic and the Republic of India are developing progressively and systematically. An Intergovernmental Commission on trade and economic, scientific, technical and cultural–humanitarian cooperation has been constituted between India and Kyrgyzstan. The ninth meeting held on November 15–16, 2019, in New Delhi was co-chaired by the Minister of Health of the Kyrgyz Republic and the Minister of Commerce and Industry of India.

On the initiative of the Embassy, on November 18, 2016, the Indo-Kyrgyz Business Council was formed, consisting of 22 member representatives of Indian business companies. The goals and objectives of the Business Council are to promote and develop mutual interest in economic relations between India and Kyrgyzstan, to conduct business meetings, conferences, seminars, meetings, organize trips of business delegations, as well as other activities that may be useful for the development of bilateral relations (MFA 2020).

Within the framework of trade and investment cooperation, events were organized that became notable events:

- Business Forum as part of the State Visit of the President of the Kyrgyz Republic to India (December 21, 2016),
- Kyrgyz–Indian Investment Business Forum (March 29, 2017),
- "Green Investment Forum", as part of the International Forum for the Conservation of the Snow Leopard and its Ecosystems (August 25, 2017, in Bishkek).

Three large-scale roadshows specifically targeted at the development of tourism and trade relations were organized and carried out in 2015, 2016 and 2017, the last of which was dedicated to the launch of the Electronic Visa of the Kyrgyz Republic system in India and the 25th anniversary of the establishment of diplomatic relations between Kyrgyzstan and India.

In recent years, Kyrgyzstan was represented at the sites of large business forums and exhibitions with the participation of delegations from many countries of the world:

- Aahar (2015, 2016, 2017),
- IITF (2015, 2016, 2017, 2018),
- Surajkund Mela (2015, 2016, 2017, 2018),
- Women's Economic Forum (May 2016 and 2017),
- Business Conference "Strengthening Strategic Partnership" of India and the CIS countries, (September 21–22, 2017), etc.

Kyrgyzstan is actively presented in India at the sites of popular, large international trade exhibitions as a partner country: at the "India International Trade Fair" – IITF 2017, the Kyrgyz Republic became the first focal country among the countries of Central Asia at the annual exhibition held by the Government of India. A variety of domestic agricultural products, traditional handicrafts, products using modern fashion and technology trends were widely presented in eight pavilions of a 90 sqm exhibition area. Over the two weeks of the international exhibition, the pavilion of Kyrgyzstan was visited by more than a million people and visitors, who expressed positive feedback on the high-quality and environmentally friendly products of the Kyrgyz Republic.

"Surajkund Mela-2018", which took place in Faridabad from February 1 to February 18, 2018. At the initiative of the Embassy, Kyrgyzstan was selected by the partner country of the 32nd annual international festival–fair of handicraft arts.

Bilateral trade during 2018–2019 between India and Kyrgyzstan amounted to $32.60 million. India's exports to the Kyrgyz Republic totalled $30.02 million, while Kyrgyz exports to India comprised $2.59 million. Indian exports registered a growth of 8.75 per cent on a year to year basis. The Kyrgyz Republic's share in India's total global exports was 0.01 per cent. India's exports to the Kyrgyz Republic among others comprise readymade garments and textile products, pharmaceutical products, agro-food products (tea, coffee and spices), essential oils and cosmetics, perfumery, electric machines, footwear, ferrous and non-ferrous metals. The Kyrgyz Republic exports to India include agro-food products (fruits and nuts), raw hides and skins, woollen products etc. There are around 20 Indian companies in the Kyrgyz Republic. There has been increasing interest among Indian entrepreneurs to explore business opportunities with the Kyrgyz Republic in sectors such as mining, agro-food, pharmaceuticals, textiles, gems and jewellery, IT etc. (Embassy of India 2019).

Prime Minister Narendra Modi visited the Kyrgyz Republic on an official visit from June 13 to 14, 2019. Fifteen agreements/documents including a Bilateral Investment Treaty, Protocol amending Agreement on Avoidance of Double Taxation and Fiscal Evasion, Memorandum of Understanding on Cooperation in Health, Information and Communication Technology, Defence Cooperation were signed. The bilateral relations were raised to the level of Strategic Partnership. During the visit, the Prime Minister also announced a line of credit of $200 million for financing development projects in the Kyrgyz Republic (Embassy of India 2019).

A 5-year Roadmap for Trade and Economic Cooperation was adopted during the visit of Prime Minister Modi in June 2019. The roadmap is aimed at the creation of favourable conditions for accelerated growth of bilateral trade, diversification of products and an increase in foreign investment.

An India–Kyrgyz Business forum was held on June 14–15, 2019. Kyrgyz President Jeenbekov and Prime Minister Modi jointly inaugurated the India–Kyrgyz Business Forum on June 14, 2019. One hundred and fifty Kyrgyz participants and 50 participants from India including a delegation from FICCI attended the event. Addressing the Business Forum, Prime Minister Modi highlighted the opportunities for investors from India in areas of medicines, textiles, railways, hydropower, mining and minerals, and tourism. The India–Kyrgyz Joint Textile Exhibition was held in Bishkek from June 13 to June 26, 2019. Both sides agreed to explore collaboration and cooperation in the fields of textiles, handicrafts, fabrics and arts. Prime Minister Modi also announced that an Indian trade show called "Namaskar Eurasia" would be organized in Bishkek. Namaskar Eurasia is scheduled from October 9 to October 11, 2019 (Embassy of India 2019).

India–Tajikistan

The traditional closeness and cordial friendship between India and Tajikistan since the Kushan days were translated into full-fledged diplomatic relations between both countries in 1992. This relationship was further cemented with the signing of the "Strategic Partnership" in September 2012, encompassing cooperation in a wide spectrum of areas including political, economic, education, health, human resource development, defence, counterterrorism, science and technology, culture and tourism (MEA 2019B).

Major political visits to Tajikistan from the Indian side have been Prime Minister Shri Atal Bihari Vajpayee to Tajikistan in 2003, President Smt. Pratibha Devisingh Patil in 2009, Vice President Shri Hamid Ansari in 2013. Smt. Sushma Swaraj, External Affairs Minister, visited Tajikistan for the Council of Heads of the Shanghai Cooperation Organization Summit in Dushanbe in September 2014. In recent years Prime Minister Shri Narendra Modi visited Tajikistan in 2015 and President Shri Ram Nath Kovind in 2018. Dr S. Jaishankar, External Affairs Minister of India, visited Tajikistan in June 2019 to attend the Fifth Summit Meeting of Conference on Interaction and Confidence Building Measures in

Asia. From the Tajik side, President Rahmon has visited India six times – in 1995, 1999, 2001, 2006, 2012 and 2016. The Tajik Foreign Minister visited India in May 2015, Tajik Defence Minister in January 2018 and Minister of Economic Development and Trade in June 2017. Several other ministers and senior civil and military officials have visited India from time to time (MEA 2019b; EOI 2019a).

During the visit of Prime Minister Shri Narendra Modi to Tajikistan in July 2015, the two sides decided to step up cooperation in the spheres of defence, connectivity and the fight against terrorism. They signed the "Programme of Cooperation in Culture and Art" for 2016–18 and decided to set up computer labs in 37 schools of Tajikistan. Apart from this, an Agricultural Workshop was also held. During his visit to India in December 2016, President Rahmon's three new cooperation agreements/MoUs were signed (MEA 2019b).

The state visit of President Shri Ram Nath Kovind to Tajikistan during October 7–9, 2018, was a milestone on many accounts. He announced $20 million grants for projects to be mutually agreed upon. An MoUs/ Programme for Cooperation in the following areas was signed: (i) Peaceful Use of Space Technology, (ii) Disaster Management, (iii) Renewable Energy, (iv) Youth Affairs, (v) Agricultural Research and Education, (vi) Unani Medicine, (vii) Programme between Foreign Ministries for 2018–21 and (viii) Cultural Exchange Programme for 2019–23. Separately, an MoU between Vivekananda International Foundation, New Delhi and the Centre for Strategic Researches under the President of Tajikistan was signed (MEA 2019b).

Among the Central Asian states, Tajikistan, apart from Kyrgyzstan, is blessed with huge hydroelectricity resources in addition to its enormous potentials in power transport, mining, the full chain of cotton processing, tourism and medical tourism. This gives Indian private investments immense opportunities to invest in various Tajik sectors. As of now, Indian investments in Tajikistan can be seen in a 5-star hotel constructed by M/s CHL Limited, India; the construction of 116 km long power transmission line from Sangtuda-1 Hydropower plant to the Afghan border in October 2010, completed by an Indian company named KEC/RPG and sponsored by ADB; BHEL supplied a 7 MW generator to the Tajik company "Pamir Energy" in 2011 on a commercial basis; Indian Company M/s Kalpataru bagged a contract worth approximately $22 million for the construction of electric transmission lines under ADB financing and finished the project in early 2017. The company won one more project worth $35 million in 2017 under the CASA-1000 power transmission project. There are other small private projects/companies/clinics which provide healthcare and other services in Tajikistan (MEA 2019B).

Although economic and trade relations between India and Tajikistan are only minuscule as yet, both countries are keen to take this relationship to a higher scale through cooperation. As of 2019, India's main exports are pharmaceuticals, apparel and clothing accessories, and handicrafts, machinery, and meat and meat products. Different types of ores, slag and ash, aluminium, organic chemicals, herbal oils, dried fruits and cotton are exported to India

TABLE 3.6 Bilateral trade between India and Tajikistan during 2011–18 (in million US$)

Bilateral trade	*2011–12*	*2012–13*	*2013–14*	*2014–15*	*2015–16*	*2016–17*	*2017–18*	*2018–19 (April–Jan)*
Export to Tajikistan	21.28	35.16	54.27	53.71	22.26	20.44	23.94	16.58
Imports from Tajikistan	8.86	12.86	0.86	4.39	9.98	21.82	50.29	4.24
Total trade	30.14	48.02	55.13	58.1	32.24	42.26	74.23	20.82

Source: MEA (2019c), India–Tajikistan Bilateral Relations, Ministry of External Affairs, Govt. Of India, available at: www.mea.gov.in/Portal/ForeignRelation/Bilateral_Brief_india_tajikistan_2019.pdf.

from Tajikistan. The bilateral trade figures during the last seven years are given in Table 3.6.

India–Turkmenistan

India and Turkmenistan have had close historical bonding since the days of the Great Silk Route. The "Turkmen Gate", built in the 1650s in Delhi, is a witness to their close friendship and superb ties. Turkmen people are very hospitable towards Indians (EOI 2019). They are very fond of Indian culture, cinema and TV serials. Similarly, their leadership is also cordial towards India politically. H.E the President of Turkmenistan, Mr Gurbanguly Berdimuhamedov visited India in May 2010. From the Indian side, Prime Minister of India Shri Narendra Modi visited Turkmenistan on July 10–11, 2015 (MEA 2019c). Several MoUs and important agreements were signed during this visit.

There have been several other visits at ministerial level including the then External Affairs Minister (EAM)'s visit in April 2015 for the Intergovernmental Commission (IGC) Meeting and the visit of her counterpart Mr Rashid Meredov, Deputy Prime Minister and Foreign Minister in 2017 and again in January 2018. The late Smt. Sushma Swaraj, the then EAM also had a separate meeting with Mr Rashid Meredov, Deputy Prime Minister and Foreign Minister on the side-lines of First India–Central Asia Dialogue held in Samarkand, Uzbekistan on January 13, 2019 (Ibid).

Major items of import by India include electronic and electrical items, machinery and woven apparel and pharmaceuticals, frozen meat and tyres. Exports by India comprise fertilizers, cotton, raw hides and inorganic chemicals (e.g. Sulpher, Iodine). Turkmenistan produces cotton, wheat, rice, and a variety of vegetables and fruits. Total trade between India and Turkmenistan for the year 2018–19 stood at $66.27 million of which exports from India stood at $45.64 million and imports to India at $20.63 million, registering a surplus of $25.01 million in India's favour. The bilateral trade relationship between both countries is presented in Table 3.7.

TABLE 3.7 Bilateral trade between India and Turkmenistan (in million US$)

Bilateral trade	*2013–14*	*2014–15*	*2015–16*	*2016–17*	*2017–18*	*2018–19*
Exports to Turkmenistan	73.63	91.98	68.53	57.60	54.31	45.64
Imports from Turkmenistan	14.10	13.05	46.97	21.32	26.15	20.63
Total Trade	**87.73**	**105.03**	**115.50**	**78.92**	**80.46**	**66.27**

Sources: MEA (2019D), India–Turkmenistan Relations, Ministry of External Affairs, Govt. Of India, available at: https://mea.gov.in/Portal/ForeignRelation/Bilateral_Brief_turkiministan_2019.pdf.

India–Uzbekistan

Among the Central Asian states, Uzbekistan shares a very unique relationship with India. Both countries are known to have deep-rooted historical and cultural relations. The frequent reference to the term "*Kamboj*" in Sanskrit and Pali language is in present-day Uzbekistan. It is believed that the Sakas participated in the Mahabharat war on the side of the Kauravas. The widely used ancient trade route "*Uttarpatha*" passed through Uzbekistan. The heart of the Silk Route passed through areas like Fergana, Samarkand, Bukhara in Uzbekistan which have been prominent trade centres since the old Silk Route days. The philosophical thought of Buddhism is believed to have passed to China through Uzbekistan. Famous and mighty kings like Amir Timur and Babur have hailed from Uzbekistan. These all show those close historical connections between India and Uzbekistan through the ages. This closeness was even maintained during the Soviet period as well. However, when the Soviet Union disintegrated in 1991, India accorded recognition to Uzbekistan as an independent state. Both countries since then have enjoyed astounding political and cultural relations. Both countries are known to host high-level political visits frequently. Prime Minister Shri P.V. Narasimha Rao visited Uzbekistan in 1993 and Prime Minister Dr Man Mohan Sing visited in 2006. Similarly, President Islam Karimov visited India on multiple occasions, in 1994, 2000, 2005 and 2011. In June and July 2015 Prime Minister Shri Narendra Modi visited to discuss bilateral issues and join the Shanghai Cooperation Organization (SCO) summit held in Tashkent. A high-level Uzbek delegation visited India, led by Mr Abdulaziz Kamilov, Minister of Foreign Affairs on June 23–24, 2017. During this visit, 22 contracts worth more than $80 million and 20 invest agreements worth over $70 million were signed (EOI 2017).

The trade relations between India and Uzbekistan are growing over the years and are governed by the Agreement on Trade and Economic Cooperation (ATEC) signed in May 1993. Both countries also entered into agreements on avoidance of double taxation in 1993 and for Bilateral Investments Promotion and Protection Agreement (BIPPA). There are several mechanisms to regulate and promote trade and economic relations between India and Uzbekistan. India–Uzbekistan Inter-Governmental Commission (IGC) on trade, economic, scientific and technological cooperation, and sector-specific Joint Working Groups (JWC) are among such mechanisms. As far as trade is concerned, the major areas of India's export to

TABLE 3.8 Bilateral trade between India and Uzbekistan (in million US$)

Bilateral trade	*2012*	*2013*	*2014*	*2015*	*2016*	*2017*	*2018*
Imports from India	163.4	217.4	249.0	260.6	318.1	291.0	261.3
Exports to India	37.8	42.2	67.0	58.7	51.9	32.6	23.3
Total trade	201.2	259.6	316.0	319.3	370.0	323.6	284.6

Source: EOI (2019b), India–Uzbekistan Relations, Embassy of India, Tashkent, Uzbekistan, August, available at: https://eoi.gov.in/tashkent/?2615?000.

Uzbekistan constitute pharmaceutical products, mechanical equipment, vehicle parts, optical instruments etc., while major imports to India are fruits and vegetable products, fertilizers, juice products, extracts and lubricants. The total trade relations between India and Uzbekistan are mentioned in Table 3.8.

Perception of Central Asian Republics on India

As previously discussed, India's relations with Central Asian states are deeply rooted historically, culturally and religiously. Its economic association with the CAR even dates back to antiquity when the Great Silk Route served as the connecting link between the two. The civilizational interactions among the regions through their mighty dynasties like Huna, Kushanas, Sakas, and Indian rulers like Ashoka, Bindusara and Khotans, and importantly the reign of Kanishka and Ashok have left an indelible impact on India–Central Asia relations. The marriage of languages has also had deep cultural impacts on India–Central Asia relations. Languages like Sanskrit, Brahmi, Pali and Kharoshti have enriched their relationship. Religious interactions between Central Asia and India through Buddhism, Sufism, Islam and Christianity have helped in cultural assimilation and thereby evolved their relationship to greater heights.

The rich historic bonding was further buttressed by the diplomatic relations both regions accorded to each other by establishing political relations. The participation of Kazakhstan in an Asian relations conference held in New Delhi in 1947; the Tashkent Treaty of 1966 signed between India and Pakistan with the mediation of the USSR; the popularity of Indian movies, TV serials and cultural artefacts throughout the CAR have certainly anchored the perspectives of Central Asian countries towards India.

Their independence in 1991 coinciding with India's reform policy also opened up vistas in their economic relations to grow desirably. Importantly, the New Great Game that has taken place in Central Asia around controlling energy resources and influencing the regional countries and global actors such as Turkey, Iran, China, Russia and the United States has largely concerned these newly independent countries and made them look up to India with hopes and aspirations. At a time when all these countries have developed competitive interests in Central Asia, New Delhi's emphasis on democracy, secularism, cultural and philosophical interactions have undoubtedly won the hearts of Central Asian people. They see India as a soft power with cultural and religious anchors to drive their bondings. India's non-aligned virtues of non-interference in the internal matters of other countries further provided an impetus to their growing relations.

Apart from the historical, cultural and soft-power chords, India's huge population and gigantic size in the subcontinent places it in a unique position, driving the Central Asian countries towards it. The economic reforms India adopted in the form of the New Economic Policy (NEP) in 1991 under the leadership of Shri P. V. Narasimha Rao, which opened up Indian markets for world goods, are viewed positively by the Central Asian states for exporting their goods to this large world market. On the other hand, the huge bases of energy in Central Asian heartlands also attracted India in its quest for energy security.

Further, the multi-vector policy of the Central Asian states, underpinned by autonomy in the political sphere and national reconstruction without being guided by any outside country, has been well challenged by the aggressive geopolitical competition taking place between the United States, Russia, China, the European Union, Turkey and Iran along with Pakistan's nefarious design to Islamize the region on political lines. This has allowed the Central Asian countries to view India as a guiding factor with its peaceful and harmonious world view.

However, the disheartening factor for Central Asian states is about India's low-level economic cooperation with the region. Although India since 1991 has done well in cultural and other aspects of its relations with the Central Asian Republics, its economic engagement with the region has been dismal. While CAR sees India as an alternative to the Chinese monopoly in the region, India's disinterest and discouraging economic profile in the region is a matter of concern. While India's trade relations with China, Russia and ASEAN countries are growing, its trade and economic relations with the CAS are minuscule.

Importantly, India's much-needed energy security can be anchored with the help of Central Asian hydrocarbon resources which in turn can help India eradicate its widespread poverty and fuel its economic growth. Given the current economic growth of India and the prospects for future growth, its demand for energy would grow manifold in the coming years. In this scenario, the hydrocarbon resources of Central Asia would not just provide relief to India but would also help Central Asia to neutralize the growing monopoly of China.

Despite India's dismal economic cooperation with the countries of the region, India's strong historical rooting, cultural connections, civilizational interactions, religious bonding and diplomatic ties buttressed with favourable people to people contacts have placed India in a unique position in the heartland of Central Asia. If India can move its economic relations with the region in a positive spirit by deepening its energy and trade dealings, it would help the overall relationship between the two regions to grow unprecedentedly well.

Through the better part of India's history, links with Central Asia were the most important in its contact with the outside world. Traditionally India aimed to take its philosophical and cultural message across Inner Asian countries up to the remote

Siberian region. During the British period, political officers, explorers, surveyors and traders, obviously for the "Great Game" postures, maintained some interest in Central Asia. However, in the post-independence period, India has grossly and perhaps consciously overlooked the studies and understanding of its non-South Asian neighbouring areas, which traditionally formed "buffer zones" against external aggression. However, from the 1970s to 1990 India's Central Asia policy was factored by the Soviet Union. Due to healthy Indo-Soviet relations, Indian relations with Central Asia were cordial and close. In the early 1990s, with the disintegration of the Soviet Union, India's focus in the region again remained poor and dismal. However, with the increasing geopolitical and strategic significance of the region for India, it directed its foreign policy formulation towards the region, which many called India's "Look North Policy" (Pradhan 2015). This policy is meant to promote democracy, secularism and peaceful coexistence in the Central Asian region. The situation has, however, been changed with evolving energy scenarios in the region. Accordingly, policy formulation of the countries has changed, responding to the region's demand, whereas India continued to see the region through its historical and cultural prisms until recently. Nevertheless, the present NDA regime under the leadership of Prime Minister Modi has consistently focused upon the Central Asian countries, not through historical, cultural or religious lenses but through the geo-economics perspective for securing India's energy quest through Central Asia.

References

Bal, Suryakant Nijanand (2004), *Central Asia: A Strategy for India's Look-North Policy*, New Delhi: Lancer Publishers & Distributors.

Blank, Stephen (2003), "India's Rising Profile in Central Asia", *Comparative Strategy*, 22(2) (April), p. 141.

Blank, Stephen (2004), "India's Continuing Drive into Central Asia", *Central Asia Caucasus Analyst*, 14 January, pp. 7–9, available at: https://www.cacianalyst.org/publications/analytical-articles/item/8655-analytical-articles-caci-analyst-2004-1-14-art-8655.html.

Burnes, Alexander (1834), *Travels into Bokhara: Being the account of a Journey from India to Cabool, Tartary and Persia*, Vol. 1, London: John Murray, Albemarle Street.

Campbell, Ivan (2013), "India's Role and Interests in Central Asia, Safeworld", October, available at: https://www.files.ethz.ch/isn/172940/indias-role-and-interests-in-central-asia.pdf.

CASAREM (2007), *Electricity Transmission and Trade Projects – CASA -1000*, Central Asia-South Asia Regional Electricity Market, July, available at: http://centralasia.usaid.gov/datafiles/_upload/CASA-1000_Briefing_Mem_Final.pdf [accessed June 10, 2010].

Chandra, Amiya (2017), *The Trade Game: Engaging with Central Asia*, New Delhi: Pentagon Press.

Dani, Ahmad Hasan (1999), "Buddhism to Islam: Cultural Links between Central Asia and South Asia", in N. N. Vohra (ed.), *Culture, Society and Politics in Central Asia and India*, Delhi: Shipra Publication, pp. 6-7.

Das, Jyoti Prasad (2012), "India's Connect Central Asia Policy", *Foreign Policy Journal*, October 29, available at: https://www.foreignpolicyjournal.com/2012/10/29/indias-connect-central-asia-policy/.

Desai, Suyash (2017), "India's SCO Challenge", *The Diplomat*, December 05.

DNA (2012), "SM Krishna Arrives in Tajikistan on Two Day Visit", *Daily News and Analysis*, 2 July 2012, available at: www.dnaindia.com [accessed March 18, 2018].

EOI (2017), "Visit of high level delegation led by Minister for Foreign Affairs of the Republic of Uzbekistan to India," Embassy of India, Tashkent, Uzbekistan, August 20-24, available at: https://eoi.gov.in/tashkent/?6349?001, [accessed March 10, 2018].

EOI (2019), *India-Kyrgyzstan Bilateral Relations*, Bishkek: Embassy of India, September.

EOI (2019a), *India-Tajikistan Bilateral Relations*, Dushanbe: Embassy of India, September.

EOI (2019b), "India-Uzbekistan Relations, Embassy of India, Tashkent, Uzbekistan", August, available at: https://eoi.gov.in/tashkent/?2615?000 [accessed March 18, 2020].

EOI (2020), *Bilateral Trade and Investment Statistics*, Nur-Sultan, Kazakhstan: Embassy of India, March.

ET (2015), "PM Modi's Central Asia Tour: India Set to Push Trade with Resource-rich Kazakhstan", *Economic Times*, available at: http://articles.economictimes.indiatimes.com/2015-07-07/news/64177846_1_kazakhstan-kazakh-economy-central-asia [accessed March 18, 2018].

Eurasianet (2015), "Central Asia: India Woos Regional Leaders", July 9.

Gafurov, Babajan (1974), *Kushan Civilization and World and Culture in Central Asia in the Kushan Period*, Moscow: Nauka.

Hopkirk, Peter (1990), *The Great Game: On Secret Service in High Asia*, London: John Murray Publishers Ltd.

Indian Express (2006), "Pak has to pass anti-terror test, Manmohan tells forces chiefs," *The Indian Express*, Thursday, 18 October, available at: http://archive.indianexpress.com/news/pak-has-to-pass-antiterror-test-manmohan-tells-forces-chiefs--------/14927/ [accessed December 9, 2008].

Indian Express (2015), "SCO Decides to Include India as a Fulltime Member", *Indian Express*, July 11, available at: http://indianexpress.com/article/india/india-others/after-over-a-decade-sco-decides-to-include-india-as-full-time-member/ [accessed on March 18, 2018].

Interfax-Kazakhstan News Agency (2005), "Kazakhstan, India set to Develop Cooperation in Oil, Gas Sector," BBC Worldwide Monitoring: International Report, January 21.

Joshi, Nirmala (2010), *Reconnecting India and Central Asia*, New Delhi: New Century Publishers.

Joshi, Nirmala (2010), "Introduction", Reconnecting India and Central Asia – Energy Security and Economic Dimensions, Central Asia-Caucasus Institute and Silk Road Studies Program.

Joshi, Nirmala (2015), *Enhancing India-Central Asia Engagement: Prospects and Issues*, New Delhi: Vij Books Pvt Ltd, pp. 134.

Kaushik, Devendra. (1970), *Central Asia in Modern Times*, Moscow: Progress Publishers, p. 13.

Kumar, B. B. (2007), "India and Central Asia: Links and Interactions", in Roy, J. N. and Kumar, B .B. (eds.), *India and Central Asia: Classical to Contemporary Periods*, New Delhi: Concept Publishing.

Lal, Rollie. (2006), *Central Asia and Its Asian Neighbours: Security and Commerce at the Crossroads*, Santa Monica, CA: Rand Corporation, p. 30.

MEA (2012), "India-Kyrgyzstan Relations", Ministry of External Affairs, Government of India, New Delhi, March.

MEA (2012a), "India-Kazakhstan Relations", Ministry of External Affairs, Government of India, February 2012.

MEA (2015a), "Bilateral Agreement between India and Tajikistan", Ministry of External Affairs, Government of India, New Delhi, July.
MEA (2015b), "Bilateral Agreement between India and Turkmenistan", Ministry of External Affairs, Government of India, New Delhi, July.
MEA (2015c), "Bilateral Agreement between India and Kyrgyzstan", Ministry of External Affairs, Government of India, New Delhi, July.
MEA (2015d), "PM Modi's Central Asia Tour Brings Region Back into Focus", July 15, Ministry of External Affairs, Government of India, New Delhi, available at: http://mea.gov.in/articles-in-indian-media.htm?dtl/25484/PM+Modis+Central+Asia+tour+brings+region+back+into+focus [accessed March 18, 2020].
MEA (2005), "Joint Statement by the Republic of Uzbekistan and the Republic of India," Ministry of External Affairs, Government of India, New Delhi, April, 5, available at: https://mea.gov.in/bilateral-documents.htm?dtl/6525/Joint+Statement+by+the+Republic+of+Uzbekistan+and+the+Republic+of+India [accessed January 10, 2008].
MEA (2016), "India-Uzbekistan Relations, Ministry of External Affairs, Government of India, New Delhi, available at: https://mea.gov.in/Portal/ForeignRelation/Uzbekistan_09_02_2106.pdf [accessed March 18, 2020].
MEA (2016a), "India-Turkmenistan Relations", Ministry of External Affairs, Government of India, New Delhi.
MEA (2017), "India-Uzbekistan Relations", Ministry of External Affairs, Government of India, available at: http://www.mea.gov.in/Portal/ForeignRelation/Uzbekistan_Jan_2017.pdf [accessed March 18, 2020].
MEA (2019), "Brief on SCO," Ministry of External Affairs, Shanghai Cooperation Organization (SCO) Division, Government of India, May, available at: https://mea.gov.in/Portal/ForeignRelation/SCO_Brief_May_2019.pdf [accessed August 22, 2019].
MEA (2019a), "Bilateral Relations between India and Kazakhstan", Ministry of External Affairs, Govt. of India, New Delhi.
MEA (2019b), "India-Tajikistan Bilateral Relations", Ministry of External Affairs, Govt. of India, available at: https://www.mea.gov.in/Portal/ForeignRelation/Bilateral_Brief_india_tajikistan_2019.pdf [accessed March 18, 2020].
MEA (2019c), "India-Turkmenistan Relations", Ministry of External Affairs, Govt. of India, available at: https://mea.gov.in/Portal/ForeignRelation/Bilateral_Brief_turkiministan_2019.pdf [accessed March 18, 2020].
MFA (2020), "Trade and Economic Cooperation, Embassy of the Kyrgyz Republic in the Republic of India", Ministry of Foreign Affairs, Govt. of Kyrgyzstan, available at: https://mfa.gov.kg/en/dm/Embassy-of-the-Kyrgyz-Republic-in-the-Republic-of-India/Menu---Foreign-/--uslugi/Trade-and-Economic-Cooperation/mbassy-of-the-Kyrgyz-Republic-in-the-India [accessed March 18, 2020].
Muni, S. D (2003), "India and Central Asia: Towards a Cooperative Future", in Nirmala Joshi (ed.), *Central Asia – The Great Game Replayed: An Indian Perspective*, New Delhi: New Century Publications, p. 110.
Niti Central (2015), "PM Modi's Central Asia Visit: Key Takeaways", *Niti Central*, July 14, available at: http://www.niticentral.com/2015/07/14/pm-modis-central-asia-visit-key-takeaways-323561.html [accessed September 11, 2018].
Patnaik, Ajay (2016), *Central Asia: Geopolitics, Security and Stability*, New Delhi: Routledge.
Pradhan, Ramakrushna (2010), *Geopolitics of Central Asia: China-US Engagement*, Saarbrucken, Germany: VDM Verlag-Muller.

Pradhan, Ramakrushna (2015), "Mapping India's Look North Policy: Why Central Asia matters", *The IUP Journal of International Relations*, October. Vol. IX, No. 4.

Rasulzade, P. N (1968), *From the History of Central Asia – India Relations: Second Half of Nineteenth and Beginning of Twentieth Century*, in Russian Nauka, Tashkent.

Rohde (2002), "Delhi Tracks Al-Qaeda, Jaish Link", in Lal Rollie (ed.), *Central Asia and Its Asian Neighbours: Security and Commerce at the Crossroads*, Santa Monica, CA: Rand, p. 30.

Roy, J. N. and Kumar, B. B. (2007), *India and Central Asia: Classical to Contemporary Periods*, New Delhi: Concept Publishing.

Sachdeva, Gulshan. (2010), "Regional Economic Linkages", in Nirmala Joshi (ed.), *Reconnecting India and Central Asia*, New Delhi: New Elegant Printers, p. 138.

Sachdeva, Gulshan (2017), "Chaining Dynamics of India-Central Asia Ties", *Bishkek Project*, April 5, available at: https://www.bishkekproject.com/memos/24.

Sajjanhar, Ashok (2013), "India-Kazakhstan Relations: Challenges and Opportunities", *Indian Embassy in Kazakhstan*, November 20.

Sajjanhar, Ashok. (2016), "India-Central Asia Relations: Expanding Vistas ofPartnership", June 22, Observers Research Foundation, New Delhi.

Sharma, Raghav (2009), "India in Central Asia-the Road Ahead", *Institute of Peace and Conflict Studies*, Special Report, No. 63, January, p. 3.

Singh, Amit Kumar (2015), "India and Central Asia: An Interpretation of Mutually Indelible Historical Relationship and Its Multifaceted Impact", *International Journal of Interdisciplinary and Multidisciplinary Studies*, 2(7).

Singh, Manmohan (2005), Prime Minister of India, "Inaugural Address", at the conference "Petrotech 2005", New Delhi, [online] January 16, 2005, available at: https://archivepmo.nic.in/drmanmohansingh/speech-details.php?nodeid=64.

Sinha Y. (2004), "India and Central Asia in the Emerging Security Environment", in K. Santhanam and Ramakant Dwivedi (eds.), *India and Central Asia: Advancing the Common Interest*, New Delhi: Anamaya Publishers, p. 6.

Srinov, T. (2000), "India and Central Asia in Pre Islamic Period", Paper Presented in a seminar: Contact between Central Asia and the Indian Subcontinents in the second millennium BC, June 12-13, Tashkant, Uzbekistan.

Stobdan, P. (2001), "Central Asia and India's Security", *Strategic Analysis*, 28(1), Jan–Mar, p. 55.

Stobdan, P. (2004), "Central Asia and India's Security", *Strategic Analysis*, 28(1), Jan-Mar, pp. 54–83.

The Hindu (2013), "India, Tajikistan Stress Stakes in Afghan Peace", *The Hindu*, April 16, available at: www.thehindu.com/news/national/india-tajikistan-stress-stakes-in-afgan-peace/article4620799 [accessed April 11, 2014].

Ufa (2015), "2015-SCO BRICS Office Group", Ufa, Russia, available at: http://ufa2015.com/

UNODC (2011), "World Drug Report 2011", United Nations Office on Drugs and Crime, United Nations.

Uzbek Embassy (2015), "Uzbekistan President Starts State Visit to India", Uzbek Embassy, New Delhi.

World Bank (2014), "Kazakhstan-Country Profile", World Bank, available at: http://web.worldbank.org/WBSITE/EXTERNAL/COUNTRIES/ECAEXT/0 [accessed April 6, 2018].

4

INDIA'S ENERGY TRAJECTORY

> *Coal was king in 1800; coal was still king in 1900; coal is a dethroned monarch in 2000. Oil is king in 2000; oil will have abdicated before 2100.*
>
> (*The Times 1999*)

Nobel Laureate Richard Smalley (2005) characterized ten prioritized problems in the context of the world's quest for sustainability. These precedence problems are energy, water, food, environment, poverty, terrorism and war, disease, education, democracy and population. He accorded the highest priority to energy among all the chronic problems the world has been facing in contemporary times (Randolph and Masters 2008: 4).

Energy tops Smalley's list not just because abundant, available, affordable, clean, efficient and secure energy would enable the resolution of all the other problems, energy, besides, is needed to reclaim and treat water, grow food and manage the environment. Once these goals are achieved, energy can be used further to arrest poverty and disease and expand education and communication. By meeting these basic needs, we can control the root cause of terrorism and war, expand democracy and stabilize population (Ibid). Therefore, energy is a decisive public, economic, social and environmental issue of high importance. It is, thus, the key for achieving a sustainable world system and a constant flow of energy is, therefore, required to maintain that order. Hence, it is no surprise that energy is certainly the keystone of nature and society.

Apart from Smalley's observation, revelations of history reflect the resultant use of energy in the advancement of human society and civilization. Energy has freed people from slave and animal labour, from an agrarian society and the constraints of space. Energy is fundamental to economic development. Without energy resources, businesses would not be able to light their stores; people and goods would not be able to enrich markets on the other side of the world; homes and schools would be more difficult to heat, and the manufacturing sector would not be able to produce any products used daily. In short, the world economy depends on energy and the largest economies of the world rely on cheap and abundant supplies of energy for the growth of human populations and economic systems.

Since growth demands energy, it is no wonder that India – with an economy expected to grow at 10 per cent for the next 25 years has developed a ravenous appetite for energy. India, accounting 2.4 per cent of the world's total land surface and around 16 per cent of the total world population, is also the third-largest growing economy in the world (India Energy Handbook 2011). With the rapid rise of population and industrialization, the main challenge before India, therefore, is to maintain a sustainable growth at a rate of 8–10 per cent GDP over the next quarter-century to meet its developmental goals for poverty eradication, food security, rural development, education and health. India had an average growth rate of GDP at 7 per cent between 2000 and 2010 and attained a growth rate of 7.1 per cent up to March 2017 despite demonetization (Economic Survey 2017). Further, to catch up with the rest of Asia and to eradicate poverty, it is essential on the part of India to continue to grow at about 8–10 per cent or more over the next 25 years or so. To maintain this pace of growth, India will have to increase its energy consumption by at least 4 per cent annually (CSIS 2006). The energy requirement for such sustained annual growth poses a major challenge. According to the Integrated Energy Policy of Government of India, it needs to increase its primary energy supply by a factor of three or four and its electricity generation capacity/supply by a factor of five to six compared to its 2004 level (Planning Commission 2006).

Since energy is pivotal for national development and plays an important role in the everyday life of individuals and society, every country strives to be energy secure both through domestic and foreign supply sources. As India's domestic energy resources consistently failed to meet the energy demands, frustrated by the dismal performance of the domestic energy sector, India's diplomatic setup has opened up its arms to be actively involved in an energy quest. Diversifying and expanding its international sources of energy has been a major Indian policy thrust for the past decade. Since then there has been a growing recognition that energy security needs to be a critical component of India's foreign policy as India's continued economic success hinges around this. It is also believed that India's energy security can be increased by (a) diversifying both its energy mix and its sources of energy imports, and (b) seriously pursuing the overseas acquisition of energy assets as oil and gas are non-renewable and are in limited quantities. So it is no surprise that energy cooperation is at the heart of India's engagement with Central Asia.

In the scenario of India's unprecedented energy requirement and stupendous foreign dependence, the energy resources of Central Asia including the Caspian Sea region will play an important role in India's energy security strategy. Further, Central Asian oil and gas are of high quality, largely untapped, the investment environment is open and very friendly. As the producing countries consume less, a major chunk of these resources is meant for export. Besides, unlike the Middle East and African energy-rich countries, Central Asia is very stable and popular uprising against outside powers is seemingly absent there. The gas of Central Asia and the Caspian has less ash in comparison to other gas-producing regions of the world. All these happen to be the driving factors behind the resource scramble by major powers in Central Asia, which many would call the "New Great Game" (Pradhan 2018). The bottom line of the New Great Game, unlike the previous version, is essentially played out around petro-politics and pipeline diplomacy. It is in this context that this chapter, after a thorough examination of the energy factor in the geopolitics of Central Asia, tries to figure out the position of India in the epic quest for energy in the traditional bastion of Russia and the new grand chessboard of China and the United States. Nevertheless, India's energy quest in Central Asia would be incomplete without a substantial energy profile of India and the dilemma New Delhi faces in arresting the four major objectives of India's National Energy Policy (NEP): access to energy at affordable prices, improved security and energy independence, greater sustainability and economic growth to support the demand of a burgeoning population and maintain the growth trajectory (NEP 2017).

Energy profile of India

In relation to its population, India is poorly endowed with energy resources. Its share in the world population is 17 per cent whereas the shares in world coal, oil and gas are only 7 per cent, 0.4 per cent and 0.6 per cent respectively (NITI Aayog 2017). This means the domestic energy resources of India are insufficient to meet the burgeoning needs. Thus, India has to depend heavily on imports despite a very low level of energy consumption. Although, India is the eighth largest producer of energy in the world with 2.4 per cent of the world's total energy production, it is also the third-largest energy consumer in the world with 3.7 per cent of the global energy consumption (EIA 2018). India's energy consumption with this rate is projected to grow at 4.2 per cent a year by 2035 as per the report of BP Energy Outlook (*The Economic Times* 2017). Figure 4.1 and Table 4.1 give a broader outlook about India's energy consumption since the 1980s. India has domestic coal reserves of 293.5 billion tonnes with an annual production of over 739.92 million tonnes (Ramachandra and Hegde 2015). Coal constitutes the largest energy source of India with almost 44 per cent followed by traditional biomass and wastes with 24 per cent and petroleum and other liquids with 23 per cent as shown in Figure 4.2; other renewable fuel sources make up a very small portion of primary energy consumption. Since the population of India after the New Economic Policy in 1991 has been moving increasingly to the cities, the fuel use pattern has shifted from traditional biomass and waste to the use of electricity for cooking, heating and lighting purposes. The power sector in India is one of the fastest-growing

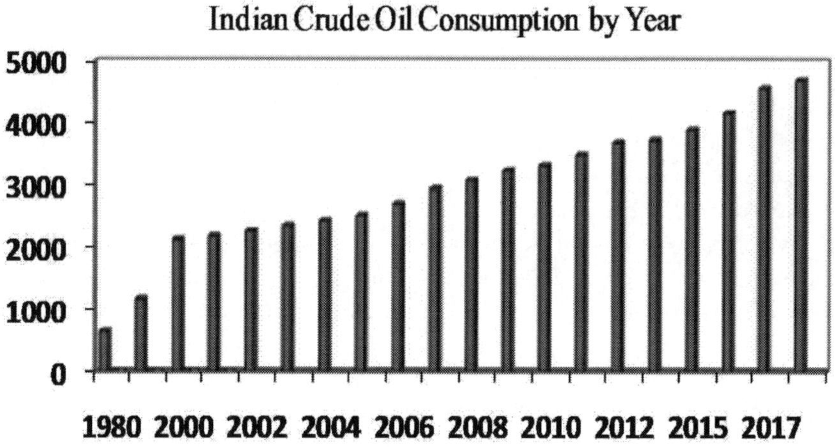

FIGURE 4.1 Indian crude oil consumption by year, 1980–2018 (thousand barrels per day).

Source: BP Statistical Review of World Energy, 67th edition June 2018

areas of energy demand, rising from 11 per cent to 15 per cent of total energy consumption between 2000 and 2013 (EIA 2018) and projected to grow at 26 per cent by 2040 (NITI Aayog 2017). Although the electrification rate in India has been growing since the NDA government came to power in 2014 under the leadership of Prime Minister Modi, yet 19 per cent of the population (240 million people) according to the IEA lacks basic access to electricity (IEA 2015). The remaining 33 per cent is met by oil and gas with more than 65 per cent of it being imported, mainly from the Middle East (NITI Aayog 2017). Given the environmental reasons, coal quality in India is the dirtiest and hydrocarbon fuel is unpurified; hence, India cannot rely on them for the long term to meet her energy needs.

Oil

India's oil and gas reserves are not sufficient to meet its rapidly growing energy needs. According to the *Oil and Gas Journal*, India had 5.7 billion barrels of proved oil reserves at the end of 2015, the second-largest amount in the Asia–Pacific region after China (EIA 2016). Although oil production in India has trended upwards slightly in recent years, it has failed to keep pace with demand. Additionally, in contrast to production, India's oil consumption has continued to be robust. India has consumed approximately 2.8 million bbl/d in 2007 which again grew to nearly 4.1 million bbl/d in 2015 (Ibid). The combination of rising oil consumption and relatively flat production has left India increasingly dependent on imports to meet its petroleum demands, as shown in Figure 4.3.

TABLE 4.1 India's crude oil consumption annual growth rate, 1980–2013

Year	*Consumption (thousand barrels per day)*	*Change (%)*
1980	643.00	NA
1981	729.00	13.37
1982	737.00	1.10
1983	773.00	4.88
1984	824.00	6.60
1985	894.90	8.60
1986	947.44	5.87
1987	987.85	4.27
1988	1,083.78	9.71
1989	1,149.78	6.09
1990	1,168.33	1.61
1991	1,190.32	1.88
1992	1,274.91	7.11
1993	1,311.07	2.84
1994	1,413.27	7.80
1995	1,574.67	11.42
1996	1,680.92	6.75
1997	1,765.49	5.03
1998	1,844.37	4.47
1999	2,031.25	10.13
2000	2,127.44	4.74
2001	2,183.73	2.65
2002	2,263.44	3.65
2003	2,346.33	3.66
2004	2,429.62	3.55
2005	2,512.43	3.41
2006	2,690.90	7.10
2007	2,800.75	4.08
2008	2,950.00	5.33
2009	3,110.00	5.42
2010	3,305.00	7.72
2011	3,461.00	4.72
2012	3,618.00	4.54
2013	3,660.00	1.16
2014	3848.754	
2015	4163.927	
2016	4559.746	
2017	4690.282	

Source: United States Energy Information Administration, 2018; CEIC, 2018.

The growing energy crunch of India is evident from the fact that in 2006, India was the seventh-largest net importer of oil in the world; in 2007 it became the sixth-largest importer and is currently in the fourth position after the United States, China and Japan (EIA 2016). India imports about 62 per cent of its total

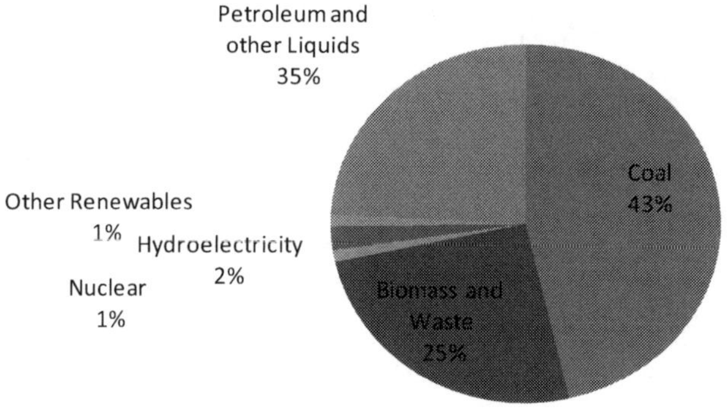

FIGURE 4.2 Sourcewise total energy consumption in India, 2016–17.

Source: International Energy Agency, 2018; MOSPI, 2018

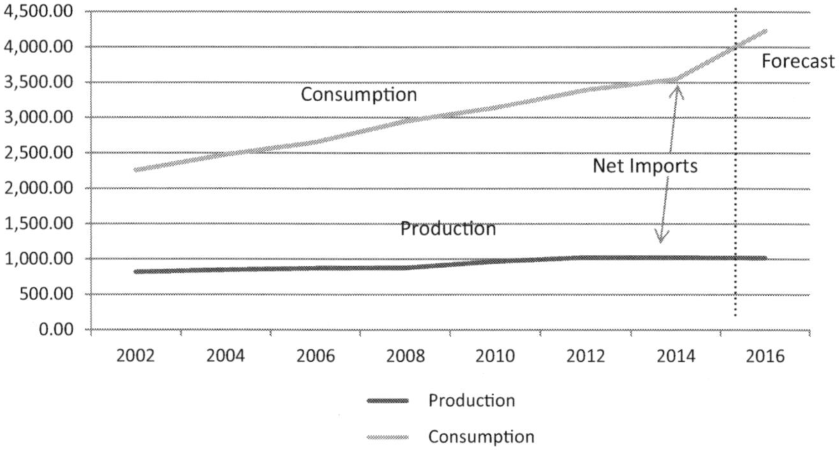

FIGURE 4.3 India's petroleum and other liquids production and consumption, 2000–17 (in million barrels per day).

Source: US Energy Information Administration, May 2016

oil consumption (NEP 2017) and met 82 per cent of its crude oil requirements through imports (Abdi 2018). It is expected to be the world's third-largest consumer of oil soon (ET 2018). India has been guzzling increasing amounts of oil, fuelling an economy that has been growing at 7–8 per cent a year since 2003 (Economic Survey 2017). Correspondingly, while global oil demand is expected to increase at an annual average rate of 1.6 per cent, India's demand for oil is expected to increase at an average rate of 2.9 per cent annually from 2002 to 2030 (IEA 2016).

In India, oil and its products are consumed mainly in the transport, commercial, industrial and domestic sectors (See Figures 4.4 and 4.5). Oil is also used

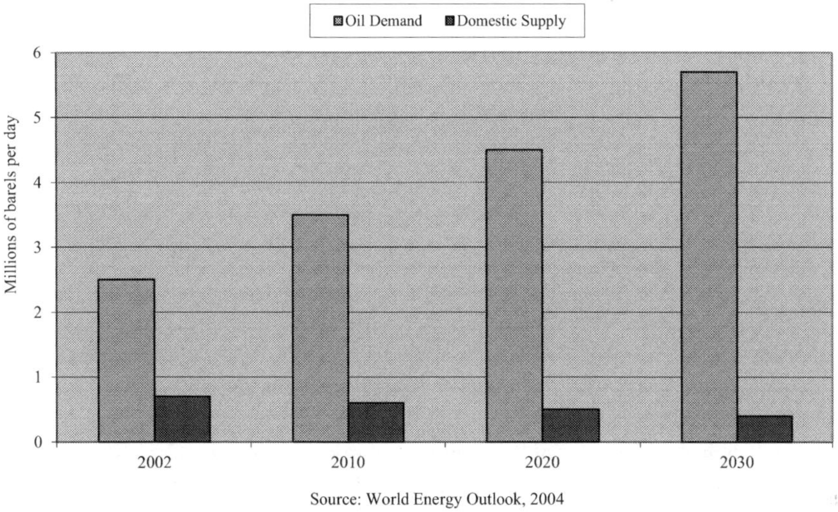

FIGURE 4.4 India's projected oil demand and domestic supply.

Source: World Energy Outlook 2014

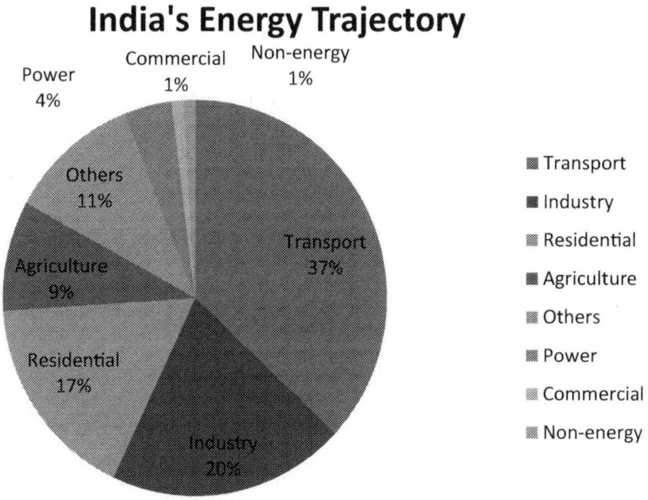

FIGURE 4.5 India's energy trajectory.

Source: Ramachandra and Hedge (2015), Energy Trajectory in India, *The Journal of Resources Energy and Development*, Vol. 12, Issue 1&2

in captive power generation as India's power grid fails to provide a reliable and consistent source of electricity. Yet, the main worry for India is its ever-widening gap between consumption and production of oil. India's domestic production of crude oil as of 2017 was about at 719,900 bl/d (CEIC 218). This records a decrease from the previous number of 720,800 bl/d for December 2016 (Ibid). It contributes only a minute per cent of the world's total output. The bulk of India's supply comes from beyond its borders.

The crude oil import partners for India until 2009–10 were Saudi Arabia, followed by Iran (EIA 2009) but with the increasing dependence of India on crude oil the trajectory changed and as of June 2018, as shown in Table 4.3, Iraq is the main import partner of India followed by Saudi Arabia and Iran. To be honest, India's crude oil imports from Iran jumped to a staggering 52 per cent to 2.57 million tonnes (MT) in June 2018 as per the fresh data sources of the Director General of Commercial Intelligence and Statistics (DGCIS 2018). The Government of India expects this geographical dependence to rise in the light of limited prospects for domestic production shortly. There have been few discoveries on the domestic front, but production from these fields is merely replacing that of older oilfields. With domestic oil production expected to account for a smaller portion of India's energy supply, it is likely to import a greater portion of the oil for its use. International Energy Agency estimation predicts that with the current level of reserves and production, India's oil dependence by 2030 is projected to grow to 91 per cent (IEA 2004: 106). Thus, India will likely be a net importer till global reserves run out.

India's dependence on foreign oil is longer standing than that of China. India either buys its oil through spot purchases (Nigeria), short-term contracts

TABLE 4.2 India's crude oil imports during the first quarter (in million tonnes)

Country	*Q1 2017–18*	*Q1 2018–19*
Iraq	10.58	12
Saudi Arabia	8.36	9.17
Iran	5.62	8.14
UAE	3.33	3.89
Nigeria	5	2.66
Venezuela	4.86	3.9

Sources: Energy World, *The Economic Times*, July 14, 2018.

TABLE 4.3 Largest crude suppliers to India: 2013–18 (in million tonnes)

Country	*2013–14*	*2014–15*	*2015–16*	*2016–17*	*2017–18*
Iraq	24.6	24.5	36.8	37.45	45.74
Saudi Arabia	38.2	35	40.4	39.33	36.16
Iran	11	11	12.7	27.14	22.59
Venezuela	21.6	24.4	23.6	21.43	18.34
Nigeria	16.4	17.8	23.4	17.70	18.11
UAE	16.4	16.1	15.7	19.30	14.29

Source: Energy World, *The Economic Times*, July 12, 2018.

(generally three months) or long-term contracts (Saudi Arabia, for a year) (Madan 2006: 11). As of 2018, it imports oil from the Middle East accounting for around 70 per cent of India's foreign oil purchases. India's largest oil suppliers are Iraq (45.74 MT), Saudi Arabia (36.16 MT), Iran (22.59 MT), Venezuela (18.34 MT), Nigeria (18.11 MT), UAE (14.29 MT) and Kuwait (11.9 MT) as shown in Table 4.3 (*The Economic Times* 2018).

Unfortunately, all these countries shown in Table 4.3 except Saudi Arabia are trouble-torn, marred by civic unrest, politically instable, and prone to ethnic violence and terrorism, with Iran battling United States sanctions, which poses serious questions for the energy security system of India. Therefore, it is natural on the part of India to look to diversifying its oil sources, particularly those available in her neighbourhood: Central Asia.

Natural gas

India is relatively a newcomer to the use of natural gas. In the 1970s and 1980s, it accounted for a very negligible part of Indian energy consumption (Madan 2006: 11). The use of natural gas, however, picked up momentum when the Bombay High field went into production in 1987 (Ibid). In 2009, India had **1076.040** billion cubic meter (bcm) of proven natural gas reserves (ENI 2018). According to the official data of the Ministry of Petroleum and Natural Gas, India's total natural gas production in 2017–18 was 32.64 billion cubic metres (bcm) (MoPNG 2018) and it had nearly **1500.792 bcm** of proved natural gas reserves (EIA 2016). According to the Ministry of Oil and Gas, about 34 per cent of the total reserves are located onshore and 66 per cent are offshore (MoPNG 2018). The bulk of India's natural gas production comes from the western offshore regions while the onshore sources are also significant sources of natural gas. Natural gas demand is expected to grow considerably, largely driven by demand in the power sector. The power and fertilizer sectors account for nearly three-quarters of natural gas consumption in India. Although India was independent in natural gas usage until 2004 the production rate has consistently started decreasing, demand has already exceeded supply and the country has been a net importer of natural gas since 2004 (EIA 2016). As of 2016–17, India's natural gas import dependence was close to 45 per cent. As of 2018, India is the fourth largest importer of liquefied natural gas (LNG) in the world (MoPNG 2018). In recent periods, natural gas is one of the fastest-growing sources of energy in India. According to the International Energy Agency (IEA), India's annual energy consumption since 2004 has been growing at a rate of 6 per cent and as of 2018, it stands at 6.2 per cent. New Delhi has set a target of 15 per cent increase in gas consumption in its energy basket by 2030 (MoPNG 2018). At present, Qatar is the biggest supplier of Natural Gas to India. In 2015, Qatar was the source of 62 per cent of India's total LNG imports. New Delhi has been an active importer of spot cargoes of LNG following interruptions in the KG-D6 field production after 2010 (EIA 2016). Also, Nigeria, Egypt and Yemen are India's largest short-term LNG suppliers.

TABLE 4.4 India's LNG import by country (bcm)

Country	*2004/05*	*2005/06*	*2006/07*	*2007/08*	*2008/09*	*2009/10*	*2016/17*
Abu Dhabi			0.09	0.08	0.13	0.16	–
Australia			0.09		0.16	1.11	1.44
Indonesia						0.08	–
Malaysia			0.09	0.09	0.08	0.25	–
Oman			0.27	0.27	0.41	0.35	–
Qatar	3.49	3.68	8.24	9.43	8.34	7.95	8.5
Algeria			0.09	0.55	0.53	0.16	–
Nigeria			0.09	0.77	0.38	0.32	–
T&T				0.24	0.23	0.68	–
Egypt			0.62	0.09	0.24	0.33	–
E. Guinea					0.42	0.25	–
Norway					0.08		–
Russia						0.68	2.85
Others					0.17		–
Total	3.49	6.98	9.59	11.52	11.16	12.31	6.5

Source: IEA, Natural Gas Information 2010, PIB, 2018.

India's primary energy supply is currently dominated by coal (37 per cent), biomass and waste (27 per cent) and oil (26 per cent). The share of natural gas in the overall energy mix is only 6 per cent (Ibid). Before 2009, gas demand potential was estimated to be 20 to 30 bcm higher than actual use as consumption had been constrained by the lack of supply over a decade (MoPNG 2009). The year 2009 marked a turning point for the Indian gas market with new supplies available, India's gas consumption increased to 59 bcm in Financial Year 2009/10, from 43 bcm in FY 2008/09 (IEA 2010: 5).

In India, natural gas is mainly used for power generation (23 per cent), in the manufacture of fertilizers (32 per cent) and the replacement of LPG for cooking oil and other uses in the residential sector (14 per cent) (EIA 2016). Transportation, agriculture and domestic uses account for the rest of the consumption. Most of India's domestic sources are offshore (off the western coast). With consumption expected to increase, the dominance of domestic gas is likely to increase. India in due course, as with oil, will become increasingly dependent on imported gas. Again, there is no other energy source like Central Asia with its huge number of gas-filled untapped resources.

From Table 4.4, it is quite clear that gas import dependence of India is increasing substantially year by year. And much of this comes from countries like Qatar, Oman, Nigeria and Trinidad and Tobago – far away from India. In this respect, the Central Asia region can prove beneficial for India because of its geographical proximity.

Hydroelectricity

Hydropower plays an important role as part of India's goal for diversifying its sources of electricity. It has an installed capacity of 148 gigawatts (GW) and generates 703 billion kilowatt-hours (EIA 2016). Nearly, all power in India is generated with conventional thermal sources, which produce over 80 per cent of electricity. Despite this, India suffers from a severe shortage of electricity capacity. According to the World Bank, roughly 40 per cent of residences in India are without electricity and besides, blackouts are a common occurrence throughout the country's main cities (Ibid). Also, compounding the situation is that the total demand for electricity in the country continues to rise and is outpacing increases in capacity. India as of 2016 is the seventh-largest consumer of hydroelectricity. This accounts for 5 per cent of the country's total consumption of commercial energy. In addition to this, more aggravating is the shortage of coal which is further straining power generation capabilities.

Nuclear energy

Nuclear energy accounts for only 1 per cent of India's primary commercial energy consumption. India has 21 operational nuclear reactors at seven nuclear power plants with a net generation capacity of 5.3 GW. The first unit of the Kudankulam power plant – India's first large nuclear plant in Tamil Nadu – became operational at the end of 2014. As of early 2016, six reactors with a combined net installed capacity of 3.9 GW are under construction and could come online soon. By 2030, it is expected to increase to at least 29 million tonnes of oil equivalent (mtoe) (IEA 2016). With the inking of the civil nuclear cooperation deal with the United States, the Indian government set its nuclear generation target from the original goal of 20,000 MW to 40,000 MW by 2020 (EIA 2009). Nuclear power holds a great deal of potential in India and the government is increasingly relying on its development to hit its power generation targets.

Coal

India is the third highest coal producer in the world with an annual production of 739.92 million tonnes (MT) (Ramachandra and Hegde 2015) while it has the fourth-largest reserve of coal in the world (BP 2005: 33). It is simultaneously the third-largest consumer of energy from coal with approximately 55 per cent of primary energy supply coming from coal and is expected to remain high at 48–54 per cent by 2040 (NITI Aayog 2017). In total, coal accounts for more than half of India's total energy consumption followed by oil, which comprises 31 per cent of total energy consumption. Natural gas and hydroelectric power account for 8 and 6 per cent of consumption, respectively. Although nuclear power comprises a very small percentage of total energy consumption at this time, it is expected to increase in light of recent international civil nuclear energy cooperation deals. According to the Indian government, 30 per cent of India's total energy needs are met through imports, which were just 17.8 per cent in 1991(Planning Commission 2006). Further, demand for oil has doubled to 2.9 million barrels per day in just a decade and is projected to reach around 7 million barrels per day by 2030, growing annually at a rate of about 4 per cent (Ibid). While coal's dominance as an energy source in India has slowly been decreasing, it is expected to continue, still accounting for more than 40 per cent of consumption in 2030. The IEA estimates that 362 mtoe of India's commercial energy will come from coal by then (IEA 2016). To arrest this relentless demand for energy, India is, therefore, required to import energy resources from external sources as its domestic sources are not sufficient to meet its energy needs in the long term. Although coal is abundant in India, it is probably also the most polluting source of energy. It is relatively cheap and considered easier and safer to transport than oil or gas. The majority of India's coal reserves are located in the eastern and central states of India – away from major energy consumption areas in the north and west. Recently, India had to start importing coal as production has struggled to keep up with consumption. The domestic coal shortage is expected to persist for a few more years with India projected to spend $6 billion a year importing coal (Ibid).

Depleting and polluted coal, rising oil imports, increasing natural gas demand, an inefficient electric system, energy-related water shortage, limited nuclear energy etc. pose serious challenges to India's energy security. But the country aims

> to meet reliably the demand for energy services of all sectors including the lifeline energy needs of vulnerable households in all parts of the country, with safe and convenient energy at the least cost in a technically efficient, economically viable and environmentally sustainable manner.
>
> *(NPTI 2017)*

The broad vision behind such energy policy is to have access to the assured supply of such energy and technologies at all times; considering the shocks and disruption that can be reasonably expected is essential to providing energy security to all. At its broadest level, India's energy security has to do with the continuous availability of primary commercial energy at an affordable price (IEA 2020).

India's future energy demand

Given the country's developmental goals and plans to maintain a high economic growth rate, various estimates indicate that by 2031, India's primary energy supply would need to increase significantly from the current levels. The Integrated Energy Policy Report estimates that under an 8 per cent GDP growth scenario, assuming alternative scenarios of fuel and technological diffusion, India's total energy requirement would be in the range of 1536–1887 mtoe by 2031 (Planning Commission 2006). The analysis by TERI (The Energy and Resources Institute), which is based on the MARKAL (MARKet ALlocation) model, indicates that under an 8 per cent GDP growth scenario, with current plans and policies of the Government of India, commercial energy needs would increase to 2149 mtoe by 2031/32 and CO2 (carbon dioxide) emissions would increase to about 7 Gt in the same year (Figure 4.6) (BP 2018). Moreover, both these estimates indicate that coal and oil would continue to account for most of India's energy requirement, even by 2031. Table 4.5 provides a vivid presentation of India's energy profile as of 2018.

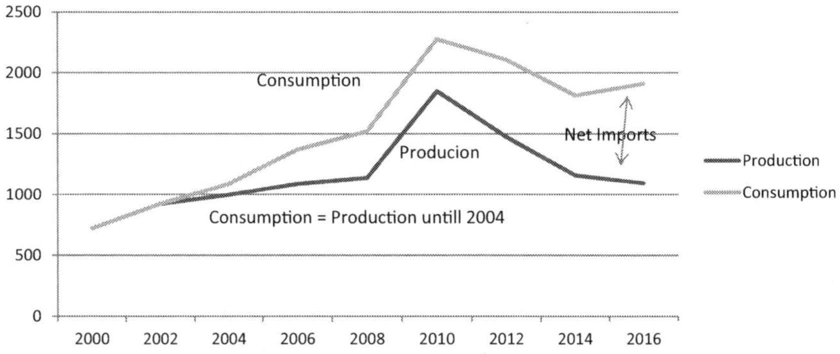

FIGURE 4.6 India's Dry Natural Gas Production and Consumption, 2000–14 (in bcf).
Source: US Energy Information Administration, 2016

TABLE 4.5 India's energy profile – 2018

Electricity access	population without electricity: 237,400,000 electrification – total population: 79% electrification – urban areas: 98% electrification – rural areas: 70% (2013)
Electricity – production	1.289 trillion kWh (2015 est.)
Electricity – consumption	1.048 trillion kWh (2015 est.)
Electricity – exports	5.15 billion kWh (2015 est.)
Electricity – imports	5.244 billion kWh (2015 est.)
Electricity – installed generating capacity	308.8 million kW (30 November 2016)
Electricity – from fossil fuels	71.5% of total installed capacity (2015 est.)
Electricity – from nuclear fuels	1.6% of total installed capacity (2015 est.)
Electricity – from hydroelectric plants	14.4% of total installed capacity (2015 est.)
Electricity – from other renewable sources	14.6% of total installed capacity (2015 est.)
Oil – production	734,500 bbl/day (2016 est.)
Oil – exports	0 bbl/day (2014 est.)
Oil – imports	3.789 million bbl/day (2014 est.)
Oil – proved reserves	4.621 billion bbl (1 January 2017 est.)
Refined petroleum products – production	4.793 million bbl/day (2014 est.)
Refined petroleum products – consumption	4.142 million bbl/day (2015 est.)
Refined petroleum products – exports	1.371 million bbl/day (2014 est.)
Refined petroleum products – imports	481,900 bbl/day (2014 est.)
Natural gas – production	31.24 billion cu m (2015 est.)
Natural gas – consumption	102.3 billion cu m (2015 est.)
Natural gas – exports	270 million cu m (2015 est.)
Natural gas – imports	18.67 billion cu m (2015 est.)
Natural gas – proved reserves	1.227 trillion cu m (1 January 2017 est.)
Carbon dioxide emissions from consumption of energy	1.887 billion Mt (2013 est.)

Source: CIA World Factbook, January 20, 2018.

According to BP Energy Outlook, India's energy consumption is set to grow 4.2 per cent a year by 2035 (ET 2018). India as of 2018 is the second biggest energy consumer in Asia after China, having surpassed Japan in 2015. It is further predicted that India is growing at a faster pace than any major energy consumer and its consumption of fossil fuel will be the highest by 2035. It is also projected that India will overtake China as the largest growth market for energy in volume terms by 2030 (Ibid). This will accentuate global demand of energy to increase by 30 per cent by 2035 and natural gas consumption will grow faster than either oil or coal, expanding at 1.6 per cent a year (ET 2018). The scenario of future energy demand as projected by the BP World Energy Outlook has been shown in Figures 4.8 and 4.9.

From the figures, it can be estimated that India's gas demand will expand by 162 per cent, followed by that of oil (121 per cent) and coal (105 per cent). Renewables will rise by 712 per cent, nuclear by 317 per cent and hydro by 97 per cent by 2035 (ET 2018). India's oil imports are projected to rise by 165 per cent and account for 56 per cent of the increase in imports. Imports of natural gas will also follow the rising pattern with 173 per cent and coal by 105 per cent (BP 2018). Figures 4.8 and 4.9 depict the trend of India's total primary energy consumption during the period 2015–35 and its projected share of global energy consumption in 2035.

Going with the current rate of growth and the future projection of BP Energy outlook, India is destined to be the numero uno in world energy consumption. A country with 68 per cent of import dependence at the current level will have to climb the Alps to meet the herculean task of energy demands. The only options before India in such a scenario seem to be diversifications of both sources and resources. As India already imports about three-fourths of its crude oil from the Middle Eastern partners, Saudi Arabia and Iran, the question that looms large now is where India will get these resources at a cheaper cost with reliable and uninterrupted supplies. The only option that comes to mind is Central Asia and the Caspian Sea energy-rich region which has emerged as the new geological landscape of energy. Hence, this chapter emphasizes the importance of Central Asian energy resources for India's present energy challenges and future energy dilemma.

India's energy crunch

India's energy sector faces some critical challenges on account of several factors that need to be carefully considered and built into strategies for the future. First, with the increase in global oil prices and India's mounting dependence on oil imports, a socio-economic dilemma presents before the government in formulating pricing policies. Unfortunately, even though the administered pricing regime, which required the government to carry out the pricing of petroleum products, was to be dismantled in 2002, the old system has continued without

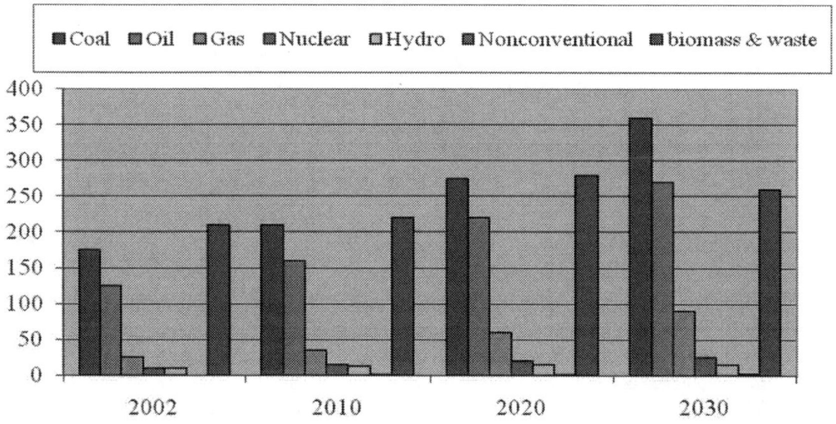

FIGURE 4.7 India's primary energy demand.

Source: World Energy Outlook, 2018

any perceptible change. Hence, the Government of India still retains responsibility for pricing petroleum products, which inevitably involves several pulls and pressures from those sections of the society which have benefited from subsidies in the past. Unfortunately, even with the higher prices of oil, the government has not been able to roll back these subsidies, and this has placed a major burden on the public sector oil companies.

India already has serious problems with the lack of access to modern forms of energy. According to the National Energy Policy, nearly 304 million Indians have no access to electricity and about 500 million people still depend on solid biomass for cooking (2017). This continues to pose a major problem, and, so far, suitable alternatives have not been found for this large part of the population, although in some limited areas, marketing of LPG at subsidized prices through Ujjawal Yojana has helped to a great extent. Millions of people in the country have no access to electricity and therefore they are virtually left with no choice but to use candles, small oil lamps based on kerosene, and other oils (Ibid). These devices not only provide inadequate lighting but also affect human health through the emission of harmful gases. Kerosene is subsidized largely because it is regarded as the poor man's modern fuel. But it is also well known that a large quantity of the subsidized kerosene does not reach those that it is meant for, and is diverted for other purposes. Even so, lack of a lifeline supply of safe and convenient energy is responsible for most of India's poor human development indices – either directly or indirectly. Illiteracy, gender inequality, disempowerment, high infant and maternal mortality rates, lack of access to clean drinking water, and poor health indicators can all be traced back to the lack of a lifeline level of safe and clean commercial energy for all Indian households.

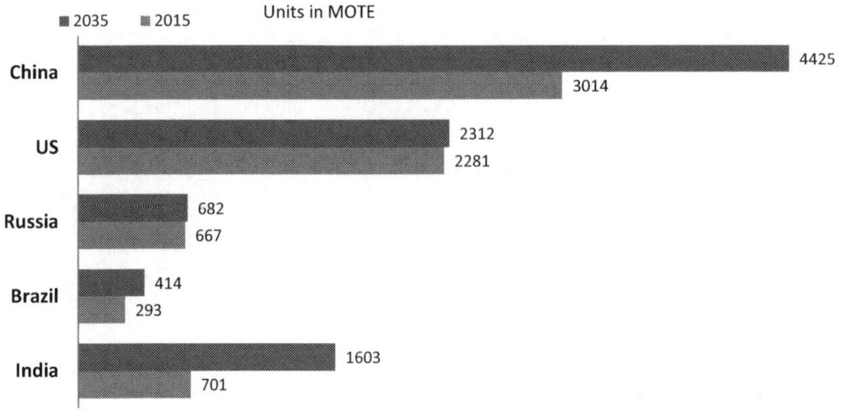

FIGURE 4.8 India's total primary energy consumption 2015–35.

Source: Author's self assessment based on the data of BP World Energy Outlook, 2018

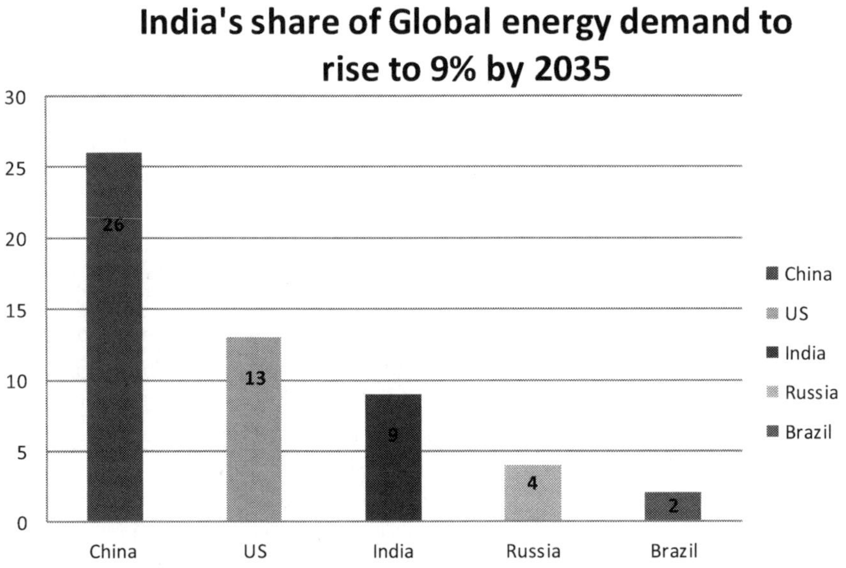

FIGURE 4.9 India's share in global energy demand by 2035.

Source: Author's self assessment based on the data of BP World Energy Outlook, 2018

India needs a consistent and inclusive 8 per cent plus GDP growth over the next 25 years to eradicate poverty and meet the millennium development goals. The emphasis on inclusive growth is essential if this aspiration is to be meaningful for all Indians. Raising access to modern commercial fuels is at the very heart of delivering such inclusive growth. The rapid growth of the Indian economy

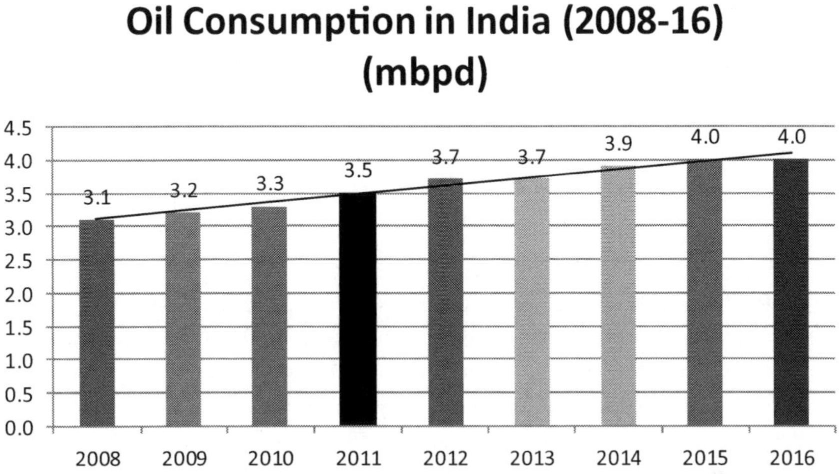

FIGURE 4.10 Oil consumption in India 2008–16 (in million barrels per day).

Sources: Ministry of Oil and Natural Gas, Govt of India and BP Statistical Review 2015

has led to increasing demand for energy, but capacity, particularly in the power sector, has not kept pace with this growth in demand. Additionally, whatever capacity exists is often utilized at very low levels of efficiency. This has resulted in substantial losses in the transmission and distribution system and generation of very low plant load factor in several cases. Overall, the energy challenge for India requires significant improvements in efficiency and the creation of options for rural areas as well as for the urban poor. This way proper access can be provided to people in the form of affordable and clean sources of energy for basic end-uses such as cooking, lighting and heating (Figure 4.10).

From the above figure, it is quite clear that India's energy consumption in each sector is growing and growing fast. Therefore, all these increasing demands would also need to be met in an environmentally sustainable manner. India must raise access to modern commercial energy sustainably, because even with a share of just four per cent of global GHG emissions, India is coming under increasing pressure to curb fossil fuel consumption. Thus, India must decouple its economic growth from growth in energy consumption while ensuring universal access to lifeline levels of energy consumption. With growing concerns on climate change and the pressure to limit emissions of greenhouse gases, this would be another consideration in devising energy solutions for the country. Overall, India has a set of complex issues to deal with in its future energy decisions. Repeating what other countries have achieved or attempted will not help.

India is already the world's third-largest consumer of energy. As its economy grows, so will its energy needs. Hydroelectricity, nuclear energy and non-conventional sources of energy will have a marginal impact on India's energy security, which will remain dependent on coal, oil and gas for the next quarter-century as predicted by the BP energy outlook. Since India's resources and production are insufficient, India will have to import large quantities of oil and gas, even coal to some extent from abroad. As of 2018, India's oil import profile from different sources has been given in Table 4.2.

Energy security strategy of India

India's appetite for energy is showing no sign of slowing down and its growth rate is expected to continue to be fairly high. Concerns about where the energy is going to come from have been increasing as the realization grows that India is not alone in this epic quest for energy. It is competing with China, Japan, Europe, South Korea and the United States. Besides, the main concern is that supply routes could be disrupted by instability in the Middle East, Africa or the Indian Ocean region. The recent civic unrest and violent protests for regime change in the Arab world have certainly rung the alarm on an upcoming grave concern for energy security from India's point of view. Worries persist over the blockage of key chokepoints like the Strait of Hormuz – a transit route for the majority of India's fuel containers. Fear looms large about the potential for domestic disruption due to the vulnerability by accident, attack, or natural disasters of onshore and offshore facilities. Being cut off from the potentially vulnerable rail and pipeline links further adds to the energy woes of India. In this scenario, Central Asia offers a healthy opportunity for India in her neighbourhood. Before looking at the Central Asian option in India's energy quest, India's energy security strategy needs to be studied broadly.

India does not have an overarching energy strategy – instead, it has several disparate policies. Because many politicians and analysts use the terms "strategy" and "policy" interchangeably, it is not always an obvious distinction. Separate vision statements have emerged from different energy-related ministries and departments. The Hydrocarbon Vision 2025 report, for example, focused exclusively on oil and gas. Even within ministries, the emphasis tends to be on specific and limited polices rather than on a long-term, integrated strategy. A former minister remarked that his job was "to make policy for next year" (Aiyar 2005: 35) which begs the question: Whose job is it to make strategy?

Dr Manmohan Sing during his tenure as prime minister said that India "must learn to think strategically" (Singh 2005). However, there is a good deal of debate about whether an energy strategy is essential. Having several policies is not thought to be a bad thing in and of itself. Meeting the country's energy needs is considered a complex problem, requiring different solutions. "There is no silver bullet" is a common refrain – especially in a country with intricate internal politicking and an energy sector that is neither purely market-driven nor entirely state-controlled (Anderson 2006).

While there continue to be debates about whether an overarching strategy is necessary, India's decision makers recognize that – at the very least – the country's disparate energy policies need to be integrated. This notion has proved problematic so far. There has been little indication of how policies should be prioritized, no plan for funding them, and often a gap between policymaking and implementation.

Despite these incongruities, there does seem to be a dominant policy trend toward diversification of sources, suppliers, pricing and technologies. Diversification is also evident in the number and variety of proposals to increase energy security for India. At its most basic level, policy diversification offers India more options, not just in terms of energy security, but in foreign policy as well. Pursuing multiple tracks also helps ensure that India is not affected by area-specific shocks (Ahluwalia 2006).

Policy diversity is not just a question of choice, but a necessity. Many decision-makers admit (though perhaps not publicly) that growing energy demands require India to explore every option – because it must, not necessarily because it wants to.

India depends for over 60 per cent of its oil needs on just four countries, namely Saudi Arabia, Nigeria, Kuwait and Iran. India is dependent on the Middle East for almost two-thirds of its oil imports (BP 2018). In pursuing India's strategy to diversify its suppliers, its overwhelming dependency on Middle Eastern oil is likely to continue for reasons based on geography and cost. However, the recent developments in the Middle East with resultant political turmoil, civic unrest, violent regime transformation and often hostile popular uprisings certainly pose a grave cause of concern for India in its dealings with these oil-rich countries. In addition to this, problems occur to transportation channels via the Suez Canal and the Strait of Hormuz as a result of the constant blockades by the littoral states due to their vested interests. This hampers business as usual and brings heavy economic losses. Yet another problem is the piracy on the Somalia coast. Therefore, India's problem is not confined to ensuring its share of oil and gas from the Middle East, it also has to deal with the resultant problems arising out of oil imports from the region. For that, India needs both economic leverage and political willingness along with flexing muscle power wherever it is required.

Notwithstanding, ONGC Videsh, the overseas arm of India's Oil and Natural Gas Corporation has purchased exploration and production blocks in oilfields in a range of countries from Sudan, Libya and Iran to Myanmar and Russia. India's private sector oil company Reliance Industries has purchased exploration blocks in Yemen and Oman. Apart from uncertainty regarding the availability of oil, India is also concerned about the possibility of a sudden increase in oil price and its negative impact on the Indian economy.

In 2004, the Indian government decided to establish strategic petroleum reserves for 15 days of consumption. It was also decided that this stock of reserves would be over and above the existing storage with the country's oil companies. The Planning Commission has also recommended that New Delhi should build and maintain a strategic reserve for 90 days of oil imports. In addition to these, concerns about availability and affordability for consumers, New Delhi is also keen to minimize the strain on its foreign exchange reserves as a result of a massive oil imports bill. Therefore, to shield India from supply disruption, price fluctuation and to reduce its overall crude oil import level in longer terms, the government decided to set up strategic storage of 39 million barrels of crude oil at three locations: Visakhapatnam, Mangalore and Padur (EIA 2016). The Visakhapatnam facility came online in June 2015. The government is now unveiling options to increase reserves for 90 days and another 91 million barrels to the state's strategic crude oil capacity in a second phase by 2020 (EIA 2016). Despite all these measures, in the financial year 2017–2018, New Delhi spent $87.725 billion on importing oil of around 219.15 MT (PTI 2018). It is estimated that India's oil import bill jumped by 25 per cent in the financial Year 2018–19 (ET 2018). The strongest heat and anger the present government of Mr Modi facing is on the skyrocketing of the prices of oil and gas. Hence, New Delhi is more particularly concerned about the increasing trend of oil prices than any other thing. Also, a drain on its foreign exchange reserves for purchasing of equity oil is the new headache for the government. Thus, India is pursuing several financial options like obtaining equity oil abroad and participating in future trading in oil to mitigate this challenge.

The Planning Commission in 2006 recommended that New Delhi purchase buying options from large oil storages in neighbouring states like Singapore to deal with emergencies (Planning Commission 2006). With investments in a special economic zone at Jamnagar in Gujarat, in 2008, India is all set to emerge as an "energy outsourcing hub" in the near future. Jamnagar already boasts the world's third-largest oil refinery and is set to emerge as the largest when Reliance Petroleum Limited begins its operation in December 2008. Several new oil fields have also been discovered from the Krishna-Godavari basin, in the coastal belt of Orissa, in Nagaland and south Tripura. There are also plenty of thorium sands available in coastal Orissa and Kerala which are well conserved by Indian Rare Earth Limited, which can be transformed into uranium; hence nuclear energy can be produced.

Besides its energy bases, India is also considering diversification of fuel sources. In this regard, the consumption of natural gas in the country is set to increase dramatically in the years ahead. India can import gas through pipelines from neighbouring states or import LNG through long-term contracts. Since a pipeline traverses several countries, it entails a complex contractual framework and has an important bearing on geopolitics. This is in stark contrast to LNG contracts that have a relatively minor impact on geopolitics.

India is interested in acquiring gas from Iran, Bangladesh and Myanmar. Since the early 1990s, India has considered various pipeline projects: Oman–India Deep Water pipeline, Iran–Pakistan–India pipeline, Turkmenistan–Afghanistan–Pakistan-India pipeline, Qatar–Pakistan–India pipeline and Myanmar–Bangladesh–India pipeline. All of these projects have run into numerous troubles due to regional and geopolitical tensions. On the other hand, India's first LNG import terminal, Dahej in Gujarat, began operation in 2004 and is importing gas from Qatar. The Indian government has approved plans for 12 possible import terminals mostly along the country's western coast (from Gujarat to Kerala). These infrastructure projects highlight the importance of the Persian Gulf in meeting the country's LNG needs.

Nuclear power constitutes only about 3 per cent of India's electricity needs. India's meagre uranium reserves and the poor quality of its ores mean that India's nuclear reactors are operating at sub-optimal levels. In the long term, beyond 2050, India's substantial thorium reserves can make the country self-sufficient in electricity production. This process can now be accelerated as New Delhi can access uranium and other civil nuclear technologies from foreign sources that accelerate the process of converting India's thorium supplies into fissile material. These technologies are currently available to New Delhi as the Nuclear Suppliers Group has passed the resolution while signalling a go-ahead to the Indo-US Civil Nuclear deal in 2008. Although India is not a signatory to the Nuclear Non-Proliferation Treaty, it can enjoy access to the services and technologies that would boost her nuclear energy potential. Meanwhile, Russia, France, Canada, South Korea, Australia and Kazakhstan have signed comprehensive nuclear agreements with India and agreed to cooperate with New Delhi on civil nuclear technology and help India with uranium supplies to power its nuclear reactors. Moreover, Russia and France seem to be at the forefront with the intent to cooperate with New Delhi in this regard.

Causes of heightened concern

Energy is acknowledged as a key input towards raising the standard of living of the citizens thereby impacting the economic development of any country. In case of India, while the main focus of the country has been to eradicate poverty, the bottom line of energy security is missing somewhere as nearly 340 million Indians are without access to electricity and about 500 million people still depend on biomass for cooking (NITI Aayog 2017). While the National Energy Policy (NEP 2017) aims to chart out the government plan of providing access to electricity to all by 2018 and universal electrification to all by 2022, India is still heavily dependent on fossil fuels.

India as of 2016 is the fourth largest consumer of energy in the world, accounting for almost 4.2 per cent of the world's consumption (BP 2018). Its total primary demand is expected to almost double by 2030 (Figure 4.11). India's total energy consumption of 15.4 quadrillions Btus, consists of coal (53 per cent), oil (33 per cent), natural gas (8 per cent), hydroelectricity (5 per cent) and nuclear (1 per cent) (Koolaee and Kalesar 2010: 84). It is predicted that India's demand for oil and gas will increase massively within the coming two decades. BP estimated that in 2018 "India's import dependence in crude oil would touch 80 per cent and in natural gas 77 per cent" (BP 2018). Supplies for this increased demand are expected largely from the Persian Gulf, Central Asia and Southeast Asia.

Apart from oil, coal and hydropower are the two main sources for India's energy consumption (NITI Aayog 2017) (see Figure 4.12). India's hydropower

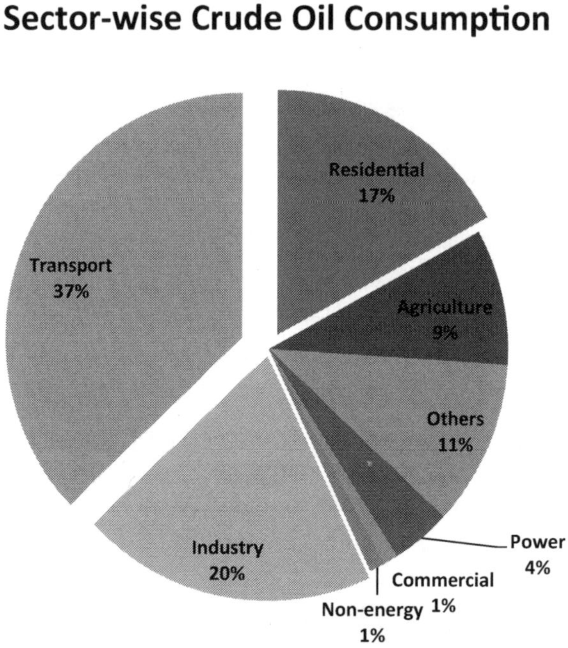

FIGURE 4.11 Oil consumption in India by sectors, 2015.

Source: Author's own analysis from the data collected from BP, 2018 and T. Ramachandra and Ganesh Hegde, 2015, *Energy trajectory in India: Challenges and Opportunities for Innovation, Energy and Development*, 12(1–2), pp. 1–24

consumption stands lower than its production level. Therefore, India consumes more than it produces in other forms of energy sources. It ranks 25th and 23rd globally in terms of proven natural gas and oil reserves (EIA 2017).

Coal is the most important source of energy for India and provides almost 51 per cent of the total energy consumed in the country. However, Indian coal suffers from low calorific value and causes considerable environmental degradation as it is high in sulphur and ash. Given its poor quality, India imports almost 25 per cent of the coking coal required by its steel industry. Nevertheless, coal is the most polluting among energy sources.

Oil accounts for roughly 34 per cent of India's energy consumption. India already imports close to 65 per cent of its oil needs and its import dependency is growing fast. It is estimated that in the worst-case scenario, almost 90 per cent of its oil consumption needs would be met by imported oil by 2030. Natural gas accounts for 10 per cent of India's energy consumption.

Moreover, it is fast emerging as a major alternative for India's poor quality coal, especially for electricity production. It is estimated that India will be dependent on imported gas for more than 40 per cent of its total gas needs by 2030 (NEP 2017).

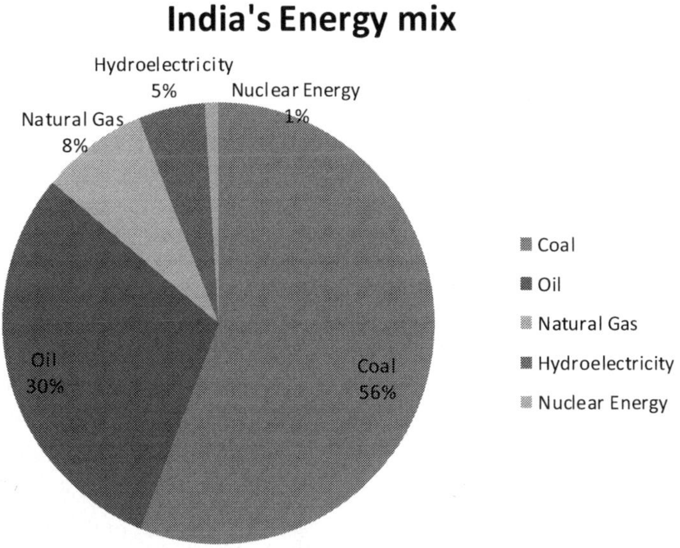

FIGURE 4.12 India's energy mix.

Source: BP Energy Outlook, 2018

The remainder of India's energy needs is provided by a mix of hydropower, nuclear power, wind power, biomass and other non-conventional energy sources. According to a recent study done by the NITI Aayog, the apex institution that formulates India's Five-Year Plans, even if hydropower, nuclear power and other renewable sources were exploited to their full potential, their best possible contribution to India's energy mix by 2030 would be around 5–6 per cent each (NITI Aayog 2017).

By 2030, India is expected to overtake Japan and Russia to become the third-largest consumer of energy. If consumption follows the current pattern and trajectory, the country is projected to run out of coal – its primary source of energy for 40 years. Furthermore, its domestic reserves of oil and gas are limited. Currently, India is importing a portion of three of its major sources of energy: oil, gas and coal. Its dependence on imported oil is already greater (as a percentage of oil consumed) than that of the United States and China and is expected to increase even further (Sachdeva 2017, Sajjhnar 2016).

There are certain other complicated factors which further perplex the situation. These are:

- Though India imports oil from more than two dozen countries, almost three-quarters of its oil is imported from five countries of the Middle East. All of these countries are located in a region that is considered fairly unstable and this trend is likely to continue.
- High oil prices which in turn seem to spur high gas prices.

- Continuing geopolitical uncertainty stoking fears of a possible supply disruption, ceasing of main chokepoints, or volatility in oil prices.
- Few or no obvious viable energy alternatives – progress in its nuclear program has regularly fallen behind schedule; large-scale development of hydroelectricity generation facilities has been stymied by financial, social and environmental concerns; and non-conventional sources are not yet considered affordable or reliable.
- India is not alone in this high-speed quest for energy – it is competing with China, the United States, Japan, Europe, South Korea etc. It has neither the political will nor the economic leverage to engage in such high profile competitions.
- Without clean, convenient and reliable energy, India will not be able to sustain a high growth rate across all sectors of the economy.
- Vulnerability to volatile prices adds to the problems, causing an increase in India's fiscal and trade deficits. There is also a certain amount of discomfort that India's economic growth "stands hostage" to imported energy at a high price from volatile regions.

The dilemma for India's energy domain comes from the following factors:

- The average quality of Indian coal is not very high. This necessitates the import of high-quality coal from abroad to meet the requirements of steel plants. This has been increasing in recent years.
- Import of coal steadily increased from 49.79 MTs during 2007–08 to 190.95 MTs during 2016–17 (MoSPI 2018).
- India is highly dependent on crude oil. Net imports of crude oil increased from 121.67 MTs during 2007–08 to 213.93 MTs during 2016–17.
- The gross import of natural gas increased from 8.32 bcm in 2007–08 to 18.63 bcm in 2016–17, recording a CAGR of 8.40 per cent (MoSPI 2018).

In the above-given scenario, as shown in Table 4.6, India will undoubtedly overtake China as the largest growth market for energy by the late 2020s with the country's energy consumption growing by more than 4.2 per cent per annum (ET Energy world 2018). According to BP Energy Outlook 2018, this rate of growth makes India the fastest among all the major economies of the world (BP 2018a). It is estimated by BP Energy outlook as stated in the Economic Times (2018) that India's demand growth of 165 per cent, nearly three times the overall non-Organization for Economic Cooperation and Development (OECD) growth of 61 per cent, also outpaces each of the other BRIC countries: China (+41 per cent), Brazil (+60 per cent) and Russia (+6 per cent) (2018).

According to the production of hydrocarbon data provided by BP Energy outlook 2018 as shown in Table 4.7, India's oil output is pegged to decrease by 40 per cent to 24 mtoe in 2040 from 40 mtoe in 2016. Natural gas production is estimated to increase by 96 per cent to 49 mtoe in 2040 from 25 mtoe in 2016. Coal production is also estimated to increase by 154 per cent to 734 mtoe in 2040 from 289 mtoe in 2016 with coal remaining the dominant fuel production

TABLE 4.6 Change in world energy consumption rate by 2035 in %

Category	*Brazil*	*Russia*	*US*	*China*	*World*	*India*
Oil	15	15	–17	61	15	121
Gas	43	–2	25	186	38	162
Coal	–16	–22	–50	–2	5	105
Nuclear	149	17	–2	644	59	317
Hydro	37	14	15	38	42	97
Renewable	157	>1000	182	673	291	712

Source: BP World Energy Outlook, 2018.

TABLE 4.7 Primary energy consumption scenario in 2016 and 2040

Primary energy	*Consumptionin 2016 (mtoe)*	*Consumption in 2040 (mtoe)*	*Energy share in 2016 (%)*	*Energy share in 2040 (%)*	*Overall growth (%)*
Oil	212	**485**	29	**25**	**129**
Gas	45	**128**	6	**7**	**185**
Coal	412	**955**	57	**50**	**132**
Nuclear	9	**44**	1	**2**	**389**
Hydro	29	**52**	4	**3**	**80**
Renewable	17	**256**	2	**13**	**1406**
Total	**724**	**1921**	**99**	**100**	**165**

Source: BP Energy Outlook 2018.

in India with 63 per cent share of total production in 2040 (ET Energy world 2018). In this scenario, India's energy consumption would grow by 4.2 per cent per annum faster than all major economies of the world. By the late 2020s, India is set to overtake China as the fastest-growing market for energy. Growth in India's energy consumption will increase by 165 per cent with India having a global share of 11 per cent by 2040. Although India's production will also increase by 184 per cent, its energy mix would be heavily dominated by coal, with fossil fuel involving 82 per cent of the total demand. The energy in transport will grow by 4.4 per cent per year and oil remains the dominant fuel source with a 96 per cent market share in 2040. Industry's share of energy consumption remains around 60 per cent of the market share during the forecast. Although, energy production increases from 56 per cent in 2016 to 60 per cent in 2040, the rising import by 141 per cent in 2040 remains a serious cause of concern (BP 2018A). In addition to this, the import of oil will rise by 175 per cent, accounting for a 65 per cent increase in energy import closely followed by gas (+2915) and coal (+79 per cent) (Ibid).

The reason for heightened concern, therefore, goes beyond the need to satisfy India's growth compulsion. It involves political, social and strategic dimensions as well. Indian political leaders, executives, decision makers and think tanks got to learn from their past mistakes and follow a broad and integrated strategy instead of several policy formulations to ensure India's energy security. To put

TABLE 4.8 India's hydrocarbon production growth in 2016 and 2040 scenario

Fuel	*Production in 2016 (mtoe)*	*Production in 2040 (mtoe)*	*Change (%)*
Oil	40	**24**	**40**
Gas	25	**49**	**96**
Coal	289	**734**	**154**

Source: BP Energy Outlook 2018.

India in its rightful place in world politics, the country needs to be energy secure. As domestic resources at hand are dismal and limited, as shown in Table 4.8, and the trend of consumption dominating the production rate, and renewable energy sources taking time, India should look at the alternate sources of energy with reliable, clean and affordable costs. Given the resource scramble in the Middle East, the resource curse in Africa, Central Asia stands out as a viable destination for India in her energy quest. Further, Peak Oil theory also suggests that Middle East oil quantity is steadily declining and is expected to diminish soon. And the same can apply to any energy-rich destinations.

The former Prime Minister of India Dr Man Mohan Singh has reiterated several times that "energy security is second only in our scheme of things to food security". Assured, uninterrupted supply of energy is critical for running India's economic engine. India's dependence on imported oil is projected to escalate from the current level of 83.5 per cent as of June 2012 to more than 90 per cent by 2030. Central Asia has an estimated 4 per cent (270–360 tcf) of the world's gas reserves; its oil reserves are pegged at 2.7 per cent (13–15 billion barrels) with Kazakhstan holding large reserves of high-quality uranium, while Kyrgyzstan has substantial amounts of nuclear waste. Uzbekistan and Tajikistan hold sizeable uranium reserves and have the potential for its enrichment.

The energy resources of Central Asia including the Caspian Sea region will play an important role in India's energy strategy. Central Asian oil and gas are of high quality and are largely untapped. The investment environment is open and friendly. Besides, Central Asia is relatively more stable than the Middle East and African energy-rich countries.

References

Abdi, Bilal (2018), "India's Crude Oil Imports from Iran Jumped 52 Percent in June", *The Economic Times*, July 24.

Ahluwalia, Montek Singh (2006), "Inaugural Address", to conference on "India's Energy Security: Major Challenges", National Conclave, Observers Research Foundation, New Delhi, February, 15.

Aiyar, Mani Shankar (2005), "Energy Cooperation: India and Its Neighbours", in I. P. Khosla (ed.), *Energy Diplomacy*, New Delhi: Konark Publishers.

Anderson, George (2006), "Managing Energy Policy in Federations: Reflections on Canadian and Other Experiences", presented at the conference on "India's Energy Security: Major Challenges", National Conclave, Observers Research Foundation, New Delhi, February, 15.

BP (2005), "Making Energy more – Sustainability Report-2005," *British Petroleum*, available at: https://www.bp.com/content/dam/bp/business-sites/en/global/corporate/pdfs/sustainability/archive/archived-reports-and-translations/2005/bp-sustainability-report-2005.pdf [accessed January 14, 2006].

BP (2018), "BP Statistical Review of World Energy", British Petroleum, March, available at: www.bp.com [accessed September 2018].

BP (2018a), "Country and Regional Insight – India", BP Energy Outlook, available at: https://www.bp.com/content/dam/bp/en/corporate/pdf/energy-economics/energy-outlook/bp-energy-outlook-2018-country-insight-india.pdf [accessed September 2018].

CEIC (2018), "India's Oil Consumption Economic Indicators 1965–2017", CEIC, December, available at: https://www.ceicdata.com/en/indicator/india/oil-consumption [accessed January 2019].

CSIS (2006), *India's Energy Dilemma*, Washington, DC: Centre for Strategic and International Studies, No. 98.

DGCIS (2018), "India's Import Data of Principal Commodities", Director General of Commercial Intelligence and Statistics, Ministry of Commerce and Industry, Government of India.

Economic Survey (2017), "An Overview of India's Economic Performance in 2017–18, Economic Survey of India", Ministry of Finance, Government of India, available at: http://mofapp.nic.in:8080/economicsurvey/ [accessed September 2018].

EIA (2009). "Country Analysis Brief – India", available at: http://www.sciencerepository.org/in_documents/IN1084.pdf, March.

EIA (2016), *Country Analysis Brief-India*, U.S Energy Information Administration, June 14.

EIA (2017), "Beyond China and India, energy consumption in non-OECD Asia continues to grow," Energy Information Administration, September 27, available at: https://www.eia.gov/todayinenergy/index.php?tg=india [accessed September 17, 2018].

EIA (2018), *World Oil Transit Chokepoints*, U.S Energy Information Administration, July 25.

ENI (2018), *World Oil Review*, Vol. 1, available at: https://www.eni.com/docs/en_IT/enicom/company/fuel-cafe/WORLD-OIL-REVIEW-2018-Volume-1.pdf[accessed September 2018].

ET (2018), "India's Oil Imports Bill to Jump by 25% in FY 2018", *The Economic Times*, March 26.

ET (2018a), "India's Energy Consumption to Grow Faster than Major Economies", *The Economic Times*, January 27, available at: https://economictimes.indiatimes.com/industry/energy/oil-gas/indias-energy-consumption-to-grow-faster-than-major-economies/articleshow/56800587.cms [accessed September 2018].

ET Energyworld (2018), "India Will Overtake China as the Largest Market for Energy by Late 2020s: BP Energy Outlook", ET Energyworld, February 22, available at: https://energy.economictimes.indiatimes.com/news/oil-and-gas/india-will-overtake-china-as-largest-market-for-energy-by-late-2020s-bp-energy-outlook/63024657 [accessed September 2018].

IEA (2004), *World Energy Outlook 2004*, International Energy Agency, available at: www.iea.org [accessed June 10, 2010].

IEA (2010), *Natural Gas in India 2010*, Working Paper, International Energy Agency, OECD/IEA, Paris.

IEA (2015), "India heading for the centre of the global energy stage, IEA says," India Energy Outlook - 2015, International Energy Agency, 27 November, available at: https://www.iea.org/news/india-heading-for-the-centre-of-the-global-energy-stage-iea-says [accessed September 18, 2018].

IEA (2016), "World Energy Outlook, 2016," International Energy Agency, November, available at: https://www.iea.org/reports/world-energy-outlook-2016 [accessed September 18, 2018].

IEA (2020), "India 2020: Energy Policy Review," International Energy Agency, Available at: https://niti.gov.in/sites/default/files/2020-01/IEA-India%202020-In-depth-EnergyPolicy.pdf.

India Energy Handbook (2011), *Demand Driven, Supply Chained*, Las Vegas, NV: PSI Media Inc, USA.

Madan, Tanvi (2006), "Energy Security Series: India", *The Brookings Foreign Policy Studies*, The Brookings Institution, November.

MoPNG (2009), "Basic Statistics on Petroleum and Natural Gas 2007–2008", New Delhi: Ministry of Petroleum and Natural Gas, Government of India.

MoPNG (2018), "Annual Report-2017-18, Ministry of Petroleum and Natural Gas", Ministry of Petroleum and Natural Gas, Government of India, available at: http://petroleum.nic.in/sites/default/files/APR_E_1718.pdf [accessed September 2018].

NEP (2017), "India's Energy Strategy: Draft National Energy Policy (NEP) 2040," *NITI Aayog*, Government of India, July 12.

NEP (2018), "India's Energy Strategy: Draft National Energy Policy (NEP) 2040", *NITI Aayog*, Government of India, July 12.

NITI Aayog (2017), "Draft National Energy Policy", *NITI Aayog*, Government of India, June 27.

NPTI (2017), "Power and Energy," National Power Training Institute, Ministry of Power, Government of India, available at: http://npti.gov.in/sites/default/files/policies-document/plg_comm_write_up_on_power_and_energy.pdf.

PIB (2018), "Import of Natural Gas", *Press Information Bureau*, July 23, available at: http://pib.nic.in/newsite/PrintRelease.aspx?relid=180889 [accessed September 2018].

Planning Commission (2006), *Integrated Energy Policy: Report of the Expert Committee*, New Delhi: Government of India.

Pradhan, Ramakrushna (2018), "China's Rise in Central Asia: The New Silk Road Diplomacy, Fudan", *Journal of Humanities and Social Science*, Springer, 11(1), March, pp. 9–29.

PTI (2018), "India's Oil Imports Bill to Jump by 25% in FY 2018", *Press Trust of India*, March 26.

Ramachandra, T. V. and G. Hedge (2015), "Energy Trajectory in India", *The Journal of Resources Energy and Development*, 12(1&2) pp. 1–24.

Randolph, J. and G. M. Masters (2008), *Energy for Sustainability: Technology, Planning, Policy*, Island Press, London: Bloomsbury Publishing.

Sachdeva, Gulshan (2017), "Chaining Dynamics of India-Central Asia Ties, Bishkek Project", April 5, available at: https://www.bishkekproject.com/memos/24 [accessed September 2018].

Sajjanhar, Ashok (2016), *India-Central Asia Relations: Expanding Vistas of Partnership*, June 22, New Delhi: Observers Research Foundation, available at: https://www.orfonline.org/expert-speak/india-central-asia-relations-expanding-vistas-of-partnership/.

Singh, Man Mohan (2005), Prime Minister of India, "Inaugural Address", at the conference "*Petrotech 2005*", New Delhi, January, available at: https://archivepmo.nic.in/drmanmohansingh/speech-details.php?nodeid=64.

Smalley, R (2005), "Our energy challenge," 27th Illinois Junior Science & Humanities Symposium, Rice University, April 3.

The Times (1999), "Troubled Waters of Oil," The Times, August 30, available at: https://www.thetimes.co.uk/news/pages/tim/99/08/30/timopnope01004.html?region=global&999 [accessed December 10, 2007].

5

INDIA–CENTRAL ASIA AND THE ENERGY QUEST

Safety and certainty in oil lie in variety and variety alone.

– Winston Churchill (1946)

The geopolitical salience of Central Asia for India was never in doubt. New Delhi has always rated the region highly since its independence. Apart from its strong historical ties, close cultural affinity and superb friendship with the CAR (Central Asian Region), the abundant natural resources of Central Asia remain of particular relevance for India, the energy deficit South Asian proximate neighbour. In a real-time scenario, India imports close to 80 per cent of its hydrocarbon requirements. For that, the country has to heavily depend on the volatile Middle East and has faced many fuel supply disruptions, price fluctuations and unprecedented monopoly from the OPEC countries. As the book is going to press, India had already imported 213.93 million tonnes (MT) of crude oil for the year 2016–17 for $70.196 billion or approximately Rs. 4.7 lakh crore in Indian currency (ET 2018). For 2017–18, the imports are pegged at 219.15 MT for $87.715 billion (Rs. 5.65 lakh crore) (PPAC 2018). India in October 2018 paid $76.90 per barrel (Markets Insider 2018). Given the trajectory, it is expected that India's oil import bill increases by the end of 2018 (The Hindu 2018). This has seriously impacted India's foreign reserves and the exhausting of those reserves, in turn, has caused the rupee to hit a record low of 74.32 to the US dollar in October. On the other hand, the exorbitant rise in the price of petrol, diesel and LPG have made people restless, allowing the opposition to strengthen and direct their attack on the government in a massive way for the first time since 2014. That is evident enough to testify the importance of energy to India's growth story and functioning of day to day life. That is perhaps the reason energy is regarded as the crux of everything, and therefore a universal currency (Pradhan 2016: 42–60). Therefore, India as part of its energy strategy to secure the sources of supply and diversify the resource base particularly under Prime Minister Mr Modi has developed a pragmatic vision towards the CAR, deviating from the old historical and cultural dimension.

To meet India's unprecedented energy requirements and to arrest stupendous import dependence on the Middle East, New Delhi started considering the energy resources of Central Asia including the Caspian Sea region as strategic resources as far as its energy calculus is concerned. What leveraged the region further are its high quality and largely untapped oil and gas resources and the investment-friendly environment. As the home countries consume less, a major chunk of these resources is meant for export. Besides, unlike the Middle East and African energy-rich countries, Central Asia is very stable and popular uprising against outside powers is seemingly absent there. The gas of Central Asia and the Caspian has less ash in comparison to other gas producing regions of the world. All these happen to be the driving factors for any country in general and India in particular in choosing the Central Asian energy hub. In fact, in the last one decade or so energy diplomacy has become the driving force of India's foreign policy and New Delhi is pretty serious about pursuing nuclear energy and diversifying its energy imports by securing supplies beyond the Middle East. Apart from Russia and Azerbaijan, Kazakhstan, Turkmenistan, Uzbekistan and other Central Asian countries could certainly play an important role in this regard.

Like China, India is also actively involved in the oil politics of Central Asia. Both China and India are expected to occupy 50 per cent of total world energy demand growth, 60 per cent of world oil demand growth, 20 per cent of natural gas and 85 per cent of coal demand growth (Hart 2016). India wanted the construction of pipelines which became clear in its support for pipelines along with six countries passing through Afghanistan, Pakistan, Bangladesh, Iran, Myanmar and Turkmenistan. India's primary energy demand is expected to grow at 6 per cent with GDP growing at 7–8 per cent. According to the international energy agency (IEA) reports, a $10 rise in crude prices would reduce India's GDP by 1 per cent which calls for the diversification of energy sources for ensuring the availability of energy at affordable rates (Hart 2016).

India with its Connect Central Asia policy has been one of the first such countries to establish strategic connections with the region in June 2012. The full membership position granted to India in the Shanghai Cooperation Organization (SCO) has further bolstered New Delhi's position in the region as an alternative to Chinese hegemony (Pradhan 2015).

India's energy diplomacy in Central Asia

Central Asia and India are deeply rooted friends and enjoy superb bonding through their cultural connections and historical linkages. Geographical proximity and geostrategic necessity further bind them together. Despite the peace, stability and regional security in Central Asia remaining critical to India's national security, New Delhi since the 1990s has been struggling to find an appropriate policy strategy to deal with the Central Asian republics. As we stand in 2020, the significance of Central Asia is even more relevant for India both from regional security and energy security points of views. However, the point of dissatisfaction has been the minuscule level of trade and economic relations between India and Central Asia despite sustained excellent rapport at the top political level and mutual respect since the mid-1990s. In addition to the geographical barriers, the challenges that come in the way of India have been the external actors like China and India's pathetic trade share with the countries of the region. It has to be seen what strategies India puts in place to address its low political linkages with the CAS so that its greater objectives of energy security and a level playing field in the grand chessboard of world politics can be fulfilled. Some of the policy strategies India so far has adopted to deepen its trade and economic relationship with Central Asia to attain its much-needed energy security are discussed in the following paragraphs.

Development of India's Central Asian strategy

The deep-rooted Nehruvian socialistic and idealistic international positioning of India's foreign policy has seen considerable recasting over the last two decades or so. The new-found pragmatism in India's foreign policy sidelining the historical and cultural silver lining has been widely acknowledged as the need of the time after the post-Cold War world order. In the post-1990 period, "India's foreign relations have been envisioned more in terms of widening circles around historical and cultural commonalities across the globe into categories viz. the immediate neighbourhood, the extended neighbourhood and the global powers" (Chandra 2017). In this framework, Central Asia has been described as India's "extended and strategic neighbour". Accordingly, India had initiated a policy process towards the region although it was not as robust as it ought to have been. Nevertheless, India has taken a firm stand towards the region in building its relationship in a greater way and started the initiative with its Look North Policy in the mid-1990s (Pradhan 2015).

Another significant transformation in India's foreign policy witnessed during the new world order was its shift from unilateralism to a proactive multilateral approach towards Central Asia. The increased bilateral exchanges and regular flow of high-level visits between India and Central Asian states have manifested in establishing meaningful and mutually beneficial ties leading to enhanced footprints of India across various Central Asian republics. New Delhi has been actively pursuing several initiatives to enable her to attain a substantial position in the energy game of Central Asia.

Importantly, India's goal to reach 5 trillion USD GDP by 2024 looks ambitious but the reiteration of Prime Minister Shri Modi on several forums clears the cloud of India's obvious aspiration (*New Indian Express* 2019). In pursuit of this objective, energy security is without a doubt an important matter, since ensuring stable access to energy resources is vital for achieving any major economic or development-related goals for a country which aims to strengthen its regional power position. The energy security perspective of India was well presented by Prime Minister Shri Narendra Modi in his address to the 16th International Energy Forum in New Delhi in 2018, by saying "my vision for India's energy future has four pillars – energy access, energy efficiency, energy sustainability and energy security" and that energy issues are pivotal for India's further growth and prosperity (IEF 2018). "Energy justice" has also become an often quoted term by India's policymakers in the past couple of years. This term is defined by Sovacool et al. as a "global energy system that fairly distributes both the benefits and burdens of energy services and one that contributes to more representative and inclusive energy decision-making" (2017: 677–691), and it has become a framework for characterizing India's vision for its energy future by its leadership. In light of the aforementioned, a pivotal question is how can India provide energy justice domestically, and to this end, how it can establish a stable supply framework with other countries for securing its imports. In other words, the latter question reads as how can India best implement an energy security-oriented foreign policy. Taking the above factors into consideration, this chapter seeks to shed light on the necessity of establishing energy ties with the Central Asian states. This quest for energy security has encouraged India to develop its Central Asian strategy.

The Look North Policy of India is one such strategy developed in the 1990s to develop cordial and superb bonding with the energy-rich nations of Central Asia. This policy was further strengthened with the visit of Shri P. V. Narasimha Rao to Turkmenistan in September 1995 when he aptly affirmed that Central Asia is a region of high priority for India (Muni 2003). In his address, he further emphasized that

> we aim to stay engaged far into the future with the Republics of Central Asia. We are an independent partner with no selfish motives. We only desire honest and open friendship and to promote stability and cooperation without causing harm to any third country.

This proclamation reflects the core of the genesis of the Look North Policy. Its vision of peaceful engagement with neighbours extending that relationship in the context of trade and business are at the heart of this policy. Moreover, the propositions of the Look North Policy point to "secularism", "democracy", and "literacy" as national strengths that India and Central Asia share (Blank 2003) and together would further help in strengthening the bonding. Ironically, such a discourse didn't find any mention in the aftermath of Narasimha Rao's government in India. Although the Gujral Doctrine for several reasons is a heartening step as far as India's relations with the neighbours is concerned it is specifically confined to South Asia only. When it comes to Central Asia, the Gujral doctrine hardly offers anything new (Pradhan 2015). That is the reason why this policy of peaceful engagement with the energy-rich nations of Central Asia should be given due recognition in Modi's policy decisions as the region offers India much in return for what India offers to them.

"The Focus CIS programme was launched by the Ministry of Commerce & Industry of the Government of India in 2003 at the time of the announcement of the Exim Policy on March 31, 2003" (Chandra 2017). This programme aims at enhancing trade relationships with at least seven countries of the CIS region, namely Azerbaijan, Kazakhstan, Kyrgyzstan, Tajikistan, Turkmenistan, Ukraine and Uzbekistan. Since 2004, the programme has been further extended to the rest of the CIS countries including Russia, Armenia, Belarus, Georgia and Moldova. This initiative is indeed an encouraging step forward to boost bilateral and multilateral trade and economic relationships with the partner countries which in turn helps India in attaining its energy quest.

CEPA is an omnibus free trade agreement between India and the member countries of the Eurasian Customs Union which aims at lowering tariffs on goods by both sides. This initiative was forwarded further by the UPA government during the visit of Dr Man Mohan Singh to Russia in December 2011 (Chandra 2017). This agreement apart from sorting out trade issues with Russia is tailor-made to fit into the Eurasian Customs Union members' requirements, especially Kazakhstan and Belarus to help Indian entrepreneurs to enlarge their businesses.

The India-Eurasian Economic Union (EAEU) has proposed to initiate a Free Trade Agreement (FTA) for expanding the trade and business interests of India and member countries of EAEU largely dominated by Russia. Despite global economic recessions,

> the bilateral trade between India and EAEU in 2014 was at US$ 11.3 billion. India's total exports o the member states of EAEU stood at US$ 1.8 billion in 2016 while its imports from the EAEU are higher at US$ 5.1 billion in the same year.
>
> *(Chandra 2017)*

It can be seen that bilateral trade between India and members of EAEU are very weak except for Russia and Kazakhstan. The objectives of India have been to diversify its Russian dominated trade relationship and expand it to other members of EAEU so that bilateral trade would benefit the members and can be expanded to other sectors with mutual interests.

Indian-Technical and Economic Cooperation (ITEC) is a flagship programme dating from the 1990s between India and the Central Asian countries to exchange students and professionals for study and training in India. Since its inception, the programme has hosted more than 3000 people from Central Asia across the professions and streams. This is a noble initiative through which people to people contact can be well developed between India and CAS and help strengthen ties between the two regions.

Despite all efforts, India's trade relationship with the Central Asian republics has been painful and discouraging. India's trade with CARs grew sluggishly from $115 million in 1996 to $738 million in 2012 (Chandra 2017). India needs to address the low level of trade relations with Central Asia which indeed hampers India's larger energy interests in the region.

Central Asia in India's energy strategy

The hydrocarbon resource of Central Asia is undoubtedly paramount for India's quest for energy security. Importantly, being an "extended neighbour", India is optimistic about strong cooperation with Central Asian republics in the energy sector. Since Central Asian states are also in favour of diversification of their energy routes to prevent any kind of monopoly from a single customer, thereby maintaining their autonomy both in the political and economic sphere which includes energy as a greater strategic asset, India is provided with an option to access Central Asian oil and gas fields and be involved in exploration and development of energy deposits in CAR. For that,

> India has made a shift from forging ties in business-to-business relations by the respective oil companies, sharing technical knowhow in the exploration of oil and gas fields and entering into joint production mechanisms. The efforts now have come to be directed more towards the creation of an energy corridor between Central Asia and South Asia.
>
> *(Chandra 2017)*

To transmit energy from Central Asia to India, New Delhi needs to seriously work towards the creation of a regional framework for energy cooperation involving Iran, Afghanistan and Pakistan; although it creates a situation where both South Asian old adversaries – India and Pakistan – will have to join hands for the sake of shared prosperity. If that happens, it would be feasible for India to transport hydrocarbon resources from the lower riparian countries such as Uzbekistan, Turkmenistan and Kazakhstan and export hydroelectricity from Tajikistan and Kyrgyzstan to India through CASAREM transiting through Afghanistan and Pakistan. The discussion has taken place and after due agreement by all sides construction of pipelines has also started involving India, Pakistan and Afghanistan to transfer gas from Turkmenistan and Iran in two variants of pipelines –Turkmenistan–Afghanistan–Pakistan-India (TAPI) and Iran–Pakistan–India (IPI) – which are under consideration.

Turkmenistan–Afghanistan–Pakistan–India (TAPI) pipeline

The Turkmenistan–Afghanistan–Pakistan–India gas pipeline is an ambitious project for transporting natural gas from the Galkynysh gas field of Turkmenistan (Central Asia) to India (South Asia). This project was initially mooted by the

Argentinean Company Bridas Corporation in March 1995 (Report 2011) involving only three countries, namely Turkmenistan, Afghanistan and Pakistan. However, "the U.S Company UNOCAL in conjunction with the Saudi Oil Company Delta, promoted an alternative project without involving Bridas and signed separate agreements with the Turkmen President Niyazov" (Kumar 2018). This led to the formation of a consortium called the "Central Asia Gas Pipeline Ltd (CentGas)" in August 1996. However, due to America's global war on terror, the project got delayed and when restarted with new agreements a new stakeholder was inducted in the form of India. The Asian Development Bank (ADB) after its feasibility study agreed to sponsor the project. Consequently, Turkmenistan, Afghanistan, Pakistan and India signed a framework agreement to buy natural gas from Turkmenistan on April 25, 2008. The intergovernmental agreement on the pipeline was signed on December 11, 2010, in Ashgabad. The proposed pipeline project is USD 10 billion (Niti Central 2015). The project covers 1040 miles (1814 kilometres) route from Dauletabad in Turkmenistan through Herat, Helmand and Kandahar in Afghanistan to Quetta and Multan in Pakistan and then on to Fazilka in India (Report 2011) passing through some of the worst conflict-ridden areas of Afghanistan and Pakistan. The pipeline is 56 inches in diameter with a working pressure of 100 standard atmospheres (10,000 kPa).

> The TAPI project is intended to transport 33 billion cubic meters (bcm) of gas per year from Turkmenistan via Afghanistan and Pakistan to India. Out of which 5 bcm will be provided to Afghanistan while 14 bcm each will be given to India and Pakistan.
>
> *(Chandra 2017)*

However,

> the construction of the pipeline has been stalled for various reasons: the prior commitment of Turkmenistan gas reserves to Russia; difficulties in engaging with the regime in Ashgabat; security risks associated with the pipeline that will run through trouble-torn Afghanistan and Pakistan; lack of financing to the gas project by international companies; India reserve concerning the security of supply.
>
> *(Reports 2011)*

Nevertheless, the recent visit of Indian Prime Minister to Turkmenistan on July 11, 2015, was able to clear the air and a joint statement was prepared to address the issue at hand. The joint statement welcomed the establishment of the "TAPI Ltd" special purpose vehicle for the project and the "leaders reaffirmed their strong commitment towards timely implementation of this strategic project" (MEA 2015). Timely completion of the project is mutually beneficial for both India and Turkmenistan. The latter currently depends on oil exports to China for revenues and would find an alternate source after the completion of this project. Greater cooperation in the area of oil exploration between the two countries – India and Turkmenistan – was also discussed and the leaders welcomed the establishment of a representative office of ONGC Videsh in Ashgabat. The standing committee on Petroleum and Natural Gas said in a report submitted to the Parliament in July 2017,

> that a consortium for Turkmenistan–Afghanistan–Pakistan–India Pipeline – TAPI pipeline Company Ltd (TPCL) – was incorporated in Isle of Man and shareholders agreement signed in December 2015. Turkmenistan will own 85 per cent of TPCL while India, Pakistan and Afghanistan will each have 5 per cent stake. The construction of the pipeline has commenced in December 2015 and is likely to be completed in about 7 years. The much-delayed project is now expected to be operational by 2022.
>
> *(Chandra 2017)*

Iran–Pakistan–India (IPI) pipeline

The idea of an overland, trans-Pakistan pipeline was first proposed in 1989 by Ali Shams Ardekani, acting Deputy Foreign Minister of Iran, and RK Pachauri, the Director-General of the Tata Energy Research Institute (TERI) in New Delhi (Temple 2007: 6). The idea received a positive reaction in Iran. Pakistan initially refused to sign the project worrying about India's long-term benefits, but later on, agreed to the project since it would profit from both access to energy and transit fees. However, the initial response from New Delhi was sceptical. India was worried about leaving her long-term energy security in the hands of hostile Pakistan and trouble-torn Afghanistan. However, the instability of political regimes in the Middle East concerned India and underlined the need to diversify its energy needs. This realization further led India to ink agreements with Iran in 1993 and Oman in 1994 (Ibid). It is with this background that the IPI (Iran–Pakistan–India) pipeline project has been taken forward.

Although the project was initiated way back, it was only in 2006 with the help of the Asian Development Bank (ADB) that a series of studies and research were carried out for facilitating the project. The Asian Development Bank also agreed to finance the project. Agreements were signed among partner countries on all elements except pricing and contractual structure of the pipeline project. The matter of pricing is the most difficult issue among all. Since the pipeline is expected to provide a stable supply of gas from Iran to Pakistan and India for the next 40 years, all three countries are wary of signing a deal that they may regret later.

So far, Iran has made several offers of pricing mechanisms that have been unacceptable to India. Initially, the Iranians wanted the gas to be priced according to Henry Hub, the American spot price index (Ibid: 27). India and Pakistan instantly rejected this option because spot prices are always substantially higher than prices for long-term deals. Iran also offered to base the price on the average of LNG prices in Japan, Korea and India. However, this proposal too was unacceptable to India and Pakistan because Japan and Korea are entirely dependent on LNG and therefore willing to pay more than other users. India has demanded that the price of gas be offered at "cost-plus", which is the cost of gas production plus transportation costs (Ibid).

Notwithstanding, the Iran–Pakistan–India pipeline project has been regarded as strategically the most important. This is the southern route from Central Asia and the Caspian Sea basin. It is also considered economically most viable of all the routes that connect India with Central Asia. Although the IPI project remains most promising when it comes to gas imports, it has also been the most controversial of the pipeline projects. Differences between India and Pakistan over transit fees, financial and security issues and the US sanctions on Iran have all contributed to the delay of this project and its future is hanging in uncertainty.

International North–South Transportation corridor

The International North–South Transport Corridor (INSTC) is a 7200 km long multimode network of ship, rail and road route for moving freight between India and Russia through Iran, Europe and Central Asia. This project was proposed and initiated by India, Russia and Iran in St Petersburg in September 2000. The objective of the corridor is to increase trade connectivity between major cities such as Mumbai, Moscow, Tehran, Baku, Bandar Abbas, Astrakhan, etc. The agreement was signed on May 16, 2002, and the first dry run of two routes was conducted successfully in 2014 (Chaudhury 2017). The result was amazing as the cost of transportation was reduced by $2500 per 15 tonnes of cargo (MEA 2017). Since India is facing roadblocks in materializing the TAPI and IPI pipeline projects due to its transit through Pakistan, INSTC offers India bounties of opportunities to sideline Islamabad by working out the INSTC option through the Bandar Abbas and Chabahar port of Iran to Mundra and Mumbai through the Arabian Sea. Also from the cost–benefit analysis point of view, this has been seen as less expensive than other available routes and importantly it is secure and free from any sort of hostages.

Recent studies show that INSTC can reduce the time and cost of container delivery by 30–40 per cent and once the flow of goods from the two Iranian ports begin the corridor will be able to move 30–50 million tonnes of goods per year (Stobdan 2017). Given the importance of Chabahar Port to Iran's infrastructure development plans and its entry points for Iran, Central Asia and India; operational capacity of two terminals at Chabahar – Shahid Kalamtari and Shahid Beheshti; greater prospects for enlarging both the operational and practical scope of Chabahar to become a vital gateway to Central Asia as it gives ready access to several trade corridors (existing and planned); India's foothold in Chabahar as a result of the 2016 India–Iran Agreement, which underscores the

Indian commitment to build, equip and operate the port (two terminals and five berths with cargo handling for 10 years), the transportation from Chabahar is not only viable but also competitive in terms of distance, cost, delivery, market access, sustainability and safety of goods and cargo to and from Eurasia. Besides, the Chabahar transit route would potentially provide the landlocked countries of Central Asia with the shortest land route to conduct maritime trade with countries in the Indian Ocean region (Stobadan 2017).

Recently, good news has come from the International North–South Transportation Corridor that India and Russia have agreed to bolster their mutual trade by overcoming their geographical distance through INSTC, bypassing Iran despite the US warning against trade activities with Iran (FT 2020; RT 2020). If things go well, then it is just a matter of time before India overcomes the greatest geographical barrier that has posed a challenge for New Delhi.

CASAREM

The Central Asia–South Asia Regional Electricity Market (CASAREM) (World Bank 2014) is based on the vision of a Greater Central Asia. This, in turn, is based on the premise that Central and South Asia are, or can become, a single integrated unit committed to economic activity and growth. This concept further strengthens the spirit of regional security and regional cooperation. The CASAREM is already connected with Afghanistan from Kyrgyzstan and Tajikistan and has the potentiality and possibility to connect other South Asian countries including India. If effective initiatives are taken, it can help India in providing electricity to its north Indian cities which are generally facing blackout during the long summer. India has been working on this direction to extend the Central Asian electric grid now at Afghanistan to India through Pakistan.

India's energy engagement in Central Asia

There can be no denying the importance of reliable access to Central Asian energy resources for sustaining India's growth trajectory. However, the growing concern is about how much India is into the energy-rich region and how far it needs to go. India is a late starter in the region. Indian companies are trying hard to get a strong foothold in the region. In Central Asia, ONGC has made significant inroads into Iran, Kazakhstan, Turkmenistan, and most recently Tajikistan. It has formally bid on Tengiz and Kashaugan oil fields and the Kurmangazy and Darkhan exploration blocks in Kazakhstan (CSIS 2006). Competition in this region is fierce, as China is pursuing the same strategy. Understanding their losses in the competition New Delhi and Beijing initially agreed to do mutual biding where possible. As China is pursuing an aggressive policy, the onus is on India to come to an agreement table. India and China, in line with Asia-wide regional cooperation in energy, are cooperating in other areas. But when it comes to Central Asian energy, competition is fierce. China always chooses to go it alone. This was clearly illustrated in late 2005 when China outbid India to acquire PetroKazakhstan – Kazakhstan's third-largest oil producer, with CNPC raising its bid to $4.18 billion (Sachdeva 2011: 122). And the recent experience in the South China Sea, where India inked an agreement with Vietnam for oil exploration, of having to face Chinese confrontation is a reminder of China's go it alone approach in terms of energy, at least in Asia.

India's footholds in the Central Asian states

Kazakhstan

In 2017, India and Kazakhstan marked 25 years of their friendship and cooperation. In the entire Eurasian landscape, Kazakhstan naturally constitutes an important ally of India as far as its energy engagement is concerned. New Delhi has been trying since 1995 to gain a foothold in the hydrocarbon sector of Kazakhstan (Sajjanhar 2013). But it was only in 2009 that an agreement was signed between ONGC Videsh Ltd (OVL) and KazMunaiGas (KMG) (Sachdeva 2017). This was followed by an exploration contract between India's Ministry of Oil and Gas and the KMG in 2010. During the visit of Indian Prime Minister Dr Manmohan Singh in 2011, the much-awaited agreement on energy cooperation was finalized. A package of three agreements – participating share assignment agreement, carry agreement and joint operation agreement – on the Satpayev exploration block was signed between OVL and the national company KMG in highly prospective waters of the north-western Caspian Sea (Sajjanhar 2013). This agreement assigned 25 per cent participating interests in the Satpayev block which holds estimated reserves of 1.8 billion barrels in the Kazakh sector of the Caspian Sea (Sachdeva 2017). It was agreed that the Kazakh state oil company would pay about $80m signature bonus for a 25 per cent stake in Satpayev where oil reserves are estimated to amount to 250 MT (Gorst 2011). During Mr Modi's visit to Kazakhstan in 2015 drilling was launched and OVL is investing about $400 million in the project, with oil expected to flow by 2020. OVL also bought a 2.7 per cent stake in the Azeri–Chirag–Guneshli oil field in Azerbaijan, along with a 2.4 per cent stake in the associated Baku–Tbilisi–Ceyhan pipeline (Sachdeva 2017).

It was also agreed that ONGC would cover all exploration costs at Satpayev, minimizing Kazmunaigas' risk in the early stages of the project that will eventually require $9 billion of investment. It has become common practice around the world for foreign companies to pay exploration costs when entering into undeveloped projects with state oil companies. India, which is heavily dependent on imported energy, has had less success than other countries in winning Kazakh oil deals. The United States and European majors secured rights to develop the vast Tengiz and Karachaganak fields in the 1990s that now accounts for the bulk of Kazakhstan's 80 MT a year oil production. China, India's main rival for global oil reserves, has accumulated a large portfolio of upstream assets in Kazakhstan and built pipelines to carry production to its north-western border (Ibid). This was clearly illustrated in late 2005 when China outbid India to acquire Petro-Kazakhstan – Kazakhstan's third-largest oil producer – by placing a bid of $4.18 billion (Sachdeva 2017).

India has been trying to catch up at Satpayev, but the deal has taken a long time to materialize. During the visit of the Kazakh President Nursultan Nazarbayev to India in January 2009, India's ONGC Mittal Energy Limited (OMEL) and KazMunaiGaz (KMG) signed a Heads of Agreement for exploration of oil and gas in the Satpayev block in the Caspian Sea (Sachdeva 2011: 122). OMEL is a joint venture between ONGC Videsh Limited (OVL) and Mittal Investments. The Satpayev block covers an area of 1582 square kilometres and is at a water depth of 5–10 metres (Ibid). It is situated in a highly prospective region of the North Caspian Sea. An additional benefit of this is that it is close to major fields such as Karazhanbas, Kalamkas, Kashagan and Donga where significant quantities of oil have been discovered. It has estimated reserves of 1.85 billion barrels. The Indian company will have a 25 per cent stake. The remaining 75 per cent stays with KazMunaiGas (*Times of India* 2009). However, the deal couldn't be materialized due to protracted delay from the Indian side and the Kazakh President, using his sovereign power, handed over the deal to China.

In 2013, however, India suffered a setback in Kazakhstan again, losing its bid to acquire an 8.4 per cent stake in the North Caspian Sea Production Sharing Agreement from ConocoPhillips. It would have given India a stake in the vast Kashagan oil field in the Caspian Sea, and OVL came very close to finalizing the deal for $5 billion after getting approval from its partners. But the Kazakh government used its legal rights to sell this stake to the China National Petroleum Corporation instead, for a sum reported to be between $5.2 and 5.4 billion (Sachdeva 2017). Altogether, by some estimates, India has lost at least $12.5 billion worth of deals to China in recent years. And when the Kazakh government reportedly offered the ONGC a stake in the mid-sized Abai oil block in 2014, India rejected the deal. With the declining oil prices, the ONGC did not find the offer particularly attractive (Ibid).

Oil and gas, of course, represent the most important areas in which both countries can collaborate to mutual advantage. Currently, India imports 70 per cent of its energy requirements. India's demand for fossil fuels and other forms of energy is expected to keep increasing because of its rapid economic growth. Currently, Kazakhstan produces about 80 million tonnes per year (1.6 million barrels per day). With the Kashagan oil field expected to come on stream later this year, Kazakhstan's oil production is likely to go up to 150 million tonnes per annum by 2015, making it one of world's top ten exporters of oil. Kazakhstan can take advantage of the rich and vast experience that India has accumulated in downstream processing and refining of crude oil to manufacture petrochemicals and other related products (Sajjanhar 2013).

OVL was hopeful that it will be able to wrest an 8.3 per cent stake in the Kashagan oil field for which it had made an offer of $5 billion. Regrettably, this share was given to the Chinese for a similar amount although India had indicated its interest in this project much earlier. This caused an avoidable psychological disappointment, shock and heartburn to the section of opinion makers and leaders in India who have been speaking out vociferously in favour of stronger strategic and economic links with Kazakhstan. However, this setback notwithstanding, it would be important to continue to identify and pursue fresh initiatives and opportunities for strengthening and deepening the bilateral partnership (Sajjanhar 2013).

Both countries agreed and signed the "Strategic Partnership" in 2009 for developing comprehensive bilateral relations on issues of security and strategic importance. The two sides are negotiating a possible uranium supply agreement as civil nuclear energy cooperation presents attractive prospects for further diversifying bilateral economic and commercial contacts. Kazakhstan already supplies India with nuclear fuel from its significant uranium deposits, while India plans to increase its civil nuclear programme, which already counts 20 nuclear reactors (Cutler 2011).

Kazakhstan also actively supported India for an unconditional waiver for international commerce in civil nuclear energy in 2009 at the negotiations at the International Atomic Energy Agency (IAEA) and Nuclear Suppliers Group (NSG). Kazakhstan is the largest producer of uranium ore currently with an annual production of around 20,000 tonnes per annum, with a projected annual output of 27,000 tonnes by 2015. India has developed nuclear reactors indigenously. Both countries can collaborate successfully to mutual advantage and benefit in this field. Kazakhstan is also keen to use India's expertise to move up the value chain in the production of nuclear fuel pellets (Sajjanhar 2016).

According to India's 12th Five Year Plan, nuclear power will play a major role in meeting the country's energy needs. The country needs an additional 100,000 MW of power during the 12th Plan (2012–17). The civil nuclear energy cooperation in this regard provides India with a diversifying energy source. Kazakhstan supported India for international commerce in civil nuclear energy in the International Atomic Energy Agency (IAEA) and Nuclear Suppliers Group (NSG) in 2009. The MoU was signed between Nuclear Power Corporation of India (NPCI) and National Atomic Company, Kazatomprom in 2009 during the visit of Nazarbayev (president of Kazhakstan). It was the initial step for future cooperation. The nuclear bilateral talks were strengthened during the visit of former Indian Prime Minister Manmohan Singh in 2011 to Astana, Kazhakstan. During his visits, Singh signed a peaceful use of atomic energy agreement with Kazhakstan. The agreement provides a legal framework for cooperation in fuel supply, reactor safety mechanism and exchange of scientific and research information, exploration and joint mining of uranium, design, construction and operation of nuclear power plants. According to the agreement, Kazakhstan supplied 2000 tonnes of uranium to India in 2014 (Pradhan 2017). Further, Kazakhstan has shown interest in allowing India to build small nuclear reactors with a capacity of 220 MW in its territory (*The Indian Express* 2017).

Turkmenistan

Being the richest country in natural gas in Central Asia, Turkmenistan is important for India's energy security. Turkmenistan is endowed with rich reserves of natural gas, crude oil, potassium and rock salts. Turkmenistan has the fourth-largest natural gas reserves in the world (WEC 2018). It also has significant reserves of crude oil.

Four countries of the region – Turkmenistan, Afghanistan, Pakistan and India – have taken an initiative to construct a gas pipeline project popularly known as the TAPI gas pipeline (Turkmenistan–Afghanistan–Pakistan–India gas pipeline). Over the years, there has been much discussion on the $7.6 billion TAPI gas pipeline (Sachdeva 2011: 123). The project has been marred by uncertainties regarding gas reserves in Turkmenistan, the security situation in Afghanistan and the strained relations between India and Pakistan. Still, all parties are considering the proposal seriously. Again, on December 11, 2010, basic documents between the four countries were signed in Ashgabat in the presence of the Presidents of Turkmenistan, Afghanistan and Pakistan and from India, the then Minister of Petroleum & Natural Gas, Shri Murli Deora (MEA 2011, MEA 2017).

This 1680 km pipeline would run from the Dauletabad gas field in Turkmenistan to Afghanistan. From there it would run alongside the highway from Heart to Kandahar, and then via Quetta to Multan in Pakistan. The final destination of the pipeline is to be Fazilka in Indian Punjab (Sachdeva 2011: 123).

The Dauletabad gas field has confirmed reserves of over 2.3 trillion cubic metres (tcm). Additional reserves of about 1.2 tcm are expected after drilling in the adjacent area. The gas production capacity of the field could be increased to about 125 million cubic metres per day (mcm/d). From the current 80 mcm/d, Turkmenistan has committed to providing sovereign guarantees for long-term uninterrupted supplies to Pakistan and India (*The Dawn* 2006).

In May 2006, the Indian government officially approved its participation in the TAPI project and authorized the Ministry of Petroleum and Natural Gas to put up a formal request for joining the project (PIB 2006). Moreover, India's continuing relationship with and participation in the project for a Turkmenistan–Afghanistan–Pakistan–India (TAPI) natural gas pipeline has contributed to increasing its profile in the region. Turkmenistan's interest in TAPI has only increased since the Nabucco project meant to pipe gas to Europe was canceled by Russia as a response to the US led western sanctions on Kremlin after the Russia-Ukraine standoff in Crimea.

Following two decades of discussion, leaders from all four countries held a groundbreaking ceremony in Mary, Turkmenistan, in December 2015 (Sachdeva 2017). The event defied many sceptics who had long considered TAPI's relevance limited to academic and diplomatic conferences. The project has enormous strategic potential: once completed, the pipeline could become a game-changer in regional geopolitics and a force for economic integration. It would also generate significant transit revenues for Afghanistan and thereby help ease its economic difficulties (Ibid).

Uzbekistan

As far as gas imports are concerned Uzbekistan holds importance for India. It has large amounts of proven reserves. It had 594 billion barrels of proven crude oil as of 2016 as per the estimates of *Oil and Gas Journal* (*Oil and Gas Journal* 2016) with a production capability of 78,900 barrels per day (EIA 2016). Roughly 60 per cent of Uzbekistan's oil and gas fields are located in the Bukhara–Khiva region accounting for almost 70 per cent of the country's oil production (EIA 2016). Apart from oil, Uzbekistan has huge reserves of natural gas. The country ranks third in gas production in the entire CIS after Russia and Turkmenistan. It produces just over 2 trillion cubic feet (tcf) natural gas annually (BP 2016).

Besides, in the last decade and a half Uzbekistan has been trying to increase export volumes and diversify export routes. The Indian public sector company Gas Authority of India (GAIL) signed an MoU with Uzbekistan's Uzbekneftegaz for oil and gas exploration and production (Sachdeva 2017). The GAIL also set up a Liquefied Petroleum Gas (LPG) plant in western Uzbekistan, mainly for Uzbek consumption. India took another step towards economic and strategic penetration into Central Asia with the visit of Uzbekistan's President Islom Karimov to New Delhi in May 2011 (Cutler 2011). The honourable President signed an agreement that would lead to India's ONGC Videsh Ltd (OVL) prospecting for oil and gas inside its neighbour's territory in cooperation with Uzbekneftegaz.

In meetings with former Indian Prime Minister Dr Manmohan Singh, both sides agreed to raise the level of bilateral relations to a "long-term strategic partnership". The heads of state signed 34 accords across a wide range of issues that, alongside the hydrocarbon sector, included cooperation in pharmaceuticals and information technology (Sachdeva 2011). Under their provisional agreement, OVL, the overseas arm of India's state-owned Oil and Natural Gas Corporation, would form working groups with Uzbekneftegaz in a view towards joint activities in third countries, allowing OVL to continue to increase access to Central Asia's vast energy resources (Ibid).

Bilateral energy cooperation between India and Uzbekistan extends to Afghanistan as well. The two countries have cooperated to supply electricity to Kabul, with Uzbekistan furnishing the power for the transmission network built by India (*The Hindu* 2011).

Karimov's unsettled authoritarian rule in Uzbekistan made cooperation with India problematic until the two sides decided to focus first of all on security and anti-terrorism issues. Since then, economic cooperation has increased markedly. Uzbekistan is the thirteenth-biggest gas producer in the world, a fact often overlooked because its large population consumes a significant proportion of the production, which is therefore not a "strategic" export as it is for Kazakhstan and, for example, Turkmenistan.

Kyrgyzstan and Tajikistan

Tajikistan is the second-largest producer of hydroelectricity in the Commonwealth of Independent States (CIS) and has more than half the hydropower resources in Central Asia. Tajikistan possesses about 4 per cent of world hydroelectricity potential and ranks eighth in the world in terms of reserves (Ministry of Energy and Industry 2015). When it come to hydropower reserves, "Tajikistan ranks 8th in the world behind China, Russia, the United States, Brazil, Zaire, India, and Canada. Specifically, it ranks 1st and 2nd in the world in terms of hydropower generation capacity per square kilometer (36,699,000 kWh/km2/year) and per capita (65,900 kWh/person/year). Besides, it is expected that Tajikistan's hydropower potential can provide sufficient energy security for Central Asia, at 527 billion (kWh/year) equivalents to three times the current electricity consumption in Central Asia" (Xu et al. 2020: 3).

As far as the hydropower potential of Kyrgyzstan is concerned, it is just behind Tajikistan and is the third largest in the CIS countries after Russia and Tajikistan. It produces 80 per cent of electricity by hydropower plants and the rest from coal, gas and oil. The five major hydro-electric power stations are situated at Kurpsay, Toktogul, Shanoldysay and Tas-kumyar. They are situated on Naryn River and together accounts for 97 per cent of the hydro capacity. As of 2015, nine major power plants were operating with a capacity of 3,646,600 kWh. In addition, two extra hydro-power plants on the Naryn River, above the Toktogul water reserve, have the potential to add to the country's production capacity. However, these plants are not yet completed due to the collapse of the Soviet Union. Both Tajikistan and Kyrgyzstan have been poor countries since the time of the Soviet regime and are still not yet developed. To exploit their water resource, Tajikistan and Kyrgyzstan and other Central Asian countries are mostly dependent on Russia, China and even India (Ministry of Energy and Industry 2015).

Kyrgyzstan and Tajikistan intensified their electricity transmission to South Asia (Afghanistan and Pakistan) through the visionary concept of the Central Asia–South Asia Regional Electricity Market (CASAREM). The existing facility in Tajikistan on the Vakhsh River and in the Kyrgyz republic on the Naryn River would supply the current available summer surplus for export (Roul 2010). Further, Uzbekistan has also achieved seventh position in terms of production of uranium as well as having hydrocarbon reserves. Indian companies like GAIL and Engineers India Limited (EIL) are working in Uzbekistan gas and oil fields. However, GAIL has taken the initiative and identified four blocks for exploration of gas.

A North–South 500 kV transmission line in Tajikistan is currently under construction with Chinese financing. Additional transmission links from the Kyrgyz Republic to Tajikistan enables electricity from the Kyrgyz Republic to be transmitted directly via Tajikistan to South Asia. A Tajikistan to Afghanistan 220 kV transmission link is also under construction. The electricity transmission and trading system project to transfer about 1000 MW of power from the Kyrgyz Republic and Tajikistan to Pakistan via Afghanistan (referred to as CASA 1000) (CASAREM 2007). Pakistan is not far from India. India can stretch its muscles and work out how to extend the CASAREM vision to Indian soil.

India and the Caspian Sea region

As per the estimates of the US Energy Information Administration, the Caspian Sea basin comprises two-thirds of the region's total hydrocarbon resources. It has proven gas reserves of around 243–248 tcf and, given its proximity to India, this could be a game-changer for its energy security dilemma (Hill and Spector 2001). Given New Delhi's close and cordial relationship with all the Caspian Sea states, especially Russia and Iran, it is an important player in the regional energy geopolitics. But ironically India has not been able to materialize on those historic ties with the regional countries by translating them into the shipment of energy resources. While Western countries especially European Union members have made significant investments in the Caspian Gas projects, they haven't been economically viable. If we see it from a longer perspective, for the Caspian countries transporting gas to the Asian market would be more feasible than to Western countries. For countries like India whose, demand for energy is ravenous, the Caspian basin could be a ray of hope.

For India, the import of gas from the Caspian basin, specifically from the gas fields in Turkmenistan and Iran, has been a viable option and a subject of curious discussion at the academic, governmental and industry level. To achieve this, pipelines would have to traverse a distance of at least 1500 kilometres from Turkmenistan and Iran to India. However, India can ease the cost by working on the already existing Iranian pipelines connecting the Caspian region with its South Asian neighbours.

India's investments in Caspian energy

State-run Oil and Natural Gas Corporation of India Ltd's subsidiary, ONGC Videsh Ltd (OVL) agreed with Hess Corporations to acquire 2.72 per cent participating interest in three oil and gas fields in the Azerbaijan sector of the Caspian Sea – Azeri, Chirag and Guneshli – along with 2.36 per cent interest in the Baku–Tbilisi–Ceyhan (BTC) pipeline for $1 billion (Rs 5500 crore) (Reuters 2012). A definitive agreement was signed to acquire this interest in the Azeri, Chirag and Deep Water Portion of Guneshli Fields in the Azerbaijan sector and BTC with due government approval in 2013. This acquisition marked OVL's entry into the energy-rich Azerbaijan. As per the press release of ONGC Videsh Ltd,

> The acquisition is consistent with ONGC's stated strategic objective of adding high-quality international assets to its existing E&P portfolio. The acquisition would bring 9 per cent additional proved reserves to OVL

> portfolio and also bears significant strategic importance to India in terms of contributing towards India's energy security.
>
> *(The Hindu Business line 2012)*

With an average production of around 700,000 bl/d of crude oil, ACG, located in the south Caspian Sea off the coast of Azerbaijan, is one of the largest producing oil fields in the world. British Petroleum operates ACG and is partnered by State Oil Company of Azerbaijan Republic (SOCAR), Chevron, Statoil, ExxonMobil, Inpex, Turkish NOC–TPAO and Itochu.

The 1768 km BTC Pipeline is one of the main export routes for Caspian crude oil production with a capacity of around 1 million bl/d to the Ceyhan terminal in the Mediterranean Sea in south-east Turkey (The Hindu Business line 2012).

As per the Perspective Plan – 2030 of ONGC, the oil and gas production of OVL would increase from the current level of 8.75 million tonnes oil equivalent (mtoe) to 20 mtoe by FY'18 and 60 mtoe by FY'30.

Sudhir Vasudeva, CMD, ONGC said, "The production from this asset during the financial year 2011–12 was about 15 per cent of OVL's crude oil production during the same period" (Reuters 2012).

As of 2012, OVL had interests in 15 countries, namely Brazil, Colombia, Cuba, Iran, Iraq, Kazakhstan, Libya, Myanmar, Nigeria, Russia, South Sudan, Sudan, Syria, Venezuela and Vietnam. For the year ending March 31, 2012, OVL produced 8.75 mtoe of oil and gas (VCCiRCLE 2012).

Through the better part of India's history, links with Central Asia were the most important in its contact with the outside world. Traditionally India aimed to take its philosophical and cultural message across Inner Asian countries up to the remote Siberian region. During the British period, political officers, explorers, surveyors and traders, obviously for the "Great Game" postures, maintained some interest in Central Asia. However, in the post-independence period, India grossly and perhaps consciously overlooked the studies and understanding of its non-South Asian neighbouring areas, which traditionally formed "buffer zones" against external aggression. However, from the 1970s to 1990s, India's Central Asia policy was factored by the Soviet Union. Due to healthy Indo-Soviet relations, Indian relations with Central Asia were cordial and close. In the early 1990s, with the disintegration of the Soviet Union, India's focus in the region again remained poor and dismal. However, with the increasing geopolitical and strategic significance of the region for India, it directed its foreign policy formulation towards the region, which many called India's "Look North Policy". This policy was meant to promote democracy, secularism and peaceful coexistence in the Central Asian region. The situation has, however, changed, along with the evolving energy scenarios in the region. Accordingly, the policy formulation of the countries changed responding to the region's demand. India also, under the current regime of Mr Modi, has attempted to remain engaged with the heartland region, keeping in mind that the huge energy resources the region possesses can satisfy the hunger of India's energy sector.

Nevertheless, the Central Asian gas market has been undergoing significant change, due to China's slowdown and Russia's declining demand. Turkmenistan currently exports gas to China, Russia and Iran – but the latter two have lately reduced their imports. Russia, in particular, was mostly re-exporting Turkmen gas to Europe, and as both energy prices and European demand declined, its long-term contract with Turkmenistan became unprofitable. After efforts to renegotiate the deal failed, Moscow unilaterally reduced its imports. For its part, Iran, too, is likely to cut gas imports now that the lifting of international sanctions allows it to build infrastructure for energy export. This means that China, already the largest export market for Turkmen gas, will only grow in importance, leaving some in Ashgabat worried about this overdependence and searching for alternative buyers. If TAPI becomes a reality, it will open new opportunities for Turkmenistan in South Asia.

Moreover, TAPI would likely also encourage Russia to send hydrocarbons to South Asia by pipeline. New Delhi and Moscow have already set up a working group to explore the possibility of bringing Russian energy to India either via the Afghanistan–Pakistan route or via China.

Finally, an emerging area of Indian and Central Asian cooperation is uranium purchases from the region. Kazakhstan has large reserves of uranium, and India is keen to import it for its growing nuclear industry. In 2011, Kazakhstan agreed to supply 2100 tonnes of uranium to India's nuclear plants by 2014, and pledged an additional 5000 tonnes for 2015–19 during Modi's visit to Astana in 2015. Similarly, the state-owned Uzbek mining firm NMMC agreed to supply 2000 metric tonnes of uranium ore concentrate to India between 2014 and 2018.

India, so far, has not achieved any success in winning deals in the Central Asian oil sector. The reasons for this are many – ranging from technical hurdles to high stake politics. The problem of inaccessibility apart, the issue of avoiding transit through Pakistan itself has become a fact of life. Therefore, it becomes essential, and inevitably so, to factor China into our energy security calculus. During British rule, the route via Xinjiang was preferred for conducting trade and commerce with Central Asia. However, the partition of India and illegal and forceful occupation of Northern Kashmir by Pakistan has blocked India's old trade route option in its transit route vision.

But with growing cooperation with China, the feasibility of constructing an oil/gas "Energy Highway" from Central Asia along western China connecting to northern India can be well assumed. If this happens, it would bring about unprecedented strategic change, let alone endowing energy supplies to the entire region of northern India. Such a project connecting Central Asia and India through China would undermine the much-hyped Turkmenistan–Afghanistan–Pakistan gas pipeline project.

Until such a time when construction of direct oil and gas pipelines becomes possible, India's interest should remain focused on the petroleum management sector. The Caspian Sea region and Kazakhstan offer enormous opportunity for Indian technicians and experts. Indian presence in the region is already growing, as hundreds of Indian technicians and skilled workers are finding their way into infrastructure development projects. About a thousand Indians are already working in Aksai and the Karachaganak-based Consolidated Construction Company (CCC) and SAIPEM Company, undertaking pipeline construction. With the increasing participation of the Indian workforce in petroleum management, the Caspian Sea region and Central Asia would inevitably become another Gulf model for India.

It is, therefore, necessary for India to evolve its perspective and understanding, and to broaden its operational scope in Central Asia. In this mission, it also needs to include Afghanistan and the frontiers of China (Xinjiang) in its greater Central Asian vision. India needs to capitalize on its entry into SCO as a full member at Ufa in 2015.

Consequently, the five Central Asian states are casting about for counterbalances against the two large Asian powers. Kazakhstan has had somewhat closer relations with India since earlier in the decade, which seemed to promise increased trade ties. It was founded for a time upon the difficult geography: on top of the transportation difficulties endemic to the region, New Delhi has no border with any Central Asian state. As for Uzbekistan, it is an old ally of India – historically connected. Turkmenistan, Kyrgyzstan and Tajikistan have maintained very close and cordial relations with India throughout the years and are expecting a greater Indian role in their region to counterbalance the growing hegemony of Russia, China and the United States.

Two and a half decades after the independence of the Central Asian states, India's relatively low profile in the region has acquired higher relief as it searches for "poles of attraction" other than Russia and China, which in the late 1990s had begun to establish a condominium.

References

BP (2016), "BP Statistical Review of World Energy", British Petroleum, March, available at: https://www.bp.com/en/global/corporate/energy-economics/statistical-review-of-world-energy.html [accessed September 8, 2018].

Blank, Stephen (2003), "India's Rising Profile in Central Asia", *Comparative Strategy*, 22(2) (April), p. 141.

CASAREM (2007), *Electricity Transmission and Trade Projects – CASA -1000*, Central Asia-South Asia Regional Electricity Market, July, available at: http://centralasia.usaid.gov/datafiles/_upload/CASA-1000_Briefing_Mem_Final.pdf [accessed June 10, 2010].

Chandra, Amiya (2017), *The Trade Game: Engaging with Central Asia*, New Delhi: Pentagon Press.

CSIS (2006), "India's Energy Dilemma", *South Asia Monitor*, Centre for Strategic and International Studies, No. 28, September 7, Washington, DC.

Cutler, M. Robert (2011), "India Raises Energy Profile in Central Asia," *Asia Times*, May 27, www.asitimes.com.

EIA (2016), *Country-Specific Analysis - India*, Energy Information Administration, available at: www.eia.doe.gov/india, March 14.

ET (2018), "India's Oil Import Bill to Jump by 25% in FY 2018", *The Economic Times*, March 26.

Gorst, Isabel (2011), "India Gains a Foothold in Kazakhstan," *European Dialogue*, April 25.

Hart, Michael (2016), "Central Asia's Oil and Gas Now Flows to the East", *The Diplomat*. August 18.

Hill, Fiona and Spector, Regine (2001), "The Caspian Basin and Asian Energy Market", Brookings, September 1, available at: https://www.brookings.edu/research/the-caspian-basin-and-asian-energy-markets/ [accessed April 16, 2020].

IEA (2016), *World Energy Outlook*, International Energy Agency. Flagship Report - November, Paris, available at: https://www.iea.org/reports/world-energy-outlook-2016. [accessed September 8, 2018].

IEF (2018), "India's Energy Future Has Four Pillars – Energy Access, Energy Efficiency, Energy Sustainability and Energy Security: PM Modi", *16th International Energy Forum*, New Delhi, April 11, available at: https://www.narendramodi.in/pm-modi-inaugurates-the-16th-international-energy-forum-in-new-delhi-539611 [accessed January 22, 2020].

Kumar, Ajay (2018), "Alternative to Turkmenistan, Afghanistan, Pakistan and India Gas Pipeline: The Gas Highway (Oman-India Pipeline)," Linkedin, February 26, available at: https://www.linkedin.com/pulse/alternative-turkmenistan-afghanistan-pakistan-india-gas-amit-kumar/.

Market Insider (2018), "Crude Oil Price Today, Oil Price (Brent, Crude and WTI)", *Market Insiders*, available at: https://markets.businessinsider.com/commodities/oil-price [accessed January 2, 2019].

MEA (2011), "India-Turkmenistan Relations," Ministry of External Affairs, Government of India, New Delhi, July, available at: http://mea.gov.in/mystart.php?id=50044534 [accessed September 1, 2018].

MEA (2015), "PM Modi's Central Asia Tour Brings Region Back into Focus", July 15, Ministry of External Affairs, Government of India, New Delhi, available at: http://mea.gov.in/articles-in-indian-media.htm?dtl/25484/PM+Modis+Central+Asia+tour+brings+region+back+into+focus [accessed September 8, 2018].

MEA (2017), *India-Turkmenistan Relations*, Ashgabat, Turkmenistan: Embassy of India, August 31.

Ministry for Energy and Industry (2015), "Ministry for Energy and Industry of the Republic Tajikistan, Tajikistan towards Development Sustainable Energy, Energy Charter, Regional Energy Cooperation in Central and South Asia meeting, Astana, 7 October.

Muni S.D (2003), 'India and Central Asia: Towards a Cooperative Future', in Nirmala Joshi, (ed.) *Central Asia – The Great Game Replayed*: An Indian Perspective, New Delhi: New Century Publications, p. 110.

New Indian Express (2019), "PMO Says Government on Track to Hit USD 5 Trillion Economy Goal by 2024 Despite Slump", *New Indian Express*, November 29, 2019, available at: https://www.newindianexpress.com/business/2019/nov/29/pmo-says-government-on-track-to-hit-usd-5-trillion-economy-goal-by-2024-despite-slump-2069019.html [accessed January 22, 2020].

Niti Central (2015), "PM Modi's Central Asia Visit: Key Takeaways," *Niti Central*, July 14, available at: http://www.niticentral.com/2015/07/14/pm-modis-central-asia-visit-key-takeaways-323561.html [accessed September 1, 2018].

Oil and Gas Journal (2016), "Oil and Gas Profile of CIS Countries", *Oil and Gas Journal*, September, available at: https://www.ogj.com/index.html [accessed September 5, 2018].

PIB (2006), "Union Cabinet Decision Press Release", Press Information Bureau, Government of India, May 18, available at: http://pib.nic.in/realease/re120lease.asp?relid=17859&kwd= [accessed August 2010].

PPAC (2018), "Rising Crude in Poll Time to Further Erode PE of OMCs", *Petroleum Planning and Analysis Cell*, New Delhi: Ministry oil and Natural Gas, Govt. of India.

Pradhan, Ramakrushna (2015), "Mapping India's Look North Policy: Why Central Asia Matters?", *IUP Journal of International Relations*, IX(4), October.

Pradhan, Ramakrushna (2016), "Geopolitics of Energy in Central Asia: Where Does India Stand in this Game?", *Contemporary Central Asia*, XX(2&3), May-December, pp. 42–60.

Report (2011), "Turkmenistan-Afghanistan-Pakistan-India Gas Pipeline: South Asia's Key Project", *Petromin Pipeliner.* April-June. www.safan.com.

Reuters (2012), "ONGC Videsh Picks Stake in the Caspian Sea Oil & Gas Block, Pipeline for $1 bln", Reuters, September 11, available at: https://www.reuters.com/article/ongc-videsh-picks-stake-in-caspian-sea-o/ongc-videsh-picks-stake-in-caspian-sea-oil-gas-block-pipeline-for-1-bln-idINDEE88A0E520120911 [accessed April 16, 2020].

Roul, Avilas (2010), "The Elusive Yet Abundant Hydropower in the Kyrgyz Republic, 2010", *ECO World*, January 15.

Sachdeva, Gulshan (2011), "Regional Economic Linkages", in Nirmala Joshi (ed.), *Reconnecting India and Central Asia*, New Delhi: New Elegant Printers, pp. 115–180.

Sachdeva, Gulshan (2017), "Chaining Dynamics of India-Central Asia Ties", Bishkek Project, April 5, available at: https://www.bishkekproject.com/memos/24 [accessed September 8, 2018].

Sajjanhar, Ashok (2013), *India-Kazakhstan Relations: Challenges and Opportunities*, Indian Embassy in Kazakhstan, November 20.

Sajjanhar, Ashok (2016), *India-Central Asia Relations: Expanding Vistas of Partnership*, June 22, New Delhi: Observers Research Foundation.

Sovacool, Benjamin, Burke, Mathew, et al. (2017), "New Frontiers and Conceptual Frameworks for Energy Justice," *Energy Policy*, 105(C), pp. 677–691.

Stobdan, P. (2017), "India Gears up to enter the Eurasian Integration Path," *Institute for Defence Studies and Analyses (IDSA)*, Issue Brief, June 7, available at: https://idsa.in/system/files/issuebrief/ib_india-eurasian-integration-path_pstobdan_070617.pdf. [accessed February 10, 2018].

Temple, D. (2007), "The Iran-Pakistan-India Pipeline: the intersection of Energy and Politics," *Institute of Peace and Conflict Studies*, New Delhi, April, p.6.

The Dawn (2006), "Delhi Invited to Join TAPI Project," *The Dawn*, March 16, available at: www.dawn.com/2006/03/16/top10.htm [accessed June 10, 2010].

The Hindu (2011), "India and Uzbekistan to Firm Up Communication and Security Link", May, 18, Wednesday.

The Hindu (2018), "India's Oil Import Bill to Jump by $26 Billion", *The Hindu*, August 16.

The Hindu Business Line (2012), "ONGC Videsh Buys Stakes in Azeri Fields for $ 1 Billion", *The Hindu Business Line*, March 12, New Delhi, available at: https://www

.thehindubusinessline.com/companies/ongc-videsh-buys-stake-in-azeri-fields-for-1-billion/article20499680.ece1?ref=relatedNews [accessed April 16, 2020].

The Indian Express (2017), "Nuclear Boost", *The Indian Express*, May 19, available at: https://indianexpress.com/article/opinion/editorials/decision-to-build-high-capacity-reactors-is-a-landmark-for-the-nuclear-programme-credit-for-which-is-shared-by-upa-4662813/ [accessed January 19, 2018].

Times of India (2009), "ONGC Mittal Signs Deal to Take 25 Stake in Kazakh Oilfields," January, 24, available at: http://timesofindia.indiatimes.com/Business/India_Business/ONGC-Mittal_signs_deal_to_take_25_stake_in_Kazkh_oilfield/article/articleshow/4027 031.cms [accessed January 19, 2011].

VCCiRcle (2012), "ONGC Videsh Picks Stake in the Caspian Sea Oil & Gas Block, Pipeline for $1B", *VCCiRcle*, September 11, available at: https://www.vccircle.com/ongc-videsh-picks-stake-caspian-sea-oil-gas-block-pipeline-1b [accessed April 16, 2020].

WEC (2018), "Oil in Uzbekistan, Energy Resources", World Energy Council, August, available at: https://www.worldenergy.org/data/resources/country/uzbekistan/oil/ [accessed December 18, 2019].

World Bank (2014), "World Bank Group invests in Energy Trade between Central Asia and South Asia," The World Bank, March 7, available at: https://www.worldbank.org/en/news/press-release/2014/03/27/world-bank-group-invests-energy-trade-central-south-asia [accessed March 21, 2018].

Xu, Zhao, Niu, Yumin, Liang, Yengze, Li, Zhigang and Iftikhor, Atoev (2020), "The Integrated Hydropower Sustainability Assessment in Tajikistan: A Case Study of Rogun Hydropower Plant," *Hindawi - Advances in Civil Engineering*, available at: http://downloads.hindawi.com/journals/ace/2020/8894072.pdf.

6

NEW GREAT GAME AND SILK ROAD DIPLOMACY

Unlike that Great Game, today's Great Game; a collision of three great powers that are trying to roll back one another's sphere of influence is global, more complex, and much more dangerous. In the renewed great game, there are more players and more rivalry than it was during the game being played out between Britain and Russia in the nineteen and twentieth century.

– G. Asgar Mitha (2008)

The fight for hegemony in Central Asia is age-old. Strategically placed between two nuclear powers – Russia and China – and geopolitically located at the heart of Eurasia – Central Asia has always remained in the global limelight. Even after the disintegration of the USSR, the geopolitical importance of Central Asia never waned, but instead emerged as a grand chessboard for the regional and extra-regional players with the immense opportunities it has offered in the form of hugely untapped natural resources and geostrategic leverages. Importantly, it has emerged as the latest geological landscape for the energy crunch countries as a potentially new and non-OPEC source of oil and natural gas. In the quest for energy security and diversity of supply sources by the energy consumers, the heartland region has witnessed a new great game in the scramble for resources. This accentuated struggle for oil and energy in the region has further led to aggressive foreign policy formulations and strategic calculation by countries like the United States, China, the European Union, Japan, Israel, Iran, Pakistan and India among which many now call it the New Great Game for not just controlling but also administering the energy resources of the region. The bottom line of the New Great Game, unlike the previous version, is essentially played out around petro-politics and pipeline diplomacy. This chapter tries to figure out the position of India in the epic quest for oil in the traditional bastion of Russia and the new grand chessboard of China and the United States.

New Great Game in Central Asia

While there are many potential customers for Central Asian energy including Afghanistan, Pakistan, India, Iran and Turkey, there are very few states that possess the capability to influence Central Asian energy geopolitics at the global level. While Russia remains an influential power, any examination of Central Asian energy geopolitics must now also consider the influence of the West and the growing reach of China. The slow progress of India also needs to be noted. The West will be dealt with first, as its entry into the region after the Soviet era marked, in many ways, the beginning of Central Asian geopolitics, threatening Russia's historical influence.

Central Asia represents both large potential producers of energy resources and a hub to connect oil and gas ducts inside Eurasia. Estimation by the International Energy Agency indicates that the Caspian Region including Azerbaijan contains 3.5 per cent of the world's proven oil reserves (Feddersen and Zucatto 2013). The bulk of those reserves are in Kazakhstan with smaller volumes in Azerbaijan and Turkmenistan. Similarly, in case of natural gas, the region also accounts for around 7 per cent of global proven reserves mostly concentrated in Turkmenistan. The main issue of concern for the energy-rich countries since independence has been the fact that they are landlocked, making them rely heavily on complex infrastructure to import and export their resources (Sachdeva 2017).

The geographical positioning of Central Asia in the middle of Eurasia has created problems for its much-needed transportation of energy resources. From the standpoint of transportation logistics, there is no easy route linking Caspian oil and gas with maritime shipping lanes leading to the world's major energy consumers (United States, European Union, China and India). To head directly westward necessitates skirting the Caspian, greatly increasing the length of any pipeline, or building an underwater pipeline which greatly increases the cost of the project. Further, the complications surrounding the heated dispute among its five littoral states add more woes to the already worrisome states. Heading east towards the Pacific Ocean is technically feasible from Turkmenistan through Uzbekistan and Kazakhstan and since 2005 the China–Kazakhstan oil pipeline and since 2009 the Central Asia–China gas pipeline have been fully functioning and there are many other pipelines under construction. Running south-east towards the Indian Ocean through Iran, Afghanistan and Pakistan is also feasible but the Hindu Kush mountain, trouble-torn Afghanistan and terror-prone Pakistan emerge as troublesome (Dekmejian and Simonain 2001).

Nevertheless, the energy crunch worldwide and burgeoning fuel demand from the native population have invited many potential consumers for Central Asian energy including the United States, China, the European Union, Japan, India and Pakistan. However, there are only a few states that possess the capability to influence Central Asian energy geopolitics at the global level. While Russia remains an influential power, any examination of Central Asian energy geopolitics must now also take into account the influence of the West and the growing reach of China. The slow progress of India also needs to be taken note of. The West will be dealt with in detail as its entry into the region after the Soviet era marked, in many ways, the beginning of Central Asian geopolitics, threatening Russia's historical influence (Johnson 2007).

Russian pipeline strategy

Central Asia has always been the traditional sphere of influence of the Kremlin. Since the Soviet days, due to its centralized planning and energy distribution system, Central Asia remained dependent on Moscow. The whole pipeline transport and communication network was integrally connected with Russia. The Soviet pipelines were used by Western companies like Chevron to reduce the cost of new infrastructure. That's why all the Central Asian countries rely on Russia to transfer their oil and gas through Russian pipelines enabling Moscow to maintain a stronghold in the region and to generate transit fees out of it. Any Western presence in the region would be a spoilsport for the Russian interests in its backyard.

Apart from security, Russia until recently was the main trade partner of the Central Asian Republics. However, the global economic crisis of 2008, its domestic compulsions and Western sanctions on Russia after the Crimean annexation in 2014 have led to a decrease in trade volumes in the last decade and a half. "Indeed in 2017, Russian trade relations amounted almost to $23 billion, while China amounted almost to $36 billion" (Raimondi 2019), as shown in Table 6.1.

Despite decreasing trade ties, Russia was able to exert control over the Central Asian energy sector in lieu of the Soviet system of centrally controlled

TABLE 6.1 Russia's trade with Central Asia

Year	*Trade volume in $ million*
1996	8.169
1999	3.825
2000	6.472
2005	12.681
2008	26.752
2010	21.497
2012	31.987
2014	29.983
2016	18.551
2017	22.860

Source: Raimondi, Pier (2019), Central Asian Oil and Gas Industry – The External Powers' Energy Interests in Kazakhstan, Turkmenistan and Uzbekistan, FEEM Working Paper, No. 006.

and connected pipeline networks from and through Moscow. That's why all the Central Asian countries even after their independence had to rely on Russia to transfer their oil and gas through the Russian pipelines, enabling Moscow to maintain a stronghold in the region and to generate transit fees from it.

Given the relevance of hydrocarbon reserves located in the Central Asian heartland, Russia had been pursuing the establishment of relations with the CAS in its energy fields since the 1990s. Gazprom – the Russian national gas company – enjoyed an absolute monopoly to regulate and control the pipelines running through Russia. Among the pipeline projects in Central Asia – "Central Asia-Centre (CAC) was most prominent and was delivering gas to Russia from Turkmenistan via Uzbekistan and Kazakhstan during the Soviet times with a total annual capacity of 90 bcm" (Raimondi 2019). However, the capacity of CAC dropped to about 44 bcm in 2009 due to lack of maintenance, and throughout 2017 Gazprom purchased 21.3 bcm of gas in Central Asia as shown in Table 6.2.

Gazprom used to buy natural gas from the Central Asian countries, not for domestic requirements but for external markets as Central Asian gas came at a low price to resell at a higher price in lucrative markets like Europe. Gazprom's policy was part of a greater Russian strategy to obtain economic and political benefits from such cooperation. However, the monopoly of Moscow over the pipelines, discrimination in the transportation of Central Asian gas to European markets, the declining economic influence of Russia in CAS, the growing role of China in the region, the increasing presence of new players, it became difficult for Russia to maintain its stronghold in CAR. Although the paramount objectives of Russia in promoting regional organizations such as CSTO, EAEU and CIS are aimed at balancing the increasing influence of China and the United States in the region, the goal is yet to be achieved.

The difficulty of Russia is not waning in the energy sector either. The primary threats to Russian energy dominance now come from the Baku–Tbilisi–Ceyhan (BTC) pipeline proposed by the West led by the United States. It is the greatest success of the West in countering Russia's energy monopoly in

TABLE 6.2 Gas purchase in Central Asia and Azerbaijan by Gazprom in bcm

Bcm	*Countries*	*2013*	*2014*	*2015*	*2016*	*2017*
For supply to Europe	Turkmenistan	10.9	11.0	3.1	–	–
	Uzbekistan	5.7	3.6	3.5	4.3	5.5
	Kazakhstan	11.9	10.9	12.9	12.7	13.8
	Azerbaijan	1.4	0.2	–	–	–
For supply to southern Kazakhstan	Turkmenistan	0.3	–	–	–	–
	Uzbekistan	3.7	3.7	2.9	1.9	1.7
For supply to Kyrgyzstan	Uzbekistan	–	0.004	*	*	*
	Kazakhstan	–	0.06	0.2	0.2	0.3

Source: Raimondi, Pier (2019), Central Asian Oil and Gas Industry – The External Powers' Energy Interests in Kazakhstan, Turkmenistan and Uzbekistan, FEEM Working Paper, No. 006.

Note: * = Less than 0.05

the region by developing an alternative energy route to Europe and the West at large. Importantly, this has encouraged the European Union to repeat its pipeline endeavours in the region, this time in the form of the Nabucco project. Since then, the Russian hold over the Central Asian energy sector has been waning steadily. The recently concluded Kazakh–Chinese pipeline is proof of the loosening hold Moscow has in its backyard (Pradhan 2019). Therefore, it is reasserting its position in the hinterland under the effective leadership of Mr Putin.

The primary threats to Russian energy dominance, then, are new pipeline routes beyond its control. The BTC pipeline is the greatest success that the West has had in creating an alternative route, a success that the European Union would like to replicate with the Nabucco project. Now, after completion of the Kazakh–Chinese pipeline as well, Russia perhaps is realizing that it does not have much time to act before other players' secure greater access to the region. Therefore, Russia is reasserting its position in the hinterland under the able leadership of Mr Putin (Reuter 2009).

As such, Moscow's main political goal is to maintain a wide range of influence over the former Soviet Republics which it labels as "near abroad". Besides, to build and institutionalize relations with Central Asian states, the Russian government also employs the legal and commercial means deemed necessary: (a) In ensuring that Russian firms participate in developing the region's natural resources and that Central Asian oil and gas exporters continue to use Russian pipelines; (b) In minimizing the involvement of the United States and European Companies in joint ventures formed with Central Asian counterparts; (c) In scaring off potential competitors by announcing or constructing alternative pipelines conducive to Russia dominated overland energy transport; (d) In splitting Western power through energy diplomacy, thus augmenting the energy dependence of the European Union upon Russia and less on the United States; and (e) In fostering selective bilateral ties with Central Asian governments within the setting of a comprehensive multilateral security umbrella (Geopolitica.ru 2013).

To strengthen its grip on European gas markets and head off a US-backed pipeline project, Nabucco, which would bypass Russia, Moscow wants to use "North Stream", the 1200 km twin pipeline that would carry a total of 55 bcm from Russia's port of Vyborg to the German port of Greifswald. Construction of the €7.4 billion project started in 2010, with the first pipeline ready for delivery in 2011 (Rising 2009). It runs from Kazakhstan's Tengiz fields to the Russian Port of Novorossiysk and is the largest current export route of Caspian oil, carrying 34 million tonnes of oil/year. There is talk of almost doubling capacity to 67 million tonnes/year by adding ten new pumping stations (EIU 2007). This pipeline (as shown in Figure 6.1) is built without crossing Ukraine and Poland, the transit countries with which Moscow has been at odds for years over Russian gas destined for the European market. For example, in January 2009 Moscow cut off gas supply via Ukraine for two weeks and caused an uproar. A mirror project "South Stream" will be built as a rival to ward off Nabucco (Rising 2009).

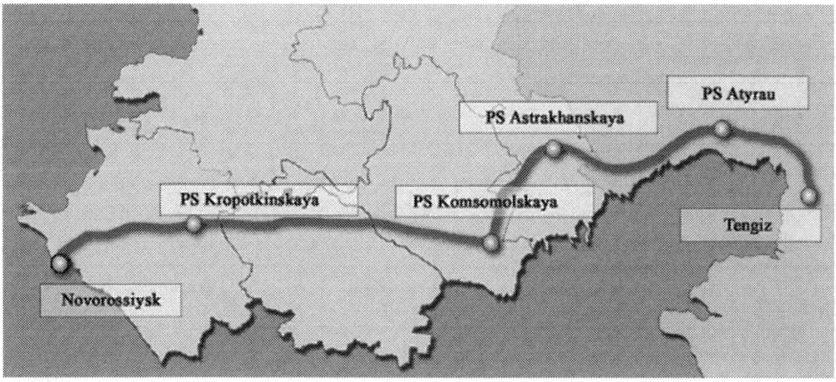

FIGURE 6.1 The Caspian Pipeline Consortium.

Source: Redrawn based on a map from the Caspian Consortium Pipeline website

Russia considers Central Asia to be firmly in its sphere of influence and would loathe losing any of its influence in the area and the benefits, especially the economic ones, which they accrue. Also, by combining the sizable Central Asian reserves with its own, Russia could become a petroleum power to rival the Middle East. Just as in the 20th century the USSR relied on its military for its superpower status, in the 21st century it will rely on its oil and gas.

The most effective strategy for Russia in its international diplomacy is to continue occasionally yielding on disputes over transit fees while continuing to implicitly (or explicitly if necessary) threaten Kazakhstan by stressing that country's dependence on it. Via this strategy, Russia should be able to guarantee that a large portion of the Caspian oil will continue to flow through its territory. However, as time goes on, Kazakhstan will likely manage to reduce its dependence on Russia. The monopoly of Moscow over transit routes and overdependence of Astana on Russia have been the driving factors of the diversification of the supply route for Kazakh oil and gas. With its penetration into Central Asia through Kazakhstan, China has managed to bargain with Russia and to a certain extent lessened Moscow's monopoly, although the steady rise of China may cause further problems for Nur-Sultan. This is what allows India to play a role in the energy sector of Kazakhstan under its multi-vector energy policy.

The United States: search for European energy diversification

It was only after the US Department of Energy in its report predicted that the estimated potential of the Caspian Sea reserves to be around 200 billion barrels equivalent to that of Saudi Arabia, that the United States started giving importance to this region (Manning 2000: 15–20). The United States with 19.4 million barrels of oil per day and 21.9 trillion cubic feet of gas per year stands as the largest energy consumer of the world (EIA 2016). Although the United States produces enormous quantities of oil and gas, it remains a net importer. It produced 12,704,000 barrels of oil daily domestically in 2015 and 368.7 tcf/y of gas in 2016 (BP 2016).

The United States with its top five energy import partners – Canada, Saudi Arabia, Mexico, Venezuela and Nigeria – is not primarily driven by the lure of Central Asian energy sources. However, it does have certain strategic and geopolitical interests in the energy resources and administration of the region. The important geostrategic necessity the United States has is in preventing the Russian monopoly and in keeping certain states (like Iran) from earning profits from Central Asian energy.

The US interest in Central Asian energy, though, is not primarily driven by a need for a new source of imports. The United States already has well-established ties with other suppliers, its top five import partners in 2016 being Canada, Saudi Arabia, Mexico, Venezuela and Nigeria. Importing crude oil from Russia is the closest the United States comes to tapping the Central Asian energy market, and Russia only ranked as the thirteenth largest import partner of the United States (EIA 2015). While the United States does not need Central Asian energy to supply domestic demand, it does have strategic, geopolitical interests in the region's energy. The United States has an interest in preventing the Russian monopolization of energy resources that might allow manipulation of prices as OPEC did in 1973, and it has an interest in keeping certain states (like Iran) from earning profits from Central Asian energy.

The United States has a basic interest in promoting the flow of oil and natural gas to Europe and Asia that has sought to limit the Russian influence over the oil and natural gas supplies from Central Asia. Despite knowing about India's urgent need for natural gas, Washington opposed the Iran–Pakistan–India and Myanmar–India gas pipelines to isolate Iran and Myanmar. Central Asia and the Caspian might be the areas rich in energy resources which too faced similar problems concerning transit, development and infrastructure of oil and natural gas reserves. Besides the above, the United States played an important role in bringing together Georgia, Azerbaijan and Turkey for building up the new pipeline project called the BTC pipeline as shown in Figure 6.2 (Sachdeva 2017).

Also, the Trans-Caspian pipeline (TCP) as shown in Figure 6.3, could be a gas, oil or combined pipeline. It would go from either Aktau, Kazakhstan or Turkmenbashi, Turkmenistan under the Caspian Sea to Baku, Azerbaijan. From there, any oil could link with the existing Baku–Tbilisi–Ceyhan pipeline (BTC) to ultimately access the Mediterranean, while the gas could be transported via the South Caucasus gas pipeline into eastern Turkey and possibly on to Europe from there via the proposed Nabucco pipeline. While the TCP is still in the planning stages, feasibility studies have shown that a gas pipeline would cost $5 billion and have a capacity of 30 bcf/year. An oil pipeline would cost $4 billion and carry 400,000 barrels/day and thus deliver 40 per cent of the BTC's total export capacity. No feasibility studies have been done for a combined TCP pipeline.

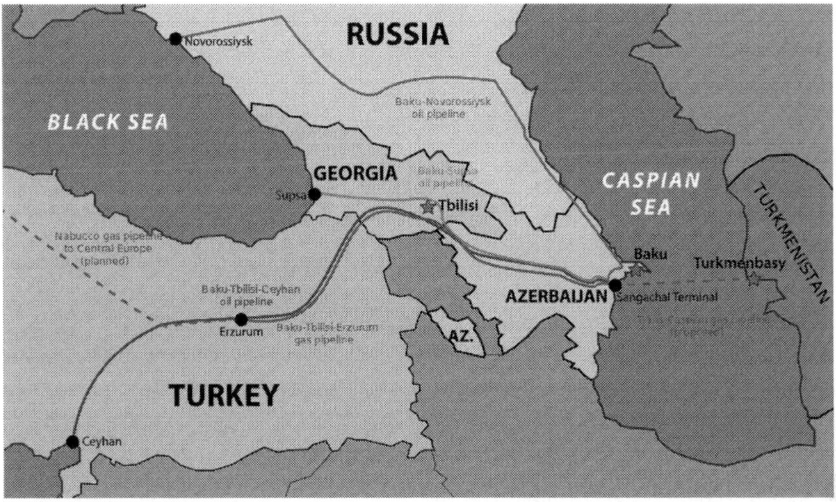

FIGURE 6.2 BTC Pipeline project.

Source: Wikimedia Commons

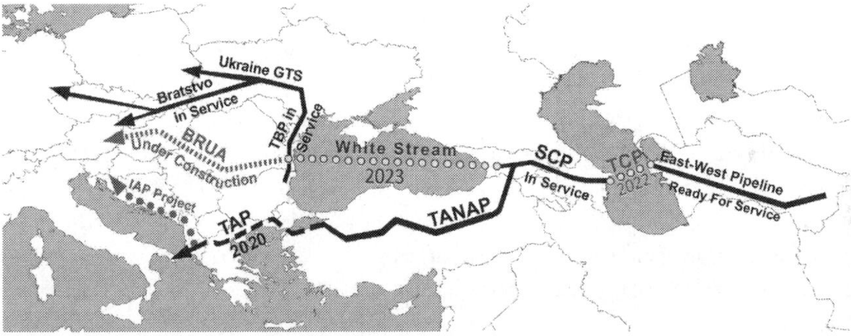

FIGURE 6.3 Trans-Caspian Pipeline.

Source: Redrawn based on a map from the Transcaspian.com website

In geopolitical terms, policymakers in Washington were unambiguous in their support for building multiple pipelines for Caspian oil and gas and for supporting American energy groups playing a significant role in the Caspian. The strategic goals which propel growing US presence in the region are self-evident: to excel in the collective game over its rivals, real or imaginary (Geopolitica.ru 2013). It is evident that the policy of successive US administrations has been to fill the power vacuum after Russia's unprecedented retreat and maintain their hegemony in Central Asia – "geopolitical pivot of Eurasia" as rightly pointed out by Halford Mackinder (1904).

In 2006, the United States has inaugurated the 1760 km BTC oil pipeline project as part of its energy venture in Central Asia with a cost of $4 billion

(Piskur 2006). This pipeline is the second longest and the world's most expensive pipeline project ever planned and executed. It runs through Azerbaijan and Georgia, proceeds through Armenia before ending at the Turkish port of Ceyhan (Escobar 2006: 42). For natural gas, the United States is working hard to ensure that a new transport route – the Nabucco Pipeline – initiated by OMV of Austria and BOTAŞ of Turkey in 2002 will materialize. Aimed at breaking Russia's monopoly, this equally costly project – estimated at $12.3 billion (Reuters 2008) – is designed to carry natural gas from Shah Deniz field of Azerbaijan to Baumgarten of Austria; it travels over a total length of 3400 km and traverses six countries en route (Geopolitika.ru). Nabucco is rated highly by the European Union for two reasons: on the one hand, it is a diversion from the traditional troublesome northern route via Ukraine and Poland – which still pumps about 80 per cent of the gas the European Union imports from Russia – and hence immune from possible disruptions in gas supply to consumers in Europe; on the other, because major gas producers as Iran, Iraq, Turkmenistan and Egypt may be included as new sources of supply (Reuters 2008). But so far the outlook of this project is not entirely clear; "Western" powers (the European Union and then United States) have been unable to organize a united front capable of withstanding the multifaceted pressure from Moscow. US vulnerability, in particular, may be accessed through several perspectives.

The United States is seriously vying for energy independence. The world oil crisis of the 1970s was the turning point for the United States and its perspectives on energy security. This oil embargo prompted the United States to get rid of Middle Eastern oil and develop energy independence. After the 9/11 terror attack, the cries for energy independence became particularly strident. Apart from the Congressional debates, US President Bush alluded to "energy independence" in his State of the Union addresses. For that, America proposed to go for alternative energy and reduced consumption to reduce its dependence on foreign oil.

China: the new pole in Grand chessboard

Brzezinski in his grand chessboard pointed out about four prominent poles playing an important role in Central Asia (Brzezinski 1998). China is one among those four poles that recently made a powerful entry into Central Asia particularly in the oil and gas sector. Sensing the geopolitical vacuum in the heartland region and disinterestedness of the Kremlin, China expressed its desire to form the Shanghai Cooperation Organization involving Russia and all Central Asian countries except Turkmenistan. To silence the widespread fear of the "China threat", Beijing reverted instead to "Peaceful Rise" as the official position on China's development path and went on investing in Central Asia heavily. Tempted by lucrative trade with China, Central Asian republics have ceded increasing mineral rights to China's state-owned enterprises such as state-owned

CNPC and Sinopec and agreed to build cross-border pipelines (Ong 2005). To shed light on this topic, the following reference is made to the widely discussed pipeline project in which Beijing collaborated with Kazakhstan and other Central Asian republics.

The Sino-Kazakh Oil Pipeline Co. Ltd (KCP), a joint venture between CNPC and KazMunaiGas, was concluded in 1997 between China and Kazakhstan (Xinhua 2005). The eastern section first started pumping oil in May 2005 from the Kumkol field of the Aktobe region, making it the first pipeline to transmit crude directly into China. On October 27, 2005, China made its first major foray into the Central Asian oil industry when the CNPC purchased the Canadian-based PetroKazakhstan Inc., owner of the Kumkol field (Chinese Embassy 2005) but China paid well over market value and was forced to sell a third of its holdings in the Kazakh state oil company KazMunaiGaz back to the government as part of the deal (Pala 2006). On completion in 2009, the Sino-Kazakh pipeline had ultimately 20 million ton/year capacity, which was about 10 per cent of China's total crude imports in 2009 (see in Figure 6.4). KCP is also designed to transport Russian crude, thus laying the base for trilateral pipeline cooperation. The question is whether LUKoil, owner of half of North Kumkol's exploration and production licence acquired from the Kazakhstani government in 1995, would use the "oil weapon" to further state interest. By the end of 2006, LUKoil managed to own the legal rights of the entire area of Kumkol North after first using litigation to drain CNPC of tens of millions of dollars. Russia's geopolitical lever matters for China for two reasons: first, Kumkol field is the primary local supply source feeding the Atasu–Alashankou pipeline; second, the Shymkent refinery that is associated with the Kumkol field is connected to the Soviet-era Omsk–Pavlodar pipeline, officially named as Central Pipeline Consortium/CPC, controlled by Russia's Transneft. This meant that Transneft combined with LUKoil had the option to regulate the volume of crude movement between CPC and KCP (Marten 2007). After all, Russia did not oppose the construction of the "Sino-Kazakh Pipeline" (Sheives 2006) virtually because it had only a symbolic meaning not significant damage on the Kremlin's grip on the Central Asian pipeline. On the other hand, Washington saw China's advance as a threat but less harmful as long as it reduced Russia's domination of the pipeline (Geopolitica.ru 2013).

Dismissing conceivable Russian sabotage, at the bilateral level, the major advantage accruing to both Kazakhstan and China may be seen in the fact that: (a) KCP provides a direct transport route between two neighbours devoid of border disputes (completely resolved in 1997); (b) there is no charge on transit fees; (c) no third country can hold Kazakhstan's oil hostage by arbitrarily raising fees or blocking the pipeline; (d) Kazakhstan is guaranteed a reliable export outlet for its superabundant oil reserve as much as China is guaranteed a stable supply to sustain its high growth momentum. Nevertheless, there are minor disadvantages as well. On this pipeline China acts as monopoly; the majority of the oil comes from the Caspian fields or even the massive Kashagan

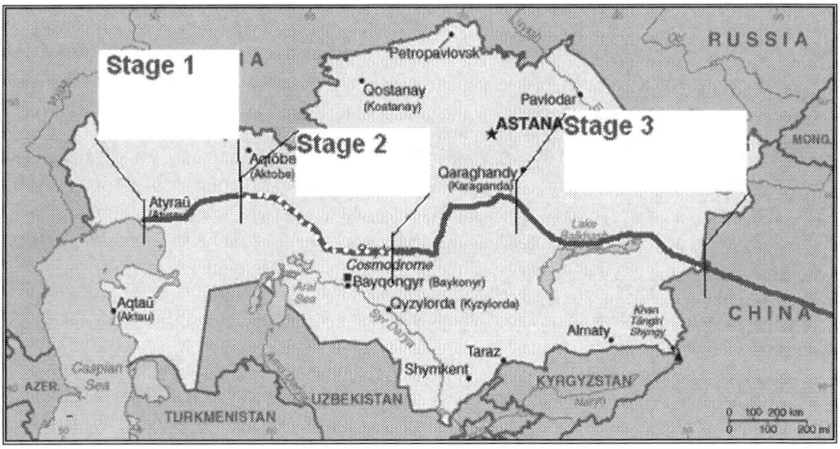

FIGURE 6.4 The Kazakhstan–China Pipeline (KCP).

Source: Redrawn based on a map from the hydrocarbons-technology.com website

field, a high-pressure field with large quantities of poisonous hydrogen sulphide located in the shallow northern Caspian Sea which freezes in winter (BP 2018). On natural gas, China has separately and jointly reached agreement with Turkmenistan, Uzbekistan and Kazakhstan in building the cross-border pipeline. The result is the "Sino-Turkmenistan" pipeline or more accurately the "Central Asia–China Gas Pipeline" (CACGP). The project was first discussed between Chinese President Hu Jintao and his Kazakh counterpart on his visit to Astana in June 2003, joined by a framework agreement signed with Turkmenistan (2006) for long-term gas supply and pipeline construction, and with Uzbekistan (2007) on building the Uzbek section of the pipeline (geopolitica.ru 2013).

Following U.S energy policy closely, China also made energy procurement its policy objective in the cold war era. Naturally, the massive industrialization of China has pushed it from an oil exporter in the 1970s to a net importer in the 1990s. In recent years, China has emerged as the net importer of both oil and natural gas. Importantly, domestic resources are not sufficient to meet the ravenous energy demands which compelled China to look for alternative supply sources. Since Central Asian countries share boundaries with China and are blessed with massive oil and gas deposits, Beijing developed a keen interest in exploiting the energy resources of Central Asia, again following the footprints of the US in the region.

China slowly but steadily deepened its energy relations with Central Asian states, initially with Kazakhstan and later on with Turkmenistan and other states of the region. In fact, China has inked agreements with Kazakhstan for the transportation of oil, and for that Beijing constructed the

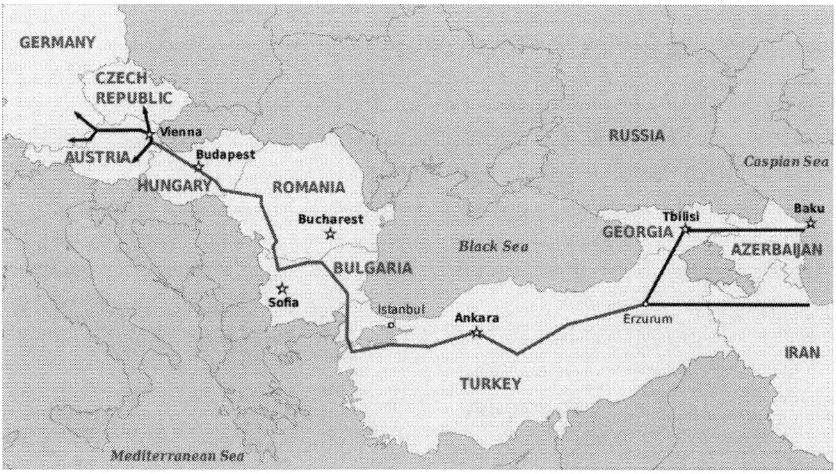

FIGURE 6.5 South Stream and Nabucco gas pipeline.

Source: https://en.wikipedia.org/wiki/Nabucco_pipeline#/media/File:Nabucco_Gas_Pipeline-en.svg

Kazakhstan-China pipeline; to import gas, China constructed the Central Asia-China pipeline connecting China with Turkmenistan, Uzbekistan and Kazakhstan in Central Asia.

The European Union: looking for energy diversification

While the United States has distant strategic interests in the energy geopolitics of Central Asia, the European Union stands to directly win or lose in the diversification of Central Asian energy exports. In 2015, the European Union consumed 18,380 tbl/d of oil and 1003.5 bcm/y of gas (BP 2016). It is a net energy importer. Even before the end of the Cold War, Europe was reliant upon energy exports from Russia. Now, with the Soviet republics as members, the European Union is finding itself even more dependent. In 2011, 33 per cent of the European Union's oil imports and 40 per cent of its gas imports were supplied by Russia, and with energy conflicts between Ukraine and Russia upsetting gas supplies to Europe, the European Union cares about Central Asian energy (EU 2011).

As a huge energy market, the European Union has the potential to be a major player in Central Asian energy. However, the European Union only recently began to harmonize the activities of its member states in the region, creating its first comprehensive Central Asia strategy paper in 2007. One of the main projects this document advocated was the construction of the Nabucco pipeline. That gas pipeline project would create a trans-Caspian pipeline link to the existing (BTE) Baku–Erzurum line and then carry gas through Turkey and into Europe. That route would avoid Russia and reduce Europe's dependency on Russian gas (Cooley 2008).

Silk Road rivalry in Central Asia

Although the recent rise of China in Central Asia is largely attributed to its Silk Road Project "One Belt, One Road", when it comes to the heartland region, neither is China the only player nor the Silk Road the only policy initiative. The struggle for control and administration over the geopolitical resources and geostrategic chokepoints has put the Central Asia region back into the limelight leading to what many like to call the "New Great Game". While the first such contest was famously chronicled by Rudyard Kipling involving the 19th-century struggle for dominance between the British and Russian empires, the second centred on the post-Soviet scramble for resources and influence in energy-rich Central Asia. Today, a third such round of geopolitical competition is emerging in Central Asia, spurred on by the vast energy potential of the post-Soviet space and the uncertain political disposition of Afghanistan; this round will be referred to henceforth as the Silk Road Rivalries between the United States, China and Russia.

In 2011 the United States launched its grand vision of greater Central Asian economic and infrastructure integration in the hope of ensuring political stability in Afghanistan in the post-2014 withdrawal period, thereby maintaining its dominance in the region. By 2013 China assertively articulated its Belt and Road Initiative (BRI), a multi-billion dollar pet project to connect China with Europe, Africa and Asia, with Central Asia being the important constituent. The Russian led Eurasian Economic Union (EEU) established in 2015 is a design to create a common customs union among the former Soviet states to keep them within the Russian geostrategic orbit. All these strategic initiatives launched in Central Asia with economic motives undoubtedly have strategic underpinning to what this book asserts is a Silk Road rivalry in the region. Thus, this section tries to investigate the competing vision of the United States and China for integrating Central Asia into their geostrategic orbit while delineating Russia's reassertion to maintain its stronghold in the geopolitical hinterland.

Analysis of the Silk Road strategies

The collapse of the Soviet Union was unprecedented and unpredictable. The sudden demise of this great landmass left both insider and outsider uncertain about how to conceptualize their approaches towards the region. This uncertainty was felt both in the United States, China, India and Russia immediately after the disintegration of the Soviet Union. To the southern periphery of the Soviet Union, a new geopolitical region emerged consisting of Kazakhstan, Kyrgyzstan, Tajikistan, Turkmenistan and Uzbekistan, collectively known as Central Asia. This region was believed to have been in the global limelight in every epoch of history for its geopolitical possessions and geopolitical locations. In every period of history, attempts were made to control and administer the region by regional and extra-regional powers to rule over the world. Even during the Tsarist period, there was a great game between the Tsarist and British to gain control of the region then known as Middle Asia and Kazakhstan (Dadabaev 2018: 30). During the Soviet period, the Marshall plan was perhaps aimed at luring the region with economic leverages and military support then known as Central Asia or inner Asia. Today, in the post-Soviet era, the region has exhibited a new kind of great game, referred to here as the "Silk Road rivalry", again to control and administer the region. It is with this rhetoric that now states of the region and beyond are striving hard to build closer engagements with the Central Asian region. We focus here on four such Silk Road narratives adopted by the United States, China, Russia and India to transform Central Asia's geopolitical landscape, demonstrating their goals and objectives, projected as "self" projecting as the best, most profitable and accommodative in comparison to the rest as "others".

The content and nature of these Silk Road strategies have changed with time and the international environment. The concept carried different meanings depending upon the country that chose the Silk Road as a brand of its foreign policy. In this sense, the static concept of traditional Silk Road got transformed into a social construction of that particular country's foreign policy engagement with the region. This paper, therefore, claims that the Silk Road is not a foreign policy doctrine but rather a discursive practice involving the grand design of the adopted country. With this premise, this paper focuses on the Silk Road narratives of the United States, China, Russia and India for their engagement with the Central Asian countries and examines their social construction to stimulate a debate that Silk Road rivalry in Central Asia involves agenda promotion through historical connotation to prevail their alternative world views of "Self" differing from the "Others".

China's Silk Road Economic Belt; America's New Silk Road strategy; Russia's Eurasian Economic Union and India's International North–South Transportation Corridor have developed competing visions for reviving ancient trade routes connecting Asia and Europe through the heartland region. The United States Silk Road strategy focuses on stabilizing Afghanistan while China's belt and road initiative hopes for economically integrating Central Asia to Bejing's geostrategic orbit. On the other hand, Russia in recent times reasserted its position through the EEU at least to play a dominant regional role whereas India has lately come up with its own version of the Silk Road known as INSTC to secure its much-needed energy security through the equity oil of Central Asia. These above stated Silk Road concepts are socially constructed to secure the interests of the respective countries by using the narrative as a proxy. Why the countries are intended to use Silk Road discourses in their recent foreign policy orientation has a reason underneath the geopolitics of Central Asia itself. Let's understand the centrality of Central Asia in the Silk Road diplomatic frameworks.

The New Silk Road of the United States

The United States came up with its own New Silk Road Strategy in June 2011 (Fedorenko 2013). This was done to maintain the United States' interests in Central Asia, to maintain stability in the region, to facilitate and enhance regional cooperation in trade, energy and transportation. It also envisions plans for joint investment projects and regional trade blocs that have the potential to bring economic growth and stability to Central Asia. Following the surge of 30,000 additional troops into Afghanistan in 2009, which President Barack Obama's administration had hoped would lay the groundwork for complete withdrawal a few years later, Washington began to lay out a strategy for supporting these initiatives through diplomatic means. These plans emphasized the need for Afghanistan to build an economy independent of foreign assistance (McBride 2015).

As then-Deputy Secretary of State William Burns outlined in a major 2014 policy address, a centrepiece of the United States strategy was building a regional energy market for Central Asia. More than 1.6 billion consumers in India, Pakistan and the rest of South Asia were increasingly demanding energy supplies of the kind that Kazakhstan or Turkmenistan, with their hydropower and natural gas reserves, were capable of providing.

A crucial next phase will be connecting private-sector investment and entrepreneurship in Afghanistan and Pakistan, says former Ambassador Marc Grossman, who served as the United States Special Representative to Afghanistan and Pakistan from 2011 to 2012. Grossman pointed to the potential for export industries like Afghani fruit and Pakistani cement that are currently restricted by trade barriers.

Major United States initiatives

Regional energy markets: The United States provided support for the CASA-1000 regional electricity grid, including a $15 million contribution following the March 2014 World Bank commitment of $526 million and support for the CASA Secretariat; more than $1.7 billion in support for energy transmission lines, hydropower plants and associated reforms in Afghanistan since 2010; and adding 1,000 megawatts to Pakistan's power grid, supplying power to more than 16 million people (USDOS 2017).

The proposed Turkmenistan–Afghanistan–Pakistan–India (TAPI) gas pipeline, which could provide major economic dividends to Afghanistan, has been a focus of the United States' policy. Turkmenistan is home to the world's second-largest deposit of natural gas, and the TAPI would allow it to diversify its exports away from China by delivering energy to India and Pakistan (Sachdeva 2017). But the $10 billion projects have been repeatedly delayed by difficulties in securing investors. Without the possibility of an equity stake, which Turkmenistan has refused to allow for foreign companies, major Western oil companies have so far baulked at the project. "It comes down to how serious the

Turkmen government is", says David Goldwyn, former State Department special envoy for international energy affairs (McBride 2015).

Trade and transport: The United States has built roads of more than 3000 kilometres in Afghanistan; provided support for Kazakhstan and Afghanistan's accession to the WTO; technical assistance for the passage of the 2010 Afghanistan–Pakistan Transit–Trade Agreement (APTTA), and support for the Cross-Border Transport Agreement (CBTA) between Kyrgyzstan, Tajikistan and Afghanistan (USDOS 2017).

Since 2010, the State Department has spent over $2 billion in Afghanistan to build some 1800 miles of national roadways. That is a small fraction of the $62 billion the United States has spent on the Afghan security forces. In 2011, the United States Agency for International Development (USAID), helped create the Almaty Consensus, a "Regional Cooperation Framework" among Central Asian nations. Its projects include reducing trade barriers, developing export capacity and supporting the World Trade Organization (WTO) accession for Afghanistan. These initiatives include the Cross-Border Transport Accord (CBTA) between Afghanistan, Tajikistan, and Kazakhstan, the CASA-1000 electricity grid, which would allow Tajikistan and Kyrgyzstan to transmit hydropower electricity to consumers in Afghanistan and Pakistan, and the Transit–Trade Agreement to allow Afghanistan to export goods duty-free into Pakistan. The United States committed $15 million to the CASA-1000 project, but its role – in contrast to China's billions of direct investments in Central Asia – is largely to facilitate these efforts diplomatically (McBride 2015).

Customs and border operations: The United States works with regional partners to reduce border wait times, increase cooperation at key checkpoints and crossings and prevent the transit of illegal and dangerous material. With United States' support: since 2009, intraregional trade in Central Asia has increased by 49 per cent; since 2011, the average cost of crossing regional borders has decreased by 15 per cent; customs procedures have been streamlined at seven Afghan border crossing points, resulting in expedited trade with average release time down from eight days in 2009 to three and a half hours in 2013, saving $38 million annually (USDOS 2017).

Businesses and people-to-people: The United States has funded university studies for hundreds of Afghan students across Central Asia; sponsored the Central Asia–Afghanistan Women's Economic Symposium and South Asia Women's Entrepreneurship Symposium in support of thousands of women entrepreneurs and business owners; organized trade delegations, meetings and conferences in Almaty, Islamabad, Kabul, Mazar-i-Sharif and Termez, resulting in over $15 million in trade deals (USDOS 2017).

Chinese Belt and Road Initiative

Chinese President Xi Jinping during his visit to Kazakhstan in September 2013 laid down his vision of the Silk Road Economic Belt in Astana (MFA

2013). The core aim of the belt concept was to initiate and strengthen bilateral trade and economic relations between China and the Eurasian region. In a significant addendum in May 2015, China and Russia agreed in Moscow to integrate the former's Silk Road Economic Belt with the latter's vision of a trade and infrastructure network across Eurasia. The Eurasian Economic Union was formally launched in January 2015, comprising the former Soviet Union states of Russia, Armenia, Belarus, Kazakhstan and Kyrgyzstan (Dijk and Martens 2016). This has reinforced Russia's own "pivot to the East" and serves to dispel the perspective that Russia and China are natural adversaries. Moreover, the Silk Road Economic Belt directly links China to the European Union; strengthening economic ties eventually raising doubt that there is any new great game in Central Asia and the Caucasus involving Russia and China in an alliance against the West. Free trade and growing cooperation in several spheres further undermine the new great game thesis (Ibid). The above-stated reasons are sufficient to assert that China has certain critical interests linked to the Central Asian geopolitics and geostrategic calculations in world politics. And the strategies it has in place makes it the most invincible and unchallenged power clashing with the West. Hence, the hitherto apprehension of a great game in energy-rich Central Asia has undoubtedly lost its character and given way to Chinese domination in the heartland region. But why the region is of such importance to China that Beijing cannot afford to lose its grip or let others stay for longer is still inexplicable.

The New Silk Road vision was officially announced by Xi Jinping in 2013. The name of the "Belt and Road Initiative" (BRI) derives from the Chinese *Yi dai Yi lu* which means One Belt One Road (Magiri 2017). It is a commitment to easing bottlenecks to Eurasian trade by improving and building networks of connectivity across Central, Western and Southern Asia, but also to reach out to the Middle East as well as East and North Africa (Amighini 2017). The Belt and Road Initiative was an attempt to revive the historical Eurasian Silk Road that is approximately 2000 years old with vigour to reconnect Europe with Asia and Africa with the use of modern transportation, thereby boosting trade, investments, economic development, and by improving diplomatic relations, scientific progress and cultural exchange for all countries and regions across the Eurasian continent. This monumental and truly grandiose initiative also gives due importance to Central Asia like its predecessor the ancient Silk Road. The New Silk Road or BRI has two separate roads: Silk Road Economic Belt (SREB), i.e. the overland part of the broader BRI, and the Maritime Silk Road. Among the number of corridors that the Silk Road encompasses, six of them are currently in some stage of planning or construction: the China–Mongolia–Russia corridor; the New Eurasian Land Bridge; the China–Central Asia–Western Asia corridor; the China–Pakistan corridor; the Indochina Peninsula corridor and the Bangladesh–China–India–Myanmar corridor (Magiri 2017). Here also Central Asia is the region most likely to receive maximum global attention.

Chinese initiatives in the region

China has multiple reasons for pursuing the Belt and Road Initiative: actualizing the Chinese dream, expansion of the Chinese market, economic solution to the Xinjiang problem and securing the much-needed energy supplies. For that, China has conceived a two-pronged strategy: development of the "Silk Road Economic Belt" through Central Asia for developing overland infrastructure and the "Maritime Silk Road Project" through the Indian Ocean and the Persian Gulf for expansion of maritime shipping routes.

Silk Road fund: In 2014 China created a Silk Road Fund of approximately $40 billion to support its Belt and Road infrastructure building activities. Xi Jinping concluded deals with Central Asian states worth $30 billion with Kazakhstan, $15 billion with Uzbekistan and $3 billion with Kyrgyzstan. It also signed a deal with Sri Lanka worth $1.4 billion to revamp the Colombo port (McBride 2015).

Asian Infrastructure Development Bank: In 2015 China planned to set up the Asian Infrastructure Investment Bank (AIIB) with an initial capital of $100 billion. The inaugural meeting held in Beijing attracted at least 57 founding members importantly including the United States' allies such as the United Kingdom, Germany and Australia.

China–Pakistan Economic corridor: In 2015 China and Pakistan signed agreements to start the multibillion-dollar infrastructure project named as CPEC (China–Pakistan Economic corridor). This multi-road energy project connects the Chinese province Xinjiang with Pakistani port city Gwadar in Baluchistan. The very objective of this project was to develop an energy corridor for Chinese vessels coming from the Persian Gulf and develop the port as a strategic asset to promote Chinese trade in the Indian Ocean region.

Eye on hydrocarbon resources of Central Asia

Central Asian countries, rich in hydrocarbon resources, were considered vital for diversifying China's domestic energy mix, especially considering its disputes in the South China Sea with Japan, Vietnam, Indonesia and the Philippines (Wani 2020: 9). Furthermore, more than half of China's supplies that come from the West Asian countries of Saudi Arabia, Iraq, Iran, Oman, Yemen and Kuwait are exposed to geopolitical risks. The transit routes for China's oil and gas trade, particularly in the Strait of Hormuz in West Asia and the Strait of Malacca in Southeast Asia, are controlled by the United States. With proven oil reserves estimated at 40 billion barrels and natural gas reserves more than 131 tcf, CARs can help China reduce its overdependence on West Asia for its energy security. Besides, Kazakhstan and Uzbekistan have uranium resources pegged at 450,400 tonnes, and another 477,800 tonnes of inferred uranium (Ibid). Apart from hydrocarbon resources, China's rapidly spiralling demand for uranium is yet another factor to have triggered China's hegemonic approach in CARs.

The Russian Eurasian Economic Union

Despite political, economic, personal and institutional links with Central Asia, Russia was not able to maintain its sway over the region due to its declining economic influence. Therefore, early post-Soviet attempts to develop regional organizations failed until a 2010 customs union among Russia, Belarus and Kazakhstan were formed. This evolved into the Eurasian Economic Union (EEU), whose Central Asian members included Kazakhstan and Kyrgyzstan in 2015.

As always, Moscow's main game is political rather than economic. The Kremlin understands too well that in the trade and finance realm, Russia's position in Eurasia is much weaker than China's. Russia's crucial strengths traditionally lie in the political–military and diplomatic domains. Hence, leaving economic initiatives to China, Moscow strives for the role of the chief architect of a Eurasian political and security order that would reflect its preferences and coincide with the basic interests of the continent's major powers.

The kind of political order Russia envisions for Eurasia is essentially one of a concert of powers, a model that hails from 19th-century Europe and places a premium on relations among a few major countries: Russia, China, India and – with some qualifications – Pakistan, Iran and maybe Turkey. Accounting for the bulk of continental Eurasia's population, landmass and military potential, the six big players should collectively manage security and economic affairs of the mega-region.

Russia aspires to be the main security and diplomatic broker in Eurasia while leaving China with the role of economic leader. As one observer put it, "China would be the bank, and Russia would be the big gun". Such an arrangement might harken back to the history of the European Community when France acted as the political leader while West Germany was the economic engine. Moscow's preference for a new Eurasian order is reflected in its diplomatic activism, such as its leading role in securing the admission of India and Pakistan into the Shanghai Cooperation Organization and in advocacy for the future membership of Iran.

Comprising Eurasia's most powerful non-Western nations, "Greater Eurasia" is being imagined as the antithesis to the Western-dominated world order. All members of the prospective Eurasian concert – with the important exception of India – are autocracies or illiberal democracies. Beijing may well like the notion of illiberal Eurasian continentalism. It is far less clear whether China accepts the Russian idea that Chinese pre-eminence should somehow be constrained and balanced within a political concert of major powers.

"The Eurasian Union is good for Russia, but offers nothing for Kazakhstan", said a businessman in north-western Kazakhstan. His view is backed by trade statistics. In the first nine months of 2016, Kazakhstan's trade with EEU member states was down by 26.4 per cent compared to the same period in 2015. Many problems were caused by the Russian economic crisis and currency volatility;

in 2014, the value of the Russian rouble compared to the US dollar more than halved, cheapening the price of Russian goods for Kazakh customers, damaging domestic producers and leading to tit-for-tat restrictions by both sides until the Kazakh tenge also was devalued.

India's Central Asia vision

Since 2014, with the Prime Minister assuming charge, it has taken several initiatives to normalize India's relationship with its neighbours: the Land Boundary Agreement signed with Bangladesh leading to the reconstruction process of Afghanistan as the fifth-largest donor; and entering into unprecedented engagements with Afghanistan, Bangladesh, Sri Lanka and Pakistan. Also, India has reinforced its relationship with West Asian countries with renewed friendship and the personal touch of the Prime Minister in enhancing friendship with UAE, Iran, Saudi Arab, Syria, Qatar, Iraq and others.

Similarly, India has re-energized its relationship with the Central Asian countries, especially in the last decade. Its constructive approach of initiating its "Connect Central Asia" policy in 2012 aimed to enhance India's political, economic, historical and cultural connections with Central Asia. Prime Minister Shri Modi's visits to all the Central Asian countries are a symbol of New Delhi's overemphasis on the heartland region. India's full membership in Shanghai Cooperation Organization (SCO) and Central Asian countries' cultural connections with New Delhi provide aspiring pictures of the future relationship between both regions.

China factor in India's Central Asia policy

One of the important agendas of China in the post-Cold War years remains energy procurement and preservation, on account of its heavy domestic demand. As a result, China has expanded its wings, starting from South Asia to Latin America. It started investing heavily in the downstream sector, building oil refineries and pipelines across the region to satisfy its domestic demands. So, its current involvement in Central Asia with which it shares 3500 kilometres of border has not been an isolated matter. China, the world's second-largest importer, has been importing pipeline or liquefied natural gas for transforming its economy. In Central Asia, Kazakhstan is the most important energy partner in China. Beijing controls approximately 20 per cent of Kazakhstan's oil production and has constructed the world's longest pipeline running 2300 kilometres from the Caspian Sea to the Xinjiang province (Pradhan 2016). Chinese National Petroleum Company (CNPC) also owns a significant stake in the Kashagan oil field. It also owns several small oil fields in Kazakhstan. Also, Kazakhstan serves as the transit route for Chinese oil transportation.

China also directly imports gas from Turkmenistan – the main gas exporter of the region. Beijing has constructed the Central Asia–China gas pipeline.

Uzbekistan also supplies gas to China through the upgraded pipeline network. Recently China and Uzbekistan inked a bilateral energy deal of $15 billion in 2013. It also financed two other refineries in Kyrgyzstan, in the towns of Kara-Balta and Tomak. The 2013 visit of Chinese President Xi Jinping resulted in the signing of an energy deal with Central Asia states worth tens of billions of dollars. Given the current energy engagement of China in Central Asia the IEA has estimated that China may be importing up to 50 per cent of the region's oil and gases by 2020, leading to a decisive shift in Central Asia's energy flow from West to East (CSIS 2016).

In the context of Central Asia–China relations, the scenarios of both confrontation and cooperation will have consequences for India. Three out of five Central Asian states share a boundary with China. This allows China to be the proximate player in the region. It is also believed in certain quarters that, although Central Asia is a Russian hinterland, it is not Russia but China whose presence worries the United States most in the region. The same is also true with India. Chinese growing presence in Central Asia and its massive economic package, military aid and political dominance in the region hampers India's strategic vision towards Central Asian geopolitics. SCO is the mechanism through which China pushes its agendas in Central Asia. Such is its dominance in Central Asia that it acts alone in the region when it comes to energy and trade while it has a cooperation mechanism with India in other areas.

China has great interests in gaining access to the rich deposits of hydrocarbon resources in the Central Asian region. Presently China is the second highest consumer of oil and gas in the world and may overtake the US very soon (Sascha 2008). Therefore, it is apparent on the part of China to depend profoundly on Central Asia, an energy hub accounting for "1.9% and 10.6% of total global recoverable resources of oil and gas respectively" (Bin 2014: 597). It has emerged as a major player in Kazakhstan's oil exploration efforts. It has been actively participating in exploring Alktyuinks and Mangyshlak oil deposits and building an oil pipeline in the Kazakhstan–Xinjiang region. One of the most ambitious projects signed by China includes a 5730 kilometres long gas pipeline project estimated at $11 billion between Turkmenistan, Uzbekistan, Kazakhstan and China in which a consortium of companies from the United States, Japan and China have already been conducting preliminary surveys for quite some time.

A normative analysis of energy game and Silk Road discourse

Halford Mackinder in his geographical pivot of history called Central Asia the "heartland" and claimed: "he who controls the heartland controls the world" (Mackinder 1904). Mackinder's hypothesis acquired renewed importance during the Second World War and Cold War, given the geostrategic significance of the region for control over Europe and subsequently the entire world. This has encouraged nations to aspire to control world politics to adopt a zero-sum game theocratic model of political realism to outdo others. Similarly, Nicholas

Spykman (1942) proposed a geopolitical model centred on the "World Island". It comprised the core of the heartland and the inner crescent, surrounded by a "rimland" which coincided with Mackinder's outer crescent. As a realist thinker, Spykman viewed international politics as a struggle for power, in which American and British security necessitated control of the rimland as a means of blocking the expansion of the World Island (Spykman 1942: 39–44). A century after the height of the Great Game between Russia and Britain, which centred on Mackinder's heartland and inner crescent, a new contest, was triggered in the far more complex milieu of the 1990s. Yet, in contrast to the territorial imperative of nineteenth-century imperial rivalries, the new Great Game is ostensibly a power struggle for the heartland's energy resources, which in reality constitute the signposts and stepping-stones of clashing hegemonic interests (Dekmejian and Simonain 2001: 6).

Zbigniew Brzezinski (1997) in his "Grand Chessboard" claimed that the region of Central Asia including the Caspian was "'the chief geopolitical prize' in the ongoing competition for international supremacy". He further maintained that "America's global primacy is directly dependent on how long and how effectively its preponderance on the Eurasian continent is sustained" (1997). A simple assessment of Brzezinski's thesis reflects the essence of the realist school of international relations underpinning the idea that "effective functioning of an international regime can only be secured based on unconditional political hegemony by one country" (Brzezinski 1997).

The leverages of huge and untapped hydrocarbon resources along with the already known geostrategic significance of the region lured the most powerful world countries to inexorably connect energy security with that of national security imperatives and therefore demand absolute control over the region leading to a hegemonic display of strategies and power (Gowa 1993). It was argued that "under hegemonic leadership of mighty powers an environment of reconciliation and accommodation will be available for all and the subordinate states will receive net benefits from participating in the international regime sponsored by such leadership" (Gilpin 1987: 87–88). However, in case of decline of hegemonic power, "the international regimes they sponsor may grow unstable and crumble under the pressure of smaller powers in the form of dissent, nationalism and beggar-thy-neighbour policies" (Keohane and Nye 2001: 35–39). The above theoretical interpretations can be intricately linked to the geopolitical transformations taking place in the Central Asian heartland right after its separation from the erstwhile Soviet Union. The great power politics it has undergone since 1991 was the result of the decline of Soviet hegemony in the region which in turn has allowed regional powers like Turkey and Iran to influence the region and ultimately resulted in the American domination over the region. The growing presence of the United States in their neighbourhood has undoubtedly concerned both Moscow and Beijing and the inching forward of NATO has made them more cautious. This in turn has invited renewed and calculated strategic engagement of both the neighbours

(Russia and China) in their backyards. However, the economic instability of Russia has allowed China to strengthen its grip over the geopolitical region to maintain its hegemony though not politically this time but certainly economically. The report of UNDP can accurately be cited to understand the predominant position of China in Central Asia as far as investment is concerned both in the energy and non-energy sectors thereby sidelining any other country including the United States from influencing the region. Although, the European Union and India have their economic and energy relations with the region, they seem largely minimal as compared to China. Albeit, the renewed great game doesn't operate under hegemonic leadership of either the United States, Russia or China, there is however no cooperation among them either. They have all been adopting beggar-thy-neighbour policies to advance their strategic objectives in the region. The recent discursive strategies of "Silk Roads" as adopted by the United States and China followed by the Eurasian Economic Union of Russia and very recent the International North–South Transportation Corridor of India is a testimony of that. Even though there is cooperation without hegemony, that cooperation is operating under anarchy in the absence of dominant ideas, norms, goals and values governing their relationship in the regional geopolitics of the Central Asian landscape.

This chapter, therefore, argues that international ethics has been put on the back burner in this resources scramble in Central Asia by the great powers, reducing the region to the grand chessboard of a new geostrategic game taking place in the region over oil and energy. The Silk Road discourse is this direction is only an extension of the New Great Game with an intensive vigour of advancing their hidden agenda in Central Asia in the disguise of economic development. In this direction, this chapter advocates in favour of a mutually agreeable international regime underlining the ethos of international relations, dominant ideas, norms, values and rules of negotiations that underscore the importance of civil society, international ethics and civilizational values. Unlike the other poles, the Indian foreign policy tradition cultivates a non-aligned culture with the spirit of non-interference in other internal matters. It also doesn't propagate any dominant narrative to promote its agenda while treating the other party as an equal member to the agreement.

To synthesize, the problems of Central Asian energy exports (oil and gas) are much clearer: they have to come into a pipeline network world and their coming will undoubtedly change the geopolitical configuration of the region as well as beyond. So, now the question is not how the energy resources will be transported, but rather the question: who will get the Central Asian energy resources? Which is perhaps the reason why the new "Great Game" in Central Asia has been going on for nearly two decades. Of the four poles, China and Russia correspond with each other the most, however, covering a variety of regional policies for one important reason: they are pregnant with the vision of multipolarity in world affairs (Walsh 1993: 273). Oil and gas loom as the cornerstone of their common initiatives, even if they have different or even competing goals in the region (Jonson and Allison 2001; (Bates and Oresman 2003). By contrast, the European Union expresses greater interest in energy security than how it may be satisfied, intent on including Iran as a potential gas supplier through Caspian pipelines that bypass Russia, a position Washington objects to strongly. To perpetuate its hegemony, the United States is strongly motivated to liquidate Russia's rule in Central Asia, restructure Eurasian space according to its own interests, thus preventing China's or Europe's rule there and progressively tightening their grip on Central Asian minerals and the pipeline infrastructures, aiming at eventually crowding out Russia's influences and curbing China's rise.

Coming to India, she did not develop any pragmatic policy towards the region until recently and used to see the region only under historical and cultural prisms. However, in the last few years, India has shown keen interests particularly since Shri Narendra Modi assumed the office of Prime Minister. Through the Reconnecting Central Asia policy and strengthening the bilateral relationship with the Central Asian States in addition to the recently acquired full member status of the SCO, New Delhi has been able to make its presence felt in the region but has not yet succeeded in removing the tag of latecomer and disinterested power as it has not done anything substantial beyond its cost–benefit analysis to remain as a prolonged player in the region. Decades after the independence of the Central Asian states, India's relatively low profile in the region has acquired higher relief as its searches for "poles of attraction" other than Russia and China, which in the late 1990s began to establish a condominium (not an apartment, but an international law term for "joint rule") over that part of the former Soviet territory.

References

Amighini, Alessia (2017), *China's Belt and Road: A Game Changer?* Milano: The Italian Institute for International Political Studies (ISPI).

Asgar, Mitha G (2008), The Last Great Game, Counter Currents, September 03, available at: https://www.countercurrents.org/mitha030908.htm, [accessed January 10, 2020].

Bates, G., and Oresman, M. (2003), *China's New Journey to the West*. Washington, DC: Center for Strategic and International Studies.

Bin, Hu (2014), "Oil and gas cooperation between China and Central Asia in an environment of political and resource competition," *Pet.Sci*, (2014)11, pp. 596–605.

BP (2016), "BP Statistical Review of World Energy", British Petroleum, March, available at: www.bp.com [accessed September 15, 2018].

BP (2018), "BP Statistical Review of World Energy", British Petroleum, March, available at: www.bp.com [accessed September 15, 2018].

BP (2018a), "Country Insight - India," Energy Outlook - 2018, British Petroleum, available at: https://www.bp.com/en/global/corporate/energy-economics/energy-outlook/country-and-regional-insights/india-insights.html [accessed September 27, 2018].

Brzezinski, Zbigniew (1997), *The Grand Chessboard: American Primacy and Its Geostrategic Imperatives*, New York: Basic Books.

Brzezinski, Z. (1998), *Grand Chessboard: American Primacy and Its Geostrategic Imperatives*, New York: Basic Books.

Chinese Embassy (2005), "Retrieved from CNPC Completes Acquisition of PetroKazakhstan", Ocober 27, available at: http://www.china-embassy.org/eng/hyzg/t218598.html [accessed October 1, 2009].

Cooley, A. (2008), "Principles in the Pipeline: Managing Transatlantic Values and Interests in Central Asia", The Royal Institute of International Affairs, p. 1181.

CSIS (2016), "India's Energy Dilemma", *South Asia Monitor*, Centre for Strategic and International Studies, Washington, DC, No. 28, September 7.

Dadabaev, Timur (2018), "Silk Road as Foreign Policy Discourse: The Construction of Chinese, Japanese and Korean Engagement Strategies in Central Asia", *Journal of Eurasian Studies*, No. 9, pp. 30-41.

Dekmejian, R. Hrair and Simonain, H. Hovann (2001), *Troubled Waters, The Geopolitics of the Caspian Region*. London: I. B. Tauris, p. 28.

Dijak, Meine Peter Van and Martens, Patrick (2016), "The Silk Road and Chinese interests in Central Asia and the Caucasus: The Case of Georgia, Maastricht School of Management", Working Paper No. 2016/12, August.

EIA (2015), "Assumption to the Annual Energy Outlook", U.S. Energy Information Administration, September 2015, available at: https://www.eia.gov/outlooks/aeo/assumptions/pdf/0554(2015).pdf [accessed September 15, 2018].

EIA (2016), "International Energy Outlook-2016," *Energy Information Administration*, May, DOE/EIA-0484, available at: https://www.eia.gov/outlooks/ieo/pdf/0484(2016).pdf [accessed September 10, 2018].

EIU (2007), "Kazakhstan Country Report", *The Economist Intelligent Unit*, January, p. 29.

Escobar, P. (2006), *Globalistan: How the Globalized World is Dissolving into Liquid War*, Ann Arbor, MI: Nimble Books.

EU (2011), *The EU Energy Interests in Central Asia*. European Union Paris.

Feddersen and Zucatto (2013), "Infrastructure in Central Asia: Energy and Transportation Controversies", *UFRGZ Model United Nations Journal*, pp. 159–181, available at: https://www.ufrgs.br/ufrgsmun/2013/wp-content/uploads/2013/10/Infrastructure-in-Central-Asia-Energy-and-Transportation-Controversies.pdf [accessed September 15, 2018].

Fedorenko, V (2013), "The New Silk Road Initiatives in Central Asia", Rethink Institute, Paper 10, August, Washington, DC, available at: http://www.rethinkinstitute.org/wp-content/uploads/2013/11/Fedorenko-The-New-Silk-Road.pdf [accessed September 15, 2018].

Geopolitica.ru (2013), "Analysis of Post-Soviet Central Asia's Oil & Gas Pipeline Issues", *Geopolitica*, available at: https://www.geopolitica.ru/en/article/analysis-post-soviet-central-asias-oil-gas-pipeline-issues [accessed January 15, 2015].

Gilpin, Robert (1987), *The Political Economy of International Relations*, Princeton, NJ: Princeton University Press.

Gowa, Joanne (1993), *Allies, Adversaries, and International Trade*, Princeton, NJ: Princeton University Press.

Hart, Michael (2016), "Central Asia's Oil and Gas Now Flows to the East", *The Diplomat*, August 18, available at: http://thediplomat.com/2016/08/central-asias-oil-and-gas-now-flows-to-the-east/ [accessed September 15, 2018].

Johnson, L., and Allison, R. (2001), "Central Asian Security: Internal and External Dynamics", in L. Jonson and R. Allison (eds.), *Central Asia Security: The New International Context*, Washington, DC: Brookings Institution.

Johnson, Rob (2007), *Oil, Islam and Conflict, Central Asia since 1945*, London: Reaktion Books.

Keohane, Robert and Joseph S. Nye (2001), *Power and Interdependence*, New York: Longman.

Mackinder, Halford (1904), "The Geographical Pivot of History", *The Geographical Journal*, XXIII(4), April, pp. 421–437.

Magiri, Palo (2017), "Introduction", in Amighini, Alessia (ed.), *China's Belt and Road: A Game Changer?* Milano: The Italian Institute for International Political Studies (ISPI).

McBride, James (2015), "Building the New Silk Road", Council on Foreign Relations, May 22.

Manning, Robert A. (2000), "The Myth of the Caspian Great Game and the New Persian Gulf," *The Brown Journal of World Affairs*, Vol. 7, No. 2, pp. 15–33.

Marten, K. (2007), "Russian Efforts to Control Kazakhstan's Oil: The Kumkol Case," *Post-Soviet Affairs*, vol. 23, no. 1, pp. 18–37.

MFA (2013), "President Xi Jinping Delivers Important Speech and Proposes to Build a Silk Road Economic Belt with Central Asian Countries", Ministry of Foreign Affairs, The Republic of China, September 23, Beijing, available at: http://www.fmprc.gov.cn/mfa_eng/topics_665678/xjpfwzysiesgjtfhshzzfh_665686/t1076334.shtml [accessed September 15, 2018].

Ong, R. (2005), "China's Security Interests in Central Asia", *Central Asian Survey*, 24(4), pp. 425–439.

Pala, C. (2006, March 12), "China Pays Dearly for Kazakhstan Oil", *New York Times*.

Patnaik, Ajay (2016), *Central Asia: Geopolitics, Security and Stability*, New Delhi: Routledge.

Piskur, M. (2006), "The B.T.C. Pipeline and the Increasing Importance of Energy Supply Routes", *Power and Interest News Report*.

Pradhan, Ramakrushna (2016), "Chinese Interests in Central Asia: Policies and Challenges", *Eurasian Report*, 3(2), p. 39.

Pradhan, Ramakrushna (2019), "Petropolitics and Pipeline Diplomacy in Central Asia: Can India afford to wait in the wings?" *India Quarterly*, No. 75, Vol. 4, pp. 479.

Raimondi, Pier Paolo (2019), "Central Asia Oil and Gas Industry - The External Powers' Energy Interests in Kazakhstan, Turkmenistan and Uzbekistan," ECONSTOR, Working Paper No. 006, March, available at: https://www.econstor.eu/bitstream/10419/211165/1/ndl2019-006.pdf [accessed December 10, 2019].

Reuters (2008), "Update 3-Nabucco Pipeline Cost Rises to 7.9 Bln Euros", May 29.

Rising, M. (2009), "Sweden, Finland OK Baltic Sea Gas Pipeline Project", Associated Press Worldstream, November 5, pp. 141–154.

Sachdeva, Gulshan (2017), "Chaining Dynamics of India-Central Asia Ties", Bishkek Project, April 5, available at: https://www.bishkekproject.com/memos/24 [accessed September 15, 2018].

Sajjanhar, Ashok (2016), "India-Central Asia Relations: Expanding Vistas of Partnership", June 22, Observers Research Foundation, New Delhi.

Sascha, Muller Kraenner (2008), *China's and India's Emerging Energy Foreign Policy*, Bonn: German Development Institute.

Sheives, K. (2006), "China Turns West: Beijing's Contemporary Strategy towards Central Asia", *Pacific Affairs*, 79(2), pp. 205–224.

Spykman, Nicholas John (1942), *America's Strategy in World Politics*, New York: Harcourt, Brace and company.

USDOS (2017), "U.S. Support for the New Silk Road", U.S. Department of States, United States of America, available at: https://www.state.gov/p/sca/ci/af/st/newsilkroad/index.htm [accessed September 15, 2018].

Wani, Ayjaz (2020), "India and China in Central Asia: Understanding the new rivalry in the heart of Eurasia," Observer Research Foundation, ORF Occasional Paper-235, February, available at: https://www.orfonline.org/wp-content/uploads/2020/02/ORF_OccasionalPaper_235_India-China-CAR_NEW-19Feb.pdf. [accessed March 1, 2020].

Walsh, J. R. (1993), China and the New Geopolitics of Central Asia, *Asian Survey*, 33 (3), 272–284.

Xinhua (2005), "China-Kazakhstan Pipeline Starts to Pump Oil", *Xinhua*, December 15, available at: http://www.chinadaily.com.cn/english/doc/2005-12/15/content_503709.htm [accessed September 15, 2018].

Xu, Zhao, Niu, Yumin, Liang, Yengze, Li, Zhigang and Iftikhor, Atoev (2020), "The Integrated Hydropower Sustainability Assessment in Tajikistan: A Case Study of Rogun Hydropower Plant," *Hindawi - Advances in Civil Engineering*, available at: https://doi.org/10.1155/2020/8894072.

7

TRANSIT ROUTES BETWEEN INDIA AND CENTRAL ASIA

Cooperation occurs when actors adjust their behaviour to the actual or anticipated preferences of others, through a process of policy coordination.

– Robert Keohane (1984)

Pipelines, in general, can be categorized into three types: domestic, cross-border and transit. The key to differentiating between the three types is the nature of their governing jurisdiction. Domestic pipelines are within an existing sovereign territory. Such pipelines are subject to the laws and regulations of that territory. Cross-border pipelines directly link the producer state of oil and gas with the consumer state. Transit pipelines, however, cross a third sovereign territory to get to the market. Normally, the terms of transit are enshrined in an agreement. This among other things determines the system of transit payments. These are payments made to the transit government. Normally payments include a transit fee. However, the concerned countries can set the terms under which the transit country can lift off the transit fee (NBR 2010: 9). The transit pipeline is of utmost importance in the given study as India is not directly connected to Central Asia, and Central Asian countries, on the other hand, are landlocked. India, therefore, has to depend on a third country to build its pipelines either through China, Pakistan and Afghanistan or through Iran to the Arabian Sea. It is in this context that this chapter examines the transit pipeline options and evaluates the importance of these pipelines for India's energy security and sustainable growth. An effort has also been made to look into the transit route option for India connecting Central Asia. It looks into the details of cost–benefit analysis in the framework of what benefits it will offer to India and what price India needs to pay for such projects. The study will also examine how viable these pipeline projects are for India as its neighbourly relations with Pakistan and China has always been strained.

Energy security and pipeline politics in Asia

Energy security is an issue which has both geopolitical and international dimensions. It is solely determined by strategic planning to ensure diversity of fuel, diversity of supply source and the efficiency and flexibility of the energy sector. This is where Asia is moving faster and is further ahead of the developed world. Asia has achieved new heights and has become ground zero in energy global markets. Its accelerated demand and incessant quest for energy has outpaced the developed countries in recent years. This shift in focus of global energy demand from mature industrial countries to developing Asia has been transforming the landscape of the global energy market and geopolitics. The latest trends are stunning.

Asia's boom in oil and natural gas demand (especially in China and India) has increasingly provoked a scramble among regional powers to secure access to and control over future oil and gas supplies. The intense competition has taken place over control of oil and gas transportation links and transit infrastructure as well. In concert with their national oil companies (NOC), national gas companies, the NOCs of key producer countries, and their state financial institutions, Asian countries like China, Japan, South Korea and India are scouring the globe to gain control over new supplies and to forge new transit routes. Central Asia is one such energy-rich region where growing competition has been taking place for control and administration of oil and gas transit facilities.

Transit pipelines: the centrality of India's energy security

India needs energy security for both domestic and foreign policy reasons. Domestically, India needs robust economic growth of around 10 per cent for the next 25 years or so. On the foreign policy front, India's foremost aim is to play a leading global role and to be recognized both economically and politically as a rising power. This is the vision that India has wanted to achieve since the term of its first Prime Minister Pt. Jawaharlal Nehru till the present day. To sustain economic growth and maintain the popular image of rising power, India needs to secure energy at a rate that outstrips its population growth. Since India is an energy supply-constrained economy, the sustainability of development and growth depends on the availability of affordable, adequate and reliable energy supplies. Therefore, there is a massive demand for oil and natural gas along with other energy resources in India's primary energy mix and the demand is still increasing. Another important point that needs to be noted here is that possible gas reserves in Myanmar and Bangladesh have probably reached the limit of gas export capacity. Future supply from the Middle East is under a scanner, given its often hostile environment and political regime change. Recent popular uprisings in the Arab world have further marked a sense of insecurity and concern among the energy consumers in the region. This insecurity is greater in the Indian context as it imports around 70 per cent of its oil from the Middle East. Besides, growing piracy and lack of government accountability in the Gulf of

Aden around the Somali Coast concerns India greatly. In this context, any other alternative that comes to mind in the India context is Central Asia. It is an Asian neighbour of India. Although not directly connected geographically, from the energy security point, it assumes looming importance for New Delhi. As a result, India is looking for transit routes that would connect it with the energy-rich Central Asian states.

Central Asia: the Asian alternative

From the geopolitical point of view, Central Asia has always been important. From the middle to the end of the 19th century, while the region was part of the Russian empire, the oil-bearing areas of Baku were producing half of the world's oil supplies. In World War II, during his campaign against Russia, Hitler tried to capture Baku and the Caucasian oil fields as part of his strategy for world domination. After the war, the Soviets retained those areas as reserves, choosing to exploit oil deposits on Russian soil, in Tatarstan and Siberia (Arvanitopoulos 2002: 1).

Following the collapse of the Soviet Union, the newly independent republics of Central Asia, especially Kazakhstan, Turkmenistan, Tajikistan, Uzbekistan and Kyrgyzstan, who have the majority share of the energy resources in the region, have been trying to exploit their natural resources. Since they consider oil to be the prime means of securing their economic and political independence, production and transport of these resources to the outside market holds the key to their growth and development. According to the estimates of geologists, the oil deposits of the Caspian Sea may not be quantitatively comparable to the deposits of the Persian Gulf, but they are still considered of excellent quality and can constitute a significant alternative source of energy in the 21st century. In particular, it is estimated that the entire Caspian Sea is a basin full of oil and natural gas, starting from Azerbaijan and continuing to the opposite shore in the territory of Kazakhstan and Turkmenistan. These deposits have taken on enormous importance due to the expected exhaustion of the deposits of Alaska and the North Sea by the year 2015.

The essence of this "new geopolitical game" in Central Asia is twofold. First, control of the production of the oil and gas, and second, control of the pipelines that will transfer the oil to the Asian and Western markets. While the issues of production have already been discussed in previous chapters, this chapter is solely concerned with the options of pipelines in Central Asia especially connecting India.

Issues of pipelines

Central Asia as a geographic entity is a land-locked region. Countries like Uzbekistan are further double landlocked. The region is also completely isolated even from its immediate neighbours outside former Soviet space. They have to depend on the Russian pipeline system for their oil and gas transportation. Central Asian oil and gas have historically flowed through Russian pipelines. For this, Central Asian states have had to pay a heavy cost. No doubt, maintaining this arrangement means that Russia will receive sizable transit fees as well as have more oil and gas with which to secure greater leverage in international politics. But it limits the Central Asian control of its resources. Further, Russia uses the pipelines for its strategic purposes causing great loss to the Central Asian economy. To exit this resource curse, the countries of the region have been looking for alternative routes as well. But the irony is that, even as countries in the Caspian sought to strengthen their newfound political and economic independence by inviting Western oil companies to rapidly develop the region's oil and gas potential, these same major oil companies saw using the old Soviet pipeline system as the easiest way to evacuate their initially low volumes to defer capital expenditure on new transportation infrastructure. The region seems to be handicapped when it comes to transportation. However, in recent times several new transit pipelines have been proposed and worked out by countries such as China, Iran and the United States.

The northern route is favoured by Russia. According to this option, Kazakhstan would expand its existing pipelines to link them to the Russian network and Azerbaijan would build a pipeline from Baku to Novorossisk. The shortcomings of this option are fear of excessive Russian control and the issue of security since the pipeline would go through Chechnya.

The western route is favoured by Azerbaijan, Turkey, Georgia and the United States. This pipeline route would bring the oil to the Georgian port of Supsa and then ship it through the Black Sea and the Bosphorus to Europe. Turkey insists that the straits cannot cope with increased tanker traffic and has proposed, instead, to construct a pipeline from Baku to the port of Ceyhan on the Turkish Mediterranean coast. However, excessive cost (around $2.9 billion) and serious security concerns (this route would pass through unstable Kurdish territory) make this option difficult to implement. Instead, Greece, Bulgaria and Russia have proposed a pipeline linking the Bulgarian port of Burgas with the Greek port of Alexandroupolis, thus bypassing the straits and Turkish territory.

The eastern route connects Central Asia with China. This pipeline would transport oil from Kazakhstan to China. It will be the costliest pipeline (covering 2000 km in Kazakhstan alone) but the Chinese consider it as a strategic decision and are willing to go through with it. China proposes to build a pipeline of about 3000 km from the Caspian oil fields across Kazakhstan and into China to feed its growing economy (Fishelson 2007: 1). Iran would pump the oil and gas south into its existing network, which would boost its efforts to obtain a regional leadership position in the Middle East. The United States, attempting to maintain its position as the world's sole superpower, but without direct geographic access to the region, would like the oil and gas to reach the open market without it falling under the control of Russia, China or Iran.

The southern route runs through Iran. Economically, this is the most viable option, since Iran already has an extensive pipeline system, and the Gulf is a good exit to the Asian markets. For the time being, however, the United States has practically vetoed this option.

The south-eastern route runs from Turkmenistan and finally connects to India. Unocal, an American oil company, has proposed the construction of oil and gas pipelines from Turkmenistan through Afghanistan to Pakistan and later to India. This route makes sense geographically but not politically since it will have to go through unstable Afghanistan. It is to be noted that, supply to the south and east can be done from Central Asia without Russian assistance. Both these routes have a larger importance for India.

Pipeline options for India

Currently, energy-hungry India is vigorously building relations with Central Asian states to gain direct access to Central Asian energy resources. India wants to do it alone and is focusing on the possibilities of opening land routes. Since India is not directly connected with Central Asia, it has to depend on its other Asian neighbours to build pipelines that would bypass either Pakistan, Afghanistan or China. Reopening of the ancient Silk Road through China's Xinjiang region is one option for Indian policymakers as well. The second possibility is the development of the North–South Corridor or road through Iran and Afghanistan. There are several transit pipeline options for India connecting Central Asia. All of them are discussed in detail below and the emphasis has been on the pipelines that are most viable as well as economically convenient to India.

Historical Silk Route

Since ancient times, Central Asia and India have been connected through land routes. Notwithstanding the great mountains of Hindukush, Karakoram, Kuen Lun and Western Himalayas, trade links were established for the socio-economic development of both regions. The caravan traders acted as the medium of exchange of art, culture, ideas and technology (Warikoo 1996: 113). Cities like Khotan, Bukhara, Badakhshan, Tibet and Kashmir were developed into major trading centres. This, in turn, helped to develop an east–west trade corridor connecting India with Central Asia. Due to its proximity to Central Asia and linkage with the Silk Routes system, Kashmir acted as an important transit linkage between the two regions.

However, Kashmir is also not directly connected to Central Asia. Whatever communication takes place, it was through the circuitous and difficult mountainous trade routes that passed through Ladakh and Chinese Turkestan on the one side and Chitral and Pamirs on the other (Ibid: 114). This route continued to be the main trading link between the two regions for quite some time. However, with the growing intensity of Anglo-Russian rivalry during the second half of the 19th century, curbs were imposed on imports from Central Asia. This further relegated the position of these transit routes to a secondary position and consequently trade from the region came to a halt. But the fact remains that the overland communication between India and Central Asia remains an important channel of communication.

With the partition of India, the trading link seems to have been closed almost entirely. But the fact needs to be stressed, indeed, that political boundaries always change, but geography remains the same along with the geographical boundaries. Karakoram pass is a natural geographical gateway for India and is going to remain so forever. It is up to the Governments of India and China to see that this natural gateway is exploited to the fullest extent. If that happens, without any doubt, the glory and importance of this geographical landmark will return once again.

Karakoram Pass – Indian gateway to Central Asia

Karakoram Pass lies exactly on the China–India border, just north of the Aksaichin area. It was illegally occupied by China in a military invasion carried out in 1962. The saddle-shaped pass is at a height of 18,172 feet and is 148 feet wide (Chandrashekhar 2010). This is the reason why this pass is known as the highest pass on any trade route in the world. What is surprising is the fact that despite being at such a height, it never snows heavily in this pass, even though extremely biting and piercing cold winds and snow blizzards are always experienced. The entire region in the vicinity of Karakoram Pass is barren, bleak, and desolate and devoid of any vegetation or grass any time of the year. Since this trade route joined Leh with Yarkand and subsequently with Kashgar, places which have always been on the Silk Route, it would help India immensely to revive its trade linkages with Central Asia. Besides, the Karakoram Pass is always negotiable at any time of the year. This allows trade to continue without any interruption all year round.

The Karakoram trade route is perhaps the only gateway to the Indian subcontinent which had never been used for any military invasion until 1962, unlike the famous Khyber or Bolan passes. In 1962 a Chinese force attacked Indian observation posts near the Daulat Beg Oldi (DBO) area. A major Chinese assault on 19/20 October overran all the Indian observation posts in that area. Since then, the international line of actual control has run just east of Depsang plains with all the eastern territory including the Aksichin area firmly in Chinese hands. However, the Chinese occupied Shahidula and the northern part of the trade route in 1949 and had stopped all caravan trade going through since then. After 1962, the Karakoram Pass and the adjoining areas became strictly no entry for all non-military personnel. After 2002, the government of India started allowing mountaineering expeditions in the DBO area and a few teams have made it to the Karakoram Pass itself in all seasons of the year.

However, time and tide wait for none. Things are changing fast in Asia. Nathu La, where guns boomed in the not very distant past, has become a busy border trade post for China and India. Is it unnatural to expect something similar for Karakoram pass? China has recently declared that Kashgar in Xinjiang would be made a free trade zone. It is already connected with good roads with the Chinese border opening to Central Asia. On the Indian side, the on-going construction of the Rohtang Pass tunnel in Himachal Pradesh would connect Delhi to Leh by an all-weather road. A good motorable road already exists between Leh up to the base of Saser La Mountain. With modern technology, if a difficult route like the Khunjereb Pass can be made commercially viable, the Karakoram trade route can certainly be made into India's grand gateway for trade and commerce to central Asia.

The significance of the Karakoram trade route is far greater for India. For many years, general thinking in India was that the Karakoram and Saser passes are the routes which could allow Chinese invaders into the Indian subcontinent. This was true to a certain extent up to 1984, when the mountain ranges west of Karakoram were not controlled by India. Now, with the Saltoro ridge firmly controlled by Indians, the Karakoram and Saser passes could be considered as gateways which would let Indians out to Central Asia.

Chinese road: Xinjiang–Tibet Highway No. 219

This is a connecting road to the ancient Silk Route that traditionally linked India and Central Asia through China's Xinjiang province. The materialization of this road would enable India to build transit pipelines from resource-rich Central Asia to its territory. The Xinjiang–Uyghur Autonomous Region (XUAR) in the process has become an important hub for any mode of transportation. It also needs to be understood here that China and Central Asian countries have already facilitated various transit transport systems to overcome their inter-regional trade problems through this region.

In the Chinese line, India and Central Asia can also think of exploring this trade route which is realistically attainable and cheaper in comparison to other routes. This is also the road that directly follows an alignment in a north–south direction along the existing railway lines and roads in Central Asia (Kazakhstan), Western China (Xinjiang) and India (Stobdan 2008: 1–3). The road includes Almaty, Korgas, Yining, Kuqa, Aksu, Kashgar, Yarkand, Yecheng (along the Xinjiang–Tibet Highway no. 219), Mazar, Shahidulla, Sumxi, Derub, Resum, Shiquanhe, Gar, Kailash, Burang and Lipu-Lekh (Ibid).

The total distance is less than 3000 kilometres as compared to the over 5000-kilometre long route via Iran. More importantly, the route under consideration (Kazakhstan, China and India) already exists and it is only a matter of cross-border connectivity.

As regards feasibility, a linkage through Ladakh in Jammu and Kashmir is arguably the shortest, but China's sensitivity to any engagement in Jammu and Kashmir may rule out that option. Alternatively, while also considering the topographical factor, Lipu-Lekh Pass in Uttarakhand, which has been open for border trade with

China since 1992, could be an entry point. Refurbishing of the road connecting to Shipkila in Himachal Pradesh and Lipu-Lekh in Uttarakhand is already in progress under the Special Accelerated Road Development Project (SARDP).

On the positive side, the proposed route involves only one country (China) as a land-link between India and Central Asia, as compared to the longer western routes traversing through Iran and Afghanistan. Importantly, the route passes through the relatively stable Xinjiang as compared to the turbulent areas of Pakistan, Afghanistan and South Central Asia. Additionally, India cannot be viewed as a factor of instability and therefore poses no threat to Xinjiang in terms of religion or ideology.

If implemented, the route will cut down transportation costs of food/fuel supplied to India's forward areas. Similarly, it would reduce the delivery costs of imports from Western China. Besides, China could earn considerable revenue from transit fees. Conceivably, arrangements for swap deals with China could also be worked out gradually.

The route needs to be viewed from a strategic consideration rather than the economic angle alone. Importantly, it could help counterpoise Pakistan's plan for an 800-kilometre-long railway line from Gwadar to Kashgar. Besides, India would gain access to the transcontinental transport corridors of Western Europe–Western China which are being developed by the Eurasian countries under various facilitation agreements.

On the negative side, the feasibility in terms of geopolitics, especially China's willingness to cooperate, is a major factor. The issue of territorial disputes between India and China would certainly get in the way. However, these apprehensions could be mitigated through the intervention by Central Asian countries. Kazakhstan holds several key leverages vis-à-vis China if it wishes to push the idea.

Iranian route

India needs Iran to achieve its varied objectives in Central Asia. Iran, for its part, sees a tremendous complementarity of interest with India. Both governments are optimistic about the commercial benefits of Central Asian markets and hope to share the benefits of the North–South Transit Corridor. Iran will require massive infrastructure investments to extract maximum benefits from it, and India is lined up to provide cost-effective intellectual and material assistance in the development of information technology networks, ports, roads and rail projects (Balooch 2009: 26).

With the completion of the Mashhad–Sarakhs–Tajan railway in 1996, the landlocked Central Asian states became linked to Iran and saw a slow decrease in their dependency on the Russian railways and road system (Ibid: 27). The Indian Government's Border Road Organization financed around $136 million for the opening of a road link between the deep ports at Chabahar in Iran and Afghanistan's main ring road highway system. The 215-kilometre road from Zaranj to Delaran was completed on January 22, 2009 (Ibid). This is part of a garland road network in Afghanistan that forms a circular route connecting Herat and Kabul via Mazar-e-Sharif in the north and also Kandahar in the south, thereby potentially connecting Afghanistan to Uzbekistan (Ibid: 28).

International North–South Transportation Corridor

India and Iran have been making progress in their commitment to build a North–South Corridor with the participation of Russia. Iran and India signed an agreement, called the Inter-Governmental agreement on International North–South Transport Corridor in September 2000 in St Petersburg (Fiar 2007: 45). India and Iran also agreed to open up a transportation route with Turkmenistan in February 1997 (Balooch 2009: 27). This agreement has provided a legal framework for the multi-modal movement of goods from India to Iran and Turkmenistan, and other Central Asian countries may also join the arrangement in the future. This North–South Corridor permits the transit of goods from Indian ports to Iran's port of Bandar Abbas, and Chabahar (Sushil 2003: 41–43) (see Figure 7.1).

As a part of the North–South agreement, India agreed to help expand the Iranian port of Chabahar. Meeting in Tehran in January 2003, Iran, India, and Afghanistan signed an MoU on the development and construction of the Transit and Transport Infrastructure with the intent of improving the route from Chabahar Port to the Afghan cities of Zaranj and Delarm (Balooch 2009: 28). Besides, an Indian consortium has been engaged by the Iranian ports and shipping companies to undertake development work at the Chabahar Port and on the Chabahar–Fahraj–Bam Railway link. Iran hopes that expanding Chabahar will relieve some of the congestion in Bandar Abbas. Part of the concerns that emanate from this activity is the ambiguity about what kind of facility or facilities will materialize at Chabahar Port. India claims that this will be a commercial port (see Figure 7.2).

However, Pakistan and China are apprehending that New Delhi would develop the Chabahar port into a naval base, and this would seriously affect the Sino-Pakistani design in the Gwadar port. It should be noted here that, Gwadar Port is located along Pakistan's Makoran Coast, only 200 kilometres distance from the Chabahar Port. Gwadar is being modernized and expanded with Chinese capital and it is hoped that this port will diminish Pakistan's vulnerability to a naval blockade of its port in Karachi. It has added importance in the light of the purported Indian and Iranian activities at Chabahar (Zeb 2003). This apprehension came true when Xi Jinping in 2015 announced the China–Pakistan Economic Corridor (CPEC) – a project worth $46 billion to connect between Gwadar port in Pakistan and Xinjiang in China.

The location of Iran is ideal for the northern neighbouring countries of Central Asia. The CAS has also been keenly interested in connection, security and low cost of transiting their goods through Iran. None of these countries

FIGURE 7.1 International North–South transportation corridor.

Source: Vivekananda International Foundation, https://www.vifindia.org/article/2016/october/24/international-north-south-transit-corridor

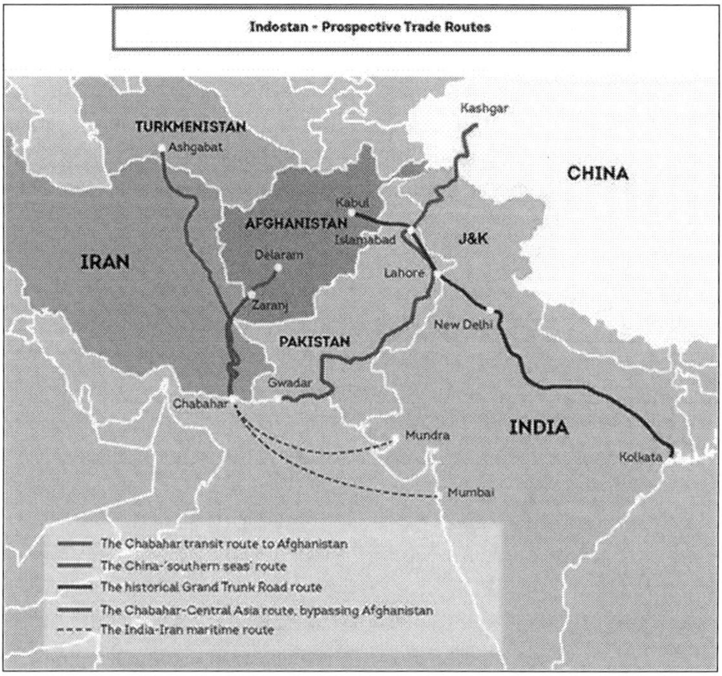

FIGURE 7.2 Chabahar Port (Iran) to Bombay (India) route.

Source: Observers Research Foundation, https://www.orfonline.org/research/india-and-china-in-central-asia-understanding-the-new-rivalry-in-the-heart-of-eurasia-61473/

has access to warm waters. The creation of the North–South Corridor is the best opportunity for Iran to expand its transit corridor to India. The idea of the North–South Corridor has multiple purposes and is, therefore, seen as an opportunity to bypass the East–West Silk Road project (Balooch 2009: 29).

Iran gains political and economic benefits from trade with Russia, Central Asia and India, perhaps at the expense of Pakistan. India, on the other hand, gets access to Russian, Central Asian, Caspian and Eastern European markets for its goods and links to a variety of energy import sources. Although India is closest to the Central Asian supply chain and could potentially be the biggest consumer of Central Asian exports, it currently has no stronghold in the region.

Lacking direct access to Central Asia, India sees Iran as a useful gateway to the markets and natural resources of that region. India can hope to diversify its energy sources from Central Asia through the Iranian route. Perhaps this route is the easiest and possibly the cheapest gateway for Central Asian goods. The route would travel some 1300 kilometres (over 800 miles) through Iran to its warm water port of Chabahar in the Arabian Sea (Ibid). The port of Chabahar is a cargo terminal with connections to Central Asia and Afghanistan and the Indian commercial capital of Mumbai. Hence, these are ideal trans-shipping points (Ibid).

Cost-effective analysis of INSTC transit option

The International North–South Transport Corridor is a 7200 km long multimode network of ship, rail and road routes for moving freights between India and Russia through Iran, Europe and Central Asia. This project was proposed and initiated by India, Russia and Iran in St Petersburg in September 2000. The objective of the corridor is to increase trade connectivity between major cities such as Mumbai, Moscow, Tehran, Baku, Bandar Abbas, Astrakhan, etc. The agreement was signed on May 16, 2002, and the first dry run of two routes was conducted successfully in 2014 (Chaudhury 2017). The result was amazing as the cost of transportation was reduced by $2500 per 15 tonnes of cargo (MEA 2017). Since India is facing roadblocks in materializing the TAPI and IPI pipeline projects due to its transit through Pakistan, INSTC offers India bounties of opportunities to sideline Islamabad by working out the INSTC option through the Bandar Abbas and Chabahar port of Iran to Mundra and Mumbai through the Arabian Sea. Also from the cost–benefit analysis point of view, this has been seen as less expensive than other available routes and importantly it is secure and free from any sort of hostages.

Recent studies show that INSTC can reduce the time and cost of container delivery by 30–40 per cent and once the flow of goods from the two Iranian ports begin the corridor will be able to move 30 to 50 million tonnes of goods per year (Stobdan 2017). Given the importance of Chabahar port to Iran's infrastructure development plans and its entry points for Iran, Central Asia and India; operational capacity of two terminals at Chabahar – Shahid Kalamtari and Shahid Beheshti; greater prospect for enlarging both the operational and practical scope of Chabahar to become a vital gateway to Central Asia as it gives ready access to several trade corridors (existing and planned); India's foothold in Chabahar as a result of the 2016 India–Iran Agreement, which underscores the Indian commitment to build, equip and operate the port (two terminals and five berths with cargo handling for ten years) makes the transportation from Chabahar not only viable but also competitive in terms of distance, cost, delivery, market access, sustainability and safety of goods and cargo to and from Eurasia. Besides, the Chabahar transit route would potentially provide the landlocked countries of Central Asia with the shortest land route to conduct maritime trade with countries in the Indian Ocean region (Stobadan 2020: 315–317).

Recently, good news has come from the International North–South Transportation Corridor (INSTC) that India and Russia have agreed to bolster their mutual trade by overcoming their geographical distance through the INSTC, bypassing Iran despite the United States warning against trade activities with Iran (FT 2020; RT 2020). If things go well then it is just a matter of time before India overcomes the greatest geographical barrier that has posed a challenge for New Delhi.

Iran–Pakistan–India pipeline (IPI)

The idea of an overland, trans-Pakistan pipeline was first proposed in 1989 by Ali Shams Ardekani, acting Deputy Foreign Minister of Iran, and RK Pachauri, the Director-General of the Tata Energy Research Institute (TERI) in New Delhi (Temple 2007: 6). The idea received a positive reaction in Iran. Pakistan initially refused to sign the project, worrying about India's long-term benefits, but later on agreed to the project since it would profit from both access of energy and transit fees. However, the initial response from New Delhi was sceptical. India was worried about leaving her long-term energy security in the hands of the frequently hostile Pakistan and trouble-torn Afghanistan. New Delhi then seemed to be less interested in allowing energy concerns to override the vagaries of its international relations with the region and outside.

However, the ashes of the Gulf War, bruises of the Iraq–Kuwait war of 1991 and instability of political regimes in the Middle East concerned India the most and underlined the need to diversify its energy needs. It is from this point that India started looking for new relationships as far as energy diversification was concerned. This realization further led India to ink agreements with Iran in 1993 and Oman in 1994 (Ibid). It is with this background that the IPI (Iran–Pakistan–India) pipeline project was taken forward.

Although the project was initiated long back, it was only in 2006, with the help of Asian Development Bank (ADB), that a series of studies and research were carried out for facilitating the project. Asian Development Bank also agreed to finance the project. Agreements were signed among partner countries on all elements except pricing and contractual structure of the pipeline project. The matter of pricing is the most difficult issue among all. Since the pipeline is expected to provide a stable supply of gas from Iran to Pakistan and India for the next 40 years, all three countries are wary of signing a deal that they may regret later.

So far, Iran has made several offers of pricing mechanisms that have been unacceptable to India. Initially, the Iranians wanted the gas to be priced according to Henry Hub, the American spot price index (Ibid: 27). India and Pakistan instantly rejected this option because spot prices are always substantially higher than prices for long-term deals. Iran has also offered to base the price on the average of LNG prices to Japan, Korea and India. However, this proposal too was unacceptable to India and Pakistan because Japan and Korea are entirely dependent on LNG and therefore willing to pay more than other users. India has demanded that the price of gas be offered at "cost-plus", which is the cost of gas production plus transportation costs (Ibid).

Notwithstanding, the Iran–Pakistan–India pipeline project has been regarded as the strategically most important. This is the southern route from Central Asia and the Caspian Sea basin. This is also considered economically the most viable of all the routes that connect India with Central Asia. This route is more political than geographical. As it would run through unstable Afghanistan and non-state terror actors marred Pakistan, this pipeline causes much concern to India when it comes to security and reliability issues.

However, the geopolitical significance of the IPI pipeline is immense. On the energy front, it would provide Pakistan and India with plentiful gas supplies for many decades. Politically, it would be a huge confidence-building measure between India and Pakistan that could create a momentum for a fundamental transformation of India–Pakistan relations. Iran too would immensely benefit from this project. As Iran, for both political and logistical reasons, cannot easily break into the European gas market, gas exports to Pakistan and India would give Iran valuable long-term customers and a steady stream of much-needed revenue. The IPI would also bring Iran important political benefits, as it would undermine the United States policy of sanctioning and isolating Iran. As a regional energy project, the IPI could form the nucleus of a regional cooperation arrangement, in the first instance between South Asia and Iran (which has become an Observer of the South Asian Association for Regional Cooperation), and later perhaps within the framework of the SCO, where Iran, Pakistan and India are Observers.

The Iran–Pakistan–India (IPI) pipeline project, though it remains most promising in terms of gas imports, has also been the most controversial of the pipeline projects. It is quite a logical project since Iran is a major producer of gas while both Pakistan and India are large consumers with growing demands. For many years, due to several reasons, India refused to continue with the idea of such a pipeline project. Since India and Pakistan were not getting along well, coupled with tensions in their bilateral relations, India could not trust Pakistan not to disrupt supplies. It was only after Prime Minister Vajpayee visited Islamabad in January 2004 and the initiation of the India–Pakistan composite dialogue to address outstanding bilateral issues that India agreed to de-link the question of the gas pipeline from outstanding bilateral issues. The country granted Pakistan most-favoured-nation treatment in trade, and therefore transit facilities through Afghanistan and Pakistan to India remained a possibility. As a result, a series of trilateral and bilateral meetings between Iran, Pakistan and India have been held over the last few years. Iran and Pakistan appear to have resolved most of the issues between them and intend to sign an agreement for an Iran–Pakistan gas pipeline regardless of whether or not India gets involved in this project.

Indian participation in the IPI, for the most part, remains uncertain. There are still some differences between India and Pakistan over transit fees. More than the financial and security issues, it is political considerations that are holding back India's participation. Despite official denials, India has given the impression that it is deliberately going slow on the IPI. When both India and Pakistan realized the importance of the IPI project, another stumbling block – the United States – emerged onto the scene which further pushed the project to the back. The new-found friendship between India and the United States forced India to go slow and even cancel the deal. The United States for that reason has linked India's participation in the gas pipeline project to the fructification of the India–United States nuclear deal, to which the present government in India attaches very high priority. India has grievously erred in succumbing to United States pressure. It has created deep mistrust and loss of credibility against India in Iran. Furthermore, this has led Iran to abrogate an attractive and significant LNG deal with India, who also lost other opportunities in Iran for investment and cooperation in the energy sector.

India must learn from its past mistakes. Iran and India have had civilizational links and cordial relationships through the ages. Also, there is no permanent friend or foe in international politics. India must exercise power to secure its national interests. As energy security is the priority of every modern state, India should not block this project which is for its betterment only. This problem of United States–Iran hostility can be resolved amicably without dragging the Indo-Iran pipeline project. Transit pipelines, whether IPI, TAPI or any other, have always been subject to dispute and conflict. However, they are not beyond resolution. These problems can be solved through political negotiations and economic bargaining. Diplomatic muscle must be flexed to deal successfully with these issues. What India needs most is strong willingness from its side to materialize this project.

Further, Western policymakers fear that if most of the Central Asian and Iranian energy resources are diverted to China and the Indian subcontinent, the West could be deprived of alternate sources of energy, thus the Western opposition to the eastward export of Iranian and Central Asian energy is understandable. NATO's continuing occupation of Afghanistan may have a link with energy exports. Perhaps, energy is also one of the causes of the West's troubles with Iran.

By playing energy politics, if the West can protect its interests, India, Iran and Pakistan or China should also probably defend their interests. The easiest way to export oil and gas from Central Asia to India and Pakistan is through Afghanistan. Iranian gas can also reach India via Pakistan and Afghanistan.

Nevertheless, it may be difficult to get technical and financial support for this pipeline project from the Western countries, as they are opposing it. But any other alternative cannot be completely ignored. It is noteworthy to mention here that Gazprom of Russia, which is rich and technically competent, has shown interest in the project. Diverting Iranian gas to markets like Pakistan and India would leave the lucrative European market free for Gazprom to continue exploiting without facing competition from Iranian gas.

The landmark gas pipeline agreement between Tehran, Islamabad and New Delhi is a great achievement for the power stricken Pakistan and energy-hungry India. The United States objections to the project are hypocritical and are part of its vicious agenda against Iran.

It is the most feasible route for energy imports to India from the former Soviet republics through Afghanistan and Pakistan. India can also export its products to Central Asian markets using the same route but the main constraint for India's access to Central Asia via Pakistan is the hostility between these two long-time rivals and instability in Afghanistan. Since the removal of the Taliban regime, India has been developing relations with Kabul but, unfortunately, New Delhi seems to be more interested in using Afghanistan as a base against Pakistan.

India enjoys warm and friendly relations with Central Asian countries. However, it cannot fully utilize the benefits of these relations and meet its energy demands without land transport connectivity with Central Asia. For that, it needs Pakistan, China, Afghanistan and Iran. Keeping all this in mind, India should proceed with the IPI project as it has multiple benefits for India both from strategic and energy security points of view.

Turkmenistan–Afghanistan–Pakistan–India pipeline (TAPI)

The Turkmenistan–Afghanistan–Pakistan–India (TAPI) pipeline, otherwise known as the Trans-Afghan Pipeline (TAP) is the biggest natural gas pipeline in South Asia. It is developed and sponsored by the Asian Development Bank (ADB). The pipeline will transport Caspian Sea natural gas from Turkmenistan through Afghanistan to Pakistan and eventually to India. The original project was started in March 1995. The project covers a 1040-mile (1680 kilometres) route from Dauletabad in Turkmenistan through Herat, Helmand and Kandahar in Afghanistan to Quetta and Multan in Pakistan and then on to Fazilka in India (Report 2011: 6).

The original project was signed between Turkmenistan and Pakistan in March 1995. However, it remained dormant until 2002 when the leaders of

Turkmenistan, Afghanistan and Pakistan signed the new deal on December 27. In 2005, the Asian Development Bank submitted the final version of a feasibility study designed by the British Company, Penspen (Ibid: 7–9). The project has strong United States' support since it will provide non-Russian transit facilities for the Western countries as well.

Finally, India joined the project in 2008. A Gas Pipeline Framework Agreement was signed by the representatives of the four participating countries on April 25, 2008 in Islamabad. At this meeting, it was decided that the route would follow the ancient trading route from Central Asia to South Asia and that construction would start in 2010 and supply gas by 2015 (Ibid: 9–12). Since this meeting, the participating countries have held numerous high-level planning meetings with the Asian Development Bank's sponsorship and multilateral support.

The intergovernmental agreement on the pipeline was signed on December 11, 2010, in Ashgabat. The proposed pipeline project is $10 billion (Niti Central 2015). The project covers a 1040-mile (1814 kilometres) route from Dauletabad in Turkmenistan through Herat, Helmand and Kandahar in Afghanistan to Quetta and Multan in Pakistan and then on to Fazilka in India (Report 2011), passing through some of the worst conflict-ridden areas of Afghanistan and Pakistan. The pipeline will be 56 inches in diameter with a working pressure of 100 standard atmospheres (10,000 kPa). "The TAPI project is intended to transport 33 bcm of gas per year from Turkmenistan via Afghanistan and Pakistan to India. Out of which 5 bcm will be provided to Afghanistan while 14 bcm each will be given to India and Pakistan" (Chandra 2017). However,

> the construction of the pipeline has been stalled for various reasons: the prior commitment of Turkmenistan gas reserves to Russia; difficulties in engaging with the regime in Ashgabat; security risks associated with the pipeline that will run through trouble-torn Afghanistan and Pakistan; lack of financing to the gas project by international companies; Indian reservations with regard to the security of supply.
>
> *(Reports 2011)*

Nevertheless, the recent visit of Indian Prime Minister to Turkmenistan on July 11, 2015, was able to clear the air and a joint statement was prepared to address the issue at hand. The joint statement welcomed the establishment of the "TAPI Ltd" special purpose vehicle for the project and the "leaders reaffirmed their strong commitment towards timely implementation of this strategic project" (MEA 2015). Timely completion of the project is mutually beneficial for both India and Turkmenistan. The latter currently depends on oil exports to China for revenues and would find an alternate source after the completion of this project. Greater cooperation in the area of oil exploration between the two countries – India and Turkmenistan – was also discussed and the leaders welcomed the establishment of a representative office of ONGC Videsh in Ashgabat. The standing committee on Petroleum and Natural Gas said in a report submitted to the Parliament in July 2017,

> that a consortium for Turkmenistan–Afghanistan–Pakistan–India Pipeline – TAPI pipeline Company Ltd (TPCL) – was incorporated in Isle of Man and shareholders agreement signed in December 2015. Turkmenistan will own 85 per cent of TPCL while India, Pakistan and Afghanistan will each have 5 per cent stake. The construction of the pipeline has commenced in December 2015 and is likely to be completed in about 7 years. The much-delayed project is now expected to be operational by 2022.
>
> *(Chandra 2017)*

The planned TAPI project offers all-round benefits to all four participating countries and would promote cooperation in the long term. For Turkmenistan, it would provide revenue and diversification of export routes. For Afghanistan, it would provide transit fees and revenue for development and gas for industrial enterprise. For India and Pakistan, it would address energy deficit. Despite all these, disagreement exists among partner countries with regards to how much gas Turkmenistan holds. According to the BP Statistical Review 2009, Turkmenistan has the world's fourth-largest natural gas reserves accounting for 7.94 tcm, exceeded only by Russia, Iran and Qatar (Ibid: 10). Turkmenistan's 2009 ranking represents a sharp rise from its 2008 profile and is expected to grow in volume in the coming years. Another area of major concern is the passage of the TAPI route through Afghanistan and Pakistan with areas of major insurgency and insecurity looming large.

It is believed that the materialization of the TAPI pipeline project would deepen India's geo-economic projection in Central Asia. It would also alter the geopolitical contours of the region, providing an artery of intensifying cooperation and for the first time integrating Afghanistan into South Asia. From the security point of view, TAPI is scoring better than its counterpart IPI. It is intended that segments of the TAPI pipeline in Afghanistan are buried to make them less susceptible to terror attacks. Local communities will be given incentives to participate in their defence. The Central Government also has ordered the deployment of some 7000 soldiers to safeguard the route in troubled areas of Afghanistan (Ibid: 12). Another benefit is that the successful operationalization of this project would not only assist in the peaceful economic development of Afghanistan but also would enable diversifying Turkmenistan's gas exports and providing resources to energy-hungry Pakistan and India. In contrast to IPI, TAPI seems to be more workable, as it has Russian support and India and Pakistan are equally relying on this project. Nevertheless, this project also suffers from insecurity syndrome. Given the myriad constraints and political problems among partner countries and insecurity in the areas of Baluchistan and western Afghanistan, India is mainly concerned about the security of supply and pipelines traversing through Pakistan and Afghanistan.

The diplomatic matrix

Among the pipeline options available for India connecting Central Asia, the Xinjiang–Tibet pipeline route ending at Uttarakhand seems to be economically the most viable and with the least security concerns. India needs to understand the strategic importance of this pipeline and engage with China positively for the materialization of this project. Unlike other projects, this Chinese route does not have many diplomatic and political hurdles. Since both countries are cooperating in several areas, particularly in the energy sector, what India needs most is to convince China to cooperate for the operationalization of this project. This would not only help India in diversifying its resources but would also provide revenues to China in the form of transit fees. Additionally, it would open a trade route between India and China which further would enable the two countries to increase trade exchanges. However, it depends on whether China agrees on this project or not. Therefore, the onus is on the Indian government to convince China of the strategic importance of this project for both the countries.

Further, this road looks more logical than any other connectivity network between India and Central Asia. Importantly, this road is also part of the ancient trade and silk route between the two regions. A journey through the Himalayan passes that would land the traders at the Xinjiang steppes is worth pursuing and is most realistic in any terms. However, the China factor cannot be discounted in realizing this project. Nevertheless, a cooperative approach from India for a regional economic integration with the Chinese support (if India supports BRI except CPEC) would yield favourable results. Importantly, China also sought India's help and support for its BRI project and hopefully would be ambivalent to open this old silk route network which would join with the China-Nepal Friendship highway bordering India.

The second most economically viable project for India connecting to Central Asia is the IPI (Iran–Pakistan–India) pipeline project. However, this project has been in a dormant state for a decade and a half. It faces numerous diplomatic hurdles. While the pipeline offers immense geo-economic and geopolitical significance for both Iran on the one hand and Pakistan and India on the other, it lacks political support from the United States, and further, the pipeline has to traverse through the trouble-torn areas of Afghanistan and Pakistan. India is apprehensive about the security of the pipeline in Pakistan and secure supply to India as the former would use it as a strategic tool against India during times of bilateral tension.

TAPI also suffers from the same problems as IPI, except for United States support. Instead, IPI has the support of Russia. Again, here also the security syndrome in Afghanistan and Pakistan is a serious matter of concern for India.

In this context, only two routes seem economically and strategically viable. One is the Xinjiang–Tibet (Chinese) route and the other is the Iranian route from Iranian Port Chabahar and Bandar Abbas along the International North–South Transport Corridor through the Arabian Sea to India.

In a nutshell, every pipeline is associated with geopolitical risks though the degree may vary. Security concerns and safety mechanisms also exist with every transit route. Diplomatic hazards are manifold everywhere, whether state-sponsored and grass-root terrorism in Pakistan, instability in Afghanistan, unreliability in Iran or the high handedness of China. However, all these risks are manageable. Steps can be taken to mitigate the majority of these risks. In the context of IPI, Iran has assured an alternative supply to India if Pakistan meddles with India's supply. It has also promised to discontinue exports to Pakistan itself if such an eventuality occurs. When it comes to TAPI, Russia has agreed to help in ensuring a safe and reliable supply of gas to India. Further, the confusion regarding the actual reserves of Turkmenistan that hindered the project, now looks promising with its production capacity increased tremendously since 2008. Additionally, it would help in bringing peace back to the region of South Asia as this pipeline is critical for all three countries of the region.

The Xinjiang–Tibet route is perhaps the most viable of all, both from economic and security points of view. As this route directly connects India with Central Asia (Kazakhstan) through western China to Tibet and then to Uttarakhand in India. Unlike Karakoram Pass and Ladakh range, the Xinjiang–Tibet route has no diplomatic disputes. Therefore, it would be easy for India to convince China to cooperate with the operationalization of this route. However, this route also suffers from one problem as it is not all-weather friendly.

But, from strategic considerations, the International North-South Transportation Corridor (INSTC) seems more feasible as it need not pass through either Pakistan or China and importantly security is not an issue. From the Iranian port of Chabahar and Bandar Abbas through the Arabian Sea, this route would connect India. But shipping in the Arabian Sea has huge security problems related to piracy along the territorial waters of coastal countries. However, the blue-water navy of India are especially trained to tackle piracy and criminal activities in the high seas and can effectively handle this.

Importantly, the recent trial runs done in the north–south corridor have yielded encouraging results with transport cost and time coming down by almost 30–40 per cent in the delivery of consignments. Also, both Iranian ports can transport around 30–50 million tonnes of goods per year. In the longer term, this route looks good for India both from a strategic point of view and also from economic considerations.

From the above understanding, it is very clear that all routes suffer from one or another constraint. But all of them are helpful for India from an energy security point of view. It also enables India to engage Pakistan and Afghanistan for their geopolitical reasons and benefits. Hence, these pipelines (IPI, TAPI) would help to generate geo-economic regional cooperation in South Asia. From a strategic angle, energy cooperation would help in bridging gaps and overcoming misunderstandings that exist among these nation-states.

Finally, in international politics, there are no permanent friends or enemies. Another important point is that political neighbours can be changed but geographical neighbours remain the same. Geography can never be changed. India has to learn from this and has to formulate a policy that would enable it to have healthy and cordial relations with her neighbours. All the outstanding problems can also be resolved amicably. As energy security is the priority of every modern nation-state including China and Pakistan, they share the same dais with India. For mutual benefits they can join hands with India or India can pursue them for its energy security concerns. What exists between India and China is mute conflict and that can be resolved in several ways. However, the only immediate solution is to introduce progressive relations without paying much heed to the past. When it comes to India and Pakistan, the relations seem to be more strained historically due to political misunderstandings. This can also be solved through mutual dialogue and broader consensus. There is another way to look at the pipeline transit routes for India through Pakistan and China. For that, the concerned countries need to push their historical enmity to the back seat and look towards progressive relations where there will be economic gains and energy self-sufficiency.

To meet its demand for gas, India is negotiating the import of gas from Iran via an overland pipeline transiting Pakistan. Apart from providing energy security to both India and Pakistan and a steady long-term customer to Iran for its gas, an Iran–Pakistan–India (IPI) pipeline would have great geopolitical significance for the region. It would be a huge confidence-building measure between India and Pakistan that could create a momentum for a fundamental transformation of India–Pakistan relations. As a regional energy project, the IPI could form the nucleus of a regional cooperation arrangement, in the first instance between South Asia and Iran and later perhaps within the framework of the Shanghai Cooperation Organization (SCO).

Despite so many uncertainties surrounding the Turkmenistan–Afghanistan–Pakistan (TAPI) gas pipeline project, India is participating in discussions on TAPI for geopolitical considerations. India would not like a gas pipeline to come up from Turkmenistan to Pakistan via Afghanistan without being involved in it. It would not be in India's interest for Pakistan to emerge as the key country with which Central Asia, including Afghanistan, is anchored economically, politically and strategically through oil and gas pipelines, roads and railways.

At the same time, it would be prudent for India to spread its risks and not rely exclusively on gas pipeline transit routes via Pakistan. The only possible alternative is gas from Russia and Central Asia via China. India must get involved in Eurasian oil and gas projects, not only for its energy security but for political and strategic considerations since Eurasia is likely to remain an important centre of global geopolitics. As a long-time trusted friend and strategic partner of Russia, India could expect the former to be positively inclined towards its quest for access to Eurasian energy. However, a hardnosed Russia is unlikely to accommodate India except as part of a larger strategic relationship and understanding. If India remains committed to an overarching India–United States strategic relationship there is not much hope for a meaningful India–Russia energy relationship.

India must have a strategic understanding of energy with China too since both are major energy consumers seeking energy from the same sources; and also because China holds the key to finding a viable alternative energy transportation route from Eurasia to India that bypasses Afghanistan/Pakistan. Although such a project faces considerable technical and political challenges, it does hold out the exciting possibility of developing a major energy corridor between Eurasia and the Indian Ocean, carrying gas from Eurasia to India via China, and oil from the Gulf to China via India. If there are insurmountable technical problems in constructing pipelines, it may be still possible to transmit electricity generated from gas or hydropower projects by transmission cables across the Karakoram and Himalayan mountain ranges. Perhaps, such a Eurasian energy project could be implemented within the framework of the India–China–Russia trilateral dialogue or the SCO. Apart from energy benefits, various long-term political, strategic, economic and environmental benefits would flow to both India and China.

In the new geopolitical realities of the 21st century, bold and innovative, even visionary, approaches are needed in inter-state relations, including in the area of energy security. The fructification of such a Eurasian energy blueprint offers the exciting prospect of transforming the Central Asian region into a strategic space uniting major Asian energy producers, consumers and transit countries in a web of interdependence. Instead of being the battlefield of a new "Great Game", Central Asia could become the crossroads of a 21st-century version of the traditional Silk Route, with gas and oil pipelines replacing caravan convoys. The Himalayas–Karakoram region could truly become a frontier zone of peace, friendship and development, rather than one of confrontation and conflict. A mega-project like this would also act as a huge stimulus for the global economy. Such a conceptual breakthrough would have far-reaching long-term consequences. It would not only bring all-round economic advantage, prosperity, social and political stability but also create a solid and enduring foundation for greater trust, confidence and understanding, extensive people-to-people ties and communication links that will hopefully lead to new, lasting and stable political and strategic relationships.

South Asia is a key region that will play an important part in the geopolitics of energy. Given its location and size, its economic and military strength and potential, and its position as a growing consumer of energy, India will be very much a part of global energy geopolitics in the coming years. If it is regarded as a responsible stakeholder and a reliable transit country, Pakistan can also become a critical player in global energy geopolitics and get many economic and political benefits. But given the current political dynamics in South Asia, the resurgence of the Taliban in Afghanistan, the rise of militant Islam in Pakistan and the military dictating the civilian government time and again, it seems impracticable to risk the pipeline run through the trouble-torn territories of Af-Pak. Therefore, the most suitable, all-weather friendly and cost–benefit transit routes for India would be through Iran's Chabahar Port to India through the Arabian Sea. Recently, discussions have been undergoing to fast track the International

North–South Transportation Corridor that connects India with Europe through Iran and Central Asia with Russia being an important constituent seems to be working out in favour of India's strategy to get reconnected with Central Asia, through which it can also mitigate much of its energy needs with the supplies of Central Asian energy resources without depending much on any of New Delhi's traditional rivals.

References

Arvanitopoulos, Constantine (2002), *The Geopolitics of Oil in Central Asia*, Institute of International Relations, March.

Balooch, Mahmoud (2009), "Iran and India's Cooperation in Central Asia", *China and Eurasia Forum Quarterly*, 7(3), October, pp. 25–29.

Chandra, Amilya (2017), *The Trade Games: Engaging with Central Asia*, New Delhi: Pentagon Press.

Chandrashekhar, A. (2010), "India's Ancient Gateway to Central Asia", *Sand Prints*, September 19, available at: https://chandrashekharasandprints.wordpress.com/2010/09/14/indias-ancient-gateway-to-central-asia/ [accessed April 10, 2019].

Chaudhury, Dipanjan Roy (2017), "International North-South Transportation Corridor for Better Indo-Russian Connectivity Inches towards Reality", *Economic Times*, April 10.

Fair, C. Christine (2007), "Indo-Iranian Ties: Thicker than Oil", *The Middle East Review of International Affairs*, Vol. 11, No. 1, pp. 41–58. March.

Fishelson, James (2007), "From the Silk Road to Chevron: The Geopolitics of Oil Pipelines in Central Asia", *The Journal of Russian and Central Asian Studies*, December, 12, available at: www.sras.org [accessed June 10, 2010].

FT (2020), "Iran Can Bring Russia, India Closer Through INSTC", *Financial Tribune*, January 12, available at: https://financialtribune.com/articles/national/101674/iran-can-bring-russia-india-closer-through-instc [accessed March 20, 2020].

Keohane, Robert (1984), *After Hegemony: Cooperation and Discord in the World Political Economy*, Princeton, NJ: Princeton University Press.

MEA (2015), "PM Modi's Central Asia Tour Brings Region Back into Focus", July 15, Ministry of External Affairs, Government of India, New Delhi, available at: http://mea.gov.in/articles-in-indian-media.htm?dtl/25484/PM+Modis+Central+Asia+tour+brings+region+back+into+focus [accessed September 15, 2018].

MEA (2017), "International North-South Transportation Corridor", Ministry of External Affairs, Government of India, May 18.

NBR (2010), "Pipeline Politics in Asia: The Intersection of Demand, Energy Markets and Supply Routes", *National Bureau of Asian Research*, Special Report 23, September.

Niti Central (2015), "PM Modi's Central Asia Visit Key Takeaways", *Niti Central*, July 14, available at: http://www.niticentral.com/2015/07/14/pm-modis-central-asia-visit-key-takeaways-323561.html [accessed April 14, 2019].

Report (2011), "Turkmenistan-Afghanistan-Pakistan-India Gas Pipeline: South Asia's Key Project", *Petromin Pipeliner*, April-June, available at: www.safan.com [accessed June 10, 2010].

RT (2020), "India and Russia Plan to Open New Trade Route via Iran Despite the Threat of U.S. Sanction", *Russia Today*, 19th March, available at: https://www.rt.com/news/483424-us-sanctions-india-russia-iran/ [accessed March 20, 2020].

Stobdan, P. (2008), "Exploring India-Kazakhstan Transport Linkages", *IDSA Policy Brief*, December 22.

Stobdan, P (2017), "India Gears up to enter the Eurasian Integration Path," *Institute for Defence Studies and Analyses (IDSA)*, Issue Brief, June 7, available at: https://idsa.in/system/files/issuebrief/ib_india-eurasian-integration-path_pstobdan_070617.pdf. [accessed February 10, 2018].

Stobdan, P (2020), India and Central Asia: *The Strategic Dimension, Knowledge World*: New Delhi.

Sushil, J. Aaron (2003), "Straddling Faultlines: India's Foreign Policy towards the Greater Middle East", *CSH Occasional*, Paper no. 7.

Temple, David (2007), "The Iran-Pakistan-India Pipeline, The Intersection of Energy and Politics", Institute of Peace and Conflict Studies, IPCS Research Paper, April, New Delhi.

Warikoo, K. (1996), "Trade Relations between Central Asia and Kashmir Himalayas during the Dogra Period (1846–1947)", *Cahiers d' Asie central*, 1(2), available at: http://asiecentrale.revues.org/index429.html [accessed September 15, 2008].

Zeb, Rizvan (2003), "Gwadar and Chabahar: Competition or Complementarily", *Central Asia and Caucasus Analyst*, October 22.

8
CONCLUSION

Energy is what keeps the world going. Throughout history – in all countries and through all ages – energy has been the driver of economic growth. It has been the main source of military power and the sole determinant of people's welfare. It is access to energy, whether human, animal or natural, that has primarily determined the scale and success of civilization or state. As we live in the 21st century, energy has become the driver of economic growth and tool of social change in every country. It is not just required to move the state and power its factories, government and office buildings, schools and hospitals but to heat homes and keep perishable foods cold. Its complexity explains its centrality. It is indeed a universal currency today.

As is observed from the study, energy has undergone a thorough transformation through the ages. In contemporary times energy has entered into an era of unprecedented revolution. Global demand for fossil fuel reserves is rising, energy price volatility is higher than ever, funding has become increasingly uncertain and climate change is firmly taking its place on the global political agenda. It is the time when the concept of energy security has come to the forefront. The term is mentioned in every policy formulation both in national and international forums. But what does it mean as Daniel Yergin puts it? Does it mean national security? Well, sort of. Does it mean energy independence? Well, sort of that too. Does it mean economic security? Yes, all of the above.

The concerns over energy security are not merely limited to oil only. Power blackouts on both the East and West Coasts of the United States, in Europe and Russia, as well as chronic shortages of electric power in China, India and other developing countries, have raised worries about the reliability of electricity supply systems. When it comes to natural gas, rising demand and constrained supplies followed by monopoly on the price regulation front in an unprecedented way has caused worries in the minds of energy-consuming countries.

Further, the age of globalization with a highly materialistic pursuit of life has led to competition among countries of the world to control and administer the energy resources essential for their survival and has become the order of the day. Hence, capturing the nerves of the world has led to an unabated drive and quest for energy. The prime focus of every major energy-consuming country has become to ensure a secure, affordable, reliable and unrestricted flow of energy to maintain its energy security system. For that, along with available domestic energy resources, having an unrestricted hold over the energy resources of foreign countries has become inevitable.

Since energy is essentially a geopolitical commodity; its availability is principally determined by geology. The geopolitics of energy today mainly revolves around oil and gas and to a lesser degree around nuclear and hydroelectricity sources. The global politics of energy is, therefore, shaped mainly by the "arc of energy" stretching from the Gulf region to the Caspian Sea, through Siberia and the Arctic region to the Russian Far East, Alaska and Canada. In this regard, it can be said that nearly 80 per cent of the world's oil and gas, including potential reserves, is located in this region.

Among these energy-rich destinations, the Middle East has always remained at the forefront. However, the region is deeply troubled by political turmoil, civic unrest and regional instability which has posed a question mark in the minds of consumer countries over the security of their supply. It is not just a matter of the trouble-torn Middle East that worries the countries of the world, civic unrest and ethnic violence in Sudan and Nigeria, political instability, regional disorder and inter-state wars in Africa and the Persian Gulf have further exacerbated the concerns of the energy consumers. In the prevailing scenario, ensuring energy security of any nation is no less than a Herculean task.

Furthermore, developed countries are not the only ones driving demands in today's world. Several energy thirsty new powers are emerging onto the scene as well. Particularly, China and India along with many smaller developing countries with steadily increasing energy demands have made their presence felt. Energy politics have become yet more complex as transport systems particularly in the United States, Europe, China and India have become largely reliant on oil. Access to energy remains critical to sustaining growth in China and India – not just to keep pace with the burgeoning population, but to avoid the failure to deliver on the hope of greater prosperity as this could unravel the governments and regimes whether democratic or not as populations become more educated and demanding.

Energy security is not straightforward to assess in this geopolitical pluralism and fierce world of oil and gas. Changes in any given factor may help or hurt energy security, depending on the specific circumstances. These factors are the diversity of supplies, level of imports and security of trade flows, international economics and political factors, nuclear proliferation risks, diversity of fuels, market/price volatility, affordability and economic impacts, energy intensity, reliability, feasibility etc.

In these circumstances, any disruption in supply puts the whole world in a bottleneck. To avoid any such future trouble countries are developing Strategic Reserves (SR). But for that as well they need more imports. This has further led to a scramble for energy for diversification.

In the process of the energy mix, consumer countries of the world have employed both progressive and aggressive policy measures to control and administer these resources. This, in turn, has disturbed the demand–supply chain as the suppliers are fewer and the consumers are unprecedentedly vast. The apparent question in this scenario that comes to mind is how long will these oil, gas and coal reserves last? According to BP Statistical Review of World Energy, the world's proven oil reserves at its 2010 rate of production would last for only 46 years. Likewise, the natural gas reserves as assumed would last for around 59 years. Also, it has been reiterated several times by the "Peak Oil" theory that Russia is producing at its peak and Saudi Arabia has limited additional short-term capacity. Due to commercial disputes, regional instability, civic unrest and political coups in the Persian Gulf, investors are thoroughly worried about their energy security concerns. In this scenario, the issues of energy security are now moving beyond the exclusive concerns of consumers. Producers too require a stable regime with a coherent demand and supply scenario.

Although global reserves have been the principal factors in influencing if not defining the energy security debate, it may be recalled that the "Club of Rome Thesis" cautioned the world community of the limited span of non-renewable sources of energy in its paper "The Limits to Growth". That is why perhaps the global scramble for oil and energy has taken a fast-track route all around the geopolitical landscapes of abundant energy resources. The agenda of climate change has further aggravated the situation by putting a reality check on the use of coal and other fossil fuels extensively. Having said this, it should also be pointed out that a major part of the 21st-century world is not yet ready to use fuels other than traditional. The use of renewable resources, though beneficial, however, requires a certain time frame as the present technology is not ready to accept it. In this situation, finding an alternative to fossil fuels looks quite bleak. In the prevailing situation, looking for diversification of suppliers and supplies has become apparent.

The geographical landscape of Central Asia in this scenario provides a ray of hope. Central Asia along with the Caspian Sea basin holds merit in terms of energy. Since the region is the least unexplored and undeveloped, its energy potential is quite promising. Despite years of under investments, engineering difficulties and the problem of piping the oil and gas to markets outside of the region, the Central Asian fields are emerging as some of the most important energy destinations in the world. This importance is not just based on the physical volume of oil and gas, estimated at 50–110 billion barrels of oil and 5–13 trillion cubic metres of gas (170–463 tcf), but on the fact that the flow of Central Asian hydrocarbons could help to meet the burgeoning world demand and provide a surplus that would help regulate world prices in times of temporary shortage.

Although Central Asian energy potential is not in a race with the Persian Gulf, it can be used as an alternative for diversification.

There is little doubt that Central Asian oil and natural gas infrastructure and reserves have come to be regarded as strategic assets. Energy resources are also the objects of rising political and economic rivalry among the regional and extra-regional powers. Today China, Russia, India and the United States, among others, are competing for influence and market shares of Central Asian energy. Many observers of Central Asia, as well as policymakers, are beginning to believe that it is only a matter of time before the region experiences an intense struggle over energy resources. Central Asian governments, for their part, have sought to mitigate the influence of the major consumer states in the region, while profiting from their need, to pursue their agendas. It may be noted here that the Central Asian energy resources have just not been able to attract outside powers, but have also helped the CAS to uplift their economic conditions.

Moreover, Central Asia today represents one of the world's last great frontiers for geological survey and analysis. It offers opportunities for the discovery, production, transportation and refining of enormous quantities of oil, gas and other energy resources. Energy is the most abundant and valuable natural resource in the countries of Central Asia. The region is rich in hydrocarbons with gas being the predominant energy fuel. While Kazakhstan is especially known for its large reserves of oil and coal and some significant amount of uranium deposits, Turkmenistan and Uzbekistan are notable for their gas reserves. Kyrgyzstan produces a significant amount of hydroelectricity power. Central Asia is poised to become a major world supplier of energy, especially in the oil and gas sectors. Since most of its reserves are undeveloped and promising; Central Asian energy excites international interests. It is in this context that the Central Asian geographical landscape has been dealt with specifically in terms of its energy potentials and capacity to meet world energy demand in general, implicating Indian energy security in particular.

India has a serious problem with its lack of access to modern forms of energy. The rural population of over 700 million people is largely dependent on biomass, including fuelwood (often in the form of twigs and green parts of trees) and animal dung. This continues to pose a major problem, and, as yet, suitable alternatives have not been found for this large part of the population, although in some limited areas marketing of LPG at subsidized prices has helped to a great extent. Almost 600 million people in the country have no access to electricity, and therefore, they are left with no choice but to use candles, small oil lamps based on kerosene and other oils. Blackouts in metropolitan cities even in the national capital have become the habit for a long time. Even so, lack of a lifeline supply of safe and convenient energy is responsible for most of India's poor human development indices either directly or indirectly. Illiteracy, gender inequality, disempowerment, high infant and maternal mortality rates, lack of access to clean drinking water and poor health indicators can all be traced back to the lack of a lifeline level of safe and clean commercial energy for all Indian households.

India needs a consistent and inclusive 8 per cent plus GDP growth over the next 25 years to eradicate poverty and meet the millennium development goals. The emphasis on inclusive growth is essential if this aspiration is to be meaningful for all Indians. Raising access to modern commercial fuels is at the very heart of delivering such inclusive growth. The rapid growth of the Indian economy has led to increasing demand for energy, but capacity, particularly in the power sector, has not kept pace with this growth in demand. Additionally, whatever capacity exists is often utilized at very low levels of efficiency, resulting in substantial losses in the transmission and distribution system and the generation of a very low plant load factor in several cases. Overall, therefore, the energy challenge for India requires substantial improvements in efficiency and the creation of options for rural areas as well as for the urban poor, whereby proper access can be provided to people in the form of affordable and clean sources of energy for basic end-uses such as cooking, lighting and heating.

If we look at India's energy profile, she is the eighth largest producer of energy in the world with 2.4 per cent of the world's total energy production. With 3.7 per cent of global energy consumption, India is in third place among the largest energy consumers of the world. With this rate of consumption, India is projected to take the second position by 2030. India's domestic coal reserves of 101,903 million tonnes with an annual production of over 400 million tonnes, accounts for 70 per cent of the country's energy needs. The remaining 30 per cent is met by oil with more than 65 per cent of it being imported, mainly from the Middle East. Given the environmental reasons, coal quality in India is the dirtiest and hydrocarbon fuel is unpurified, hence, India cannot rely on them for the long term to meet her energy needs. On the other hand, the country's consumption of energy as per the government estimates doubled in 2015 based on the 2005 level. This unwarranted situation at hand compels the country to seek diversification of energy sources, particularly from abroad, especially from Central Asia – constituting "India's extended neighbour".

Moreover, former Prime Minister Dr Man Mohan Singh observed several times that "energy security is second only in our scheme of things to food security". With energy increasingly being viewed as a vital component of what is now broadly defined as "national security", cultivating alternative sources of energy and reducing dependence on the volatile Middle Eastern region has become a vital concern for India. Assured, uninterrupted supply of energy is critical for keeping India's economic engine in motion. Its dependence on imported oil is projected to skyrocket from the current levels of 72 per cent to 83 per cent by 2030; hence, the anxiety to reconceptualize its strategic perspective. What can be more viable a destination for India than Central Asia – home to an estimated 4 per cent (270–360 tcf) of the world's gas reserves, and 2.7 per cent (13–15 bbl) oil reserves?

In this scenario, the geopolitical salience of Central Asian energy for India undoubtedly holds significance. Central Asia is an extended and strategic neighbour of India. In this context, Central Asia constitutes a natural ally of India, given its geographical proximity, shared history and cultural affinity. India's engagement with Central Asia is a function of historical interactions with the region through the ages. Both Asian neighbours share an exceedingly superb bonding and thorough friendship through the sands of time. Thus, the long-standing historical ties encompassing the political, cultural, economic and religious dimensions constitute the basis for the international relations between New Delhi and the individual Central Asian states. The historical span of these contacts further illustrates that the relationship between India and Central Asia are "multi-dimensional, deep rooted and continuous".

However, the main concern here is not about India's engagement with Central Asian states. It is about access to the Central Asian energy hub to meet India's energy needs at least partially. Currently, energy-hungry India is vigorously building relations with Central Asian states to gain direct access to Central Asian energy resources. India wants to do it alone and is focusing on the possibilities of opening land routes. Since India is not directly connected with Central Asia, it has to depend on its Asian neighbours to build pipelines that would bypass either Pakistan, Afghanistan or China. Reopening of the ancient Silk Road through China's Xinjiang region is one option for Indian policymakers as well. The second possibility is the development of the International North–South Transportation Corridor through Iran and Afghanistan. There are several transit pipeline options for India connecting Central Asia such as Iran–Pakistan–India (IPI) pipeline, Turkmenistan–Afghanistan–Pakistan–India (TAPI) pipeline etc.

However, all these transit routes suffer from one or other problem. Often hostile neighbours around India, instability in Afghanistan, terror threats to the pipeline in Pakistan, diplomatic downturn with China and geographic barriers like the great Himalayas have stood as great stumbling blocks for India. Moreover, most of these issues among India and her neighbours are either political or geographic, but none of them is economic. Hence, diplomatic initiatives need to be taken care of while dealing with her neighbours.

Among the pipeline options available for India connecting to Central Asia, the Xinjiang–Tibet pipeline route ending at Uttarakhand seems to be economically the most viable and with least security concerns. India needs to understand the strategic importance of this pipeline and engage with China positively for the materialization of this project. Unlike other projects, this Chinese route doesn't have many diplomatic and political hurdles. Since both countries are cooperating in several areas, particularly in the energy sector, what India needs most is to convince China to cooperate for operationalization of this project. This would not only help India in diversifying its resources but would also provide revenue to China in the form of transit fees. Additionally, it would open a trade route between India and China which further would enable the two countries to manifold increase their trade exchanges.

The second most economically viable project for India connecting Central Asia is the Iran–Pakistan–India (IPI) pipeline project. However, this project has been in a dormant state for a decade and a half. It faces numerous diplomatic hurdles.

While the pipeline offers immense geo-economic and geopolitical significance for both Iran on the one hand and Pakistan and India on the other, it lacks political support from the United States. India must learn from its past mistakes. Iran and India have had civilizational links and cordial relationships through the ages. Furthermore, there is no permanent friend or foe in international politics. India must exercise power to secure its national interests. As energy security is the priority of every modern state, India should not block this project as this is meant for its betterment. The problem of United States–Iran hostility can be resolved amicably without dragging the Indo-Iran pipeline project into conflict. As this project offers immense geopolitical and strategic significance, operation of this pipeline perhaps would be able to ensure peace and transform the regional dynamics by offering relatively better economic and energy benefits to all. These above mentioned two routes seem both economically and strategically viable for India.

Again, every pipeline is associated with geopolitical risks; the degree may be low or high. Security concerns and safety mechanisms also coexist with every transit route. Diplomatic hazards are manifold everywhere, whether it be state-sponsored terrorism in Pakistan, instability in Afghanistan, unreliability in Iran or high handedness of China. However, all these risks can be managed. Steps can be taken to mitigate the majority of these risks. In the context of IPI, Iran has assured an alternative supply to India if Pakistan meddles with India's supply. It also has promised to discontinue exports to Pakistan itself if such an eventuality occurs. When it comes to TAPI, Russia has agreed to help in ensuring a safe and reliable supply of gas to India. Further, the confusion regarding the actual reserves of Turkmenistan gas fields adds to the prolongness of the TAPI project. However, with the increasing trend of gas production by Turkmenistan the project again accentuated its significance for India like never before. Additionally, it would help in bringing peace back to the region of South Asia as this pipeline is critical for all the three countries of the region.

Hence, the question arises, what prevents India from its engagement in the above-mentioned transit routes. Why is it not progressive and active in the region, unlike its counterparts? Perhaps India lacks promptness in its energy engagement with Central Asia.

Among several other things, what strikes the mind first is that it is possible India lacks an overarching energy strategy – instead, it has many disparate policies. In fact, Mani Shankar Aiyar, a former minister in the Government of India remarked that his job was "to make policy for next year", which then begs the question: Whose job is it to make strategy?

The prime minister has reiterated several times that India "must learn to think strategically"; however, there is a good deal of debate about whether an energy strategy is essential. In this discourse, it can be mentioned here that having a number of policies is not thought to be a bad thing in and of itself. Meeting the country's energy needs is considered a complex problem, requiring different solutions. Hence, it is no longer hypothetical whether Central Asia is able to meet India's energy needs. It is very much evident, as discussed in this study, that

Central Asia has plenty of resources in its kitty to provide for India. On her part, what India perhaps needs to do is to formulate a clear strategy towards the region with a long-term vision.

A modest amount of cooperation

India considers Central Asia to be its extended neighbourhood. It has, since 1991, made efforts to cultivate very good relations with all the CARs. Prime Minister Shri P. V. Narasimha Rao visited four Central Asian states except Tajikistan, realizing their importance. When Atal Bihari Vajpayee became Prime Minister, he visited Tajikistan in 2003. But nothing substantial was done to cement India–Central Asia relations. When United Progressive Alliance (UPA) came to power, Dr Man Mohan Singh as Prime Minister paid his first official visit to Central Asia in 2006 to Uzbekistan and Kazakhstan in 2011. It was during the UPA regime that India's "Connect Central Asia Policy" (CCAP) was first unveiled. The then Minister of State for External Affairs, Mr E. Ahmed took the initiative of this policy at the first meeting of the India–Central Asia Dialogue, a Track II initiative organized on June 12–13, 2012 in Bishkek, Kyrgyzstan. The purpose of this policy was to fast track India's relations with Central Asian Republics. As part of India's soft power strategy in Central Asia, this policy called for setting up universities, hospitals, information technology (IT) centres and e-networks in telemedicine connecting India to the CARs, joint commercial ventures, improving air connectivity to boost trade and tourism, joint scientific research and strategic partnerships in defence and security affairs. During SM Krishna's visit to Tajikistan on July 2–3, 2012, the former Foreign Minister expounded the unfolding policy under the rubric of "commerce, connectivity, consular and community". This policy initiative if properly channelized would enable India to attain centre stage in Central Asia which would further help India to attain its basic objectives of engagement in the greater Central Asian region. However, the region remained under perceived negligence and policy paralysis until Mr Modi came to power.

In line with India first, internally, Mr Modi expounded neighbourhood first to cultivate a close relationship with the proximate neighbours. Modi's extended visit to five Central Asian countries in July 2015 marked a new start in India's re-engagement with the region, ending age-long perceived negligence. As he travelled across the region, his regional engagement acquired a new name, "Reconnecting Central Asia". Distancing itself from the Russian and Chinese geostrategic influence, India has discovered a new trajectory for its renewed commitment with the region. This was followed by India's inclusion into the Shanghai Cooperation Organization (SCO) as a full member state along with Pakistan. This has left Beijing jittery as its new sphere of influence has been ventured into by India – its traditional rival. While such nimble diplomacy might turn the region to New Delhi's advantage temporarily, Modi must develop a long-term strategy to overcome the enduring constraints on India's role in Central Asia.

Shift in policy

Several significant shifts in policy and outlook have taken place on the Indian side in her dealings with the neighbours only recently. Modi's decisive visit to Central Asian states in 2015 after the BRICS and SCO meeting at Ufa in Russia has given oxygen to the already dormant relationship. The induction of India along with Pakistan into SCO as full member states in July 2015 and the support the Central Asian states have offered, especially Kazakhstan and Uzbekistan, testifies to India's growing closeness with the region. The commencement of the construction of the TAPI pipeline project in December 2015, membership of the European Economic Union and discussion on speeding up the construction and processing of the International North–South Transport Corridor (INSTC) are evidence to the fact that a major policy shift is taking place in New Delhi with hearts open to the Central Asian states.

Nevertheless, the close political relations and solid diplomatic ties have not offered much in terms of economic cooperation; although India and the Central Asian countries have maintained stable trade and economic cooperation, albeit at a very modest level. Kazakhstan is the only country in the region to have a trade turnover of more than $1 billion with India while other countries are significantly behind.

To strengthen its position in India needs to put weight into its "Connect Central Asia Policy" and "Extended Neighbourhood" and activate its economic engagements with the region.

India's geopolitical interests

India's relations with Central Asia cannot be seen in isolation from its greater engagement in world politics. Its approach to Central Asia is in close connection with her policies towards South Asia and its multilateral engagement with countries including China, Russia and the United States. The role of regional countries like Iran, Pakistan and Afghanistan too is being closely followed to construct India's Central Asian strategy. One needs to look at the contours of India's Central Asian engagement through its regional and extra-regional sketches.

India–Pakistan

India's relations with Central Asian countries are strongly influenced by its relations with the countries it surrounds. To quote Robert D. Kaplan, "India's history is the story of invasion from a north-westerly direction, and this explains why Central Asia continues to be seen more as the source of threats than of opportunities". That is to say, India's approach to Central Asia is conditioned by its profound distrust of and tension with Pakistan. India's ability to access Central Asia is conditioned by Pakistan policy towards New Delhi. The vulnerability of India to link directly with the region comes from its apprehension about Pakistani strategy to obstruct India and at times to cut off New Delhi from the region. This is the reason probably why ambitious projects like TAPI, IPI and CASAREM, though initiated with high vigour and indomitable spirit, could not be materialized to date.

Further, Afghanistan's proximity with Pakistan and their troubled history of giving shelter to militant groups and at the time pursuing terrorism as a state policy has created lots of concern in Indian diplomatic quarters with regard to her national security. Afghanistan is not just a springboard for anti-India groups but also a rear base for Pakistan to use the territory of Kabul against India through its terror networks like the Taliban and Hakkai.

On New Delhi's part, Afghanistan is a part of the Indian subcontinent and linked organically to India on account of the record of empires past. Afghanistan also considers India a valued partner of Kabul. Both countries in the post-Taliban period have worked together in the reconstruction of the ruined state. India has credit for being the largest donor among the regional countries to Afghanistan's reconstruction and sixth largest worldwide. It has also extended support in training the military of Afghanistan in India. India's aid to Afghanistan includes in areas like education, health, road and transportation, water and sanitation and energy. That is why India fears that Afghanistan may fall under the sway of militant groups and the ill designs of Pakistan, giving rise to anti-India activities threatening New Delhi's national security. Conversely, an Afghanistan at peace and governed along secular lines would strengthen India's position vis-à-vis Pakistan.

India–China

India–China relations are equally significant in geopolitical terms in defining New Delhi's relationships with Central Asian Republics. Since China shares a long land border with the republics of Central Asia and established very good diplomatic relations with them in 1992, Beijing enjoys leverage in relationship with the CARs. Besides the economic muscle of China, Central Asia provides investment opportunities which bind them together. The political willpower of China to engage in Central Asia and its economic strength to push its strategies further through economic diplomacy outpace New Delhi in terms of trade, investment, energy acquisition, transportation building and network development and, importantly, narratives. While China's trade volume with Central Asian countries in 2017 amounted to $30 billion, India's trade volume was estimated in the same year at around $1.5 billion. China has regularly beaten several countries including India when it comes to energy acquisition. It is the invincible player in the energy sector because it consolidated transport networks while India was busy calculating its cost–benefit analysis. However, this shouldn't give an impression that all is well with Chinese penetration into Central Asia. The recent visit of the Indian Prime Minister to the landlocked region created lots of enthusiasm in the region and many believed that New Delhi would provide Central Asia with an alternative to China. To quote Kazakhstani political expert Aidos Sarym, "The way India is trying to become a more important player in

Central Asia, Russia and China will probably not be altogether glad to see India here". It clearly shows that India and China have some shared concerns in the region, especially where issues of security are concerned. Though India cannot match the firepower of China, its soft power image will certainly provide New Delhi leverage to play an active role in the region in the years to come.

India–United States

The United States from the very beginning was in favour of a larger role of India in Central Asia. Its support has grown even more with America's withdrawal from Afghanistan in 2014. The United States considers India a valued partner and integral to the peace process in Afghanistan. In fact, when the New Silk Road project was launched by the United States in 2011, India was placed emphatically in an important position with an aim to establish stability in the larger region. It is also true that the United States wants to sustain its economic interests in Central Asia, bypassing Russia, Iran and China, and looks to link India with Europe through Central Asia, thus providing new investment opportunities for the United States and undermining Chinese and Russian influence through Indian counter. Robert D. Kaplan has rightly quoted, "As the United States and China become great power rivals, the direction in which India tilts could determine the course of geopolitics in Eurasia in 21st-century India, in other words, looms as the ultimate pivot state".

India–Russia

Historically, India's relations with Russia have always been close, which led New Delhi to cultivate superb bonding with the Central Asian Republics. However, between 1917 and 1991, India's contacts with Central Asia were largely mediated through Russia. Although, India during this period had maintained certain privileged links with Central Asia that too were filtered through Moscow and the 1971 Indo-Russian Treaty of Peace, Friendship and Cooperation in which India was the junior partner. In the aftermath of the dissolution of the Soviet Union, New Delhi maintained proximity with the republics of Central Asia but Russia never preferred to allow any country including India to play a significant role in its backyard. Central Asia is the geostrategic comfort zone of Russia and Kremlin in no situation would want any other country to disturb the regional balance. However, the recent Chinese dominance over the region through economic packages has outpaced Russian influence in its traditional hinterland. That is why perhaps Kremlin has strongly advocated for the full membership of New Delhi in the Central Asian Organization SCO to strike a balance in Asia and to counter the Chinese upper hand through New Delhi's Central Asian venture.

China factor

Three out of five Central Asian states share a boundary with China. This allows China to be the proximate player in the region. It is also believed in certain quarters that, although Central Asia is a Russian hinterland, it is not Russia but China whose presence worries the United States most in the region. The same is also true with India. Chinese growing presence in Central Asia and its massive economic package, military aid and political dominance in the region hamper India's strategic vision towards Central Asian geopolitics. SCO is the mechanism through which China pushes its agendas in Central Asia. Such is its dominance in Central Asia that it goes alone in the region when it comes to energy and trade while it has a cooperation mechanism with India in other areas such as Africa.

China has great interests in gaining access to the rich deposits of hydrocarbon resources in the Central Asian region. Presently China is the second highest consumer of oil and gas in the world and is importing 50 per cent of the region's oil as of the end of 2020. Therefore, it is apparent on the part of China with a population of 1.4 billion to depend profoundly on Central Asia; an energy hub accounting for proven oil reserves of 9–40 billion barrels and natural gas reserves possibly exceeding 131 trillion cubic feet (tcf). Since most of its reserves are untapped and promising, Central Asian energy excites international interests. Therefore, it is no wonder China wants to go it alone in Central Asia while it has well-placed collaborations with India in other areas such as Africa and Latin America. China's major energy partners in Central Asia are Kazakhstan and Turkmenistan with whom it shares a 1700-kilometre land border. As of August 2016, China is in control of 20 per cent of the Kazakh oil production and has constructed one of the world's longest pipelines running about 2300 kilometres from the Caspian Sea to the Xinjiang province. Beijing has also been actively participating in exploring Alktyuinks and Mangyshlak oil deposits and building an oil pipeline in the Kazakhstan–Xinjiang region. The Chinese National Oil Company CNPC owns a significant stake in the Kashagan oil field in the Caspian Sea while several other Chinese companies own and developed several key oil fields in the western city of Aktobe. With Turkmenistan – the major gas producer and exporter of the region – China has negotiated to directly transfer the gases through the Central Asia–China gas pipeline. One of the most ambitious projects signed by China includes a 5730-kilometre long gas pipeline project estimated at $11 billion between Turkmenistan, Uzbekistan, Kazakhstan and China in which a consortium of companies from the United States, Japan and China have already been conducting preliminary surveys for quite some time. In 2013 alone China invested 15 billion dollars in energy deals with Central Asian states. Also, it financed two refineries in Kyrgyzstan, in Kara-Balta and Tomok. These refineries are supplied by CNPC-run oil fields in neighbouring Kazakhstan and produce 1.35 million barrels of refined products annually. The Chinese inroads into Central Asian energy markets have decisively diverted the flow of oil and gas from Central Asia eastward and have undoubtedly established Chinese dominance in the region. The recently concluded Belt and Road Initiative in Beijing where 130 countries across the world participated along with all the Central Asian countries beyond doubt proves the looming Chinese hegemony over the geopolitics of Central Asia. At this juncture India – a competitor of China with a population of 1.26 billion cannot afford to be a mere spectator. It needs to provide urgent attention to the inner Asian region in order not just to take care of its energy security concerns but also to address its security risks emanating from the region. Any overlooking of the developments in the region will prove self-defeating for New Delhi. Hence, New Delhi needs to follow a robust policy towards the region with an obvious strategy in mind to maintain a balance in the region vis-à-vis China.

Policy options

Like China, India is also actively involved in the oil politics of Central Asia. Both China and India are expected to occupy 50 per cent of total world energy demand growth, 60 per cent of world oil demand growth, 20 per cent of natural gas and 85 per cent of coal demand growth sooner than later. India wanted the construction of pipelines that became clear in its support for pipelines along with six countries passing through Afghanistan, Pakistan, Bangladesh, Iran, Myanmar and Turkmenistan. India's primary energy demand is expected to grow at 6 per cent with GDP growth at 7–8 per cent. According to the international energy agency (IEA) reports, a $10 rise in crude prices would reduce India's GDP by 1 per cent which calls for the diversification of energy sources for ensuring the availability of energy at affordable rates.

India's Connect Central Asia policy

India with its Connect Central Asia policy was one of the first such countries to establish strategic connections with the region in June 2012. The full membership position granted to India in the Shanghai Cooperation Organization (SCO) further bolstered New Delhi's position in the region as an alternative to Chinese hegemony. As part of the Connect Central Asia policy, Mr Modi's six-day visit to five countries of the region in 2015 put the heartland right into New Delhi's global focus. He signed several agreements with all the countries in bilateral engagements, respectively. These are:

India–Uzbekistan (MEA 2015e)

1. Economic and Strategic ties: Enhance strategic, economic and energy ties along with reviewing key regional issues including the situation in Afghanistan.
2. Joint Working Group on Counter-Terrorism: To intensify security cooperation and exchanges for combating terrorism, promoting regional integration and advancing stability in the region.
3. Defence and Cyber Security: Enhance cooperation in the fields of defence and cyber security.

4. Uranium Supply Contract: Implement the contract which was signed in 2014 for the supply of 2000 metric tonnes of uranium from mineral-rich Uzbekistan to India.
5. Strengthening cooperation: In the areas of information technology, agriculture and energy.
6. International North–South Transport Corridor (INSTC): India asked Uzbekistan to be part of INSTC, similar to the Ashgabat Agreement which is a transit pact between Uzbekistan, Iran, Turkmenistan and Oman, established in 2011. It should be noted that INSTC is a ship, road and rail route for moving freight between India, Iran, Russia, Europe and Central Asia.

India–Kazakhstan (MEA 2015f)

1. Agreement on Defence and Military: Both nations will form a joint working group (JWG) on counter-terrorism, defence training, exercise and production of defence equipment.
2. MoU on Cooperation on Physical, Cultural and Sports: It was signed between India's Ministry of Youth Affairs and Sports and Kazakhstan's Ministry of Culture and Sports.
3. MoU on Technical Cooperation in the field of Railways: It was signed between India's Ministry of Railways and Kazakhstan's Temir Zholy.
4. Agreement on Transfer of Sentenced Persons: It will facilitate swapping to prisoners from both countries to serve their remaining sentence in the home country.
5. Agreement on the Supply of Uranium to India: Kazakhstan, the world's largest producer of uranium supplied a total of 5000 tonnes of natural uranium to India during 2015–19.

India–Turkmenistan (MEA 2015g)

1. MoU on Supply of Chemical Products: It was signed between India's Rashtriya Chemicals and Fertilizers Limited and Turkmenistan's Turkmenhimiya.
2. MoU Foreign Service Institutes of both nations: It was signed between Foreign Service Institute of the Ministry of External Affairs of India and Institute of International Relations of the Ministry of Foreign Affairs of Turkmenistan.
3. Agreement on Cooperation in the field of Sports: It was signed between Union Ministry of Youth Affairs and Sports of India and State Committee for Sport of Turkmenistan.
4. Programme of Cooperation in Science and Technology: It was signed between both governments for two years viz. 2015–17.
5. MoU on Cooperation in Yoga and Traditional Medicine: It was signed between respective entities of both governments.

6. MoU on Cooperation in the field of Tourism: It was signed between respective entities of both governments.
7. Agreement in the field of Defence: It was signed between respective entities of both governments.

India–Tajikistan (MEA 2015h)

1. Programme of Cooperation (POC) in the field of Culture: It was signed between Ministries of Culture of India and Tajikistan for the years 2016–18. It envisages cooperation in the field of culture between both nations through the exchange of expertise for protection, preservation and promotion of cultural heritage.
2. Exchange of Note Verbale (NV) on setting up of Computer Labs: It conveys the intention of India to set up computer labs in 37 schools in Tajikistan.

India–Kyrgyzstan (MEA 2015i)

1. Agreement on Defence Cooperation: It was signed to deepen cooperation between both countries in matters relating to security, defence, military education and training. It also covers provisions to conduct joint military exercises, exchange of military instructors, exchange of experience and information and observers etc.
2. MoU on Cooperation in the field of Elections: It was signed to deepen cooperation in matters relating to legislation on elections and referendums. It also covered the rights of elections process stakeholders, modern systems and technologies as well as other issues of election administration.
3. MoU on Cooperation in the sphere of Standards: Seeks to strengthen and enhance technical cooperation in the fields of conformity assessment, standardization and sharing of expertise on mutual trade. It also aims at exchanging necessary information and expertise in this regard between the two parties. Signatory parties are the Ministry of Economy of Kyrgyzstan and the Bureau of Indian Standards (BIS).
4. Agreement on Cooperation in Culture: To deepen cultural cooperation between both countries in areas such as preservation of cultural heritage, theatre, youth festivals and organization of folk arts. It also seeks to boost cooperation in publishing and translation of literature, culture, sports and physical exchange of archival materials, geography, history etc.

These bilateral policy initiatives if properly channelled would enable India to attain centre stage in Central Asia which further would help New Delhi to attain its basic objectives of engagement in the greater Central Asian region.

In general, India's overall relationship with the Central Asian states is cordial and close. It has a fairly strong position in Central Asia. In recent years India has enhanced its engagements with Central Asian countries and its participation in the activities of SCO has intensified its position in the region. The persistent attempts of the Modi government to overcome the geopolitical barriers to establish reliable land communication with the CAS primarily to implement the interregional projects, especially energy and transport communication, have further reinforced India's Central Asian strategy. However, the lack of direct access to Central Asia and uncanny neighbours has troubled India in its regional aspirations. One thing is sure, that India's appeal is quite obvious in Central Asia but its low-level economic engagements don't allow it to defend its national interests in the region. No doubt India's greater engagement won't change the geopolitical dynamics of Central Asia, dominated by Beijing and Moscow, but at least that would compel the other players to negotiate and come to terms with India in the fierce regional competition. For that, India needs to do the checklist first and plan the way out to remain engaged with the region far into the future.

Recommendations

1. It is, therefore, necessary for India to evolve its perspective and understanding, and to broaden its operational scope in Central Asia. In this mission, it also needs to include Afghanistan and the frontiers of China (Xinjiang) in its greater Central Asian vision.
2. India should also look into capitalizing the entry to SCO. It could be imprudent for India to join the organization and broaden its deftness. A subregional framework involving India, China, Kyrgyzstan, Tajikistan, Kazakhstan and Afghanistan could form a viable option for long-term cooperation. Like China, it could also use the SCO mechanism to garner its interests in the region, even though not on a par with China.
3. To continue to build on our strong political relations through continuous and consistent exchange of high-level visits at bilateral and multilateral forums.
4. To show the political will and economic strengths to take on the financial risks involved in overseas investments.
5. To establish physical connectivity with each of the Central Asian states.
6. To step up multilateral engagement with CAS using the existing multilateral forums like SCO and Eurasian Economic Community (EEC).
7. India has to take a leaf out of Chinese economic diplomacy and encourage economic interests to lead other political and security objectives in place in the region.
8. The focus needs to be shifted from import orientation to export promotion of Indian goods in CAS.
9. More concentration should be given on trade in services than on trade in goods.
10. One of the major reasons for trade relationships not moving to potential is the absence of private investments. Therefore, the Indian government must come forward and provide a certain level of assurance to tackle the risks

involved in the trading system to encourage private entrepreneurs to play an important role in strengthening the relationships in the trade and economic sector which eventually would spread to sectors like energy and security.

11. Public enterprises like ONGC, SAIL, BHEL, BSNL, CIL etc. must come forward and play on the front foot as far as investments in strategic collaborations and joint ventures are concerned in the energy and power sector, minerals and oil exploration etc.
12. Importantly, India needs o come out of its "one size fits all approach". Instead of formulating a general trade policy for a region, New Delhi needs to formulate and have country-specific trade strategies.
13. Market mapping, analysis, creating data banks for raw products, consumer and capital goods is critical for Indian exporters. Hence an updated and critical information network must be created for better business ties with CAS.
14. Language barriers need to be dismantled by encouraging student exchange programmes and provisioning of translator facilities by the government.
15. India needs to work on an alternative logistic route like Chinese One Belt, One Road (OBOR) and hence must reactivate land connectivity at the earliest through INSTC.
16. To be precise, the problems of Central Asian energy exports (oil and gas) are much clearer: they have to come into a pipeline network world and their coming will undoubtedly change the geopolitical configuration of the region as well as beyond. India needs to work on that front to use both the INSTC other alternatives to transport the Central Asian hydrocarbons.
17. Since the last five years and so, India has invested heavily in INSTC Project and has made tremendous progress by joining the Customs Convention on International Transport of Goods under the cover of TIR Carnets (TIR Convention). The cargo transport through this route has taken an upward surge since 2017 and is expected to transport more than 600,000 cargos per year. Kazakhstan has already constructed its part of the road that would connect with Chabahar and Turkmenistan and is making steady progress on this front. Once the Chabahar Port and Bandar Abbas start their full-fledged operation, this can yield unprecedented results in favour of India.
18. India needs to expedite the Free Trade Agreement with EAEU (Eurasian Economic Union) which constitutes the bulk of the Eurasian landmass with a GDP of approximately $5 trillion. Since Russia is keen to involve India, it will not be a stupendous task for New Delhi to work out the formalities to enable India to have direct access to the hydrocarbon resources of Eurasia and the markets for Indian goods.
19. Central Asia's multi-vector foreign policy and India's Connect Central Asia policy can be cornerstones in bringing both regions closer if India can take purposeful actions to translate the policies in practice. Given the anti-Chinese sentiment widespread in Central Asia and the sporadic violence taking place between Chinese workers and the Central Asians, a serious trust deficit has developed in their relationship which needs to be capitalized on by

India, complemented with increasing its exports and diversifying its sectors in total trade with the CAR.

20. Instead of adopting a cost–benefit analysis, India must adopt a rate of return policy for longer-term benefits. New Delhi must not be conservative in investing in the high stake energy projects in Central Asia just looking for immediate benefit; rather it should aim for greater goods in the longer term. India needs to learn this art from Chinese investment strategy in Central Asia.
21. Importantly, India should maintain a rock-solid relationship with Iran without being conditioned by its relationship with Washington. Since Iran is the heart of India's energy transportation, New Delhi has to adopt an uncompromising policy in this direction.
22. New Delhi will have to encourage the private industrialist to invest in Central Asian energy and markets and whenever needed must provide them with tax rebates.
23. Furthermore, India needs to take energetic steps to enhance its trade and investment levels with CARs, which are currently insignificant. Apart from trade in goods, service sectors including Education and Training, IT-software, health-care, and hotels appear to be promising areas for Indian trade and investments in this region and need to be aggressively pursued.
24. Central Asia's rich natural resources endowment, including significant reserves of oil, natural gas and uranium deposits would enable India to meet its burgeoning energy needs. To meet its current and future energy needs, Indian firms need to participate in oil and gas exploration ventures in the region, perhaps by joining the relevant international consortia.
25. India should develop a Russian strategy in its Central Asian engagement. Since India's economic and energy relationship with the CAR is not deep-rooted, New Delhi has to take Russia – a reliable friend of India to pursue its energy agenda in the region. It should be noted here that, despite being independent, the foreign policy choices of Central Asian countries are not flexible. In fact, the countries of the region pursue their policies in consonance with Russia and the guidance of the security policy of Moscow.
26. Importantly, there is a silent competition between Russia and China in Central Asia both in policy and institutional level to maintain their influences. While Chinese economic domination in the region is aimed to decoupling Russian hegemony in the region, the Russian political control and security directions are meant to not to allow China to have an upper hand in the Russian backyard. The undercurrents of the competition though not quite visible from the outset has deepened in recent years. In fact, the anti-American agenda is bringing them together despite their bilateral issues of concern in he region. India needs to capitalize on this and maintain cordial relationship with Moscow and take guidance especially in her Central Asian affairs.
27. Logically, Ladakh-Xinjiang Road is more convenient for India-Central Asia trade and therefore should be strategically considered. However, Chinese

policy decision in this matter has been very clear to not to allow India access through the Xinjiang route. In such a scenario, the Iranian route seems more feasible. But the recent Chinese moves in Iran to counter Indian investment projects especially transportation networks like ports, railways and roads has worried India. But, New Delhi can overcome this crisis by proactively engaging with Iran and seeking the support of Russia which enjoys supreme relationship with Tehran.

28. We are living in the age of institutions and greater engagements with them certainly yields favourable results. The case of China in Central Asia is worth mentioning as Beijing has effectively used organizations like SCO (Shanghai Cooperation Organization) to pursue its nationalistic agenda in the disguise of regional peace and security. In fact, the recent Belt and Road Initiative is a step forward to deepen its engagement in the region and establish its supremacy through economic penetration and infrastructure developments. India needs to take a leaf out of the Chinese actions in Central Asia and master its institutional collaboration both bilateral and multilateral to garner its national interests albeit in soft-power cord. Here also, New Delhi can count the support of Russia by joining Moscow strategic narrative EAEU and inviting Russia to SAARC as an observer.

Therefore, any Central Asian policy by New Delhi without taking Russia into confidence or in consent of Moscow would be a utter failure which India must need to understand. Although for India, geography remains the single most important factor in her relationship with Central Asia. Make no mistake, Russia too will remain a key factor in New Delhi's Central Asia Policy. Therefore, the premature decision of discounting Russia by the previous governments needs rectification by Prime Minister Modi.

Through the better part of India's history, links with Central Asia had been the most important in its contact with the outside world. Traditionally, India had aimed to take its philosophical and cultural message across Inner Asian countries up to the remote Siberian region. During the British period, political officers, explorers, surveyors and traders, obviously for the "Great Game" postures, maintained some interest in Central Asia. However, in the post-independence period, India grossly and perhaps consciously overlooked the studies and understanding of its non-South Asian neighbouring areas, which traditionally formed "buffer zones" against external aggression. However, during the 1970s to 1990s India's Central Asia policy was factored by the Soviet Union. Due to healthy Indo-Soviet relations, Indian relations with Central Asia were cordial and close. In the early 1990s, with the disintegration of the Soviet Union, India's focus in the region again remained poor and dismal. However, with the increasing geopolitical and strategic significance of the region for India, it directed its foreign policy formulation towards the region which many called India's "Look North Policy", to promote democracy, secularism and peaceful coexistence in the Central Asian region. The situation has however been changed with the evolving energy scenario in the region. Accordingly, the policy formulation of the countries has changed, responding to the region's demand.

India, so far, has not achieved any success in winning any deals in the Central Asian oil sector. The reasons for this are many – ranging from technical hurdles to high stake politics. The problem of inaccessibility apart, the issue of avoiding transit through Pakistan itself has become a fact of life. Therefore, it becomes essential, and inevitably so, to factor Iran in our energy security calculus. The INSTC route is the only hope for India as of now. Given the pace of its development in collaboration with Iran and Russia, it seems that very soon Central Asian energy will connect with the Indian route.

Until such a time when construction of direct oil and gas pipelines becomes possible, India's interest should remain focused on the petroleum management sector. The Caspian Sea region and Kazakhstan offer enormous opportunity for Indian technicians and experts. Indian presence in the region is already growing, as hundreds of Indian technicians and skilled workers are finding their way into infrastructure development projects. About a thousand Indians are already working in the Aksai and Karachaganak-based Consolidated Construction Company (CCC) and SAIPEM Company, undertaking pipeline construction. With the increasing participation of the Indian workforce in petroleum management, the Caspian Sea region and Central Asia would inevitably become another Gulf model for India.

BIBLIOGRAPHY

Books

Akihiro, Iwashita (2007, edit), *Eager Eyes Fixed on Eurasia*, Sapporo: Slavic Research Centre, Hokkaido University.

Alexander, Yonah and Ebinger, Charles K. (1982, edit), *Political Terrorism and Energy: The Threat and Response*, New York: Praeger.

Amineh, Mehdi Parviz, and Houweling, Henk (2005, edit), *Central Eurasia in Global Politics: Conflict, Security, and Development*, Leiden: Brill.

Banuazizi, Ali and Weiner, Myron (1994, edit), *The New Geopolitics of Central Asia and Borderlands*, London: I.B. Tauris.

Black, J. L. (2004), *Vladimir Putin and the New World Order: Looking East, Looking West?* Lanham, MD: Rowman & Littlefield.

Carlsnaes, Walter (1998), *Energy Vulnerability and National Security: The Energy Crisis, Domestic Policy Responses, and the Logic of Swedish Neutrality*, London: Pinter Publishers.

Chandler, William (2000), *Energy and Environment in the Transition Economies: Between the Cold War and Global Warming*, Boulder, CO: West View Press.

Chopra, V. D. (2002, edit), *Global Challenge of Terrorism*, New Delhi: Gyan Publishing House.

Clawson, Patrick L. (1995, edit), *Energy and National Security in the 21st Century*, Washington, DC: National Defense University Press.

Cohen, Ariel (2005, edit), *Eurasia in Balance: The US and the Regional Power Shift*, Burlington, VT: Ashgate.

Cohen, S. B. (2015), *Geopolitics: The Geography of International Relations*, 3rd ed., London: Rowman & Littlefield.

Conant, M. and Gold, F. (1978), *The Geopolitics of Energy*, Boulder, CO: Westview Press.

Johnson, Lena (2004), *Vladimir Putin and Central Asia: The Shaping of Russian Foreign Policy*, London: I.B. Tauris.

Keith, Ronald C. (1986, edit), *Energy, Security, and Economic Development in East Asia*, London: Croom Helm.

Legvold, Robert (2003, edit), *Thinking Strategically: The Major Powers, Kazakhstan, and the Central Asian Nexus*, Cambridge: American Academy of Arts and Sciences.

Lo, Bobo (2005), "Vladimir Putin and the Evolution of Russian", *Foreign Policy*, Oxford: Blackwell Publishing.

Mitchell, John (2001), *The New Economy of Oil: Impacts on Business, Geopolitics, and Society*, London: Royal Institute of International Affairs, Energy and Environment Programme.

Muni, S. D. (2005), *India's Search for Energy Security: Prospects for Cooperation with the Extended Neighbourhood*, New Delhi: Rupa &Co. in association with Observer Research Foundation.

Olcott, Martha Brill (2005), *Central Asia's Second Chance*, Washington, DC: Carnegie Endowment for International Peace.

Ong, Russel (2007), *China's Security Interests in the 21st Century*, New York: Routledge.

Rahul, Ram (1995), *China, Russia, and Central Asia*, New Delhi: Vikas Publishing.

Ray-Dawal, Shebonti (2002), *Rethinking Energy Security in India*, New Delhi: Knowledge World.

Rumer, Boris, and Zhukov, Stanislav (1998, edit), *Central Asia: The Challenges of Independence*, Armonk: M.E Sharp.

Rutledge, Ian (2006), *Addicted to Oil: America's Relentless Drive for Energy Security*, London: I.B. Tauris.

Vansant, Carl (1971), *Strategic Energy Supply and National Security*, New York: Praeger.

JOURNALS

Abashin, Sergei (Sep. 2006), "Logic of Islamic Practices: Religious Conflict in Central Asia", *Central Asian Survey* 25(3), pp. 267–286.

Akataeva, Alia (Oct-Dec. 2006), "Kazakhstan-China Trade and Economic Relations", *Himalayan and Central Asian Studies*, 10(4), pp. 45–56.

Akatayeva, Aliya (Aug-Dec. 2005), "Security Issues in Central Asia and the Shanghai Cooperation Organization", *Contemporary Central Asia*, 9(2–3), pp. 42–50.

Andrews, Philip (Mar-Apr. 2000), "China's Involvement in Central Asian Petroleum: Convergent or Divergent Interests?", *Asian Survey*, 40(2), Mar-Apr, pp. 377–397.

Andrews, Philip (2006), "Strategic Implications of China's Energy Needs", *Adelphi Papers*, 380, pp. 380–423.

Baev, Pavel (May 2007), "Russia Aspire to the Status of 'Energy Superpower'", *Strategic Analysis*, 31(3), pp. 447–465.

Bahgat, Gawdat (Sep. 2006), "Europe's Energy Security: Challenges and Opportunities", *International Affairs*, 82(5), pp. 961–975.

Becker, Abreham S (2000), "Russia and Caspian Oil: Moscow Loses Control", *Post-Soviet Affairs*, 16(2), pp. 91–132.

Belyi, Anderi V. (Dec. 2003), "New Dimensions of Energy Security of the Enlarging EU and Their Impact on Relations with Russia", *Journal of European Integration*, 25(4), pp. 351–369.

Bhadrakumar, M. K. (Apr. 2006), "America's Energy Diplomacy in a Multipolar World", *Seminar*, 560. [online] Available at: https://www.india-seminar.com/2006/560/560%20m.k.%20bhadrakumar.htm

Bhagat, Gawdat (Mar. 2006), "Central Asian and Energy Security", *Asian Affairs*, 37(1), pp. 1–16.

Blank, Stephen (1999), "Every Shark East of Suez: Great Power Interests, Policies and Tactics in the Transcaspian Energy Wars", *Central Asian Survey*, 18(2), pp. 149–184.

Bovingdon, Gardner (2010), *The Uyghurs: Strangers in Their Own Land*. New York: Columbia University Press.

BP (2008), *BP Statistical Review of World Energy*, British Petroleum, June 2008, available at: http://www.bp.com/staristicalreview [accessed January 20, 2009].

Brower, Dreek (Jan. 2007), "EU: Energy Security: Wishful, Native Thinking", *Petroleum Economist*, 74(1), pp 1–16.

Brower, Dreek (Apr. 2007), "European Union: Impossible Bedfellows", *Petroleum Economists*, 74(4) 7–15.

Brummer, Matthew (Spring-Summer 2007), "Shanghai Cooperation Organization and Iran: A Powerful Union", *Journal of International Affairs*, 60(2), pp. 185–198.

Buchan, David (Autumn 2002), "Threat within: Deregulation and Energy Security", *Survival*, 44(3), pp. 105–116.

Bulat, Khusainov (2006), "Macroeconomic Indicators of the Central Asian States' Development", report presented at the *International Conference "Security and Democracy in Central Asia"*, Almaty, March 6.

Burakovsky, lgor V. (Jan. 1998), "Ukrainian Energy Sector: Current Problems and Perspectives", *Problems of Economic Transition*, 40(9), pp. 35–55.

Calabrese, John (Summer 1998), "China and the Persian Gulf: Energy and Security", *Middle East Journal*, 52(3), pp. 351–356.

Chang, Felix K. (Summer 1997), "China's Central Asian Power and Problems", *Orbis*, 41(3), pp. 401–425.

Chung, Chien-peng (Dec. 2004), "Shanghai Co-operation Organization: China's Changing Influence in Central Asia", 180. The China Quarterly (pp. 989–1009).

Cook, Robert L (Spring 2006), "Oil and Gas Drilling-A Cause of Earthquakes and Bad Weather", *World Affairs*, 10(1), pp. 88–96.

Corneli, Svante E. (Jan. 1998), "Turkey and Conflict in Nagorno Karabakh: A Delicate Balance", *Middle Eastern Studies*, 34(1), pp. 51–72.

Das, Bijay Kumar (Jun. 2004), "US Interests in Central Asia Since the Disintegration of Soviet Union", *Journal of Peace Studies*, 11(2), pp. 33–35.

Desai, Nitin (Jan-Mar. 2008), "New Race: Energy and Climate Change", *India Quarterly*, 64(1), pp. 79–105.

Downs, Erica S(Mar. 2004), "Chinese Energy Security Debate", *China Quarterly*, 177, pp. 21–41.

Druckman, Daniel (Nov. 1999), "Hurting Stalemate or Meditation? The Conflict Over Nagorno-Karabakh, 1990–95", *Journal of Peace Research*, 36(6), pp. 709–727.

Dutta, Sujit (2003), "China's Emerging Ties with Central Asia", in Nirmala Joshi (ed.), *Central Asia: The Great Game Replayed*, New Delhi: New Century Books, p. 3.

Dwivedi, Ramakant (July-Sep. 2006), "Dark Side of the West's Global War on Terror", *Strategic Analysis*, 30(3), pp. 675–680.

EC (2006), *Energy Strategy, Green Paper: A European Strategy for Sustainable, Competitive and Secure Energy*, European Commission, March, available at http://ec.europa.eu/energy/strategies/2006/2006_03_green_paper_energy_en.htm [accessed on December 29, 2010].

EIA (2005), *Review of EIA Draft Notification*, Energy Information Administration, available at http://www/eia.doe.gov [accessed on February 12, 2008].

EIA (2015), "The Assumption to the Annual Energy Outlook", U.S. Energy Information Administration, September 2015, available at https://www.eia.gov/outlooks/aeo/assumptions/pdf/0554(2015).pdf [accessed on 15 August 2017].

EIA (2017), "Short-Term Energy Outlook", U.S Energy Information Administration, April [accessed on 15 August 2018].

EIU (2008), "Kazakhstan: Country Report", *The Economist Intelligence Unit*, February 1, 2008, available at http://www.eiu.com/index.asp?layout=displayIssueTOC&toc2=no&issue_id=1832973568&publication_id=520000852 [accessed on February 7, 2008].

ENI (2008), "World Oil and Gas Review", available at http://www.eni.com/en_IT/home.html [accessed on July 7, 2010].

Ercilasum, Konuralp (Dec. 2004), "China in Central Asia: A Case Study of the Relationship between China and Kazakhstan", *Contemporary Central Asia*, 8(3).

Estrada, Aurelia Mane (2009), "Central Asia: Moving Towards an Alternative Vision of Energy Relations?", WP. 56/2009, available at www.ealinstitutoelcano.org/wps/.../Content?... [accessed on July 7, 2010].

Evans, Graham and Newnham, Jeffrey (1998), *The Penguin Dictionary of International Relations*, London: Penguin Books Pvt Ltd, pp. 197–198.

Fesharaki, Fereidun (Fall 1999), "Energy and Asian Security Nexus", *Journal of International Affairs*, 53(1), pp. 85–99.

Filimonovic, Miljan (Jan.-Jun. 2007), "Causes of the Russian Policy Offensive", *Review of International Affairs*, LVII(1125–1126), pp. 143–171.

Frankopan, P. (2015), *The Silk Roads: A New History of the World*, London: Bloomsbury.

Fumagalli, Matteo (Jun. 2007), "Framing Ethnic Minority Mobilization in Central Asia: The Cases of Uzbeks in Kyrgyzstan and Tajikistan", *Europe-Asia Studies*, 59(4), pp. 829–846.

Ghosh Prodipto, Chopra S. K., Sethi Surya, P., and Preeti, Bhandari (Spring 2006), "A Partnership for a Decarbonised Energy Future", *World Affairs*, 10(1), pp. 140–165.

Gorst, Isabel (Feb. 2007), "Pipelines: Russia: Price War Settled, for Now", *Petroleum Economist*, 74(2), pp. 8.25.

Huasheng, Zhao (Apr.-Aug. 2004), "China's Energy Interest in Central Asia", *Contemporary Central Asia*, 8(1–2), pp. 170–172.

Hueper, Paul (Sep. 2007), "Energy Security: Evaluating Global Threats", *Petroleum Economist*, 74(9), pp. 111–135

Iper, Pinar (Nov. 2007), "The Role of Oil and Gas in Kazakhstan's Foreign Policy: Looking East or West", *Europe-Asia Studies*, 59(7), pp. 1179–1199.

Iqbal, Humera (Autumn 2007), "Democracy and the Central Asian States", *Regional Studies*, 25(4), pp. 66–99.

Kaushik, Devendra (Aug.-Dec. 2005), "Caspian Cauldron: New Geopolitical Game", *Contemporary Central Asia*, 9(2–3), pp. 5–15.

Kavalski, Emilian (Jan-Mar. 2007), "Whom to Follow?: Central Asia between the EU and China", *China Report*, 43(1), pp. 839–856.

Kazakhstan Times (2007), "Contract Terms Implementation by Mineral Resource Users is Generally Unsatisfactory – Massimov", January 18, available at http://www.zakon.kz/our/news/news.asp?id=30084835 [accessed on December 20, 2007].

Kazakhstan's News Bulletin (2007), Embassy of Kazakhstan to the USA and Canada, "Amendments to the Legislation on Subsoil Have Been Signed into Law", October 14, available at http://www.kazakhembus.com/NB14-103107.html [June 10, 2008].

Kemp, Geoffrey (Winter 1998), "Persian Gulf Remains the Strategic Prize", *Survival*, 40(4), pp. 132–149.

Kerr, David with Swington, Laura C. (Mar. 2008), "China, Xinjiang, and the Translational Security of Central Asia", *Critical Asian Studies*, 40(1), pp. 89–112.

Khusianov, Bulat (2006), "Macroeconomic Indicators of the Central Asian States' Development", report presented at the *International Conference "Security and Democracy in Central Asia"*, Almaty, March 6.

Khojaev, Ablat (2007), "China's Central Asia Policy", *Central Asia and the Caucasus Journal, Sweden*, available at http://www.ca-c.org/journal/2007-03-eng/03.shtml [accessed on April 15, 2008].

Kramer, Andrew E. (2009), "Putin's Grasp of Energy Drives Russian Agenda", *New York Times Online Edition*, January 28, http://www.nytimes.com/2009/01/29/world/europe/29putin.html? [accessed on January 28, 2010].

Kuchins, Andrew (Oct. 2007), "Russia and China: The Ambivalent Embrace", *Current History*, 106(702), pp. 321–327.

Kurganbayeva, Aigul (Oct.-Dec. 2006), "Geopolitical Realities of Central Asia", *Himalayan and Central Asian Studies*, 10(4), pp. 9–12.

Leal, C. M. (2011), *As Relações Energéticas entre Portugal e a Nigéria: Riscos e Oportunidades.* IDN Cadernos No 3. Instituto da Defesa Nacional, available at http://www.idn.gov.pt/publicacoes/cadernos/idncaderno_3.pdf [accessed on January 30, 2017].

Luong, P. J. (Mar-Apr. 2002), "New Friends, New Fears in Central Asia", *Foreign Affairs*, 81(2), pp. 61–70.

Luzyanin, Sergey (Apr-Jun. 2007), "Central Asia in Trilateral Cooperation: Regional Potential and Resources of SCO", *China Report*, 43(2), pp. 237–243.

Macfarlane, S. Neil (May 2004), "The United States and Regionalism in Central Asia", *International Affairs*, 80(3), pp. 447–461.

Maio, Susannah (Apr. 2007), "Energy Security in an Interdependent World", *OPEC Bulletin*, 4, pp. 27–29.

Maitra, Ramtanu (Spring 2006), "Thorium: Preference Nuclear Fuel of the Future", *World Affairs*, 10(1), pp. 98–110.

Mary, Kaldor, Karl, Terry Lynn and Said, Yahia (2007, edit), *Oil Wars*, London: Pluto, pp. i-304.

Menon, Rajan (Summer 2003), "New Great Game in Central Asia", *Survival*, 45(2), pp. 187–204.

Milani, Abbas (Oct. 2007), "Russia and Iran: An Anti-Western Alliance?", *Current History*, 106(702), pp. 328–332.

Misra, S. S. (May-Jun. 2001), "Chinese Perspective on Central Asia: Threat of Uighur Separatism", *Journal of Peace Studies*, 8(3), pp. 37–56.

MoE (2018), "Kazakhstan Seeks New Coal Export Markets", Ministry of Energy, Republic of Kazakhstan, February 4.

Mohapatra, Nalin Kumar (Apr-Jun. 2007), "Political and Security Challenges in Central Asia: The Drug Trafficking Dimension", *International Studies*, 44(2), pp. 157–174.

Mokhtari, Fariborz (Spring 2005), "No One Will Scratch My Back: Iranian Security Perceptions in Historical Context", *Middle East Journal*, 59(2), pp. 209–229.

Morse, Edward L. (Mar-Apr. 2002), "Battle for Energy Dominance", *Foreign Affairs*, 81(2), pp. 16–31.

Morse, L. Edward and Richard, James (2007), "The Battle for Energy Dominance", *Foreign Affairs*, March-April 2002, available at http://www.foreignaffairs.org/20020301faessay7969/edward-l-morse-james-richard/the-battle-for-energy-dominance.html, December 20 [accessed on October 12, 2004].

Muzalevsky, Roman (2016), "China's Long March into Central Asia", *Stratfor, WorldView*, April 27, available at https://worldview.stratfor.com/article/chinas-long-march-central-asia [accessed on September 15, 2018].

Noel, Pierre (Winter 2006–2007), "New US Middle East Policy and Energy Security Challenges", *International Journal*, 62(1), pp. 43–54.

Olcot, Martha Brill (Oct. 2005), "Great Powers in Central Asia", *Current History*, 104(684), pp. 331–335.

Olcott, Maratha Brill (Oct. 2007), "The Shrinking US Footprint in Central Asia", *Current History*, 106(702), pp. 333–339.

Pant, Girijesh. (Dec. 2004), "Caspian and Central Asian Energy Architecture in Emerging Frontiers of Global Energy Space", *Contemporary Central Asia*, 8(3), pp. 1–8.

Parthasarathi, Ashok (Spring 2006), "Renewable Energy Sources: Situation and Prospects", *World Affairs*, 10(1), pp. 112–138.

Platte, Erika (Jun. 1996), "Role of China in Japan's Quest for Energy Security", *Hitotsubashi Journal of Economics*, 37(1), pp. 69–86.

Prabhakar, Akhilesh Chandra (Apr-Jun. 2005), "Energy Security Cooperation and Geopolitics", *Dialogue*, 6(4), pp. 124–142.

Pradhan, Ramakrushna (2019), "Petropolitics and Pipeline Diplomacy in Central Asia: Can India Afford to Wait in the Wings?", *India Quarterly*, 75(4).

Raczka, Witt (Sep. 1998), "Xinjiang and Central Asian Borderlands", *Central Asian Survey*, 17(3), pp. 373–407.

Rieff, David (Mar.-Apr. 1997), "Nagorno-Karabakh: Case Study in Ethnic Strife", *Foreign Affairs*, 76(2), pp. 71–103.

Rutledge, Ian (Nov. 2007), "New Labour, Energy Policy and Competitive Markets", *Journal of Economics*, 31(6), pp. 901–925.

Rzayeva, Esmira (2014), "Turkmenistan's Energy Policy", *IPPR Blog, ULC*, December 05, available at https://blogs.ucl.ac.uk/ippr/turkmenistans-energy-policy/ [accessed on April 14, 2019].

Saidolimov, Saidkhon (Jan.-Mar. 2007), "Central Asia in the New World System", *Dialogue*, 8(3). [online article]. see the link: https://www.asthabharati.org/Dia_Jan%2007/Said.htm

Satish, Chandra (Apr. 2002), "Central Asia: The New Great Game", *Journal of Indian Ocean Studies*, 10(1), pp. 165–177.

Schaaatz, Edward (Oct. 2002), "Islamic and Anti-American in Central Asia", *Current History*, 1(657), pp. 127–129.

Shaffer, Brenda (Nov. 2002), "Is There a Muslim Foreign Policy? The Case of the Caspian", *Current History*, 101(658), pp. 382–387.

Shah, Chirag (16–22 Jun. 2007), "Shifting the Focus for Oil Security", *Economic & Political Weekly*, 42(24), pp. 16–22.

Sharma, R.R. (Apr.-Aug. 2004), "Regional Order and Security: Role of External Powers in Central Asia and Caspian Region", *Contemporary Central Asia*, 8(1–2), pp. 8–15.

Sharma, Raghav (2009), "India in Central Asia, the Road Ahead", Institute of Peace and Conflict Studies. Special Report. No. 63, January, p. 4.

Sheives, Kevin (Summer 2006), "China Turns West: Beijing's Contemporary Strategy towards Central Asia", *Pacific Affairs*, 79(2), pp. 205–224.

Shlapentokh, Vladimir (Jan. 2007), "China in the Russian Mind Today: Ambivalence and Defeatism", *Journal Europe-Asia Studies 59*(1), pp. 1–21.

Shokri, Ghanem (2008), "Are the World's Oil Resources Limited? An OPEC Point of View", *Energy Bulletin*, October, available at www.energybulletin.net [accessed on December 10, 2010].

Shri, Prakash (Jan-Mar. 2003), "US Involvement in Afghanistan: Implications for the Future", *Journal of Peace Studies*, 10(1). [online], http://www.icpsnet.org/admin/photo_banner/2003Jan-Art4.pdf

Simpson, Adam (2007), "Environment Energy Security Nexus: Critical Analysis of an Energy' Love Triangle' in Southeast Asia", *Third World Quarterly*, 28(3), pp. 517–541.

Smith, Jeff and Berman, Ilan (2011), "Central Asia's Energy Bazaar", *The Wall Street Journal*, January 27, available at: www.wsj.com/articles/SB10001424052748703398504576101063649062424 [accessed on April 25, 2015].

Sorokodum, E. (Spring 2006), "Extraction of Low- Potential Energy from the Environment: The Solution to Energy and Ecological Problems", *World Affairs*, 10(1), pp. 166–183.

South China Morning Post (2017), "Belt and Road: 2107 Summit", China: South China Morning Post, available at http://www.scmp.com/topics/belt-and-road-2017-summit [accessed on September 15, 2018].

Spykman, Nicholas (1942), *America's Strategy in World Politics: The United States and the Balance of Power,* New York: Transaction Publishers.

Spykman, Nicholas (1944), *Geography of Peace and Foreign Policy of the United States*, New York: Harcourt Brace and Company.

Stobdan, P. (Jun. 1998), "China's Central Asia Dilemma", *Strategic Analysis*, 22(3), pp. 399–408.

Swanstrom, Niklas (2015), "The Security Dimension of the China-Central Asia Relationship: China's Military Engagement with Central Asian Countries", *Institute for Security and Development Policy*, March 18. Available at www.isdp.eu.

Trenin, Dmitry (Autumn-Winter 2003), "Farewell to the Great Game? Prospects for Russian –American Security Cooperation in Central Asia", *European Security*, 12(3–4), pp. 21–35.

Umarov, Kairat (Apr-Aug. 2004), "Energy, Security and Development: The Kazakh Experience", *Contemporary Central Asia*, 8(1).

US DOE (2006), *The US Energy Strategic Plan*, US Department of Energy, available at http://energy.gov/downloads/us-department-energy-strategic-plan [accessed on February 11, 2011].

Valencia, Mark J. (Autumn 1997), "Energy and Security in Asia", *Survival*, 39(3), pp. 86–113.

Verma, Shiv Kumar (Oct-Dec. 2005), "Central Asian Potential and Geopolitics of the Future", *Journal of Peace Studies*, 12(4), pp. 3280–3301.

Wadlow, Rene (Summer 2006), "Shanghai Cooperation Organization: A Balance of Opportunity", *World Affairs*, 10(2), pp. 56–59.

Wall, David (Jun. 2006), "Shanghai Cooperation Organization: Five Candles, Three Evils", *World Today*, 62(6). [online], https://www.chathamhouse.org/publications/the-world-today/2006-06/shanghai-cooperation-organisation-five-candles-three-evils

Waugh, Daniel C. (Jun. 2007), "Making of Chinese Central Asia", *Central Asian Survey*, 26(2), pp. 232–250.

WB (2020), "Country Profile – Kazakhstan", World Bank data, available at https://data.worldbank.org/country/kazakhstan [accessed on 17th April 2020].

Weston, N. J. (Oct. 2004), "Central Asia: China Looming Presence", *Petroleum Economist*, 71(10), pp. 249–259.

Wicks, Malcolm (Jan. 2008), "Energy Security: Opinion: Caspian Engagement", *Petroleum Economist*, 75(1), pp. 20–25.

Wilfrid, L. Kohl (1983, edit), *After the Second Oil Crisis: Energy Policies in Europe, America, and Japan*, Lexington, MA: Lexington Books.

Winrow, Gareth M. (Winter 2003), "Pivotal State or Energy Supplement? Domestic Structure, External Actors, and Turkish Policy in the Caucasus", *Middle East Journal*, 57(1), pp. 89–91.

Wishnick, Elizabeth (Jan-Feb. 2007), "Russia and the CIS in 2006: Asserting Russian Interests on Korean Security, Energy, and Central Asia", *Asian Survey*, 47(1), pp. 58–67.

Wood, Steve (Mar. 2008), "Energy and Democracy: The European Union's Challenges", *Current History*, 107(707), pp. 133–138.

Wu, Jianmin (2015), "One Belt and One Road-Far-Reaching Initiative", *China-US focus*, http://tinyurl.com/chinaUSbeltroad [accessed on September 15, 2018].

Wu, Junfei (24–30 Sep. 2005), "Will SCO Become Another Warsaw Pact?" *Economic & Political Weekly*, 40(39). September 24, Available at: https://www.epw.in/journal/2005/39/book-reviews/will-sco-become-another-warsaw-pact.html

Yavuzalp, Osman (Winter 2001–2002), "On the Front Line", *NATO Review*, 49, pp. 24–25.

Yazdani, Enayatollah (Apr.-Jun. 2007), "US Democracy Promotion Policy in the Central Asian Republics: Myth or Reality?", *International Studies*, 44(2), pp. 141–155.

Yergin, Daniel (Mar./Apr. 2006), "Ensuring Energy Security", *Foreign Affairs*, 85(2), pp. 69–82.

Yi-chong, Xu (Jun. 2006), "China's Energy Security", *Australian Journal of International Affairs*, 60(2), pp. 265–286.

Zhi, Wang (2016), "China's New Silk Road Strategy and Foreign Policy towards Central Asia", *Southeast Review of Asian Studies*, 38, pp. 69–77.

INDEX

Page numbers in "italic" indicate a figure and page numbers in "bold" indicate an illustration.

Made in the USA
Las Vegas, NV
31 October 2024

7e49fbad-ef4b-4521-8ce9-1d1701a1dbb6R01